Conscience in Recovery from Alcohol Addiction

Conscience in Recovery from Alcohol Addiction

Exploring the Role of Spirituality
in Conscientious Transformation

Yordan Kalev Zhekov

Foreword by Geoffrey M. Stephenson

RESOURCE *Publications* • Eugene, Oregon

CONSCIENCE IN RECOVERY FROM ALCOHOL ADDICTION
Exploring the Role of Spirituality in Conscientious Transformation

Copyright © 2013 Yordan Kalev Zhekov. All rights reserved. Except for brief quotations in critical publications or reviews, no part of this book may be reproduced in any manner without prior written permission from the publisher. Write: Permissions, Wipf and Stock Publishers, 199 W. 8th Ave., Suite 3, Eugene, OR 97401.

Resource Publications
An Imprint of Wipf and Stock Publishers
199 W. 8th Ave., Suite 3
Eugene, OR 97401
www.wipfandstock.com

ISBN 13: 978-1-62032-498-1
Manufactured in the U.S.A.

Contents

Foreword vii

1. Introduction: defining conscience and its relationship to immorality, addiction, morality, spirituality, and recovery through a survey of relevant scholarship 1

2. Methodology 13

3. John's personal interview 18

4. Results 35

5. Discussion 79

6. Conclusion 90

References 93
Appendices 99

Foreword

THE PUBLICATION OF YORDAN Zhekov's book is a welcome event that contributes to a resurgence of interest in the role of spirituality and the moral dimension in our understanding of the nature of addiction, and of how problems of addiction should be tackled by psychologists. I will try to place it more specifically in context.

Psychology has generally striven to be value free, to describe what is, and not what ought to be, and to emphasise management of misconduct and not its condemnation. Indeed, the concept of misconduct has largely been alien to mainstream psychology. Behaviour has been the operative construct in the description of human actions, not conduct. The concept of "behaviour" as employed by Behaviourists was neutral as to responsibility for actions, and fostered the belief that referring to behaviour as "conduct" implied a sphere of moral responsibility that was irrelevant to psychology as an objective scientific enterprise. The neglect of what might be termed "character" over many decades was one unfortunate consequence, but happily there are serious attempts now being made, particularly in the area of "positive psychology," to remedy previous neglect. Zhekov's elucidation of the way in which spirituality can lead to a regeneration of conscience in the recovery of those with problems of addiction is a welcome contribution to this movement.

Another example of the changing scene can be taken from social psychology. One of the most influential theories in mainstream social psychology is the Theory of Cognitive Dissonance, first promulgated by Leon Festinger. Dissonance is said to occur when, for example, our awareness of what we do (let's say, smoke tobacco) is contradicted by evidence of its effects on health, or perhaps our family finances. These cognitions suggest that we should break with the habit. Festinger characterised our response to such "cognitive dissonance" as a feeling of "discomfort," which we are motivated to reduce, perhaps, in the smoking example, by the creation of comforting beliefs about the social benefits of smoking (not so easy now it is banned in public settings), or by "denial" as in the case of addicts more generally. "Discomfort," however, is another of those morally neutral constructs that has increasingly been shown to be inadequate as a description of what generally motivates the reduction of dissonance in the various paradigms that have guided research. A recent review (*) shows rather that it is feelings of *guilt* that drive the individual to seek, by whatever dubious stratagems, to change their perceptions of the conflict between what we do and what we ought to be doing.

Zhekov's work is consistent with this new emphasis, showing how addiction can become a stratagem for the management of guilt. The escalation of excessive behaviour, well revealed in his interviews, shows clearly the process whereby conscience and the capacity for moral judgement may be progressively, and remorselessly undermined. His development of the notion of "conscience therapy" is remarkable for the fact that it shows in a vivid way that a spiritual awakening can revive the functioning of conscience, and motivate the practice of choice guided by moral values. Zhekov would reject the lamentable "moral model" which passes moral judgement on the addict, and he respects the abundant mainstream research into the "biopsychosocial" underpinnings of addictive behaviours which has so effectively undermined that approach. What Yordan Zhekov has achieved is to expand more thoroughly than has been achieved in the past, the role that spirituality can play in transforming the lives of addicts through a revitalised sense of conscience. This is a significant achievement that contributes effectively to the development of a more humane and responsible understanding of the psychology of addiction.

Geoffrey M. Stephenson
Emeritus Professor of Social Psychology,
University of Kent, Canterbury, UK

July 2012

* Kenworthy, J. B., Miller, N., Collins, B. E., Read, S. J., and Earleywine, M. (2011). A trans-paradigm theoretical synthesis of cognitive dissonance theory: Illuminating the nature of discomfort. *European Review of Social Psychology* 22, 36–113.

1.

Introduction

defining conscience and its relationship to immorality, addiction, morality, spirituality, and recovery through a survey of relevant scholarship

ALCOHOL ADDICTION IS A complex phenomenon and scholarly attempts to formulate it have produced diverse results. These may even stay in tension when considering the issue of manageability as in the case of the historical perspectives of moral failure and illness (Raskin and Daley, 1991). The view of addiction as a disorder underlines a cognitive and behavioural preoccupation with the substance, impaired control, and disregard of damaging effects (ICD-10, 1993). The negative consequences of addictive behaviour are perceived as established through continuous bonding to substance related contextual stimuli (West, 2001). The relationship between cognition and environmental stimuli (Albery, Sharma, Niazi, and Moss, 2006) clarifies addiction processes through automaticity (Bargh, 1997) and attentional bias (Sharma, Albery, and Cook, 2001). Excessive desire is considered as the central addictive force leading to repetitive unpredictable behaviour underlined by conflict (Orford, 2001). These approaches stressing moral unwillingness, disease inability, unhealthy attachment, contextual dependence, and intemperate appetite, enlighten various aspects of alcohol addiction but also highlight disunity. The diversity creates a methodological and pragmatic gap which requires a unifying concept suggested as conscience and its relation to morality and spirituality. These core elements of transformation on the road to a successful recovery are overlooked by the contemporary scholarship (Orford, 2001).

Spiritual conversion is underrepresented in psychology and counselling studies (Mahoney and Pargament, 2004). Further research is needed to clarify the relationship between an individual's holistic spirituality and alcohol treatment (Piderman, Schneekloth, Pankratz, Maloney, and Altchuler, 2007; Patock-Peckham, Hutchinson, Cheong, and Nagoshi, 1998) and between religiousness and conscience (Chau, Johnson, Bowers, Darvill, and Danko, 1990).

The present proposal suggests that spiritually empowered conscience leads to moral effectiveness, conscious control, and physical, cognitive, spiritual, and virtuous manageability of the addictive behaviour. Conscience which has been deadened and morally inactive is empowered and renewed through moral reformation and spiritual edification making it ethically sound, consciously involved, and spiritually active to enable decisions which break the addictive behaviour patterns. This model requires an understanding of the nature of conscience, its suppressed state, spiritual empowerment, and virtuous development.

1.1. Conscience's nature and functioning: cognitive, emotive, and conative elements

Conscience is considered as defined by three elements, namely, cognitive, emotive, and conative (Koops, Brugman, and Ferguson, 2010). Cognitively conscience forms a decision about behaviour based on morally defined assessment (Koops, Brugman, and Ferguson, 2010). The moral reasoning is strengthened through one's belief system with absolute qualities grounded on divine perfection leading to fulfilment of personal, spiritual, and social responsibilities (McCosh, 1887). The theological notion of righteousness defines the divine influence on conscience through the Bible as a literary source of authority (Wall, 1996). One's self-understanding also shapes conscience (Wall, 1996). The latter is crucial for resolving internal personal conflicts (Miller and Jackson, 1995). Conscience and its relationship to the unconscious and conscious find their historical roots in Freud's work (Natsoulas, 2005. *Freud's phenomenology*). Conscience is a guide for conscious processes and automatic behaviour through developing affective familiarity to the context by conscious employment of conscientious behaviours (Martin, 2006). The importance of conscience in a health care context (Ladd, 2007; Cook, 2007) for both professionals (Dahlqvist, Eriksson, Glasberg, Lindahl, Lutzen, Strandberg, Soderberg, Sørlie, and Norberg, 2007) and patients (Cook, 2007) may underline its potential to impact addiction related automaticity leading to conscious behavioural change.

Conscience defines the emotions accompanying ethical deduction and wilful inclination (Koops, Brugman, and Ferguson, 2010). The affective conscience responds to the self-assessment of internal thoughts and external actions according to their moral or immoral nature with the experience of positive or negative emotions (McCosh, 1887). A negative result from retrospective self-assessment of behaviour leads to troubled conscience defined through the experience of guilt and shame (Glasberg, Eriksson, Dahlqvist, Lindahl, Strandberg, Soderberg, Sørlie, and Norberg, 2006). Guilt resonates from the conflict between morals and actions (Wall, 1996; Johnson, Danko, Huang, Park, Johnson, and Nagoshi, 1987). Shame is triggered by the interpretation of the social reflection of one's behaviour (Johnson et al., 1987). The emotive element links both cognitive and conative aspects of conscience (Koops, Brugman, and Ferguson, 2010).

Conative conscience describes the striving to continue morally sound behaviour and to cease immoral behaviour (Koops, Brugman, and Ferguson, 2010). Religiousness and spirituality play a significant role in this process. The study of religious narratives promotes morality and encourages spirituality (Canda, 2009). The stress derived from the experience of troubled conscience (Glasberg et al., 2006) is managed through spiritual edification (Maton, 2004). Spiritual strivings, focused on aspired personal relationship with the divine, support motivation, goals, and well-being, shape personality, and improve personal, social, and marital life (Emmons, 2003).

The function of conscience is defined by the relationship of the three elements within the particular context and in relation to the durability and adaptability of the whole system. The emotive element generates feelings of guilt and shame when one moral framework is challenged leading to the engagement of cognitive and conative elements to redefine one's stand and behaviour (Koops, Brugman, and Ferguson, 2010). The function is also a self-reflective process of reassessment and development of moral character and behaviour (McCosh, 1887). Conscience's functionality is supported by spiritual-moral formation (Peterson and Seligman, 2004) and edification of character virtues and strengths (Pargament, 2009).

Conscience from a lay person's point of view is the perception of moral behaviour. It is primarily expressed through language which attempts to depict the physical symptoms of one's struggle or content with conscience's role according to one's moral or immoral interactions with the context. The language also reflects the roles and collaborations of the conscience's three elements (Koops, Brugman, and Ferguson, 2010). Morality is closely linked to spirituality (Orford, 2006). Moral formation is shaped through spirituality and religiousness and its application is defined through faith and personal relationship with the divine (Emmons, 2003). Spirituality and religiousness also play a significant role in recovery from alcohol addiction (Delaney, Forcehimes, Campbell, and Smith, 2009). The latter, on the other hand, impairs spirituality (Piderman et al., 2007) and morality (Raskin and Daley, 1991) leading to the inhibition of conscience (Miller and Jackson, 1995). Hence a closer look is required at the relationship between inactive conscience, immorality, and addiction.

1.2. Conscience's relationship to immorality: moral disempowerment during addiction

Conscience is suppressed or deadened when the conflict between external and internal moral standards leads to the continuous failure of the application of the latter (Dahlqvist et al., 2007; McCosh, 1887). Inactive conscience is associated with psychopaths (Stephenson, 1998) and may be linked to antisocial personality disorder, continuous criminal behaviour and substance abuse (Miller and Jackson, 1995). Alcohol addiction impairs one's moral judgment (Kingery-McCabe and Campbell, 1991).

Psychological research establishes a clear link between immorality, cognition, affect, and behaviour (Klass, 1978). Morality is a holistic dimension of one's life which forms an attitude of responsibility for behaviour towards oneself and others (Klass, 1978). The immoral behaviour of the perpetrator leads to negative psychological impact underlined by guilt which requires resolution taken either as self-justification, attempt for reparation, or self-punishment (Klass, 1978). Schimmel (1997) argues that historically addiction is understood as moral illness underlining a frail spiritual condition which symptoms are manifested in vices. According to him the disease model of addiction dissociates vices from responsibilities leading to the diminishing of self-control and healthy guilt.

Orford (2006) maintains that the moral failures of character are closely related to the addiction problem. The latter is characterised by passionate attachment to a pleasurable activity forming an unmanageable excessive desire for continuous indulgency in that activity leading to internal and external conflicts (Orford, 2001). This view comes close to Fairlie's (1979) perspective of the seven deadly sins as failure to manage love. Pride, envy, and anger appear to build self-love through destroying others while sloth, greed, gluttony, and lust present attractiveness gone to an extreme (Fairlie, 1979). Schimmel (1997) underlines the relevance of the seven deadly sins to the modern man from the perspective of psychology, theology, and philosophy. He defines these vices as the core of all human moral failures as well as the roots of various psychological disorders. The underlying force behind vices is failure to manage one's selfish desires through self-control and development of virtuous character (Schimmel, 1997). Hence the importance of understanding the relationship between addiction, immorality, morality, virtue, and vice requires further analysis of the latter.

Categorising of vices may be guided through the study of vices' traditions completed by DeYoung (2009) which incorporates the tradition of the seven deadly sins and formulates a list of seven main vices as the core categories of moral failures. These vices are to be understood as the general source of all other vices or moral failures. DeYoung (2009) provides the list of capital vices which includes vainglory, avarice, anger, lust, gluttony, envy, and sloth. This same list is mentioned by Xavier (2010) using the synonyms of pride, greed, and wrath for the first three terms. DeYoung (2009) prefers the title of vices over deadly sins due to the specific nature of the former related to human character and the dogmatic connotation of deadly. Nevertheless, the titles' significance is overshadowed by the similarity of their nature based on one's attitude towards them which shapes character. An attitude of accommodating the vice as part of character and as such shaping cognitive, emotive, and behaviour responses to life establish inactive position towards God and spirituality. The deadly sin mentioned in 1 John 5:16–17 is contextually defined as a continuous sinful behaviour that leads to spiritual death (cf. 1 John 5:18, NIV), which in the broader context may be understood as an attitude to lifestyle underlined by unrepented sin (cf. 1 John 1:8–10). DeYoung (2009) provides direct connection between practicing spirituality and resolving vice which defines the expansion of the latter in the absence of the former.

The seven vices characterise moral failure due to the diminished activity of conscience and expose clear links to addiction. In the context of the latter Xavier (2010) views the vices as character flaws caused by the superfluous supply of needs in disregard to conscience. A short description of each vice will provide the grounds for their identification and relation to the addictive behaviour in the interviewees' transcripts.

The list of vices includes pride, anger, greed, lust, sloth, envy, and gluttony. Pride is the complete absorption with individual power and the capacity to control others and the world according to one's desires leading to boastful arrogance of personal superiority in thought, affect, attitude, and behaviour (Fairlie, 1979), as well as failure to accept one's limitations and embrace humbly an ultimate authority of a divine being (Schimmel, 1997). Anger is an emotional response to suffering from injustice which transforms into a vice when uncontrolled; constructively forming a vengeful attitude which is cognitively shaped and behaviourally expressed through violence against the perceived carrier of the injustice (Schimmel, 1997). Research reveals that serial killers maintain high cognitive involvement with planning and executing crimes but fail to manage their evil inclinations due to inactive conscience which may also explain their experience of continuous anger and lack of guilt (Schimmel, 1997). One way to define greed is as an egoistic interest in obtaining finances through immoral means for the provision of substances which satisfy one's desires for pleasure (Schimmel, 1997). Lust is understood as a selfish sexual gratification through the exploitation of another involving promiscuous thinking (DeYoung, 2009) and an attitude of a deceitful seduction leading to abuse and rape (Schimmel, 1997). Schimmel (1997) argues that substance abuse may play a significant part of shaping one's lustful desires. Sloth is identified as an intentional refusal of one's moral and spiritual duties and commitments (DeYoung, 2009) leading to selfish inconsideration of the needs of others and loss of hope, purpose, and meaning of life (Schimmel, 1997). Envy is the acquisition of self-worth, self-love, and self-approval through comparative demeaning of others underlined by the endeavour to elevate one's own position over them (DeYoung, 2009) and obliterate their valuable qualities, possessions, or status (Schimmel, 1997). Envy disintegrates all relationships through the selfish strive to undermine others and exalt self (Fairlie, 1979). Finally, gluttony may be defined as unmanageable desires, thoughts, and behaviours for excessive consumption of food or drink which establish complete control over one's life for its provision and intake and may lead to immorality and disregard of one's responsibilities and social role (Schimmel, 1997). Fairlie (1979) argues that alcohol and drug addictions should be treated as forms of gluttony since the behaviour is developed through consensual submission to one's desire and the controlling power of the substance. Hobbs (2005) associates the vice of gluttony with the underlining attitudes towards alcohol consumption. He argues that it is the alcohol industry promoted through government economic ambitions that cultivates an environment related to the abuse of alcohol. Thus gluttony shapes both the attitudes of the drinker for higher consumption and of the producer for higher earning. The moral model of addiction treats alcoholism as vice (Jaffe and Meyer, 2001). The direct relationship between immorality, development of vice, lack of spirituality, and degradation of character underlines the absence of virtues and character strengths which may establish an environment for the development of addiction.

DeYoung (2009) maintains that vices and virtues belong to character and are developed through employment of a continuous behaviour of moral progression or regression. Both sins and vices are moral problems for which a solution can be found in the practice of spiritual disciplines. DeYoung (2009) argues that reshaping our character morally from vices to virtues requires continuous practice of spiritual disciplines to establish an habitual behaviour of moral value which incorporates cognitive and emotive involvement. Xavier (2010) maintains that the main role in establishing this virtuous habitual behaviour is to be attributed to one's conscience. This is achieved through continuous conscientious engagement with context and a consistent moral inventory. According to McCosh (1887) the development of habitual conscientious behaviour is promoted through positive self-affect. Spirituality appears to play a crucial role in the involvement of conscience in developing virtuous character and influencing behaviour positively.

Spirituality impacts the formation and integration of one's moral values in one's life (Peterson and Seligman, 2004). Spiritual change is strongly associated with, and even made equivalent to, moral transformation and is acknowledged as a viable solution for addiction problems (Orford, 2006). Spiritual-moral empowerment enables resistance to alcohol addiction (Delaney, Forcehimes, Campbell, and Smith, 2009). The process of positive spiritual influences on conscience is an integral part of 12-step facilitation underlining the relationship with a higher power and moral transformation (Seppala, 2001). The connection between conscience, virtue, and spirituality requires further examination.

1.3. Conscience's relationship to morality: spiritual empowerment, virtue, and recovery

Langston (2001) maintains that conscience is a multidimensional entity which provides synchrony between cognitive, attitudinal, emotive, and behavioural moral responses of the individual to oneself and the context. The person's conscience develops with the input of the parental and societal moral framework through communication of principle, narrative, and modelling guidance. During this process virtues are integrated as promoters of morally persuaded goals. The consistency and continuity in using conscience in shaping moral and virtuous thinking and action lead to development of habitual moral behaviour. The latter develops a character which integrates and further develops virtues. The core element in conscientious functionality is the character strength of prudence, the practical wisdom gained through the experience of conscience by application of moral choices in real life situations. Practical wisdom is understood as the framework of applying other virtues in life through the assessment of context according to its ethical demands (Fowers, 2009). A core guiding principle of conscience is a selfless attitude towards others shaped through one's perception of self in the place of others and openness to their opinions. This shapes morality with respect to the needs of others leading to its universally justifiable applications. The latter underlines a personal moral framework which reflects a desire for social ethical response. Conscience shapes behaviour through encouraging purpose-oriented supporting actions developing a moral goal and discouraging the ones which deviate from it. The relationship between conscience and virtue is mutually inclusive. Conscience inaugurates and promotes virtue which matures the conscience and stimulates its functionality (Langston, 2001).

Xavier (2010) argues that conscience is different from the super-ego. The latter is defined by Freud as a carrier of judicial and ideal faculties dictating behaviour towards right and wrong. According to Freud conscience is only dealing with negative behaviour, and therefore is diminished to insignificant and punitive. Xavier (2010) defines the super-ego as a judicial mechanism based on the accumulation of knowledge through positive and negative reinforcement from parents and society. On the other hand, conscience is the imbedded spiritual nature in oneself which is shaped by a balanced cognitive response to self and others based on the "Golden Rule" of treating others according to one's reciprocal expectations (Xavier, 2010).

The functionality of conscience is defined by Xavier (2010) as the employability of virtues within the fourfold framework of conscious evaluation, decision formation, consequent application, and consequential re-evaluation. The individual is using conscience through becoming acquainted with the evidence according to the needs involving intellect, feelings, and experience leading to establishing a decision which is acted upon and the consequences of the actions being evaluated and redefined. All these elements of the process operate with the input of virtues and character strengths such as awareness, love of learning, open mindedness, insight, wisdom, empathy, compassion, love, peace, discipline, moderation, self-control, and courage (Xavier, 2010).

The understanding of conscience, its nature and function, as defined through the connection between virtue, character strengths, and spirituality leads to further examination of these concepts and their relationship. Peterson and Seligman (2004) provide a classification which defines six virtues shaped by 24 character strengths.

The virtue of wisdom and knowledge refers to the acquisition, assimilation, and management of information (Park, 2009) supported through the strengths of creativity, curiosity, open-mindedness, love of learning, and perspective (Peterson and Seligman, 2004). Creativity involves originality in theory and application. Curiosity defines interest in obtaining and managing knowledge within a novel context. Open-mindedness provides a balanced and unbiased framework of assessment. Love of learning focuses intellectual capacity onto a particular field of study. Finally, perspective defines one's worldview to enable practical wisdom for life (Peterson and Seligman, 2004).

The virtue of courage delineates the pursuing of moral aim in spite of the unfavourable context and the uncertainty of the outcome (Pury and Woodard, 2009). The four contributory strengths are bravery, persistence, integrity, and vitality (Peterson and Seligman, 2004). The nature of bravery shows the defence of an individual's moral beliefs in a hostile environment. Persistence defines one's ability to persevere for the achievement of established objectives. Integrity underlines a person's genuine representation of self. Finally, vitality regenerates the desire to continue one's commitments in life.

The virtue of humanity shapes life's relationships underlining the value and importance of others (Peterson and Seligman, 2004). Love, kindness, and social intelligence characterise a person's character. Love in all its forms constitutes the core of mutually respectful relationships. Kindness shapes one's motivation to offer unconditional support. Finally, social intelligence defines the individual's skilful accommodation to context and others based on perceptive interpretation (Peterson and Seligman, 2004).

The virtue of justice shapes one's moral principles with equality in respect to others in organisational and community life. The strengths of character are citizenship, fairness, and leadership. Citizenship provides the fulfilment of social responsibilities. Fairness demonstrates in practice an individual's unbiased and respectful attitude to others. Finally, leadership provides the guidance for collective achievement managing relationship difficulties in a mutually respectful manner (Peterson and Seligman, 2004).

The virtue of temperance defines a balanced management of one's life, promoting wellbeing and diminishing vices of excess. Character strengths include forgiveness and mercy, humility and modesty, prudence, and self-regulation. Forgiveness and mercy formulate an attitude towards the carrier of an injustice through the perception of human imperfections and acceptance of repentance without vengeance (Peterson and Seligman, 2004). Forgiveness is a process of spiritual enlightenment which defines moral response, requires dedication (Sanderson and Linehan, 1999), and helps addiction treatment (Witvliet, 2009). Humility and modesty shape one's consideration of achievements with perception of limitations, openness for correction and appreciation of other's worth (Tangney, 2009). Prudence refers to the formation of decisions through assessment of outcomes and risks (Peterson and Seligman, 2004). Finally, self-regulation provides a balanced framework for continuous monitoring and modification of cognition, emotion, and behaviour, leading towards the achievement of a particular goal (Peterson and Seligman, 2004; Maddux, 2009).

The virtue of transcendence shapes one's meaning in life and approach to the world, the universe, and the metaphysical (Peterson and Seligman, 2004; Park, 2009). The underlining character strengths are the appreciation of beauty and excellence, gratitude, hope, humour, and spirituality (Peterson and Seligman, 2004). Appreciation of beauty and excellence characterises a person's approach to life's exquisiteness, culminating in awe with the experience of something exceptionally profound and leading to spiritual enlightenment (Sundararajan, 2009). Gratitude shapes one's perspective of life inspiring moral behaviour and through the person's spirituality resonates in reverence to a divine benevolence (Emmons, 2009). Hope provides positive perspective on the future engaging resourcefulness to overcome challenges and achieve the desired goal (Edwards, 2009). Humour underlines a person's engagement with the joyful side of life and leads to psychological benefits through cognitive, emotive, and behavioural social interactions (Martin, 2009). Finally, spirituality constitutes a belief system which defines one's worldview, moral framework, and life's relationships, providing content and stability of daily engagements (Peterson and Seligman, 2004). Spirituality is based on the individual pursuit and acceptance of the sacred in life through a personal relationship with the divine leading to the formation of character and approach to life (Pargament, 2009).

Spirituality in light of its connection to religiousness is identified as significant for the development of character strengths and virtues. The closeness between spirituality and religiousness is established through their focus on a relationship with the divine shaping one's purpose in life, morality, belief system, and transcendent experiences (Emmons, 2003). The overlap of both concepts comes from their tradition, personal and interpersonal aspects (Pargament and Mahoney, 2002), and the individual's spiritual commitment (Moberg, 2010). Spiritual wellbeing resourced through one's relationship with God and religious belonging improves psychological, physical, and social wellbeing (Pargament, 2009) and promotes successful relationships and personal growth (Canda, 2009). Spiritual fulfilment is behind the development of virtues (Pargament, 2009). The understanding of virtues benefits from spiritual and religious language (Pargament and Mahoney, 2002) as well as from the study of religious literature (Watts, Dutton, and Gulliford, 2006). Christian spirituality also encourages virtuous character (2 Peter 1:5–7) through the acceptance of God's love in Jesus underlined by repentance, faith, and gratitude leading to altruistic relationships with one's neighbour (Waltke, 1988) and personal edification based on the model of Jesus (Wiersbe, 1989). Spirituality is essential for the progress of recovery from addiction (Pargament, 2009; Miller and Thoresen, 1999; Hodge, 2011; Carter, 1998). Spiritual conversion is a transforming internal experience of reorienting one's life to God and modifying one's entire self and moral system that promotes recovery from addiction (Mahoney and Pargament, 2004). The importance of spirituality for morality, conscience, and recovery underlines the research rationale for the present study.

1.4. Research rationale: formulation of the study goal and questions

The survey of literature reveals a threefold relationship between conscience, morality, and spirituality in the context of alcohol addiction. First, the nature and function of conscience formulated through its cognitive, emotive, and conative elements define one's moral perception and behaviour. Spirituality plays a crucial role in the process and may be identified as part of the very nature of conscience. Hence the question arises of the relationship between spirituality and the elements of conscience in the interviews and its outcomes for recovery from alcohol addiction. Could cognitive conscience, empowered through spirituality, resolve the issue of attentional bias and automaticity in alcohol addiction? Second, it is evident from the review that alcohol addiction manipulates conscience leading to the development of immorality and vice. This formulates the question as to whether there is evidence of such demoralisation of conscience due to alcohol addiction in the interviews. Third, it is clear from the literature that spirituality influences conscience leading to moral enhancement and character edification with the formation of virtue. This provides the grounds for examining the narratives for such a relationship considering its influences on the recovery. This threefold query defines the goal of this study which is to examine the relationship between conscience, morality, and spirituality within the framework of alcohol addiction treatment and its role in improving recovery. Derived from this goal is the main research question: Does the relationship between spirituality and conscience lead to positive impact on recovery from alcohol addiction? The methodology for answering this question is presented in the following chapter.

2.

Methodology

THE METHODOLOGY FOR THE present research is qualitatively defined in order to achieve effective results in the study of conscience, morality, spirituality, and their impact on recovery from alcohol addiction. Personal narrative with its enlightenment of individual experiences and holistic framework defines the focus of the methodology. Autobiography is one of the appropriate methodologies for studying conscience (Stephenson, 1998). Individual's story is at the centre of the approach to quantum change, a sudden personal transformation (Miller and Baca, 2001; Baca and Wilbourne, 2004; Kurtz, 2001). Moral, religious, and spiritual characteristics underline quantum change (Miller and Baca, 2001; Baca and Wilbourne, 2004). The narratives from the Big Book of Alcoholics Anonymous (AA) define recovery from alcohol addiction through moral and spiritual transformation with the stages of acknowledging one's failures, willingness to change, and acceptance of God's leading role in life (Forcehimes, 2004). The study of one's narrative formulates the present methodology in relation to design, participants, apparatus, and procedure.

2.1. Design

Narrative Analysis (NA) is used to deal with a particular segment of the individual's life story (Langdridge, 2004). The method provides the format for analysing each story which is significantly disrupted by dramatic events. The narrative is defined through its main elements, namely, events, characters, action sequences, and personal transformation. These are connected through the narrative plot which develops the story from its beginning to the end passing through various diverse stages and leading from problem to solution (Howitt, 2010).

The data is collected through a semi-structured interview. The interview protocol involves an introductory guidance and subsequent questions with sub-questions. The first part of the protocol provides a brief guidance for the interviewee pointing to the research topics and the possible format of the story underlining the creative freedom of the interviewee. The predominantly non-conversational nature of the interview provides the necessary space for the narrator to develop the story (Howitt, 2010). The second part involves 11 questions with three or four sub-questions which are asked after the presentation of the narrative for further clarification of the research topics as a part of the individual story. The questions' content is conceptually based on the research rationale leading to the identification and understanding of important experiences and their transformative role in one's life (Langdridge, 2004). The interview schedule is presented in the appendices.

2.2. Participants

Due to the extensive nature of the interviews and their in-depth analysis (Howitt, 2010) the study involves 12 interviewees. The interview was conducted through the necessary interpersonal skills (Howitt, 2010) within an ethically sound framework protecting the participants' confidentiality (Langdridge, 2004). The latter was further implemented through replacement of all real personal names with fictional ones and omission or substitution of sensitive information in the interview transcripts (see appendices).

The grounds for participation were defined through four-dimensional selection criteria. First, the potential participants were expected to have had a history of alcohol addiction. Second, their present state was to be characterised by successful achievement of abstinence and progressive recovery. Third, the realisation of this state was believed to have been attained through a transformative experience which predominant characteristics reflect moral, spiritual, and/or religious nature. Fourth, the present actualisation of this experience was understood to be delineated by maintaining moral, spiritual, and/or religious edification.

The participants were recruited through introducing the research project in two residential rehabilitation centres, a homeless charity, a community rehabilitation centre, and in consultation with colleagues from the fields of addictions and homelessness. The participants who responded may be considered as self-selected since they identified their stories as

Methodology

corresponding to the selection criteria. Hence, the shared characteristics of the contributing group generally reflect the four dimensions of the criteria and as such underline its homogeneous nature. Several interviewees came from the two residential rehabilitation centres. Three participants were invited from the homeless charity and two came from the community rehabilitation centre. One interviewee responded positively after the project was introduced to him by our mutual acquaintance. Permissions for the interviews and their locations were obtained from the management of the rehabilitation centres, the homeless charity, and the community centre. The study is publicised through a website (www.consciencetherapy.com) which provides an overview of the research and an email address for communication with the participants.

The twelve participants represent a demographically diverse group. The latter includes 10 males and two females, whose age varies from 36 to 56. Their educational background ranges from NVQ-2 to BA and BSc degrees. The ethnic origin of the interviewees includes seven white British and five others comprising two black Africans and three white Europeans. Diverse occupations from various industries are revealed with predominant representation of the social care sector with a substance misuse counsellor, a support worker, a worker in a residential rehabilitation centre, and a managerial position in a homeless hostel. The interviewees' data is presented in the appendices.

2.3. Apparatus

The equipment used for conducting the study involved Olympus digital voice recorder WS-560M with internal memory, SONY type PC, Microsoft Word processor 2010, Express Scribe Pro transcription software, Dragon Naturally Speaking software and MAXQDA. The latter requires a further clarification.

MAXQDA is a CAQDAS (Computer Assisted Qualitative Data Analysis Software) package chosen for conducting the qualitative analysis of the data in light of the Saillard's (2011) conclusion that the diverse availability of tools improves the researcher's interactions with the text leading to establishing solid theoretical models. The similarity of operational structures and functionality of CAQDAS packages (Lewins and Silver, 2009) led to identification of NVivo 8 and MAXQDA 10 as suitable choices. The selection of the latter is based on its advance tools for memo writing, managing text's structures (Schönfelder, 2011), presentation of codes, easy access to annotations, and flexibility for close interactions with the texts (Saillard, 2011). The software offers constructive workspace and a comprehensive set of tools for effective examination of the texts through coding, annotating, browsing, establishing variables, and retrieving results (MAXQDAplus [Version 10]; VERBI GmbH, 2011; *The top 10 changes in MAXQDA 10*, 2010). MAXQDA provides the necessary means for conducting the textual analysis of the narratives and developing the theory of the present research.

2.4. Procedure

The research covers the stages of interviewing, transcribing, analysis of the narratives, and presentation of the findings in a research report. The project commenced after its ethical approval by the London South Bank University. All the interviews were carried out in locations of the organisations involved in the recruitment, namely, the residential rehabilitation centres, the homeless charity, and the community rehabilitation centre. These secured the confidential nature of the interviews and the personal safety of the interviewer. The interviews began with signing of the Informed Consent Form (constructed according to Howitt, 2010) by the interviewees. The document presented the study, defined the responsibilities and benefits for the interviewees and the interviewer, and explained the ethical framework of the research. The semi-structured interviews were opened with short introduction leaving the interviewees to develop their personal narrative freely (see the short introductory guidance from the Interview Schedule in the appendices). The clarification questions followed the personal story and were answered at the initiative of the interviewee to elaborate and enlighten its elements (see the questions and sub-questions from the Interview Schedule in the appendices). A debriefing led the interview to completion. During this stage the interviewees were provided with a Debriefing Form which included the website dedicated to the project and organisations offering counselling and other type of support (see appendices). The purpose of this document was explained and the interviewees were given the opportunity to get acquainted with its content, express any consideration, and show emotional and physical readiness to engage into normal daily activities. The data obtained from the semi-structured interviews was transcribed and introduced to MAXQDA where it was further analysed through the use of analytically developed coding system (see appendices).

Methodology

The codes were created in a fourfold manner, namely, in light of the literature review, through the perspective of the research rationale, on the basis of the interview questions, and from the reading of the collected data. Every transcribed interview was read thoroughly and divided into paragraphs which were automatically numbered by the software (the numbering in MAXQDA commences from the title of the interview). The paragraphs' content was analysed and the main subject designated with a colour code from the system. Relevant notions from each paragraph also received colour codes. I introduced paragraphs' memos next to the codes to elaborate the important aspects of the content. The codes and memos with their locations in the interviews are presented in the appendices. I will offer a complete interview transcript in the following chapter to enable the reader to establish an individual perspective of the data collected from the interviews. The rest of the interview transcripts are accessible in the appendices.

3.

John's personal interview

THE FOLLOWING INTERVIEW IS selected as a typical example of participants' responses to the semi-structured interview protocol. The audio material is transcribed and divided in paragraphs. The roles of the interviewer and interviewee are identified accordingly.

John (2011). Personal interview (Conscience in recovery from alcohol addiction), 15 November.

Interviewer (I): John, these are the guidelines. I will read them for you. Structure your life story in chapters. Think about their names, summaries, and progressive links. Without interfering with the genuine character of the story can you identify the role of the following topics in your life narrative: conscience; alcohol addiction; morality; spirituality; religiousness; moral reformation; spiritual transformation; religious conversion and/or affiliation; the relationship between morality, spirituality, religiousness, and conscience, and recovery from alcohol addiction. How will you summarise each of these chapters? What progressive links will you make between these chapters?

John (J): Okay.
I: Start with your name and so on.
J: Okay. Yeah.
I: Thank you.
J: My name is John. I'm now ... (age omitted due to confidentiality). I come from a privileged but not wealthy family; lovely parents, you know, kind, considerate, loving; very large extended family. I had, what would describe as a pretty idyllic childhood: a lot of grandparents, grandmothers, and holidays in this country, and also in the Isle of Wight. I was brought up in the North East of England. And everything was going pretty well

John's personal interview

in most of my life. My father was a grammar school teacher in a private school. I was lucky enough to go to that school. At the time it was in the top 10 in the world, in the country rather. I didn't make much of it. I played rugby. I played rugby to very high standard. I had an England trial at one point. But sadly one of the things that . . . . Well during that time my eyes got progressively worse to the point that I had to wear . . . . I wore specs since I was about three years old. But to the point I couldn't play rugby because I couldn't see the ball at all. So that's when I look back on it was a bit of, a bit of a blow. But never mind.

The main focus of our life was a very large tennis club which we were brought up in. We had home and things. My father was an excellent world tennis player. And as well as being a teacher he was heavily involved in the tennis club which is where our lives evolved, my brother, my sister, and I. And I am the oldest one of the family. And it was great fun. We had tennis. And we had squash. And the run of the place. And it was really good fun. There was obviously also a barley. In coming from the North East of England it is the drinking capital of Britain and goes with the culture. I was drinking in quite an early age. Partying in front of people, you know, I was being allowed to have shandy or something like that. Rightly or wrongly some people try it some people don't. But by the time I was 13 the alcohol began to get a grip on me for a variety of different reasons. One is the eyesight. Another is that I felt quite ugly. I used to have a very large mole sprouted hairs on my chin which was removed because as I became a man, I was going through puberty, I couldn't shave because of it. And I just sort of felt uncomfortable with myself. Other thing I suppose that came about, again looking back, is the expectations of me as the eldest. Not just with my brother and sister but within the whole of my family. There are 40 or 50 cousins and I am the eldest out of them. We don't know that's a need to realise that at the time.

One thing my dad would do, lovely bloke, but he would ask me on the Sunday morning, but he has been teaching all week and things like that, heavily involved in the tennis club, to go open up the tennis club. Which is fine! So he's got the responsibility of alarms. At this day and age it's 50–60 million pounds worth of clubhouse and grounds and also . . . . I didn't mind that. That was good fun. It would renew me. But I will get there at eight o'clock and the first members would come to play squash at 9:30 or 10. And by that time I'd already drunk half a bottle of gin, you know, or gin and orange or gin and Scotch. And it made me feel good I suppose. It just became, became the norm. I worked behind the bar. I helped in the stocking up. All that sort of thing. A lot of this evolved around my father which I know now with hindsight, I didn't realise at the time. He's kind, he's loving, he's gentle. He is not demonstrative. He doesn't show affection very well. He's got much better as he's got older with grandchildren and things. But in our family on the male side we can go back to the end of the nineteenth century and there is an alcoholic in every single generation. What science makes of genetics and all that kind of stuff I don't know. And he had quite a tough childhood. He never talks about it. I've only gleaned bits. But his father was an alcoholic and used to get him and his younger brother, my uncle, up at the middle of the night make him get dressed, make him stand to attention. He was in the Royal Navy. When he was drunk, you know. That's just about the only think I really, really know about it. He wasn't violent or nasty to them. So any sort of time I got to spend with my dad became very sort of precious, you know. He was busy. He was very much his own man. He does his own thing. Probably here I've got a quite deep voice. His is even deeper. And it is more rounded. He's a brilliant tennis player. He's very intelligent. So in my own head I got a kind of, very false image. And like most sons I suspect would like to, would want to love their dad, would like to emulate him. I discover that I didn't just want to be a bit like him I actually wanted to be him. So I stopped being me and tried to be him. And obviously, subconsciously I knew I couldn't do that so I drank.

The drink gave me confidence about the way that I looked, about my eyesight. That sort of thing. So by the time I was 15 or 16 I thought it was cool to drink large amounts of alcohol, to smock very heavily. I would steal from the tennis club. I would open up the fruit machines and steal money from there; steal from my dad; steal from the tills; steal from the bar. And I didn't think anything about it. Nobody reproached me for because it was all done. There was lots of money there. So nothing from the amounts I was pinching, still a lot of money, weren't really noticeable or anything like that. And with alcohol it sort of became the norm, I suppose. One of the other major problems I had was that I was never knowing what I wanted to do. I can play rackets' sports to a greater or lesser degree but again my eyesight, I blame it on it but it did stop to a certain extent my ability to play. My brother and sister younger than I am are phenomenal rackets force players. They were both under the age of 15 senior champions at both tennis and squash. Absolutely amazing, they are really, really good. When my dad took over the tennis club as a manager and he stopped teaching they were at the right age so it was all falling into place for them. I'm not jealous

John's personal interview

of them. I'm very proud of them. But there was a degree of envy there as well and I felt rather useless with it.

Time goes on and the first proper job I had was through my uncle who is also another alcoholic. He hasn't drunk now for about 10 years, I don't think. He was a solicitor in this south coast English city (TSCEC, name substituted due to confidentiality), or is a solicitor, and he got me a job running a bar and a casino. Great! Nobody really caught on to the fact, at least not me, how much I actually drank. And I did that successfully. I was a good barman as in the service and the communication, all like that, I think. I was terrible with the stock control because I was drinking most of it. A lot of what I was doing, any kind of relationships I built were based around alcohol. I couldn't; it was all in pubs and clubs and things like that. I was never short of female company. No matter what I thought, I was ugly etc. There always seemed to be a girlfriend or a woman around or something like that, which wasn't a problem. But it was always . . . . This is all looking back. But there was always a complete emptiness inside because I wasn't being fulfilled. I didn't have any goals. I didn't know who I was. I didn't know what I wanted to do. I felt absolutely useless basically. So I did the job at the casino. I got fired from that. I worked for a removal firm. I did all sorts of jobs. It was quite a long time ago now. But even at that stage everything was pretty much related to: "Where is my next drink coming from?"

It had to, it's coming to a residential rehabilitation centre (RRC, name substituted throughout the transcript due to confidentiality) that, and going into my past I had to be reminded at the age about 24 I got married which I'd completely forgotten about. It was a marriage of two lonely people who met because we moved into a shared house where I used to work for staff agency. I started off as a temp doing all sorts of different jobs there. Then I became somebody who works in an office where any other people have to work. Then I became a manager of offices. So actually I was relatively successful at that. I hated every minute of it but I was very successful. So I met this lady, lonely. I got married because that's what people do. It's completely wrong. We were totally unsuited. It was quite good because I lost the job with the staff agencies because I've been fiddling the funds, fiddling the money to get drink and things. Lucky not to go to prison for it, I suppose. And it was also good; it got me out of the South of England where I was basically desperately lonely and very, very unhappy. And got me back to the North East of England with my family which sounds good. And I did any number of different jobs. I was in sales mostly. Sadly I was really good at it. Sales isn't about lying. Sales isn't about misinterpretation. But it is about putting a slant on things, fabricating a story, making you seem better than everybody else. So again it was just an extension of myself. It was just lying. And I hadn't realised how far the alcohol had got. And how arrogant, bombastic, rude, know it all, I was a creak basically. Lots, lots of relationships were going on at that time; some lasting two years; some lasting three; promises of marriage. All kinds of crap that addicts come out with. It is great looking back from where I sit and I can see what a lot of rubbish it was. Basically I had a good childhood with kind, loving parents. I got stuck into my own head what we call here, "self-talk tapes": that I was worthless, that I had no self-esteem, that I couldn't do anything, that the only way I could really survive was through alcohol. That alcohol was my friend. This is stuff looking back obviously that I understand. That the only way I could progress was to drink. It was great fun. Everybody did it. And it started to get to the point where it was becoming untenable even in my own twisted, immoral mind.

And I can't remember how it came about but I made myself homeless. At least I thought I made myself homeless. And I had some drinking buddies from really rough pubs in this north east English city (TNEEC, name substituted throughout the transcript due to confidentiality). And they were good people. There is a kind of underclass in this world that you come across when you are an addict. And they do look after themselves. They look after each other. It's your turn for the doll cheque. See to buy everybody a drink. When is their turn they buy you a drink. That sort of thing. So I slept on floors. I wouldn't tell my parents where I was. Put them through hell. Eventually I got myself a flat in a really grotty part of TNEEC. I get drinking, thinking I was on the out fabricating the story: "All things are gonna get better. It's jam tomorrow etc." And it really was getting worse and worse. And I can't remember where I was but somebody gave me a telephone number. And I phoned that number. I've jumped ahead. I had to go back again in a second. I beg your pardon. I phoned that number. And it was a Drug and Alcohol Team in TNEEC. I never even heard of one. They are part of the detoxing unit within TNEEC. And I detoxed three times but never for myself. In other words, it was always to please parents, to please work, to please somebody else. And yeah, you feel great when you come out of detox but it's done absolutely nothing to do with addiction. All you've done is just clean your body above. There was a period of a fortnight or so. And of course you feel so good you go back straight on the drink again. By the third time we realised that the things

John's personal interview

were really, really desperate. My parents really started to ask questions: "Where can we send our son?" They can't afford the Priory or anything like that. I think, I began to realise I was, I was reaching the end. I couldn't do it. My whole life just evolved around alcohol. I was under 10 stone, you know. I would if I could have it and I had the money I'd drink up to two litres of vodka a day plus beer and all that kind of stuff. And it was just a rat race, a rabbit run. All the time go around, around the same stuff. And the days I didn't have alcohol, cigarettes, or food I would just sit in my grotty flat shivering, shaking, retching, and vomiting, and feeling sorry for myself basically. And anyway so I got this telephone number. Where it came I don't know. It was the Drug and Alcohol Team. I went for an interview with a lady there. The lady organised a telephone interview with the RRC, where I'm sitting now. I did that telephone interview. And within a very short period of time, in my mind I think it's about two weeks, it could have been even less, I was down here.

And as soon as I walked through the doors I knew this is where I needed to be, where I wanted to be. And I felt something at that point: a real buzz, a real high, a real sense of comfort, a real sense of peace. All sorts of different adjectives I can use here. I know now it was Christ. And I can look back that whoever gave me that telephone number that's when Christ had come into my life. I had reached the bottom, you know. My only other place that I was gonna go was death in a matter of time. So I got here and one of the first questions, one of the first things you have to do is you get strip-searched. Your bags are all searched, obviously. They don't want anything being brought in. And I was asked, you know: "Have you had a drink today?" And I denied it emphatically as addicts do cause we lie through our back teeth. But what I had had just to stop the shakes and things like that was three litres of White Lightning cider in the morning before coming down from TNEEC. And I think that was just about the last time that I told a dirty, great, big, black lie. Social untruth like: "How are you," and all that kind of stuff I will whitewash over those a little bit. I got here and I got what I craved. And I think what a lot of alcoholics crave, certainly most addicts crave is order, is the end to the chaos, to the way your mind works. I mean it takes a long time for your mind to settle down but you have an order, you have a routine here, you're loved, you're cared for. Words the men don't use. You don't have to be a man here. You don't have to show your muscles, the tattoos, and swaggle, and strength as some of the men still do. But you are actually allowed to be yourself. You actually find out who you are through process of counselling. Through your peers you learn so much about yourself, through your peers. Cause we all have a shared experience. We had it through so many different angles. You obviously get counselling. One of the things I liked was, it's not like a prison camp or anything, but you have a bell. I can't remember the routine, I should, but is something like 7:45 the bell goes, you know, you've got to come down and do X. At eight o'clock is breakfast. The bell rings quarter past etc. And it just gives you order. You can sleep because you're not worried where your next drink is coming from, your next injection, your next needle, or anything like that. You get fed. We call it the RRC belly. I put on two stone in three months. Good, you know. Good weight! So I felt better about my physical self.

You get reassurance, you get compassion. The majority of the counsellors when I was here, and still two or three of them are, are recovering addicts or healed addicts and they did it, they've done the programme. So you can't lie to them. You can't pull all over their eyes. They know exactly what you're talking about. And if you do try and lie they just pull you apart in a nice way. I told my counsellor, looking back he's very, very clever with it but he let me talk, just as I'm talking to you. He chipped away the foundations of the walls I built in my head that I thought were protecting me but they were doing exactly the opposite. I took a venture, I broke, you know, and cried, and got rid of all of the angst. And then we were able to really work on whatever the issues were which as I mentioned at the beginning was that: a father fixation, feeling uncomfortable about myself, with low self-esteem, self-respect all of those sorts of things that go along with addiction.

Other things I loved here was that it's a work-based programme. I like using my hands. I've been a salesman and in offices and in cars for the most of my life. It was great to get out on the land. I was given responsibility quite quickly because I was a relatively well-educated. I was proved to be trustworthy. For somebody to give you trust when you don't even trust yourself makes, you know, makes a huge difference. I was shown respect by my peers which gave me a bit more self-respect. Not by all of them. You can't get on with all the people all the time by any stretch of the imagination. One of the most important things for most men who come here—everybody comes here because of Christ. Whether accept him or not is a different kettle of fish. And I know I am right because I met Christ. You have to go to church. Which is a bit of a penance to start with because a lot of us will react because we've been doing things our own way for so many years. We were right and everybody else was wrong, that kind of attitude. And I tried to intellectualise it. And my counsellor gave me a book: Josh McDowell, *Evidence that demands a verdict*. It was all very, very . . . . Just quotes from very, very famous people. We all heard of why they believed in Christ, why they knew him. People like Napoleon. You know things like that. He might have banned religion and that kind of stuff but he still believed in Christ. Einstein still believed in Christ. All that sort of things. So that started to help. And then on July the 23rd, 2007 I was in the church called ". . ." which is in . . . (names omitted due to confidentiality). For some reason I knew all the hymns which is unusual for me. I can't sing a note but I like to join in. And the pastor or preacher or leader, I don't know all the terminology, the vicar at the front after his sermons said: "Would anybody like to be filled with the Holy Spirit." And my body stood up. I didn't. I'm British. I am reserved. I was wearing a black yellow rugby shirt and things like that. I was going "hrrrr" inside. "What are you doing, everybody is looking at you." Of course nobody was looking at me. So couple of people came and prayed over me. And at that one moment quite literally all of my angst, all of my sin, all my shame, all of my guilt were lifted off my shoulders, there and then. Done. And the release was absolutely phenomenal. All right, it was a process. My counsellor was part of that process. Being here was part of that process. My own willingness was part of that process. But that, that one moment I've been filled with the love of Christ. Meeting him and the Holy Spirit is just, it is inexplicable. If it has happened to you, you would understand what I'm talking about. And the intriguing thing is, it's such a wonderful feeling, I don't know, like taking heroin or like having a lovely, big, large vodka and tonic or something. You know that's a nice drink etc. It's a pleasurable feeling. But I will chase after that all the time. The Holy Spirit, I'm quite happy to wait for him to come. I am happy to be. I know that it's there all the time. I know that Christ is always looking after me no matter what I do wrong. And that is such a wonderful feeling.

I am just having a look through the list here to see if I'm getting what you want. I mean if you look at conscience which in my mind is basically: every human being is born with the conscience, it is called the Holy Spirit—right and wrong. No matter where you come from, where about in the world you are, what religion you're brought up in, what political state you're brought up in, we all know right and wrong. That's the Holy Spirit. And one of the things that we addicts do is suppress that conscience. We know really that what we're doing is wrong unless you have specifically Asperger's or something like that, you don't grasp that for medical reasons. So your conscience is brought back to life again, your morality which is right—wrong, your conscience. The spirituality: I'm not particularly spiritual person. And I'm certainly not religious. I go to church. I love going to church. I like being with like-minded people. I'm not very good with my hands in the air and all that dancing stuff. And I don't get, I don't speak in tongues. And I'm far more practical with my Christianity.

"The relationship between morality, spirituality, religiousness, and conscience, and recovery from alcohol addiction." One of the biggest holes in anybody's life, addict or not, is that the majority of people that I come across who are unhappy, are unhappy because they have a spiritual hole in them. And no other reason. They try all sorts of things, whether is: "I need a better car, or I need a better looking wife, or I need a bigger house, or I need alcohol, or I need sex," whatever it is it doesn't fill the hole. Because you don't know who you are. Those are things that are extra to what we are as human beings. We have a God-shaped hole in us. And we had to fill that hole. Once you fill that hole; I'm not saying it's easy; but it becomes easier to know who you are to deal with some other things. I realise that. Yes, it's nice to have a Ferrari. It's nice to have big, busted, blonde wife, or whatever. But that doesn't matter. It's not important. It's who you are. Are you having a nice time? Are you enjoying your life? Are you being productive with your life as in not making millions and millions of pounds? Are you fitting into society? Are you helpful? Are you kind? Are you generous? Are you compassionate? Do people love you, like you? Will they remember you? All those sorts of things. Being able to express and have real feelings. To be able to enjoy looking out at the sun coming through that window and the trees. Not having to have LSD or whatever to experience it. Not having to have a few pints outside the county pub to enjoy it.

I suppose I can summarise by: I was really blessed. When I was on the programme there was a guy coming to do a Bible study with whom I got really well. At that time we had an access to a tennis court which was great for me and my recovery. Because I was a tennis player I was quite good at it. Not very shy, I was able to meet with my other residents and enjoy life at that. I was invited by this guy for Sunday teas and Sunday lunches with his family. And they invited me to come and stay with them when I finished the programme, which was a huge weight off my shoulders again. Because from the second part of the programme, . . . (name omitted due to confidentiality), a lot of your worries are: "What I'm gonna do next? Where I am going to go?" And one of the things they encourage you to do is to stay in the area because you hopefully have made good, clean, living friends rather than people you know from where you come from.

I could never go back to TNEEC. I love the North East of England but I can't go back there. It would be a recipe for disaster. Maybe not now but it would have been if I would have gone straight from here. So from the second stage of the residential rehabilitation programme (SSRRP, name substituted throughout the transcript due to confidentiality) I knew where I was going. The guy was a very spiritual man. He was a gardener. I was doing part-time work and living with him rent-free.

My life was a double. For an addict I had lots, lots of money in my pocket. I had lots of support around me. I got temptations, big temptations, big cravings for alcohol and things. But putting into perspective of what I learned here, which is phoning somebody and saying: "I got a big craving." Speak it and the power goes out of it. One way of expressing it is that the devil is having a go. He doesn't want me to be happy. He doesn't want an addict to be happy. He doesn't want Jesus to have us. He wants us. And I was doing a part-time job. I was doing Alpha at church which I really, really enjoyed.

And once I was in the SSRRP here. It is a really an awkward place to get into . . . (name omitted due to confidentiality). Especially it was October–November time. It's dark, it's wet, it's cold, it's miserable and Alpha finished late. So getting a train back at 11 o'clock to get me back here I would have broken the rules. Cause I don't like breaking the rules. So I asked in my group as I have been told to by here: "Humble yourself and ask." "Is there anybody who can give me a lift?" And a lady said: "I can." Who has just discovered where the RRC was by accident earlier. I left the SSRRP in March 2008 and married that lady in June, sorry, July. Which is totally against the rules of recovering addicts: "When you leave the rehab don't under any circumstances get involved with a member of an opposite sex." Not that is anything wrong with women, obviously not, but it can really confuse the issue of your recovery. Well Lynn basically is not. She is, she's . . . . God put her in an Alpha group for me or for both of us. She was a widow for 13–14 years. If I look at women, the ones I like are tall, leggy brunettes. Lynn is a little, blonde, midget. And I love her to bits. She's absolutely wonderful. She's got a completely new list of life now as well. She's 15 years older than me. She is now in her 60s. Widow for a long time she thought, never thought she'd had a relationship again.

And with her support and with the knowledge that I gained here, it was other people's idea but because of the facilities I've got, I started to organise a recovery addicts group which meets the first and the third Tuesdays in the month. There is one this evening. It is the majority of ex-RRC lads. And we meet. And it's not formal, it's informal. We got some cakes and coffee and we just tell each other how we're getting on. So we have a lad who comes and is eight–nine years clean of heroin. That's me coming up towards five years sober. And then we have lads from the SSRRP who need, you know. And it's frightening out there, you know, you get nervous, we need to know that there is support. We are all out there for each other. We're looking out for each other. We're just a phone call away. And it has helped quite a few people. I facilitate it. I don't run it. It's not my idea so I'm not claiming anything on it. It's just one of the things that I'm able to do from what I learned here.

I worked for the council, the local council, for a while when we first got married. And quite frankly it was so boring. Out of the eight hour shift I do about hour and a half work. And I am a busy sort of person. It was driving me nuts. And I could see that it was going to lead to me getting tempted because I'd be bored. And boredom is an absolute killer when it comes to recovering addicts. I would have been tempted to start using alcohol again. So a little old lady, which is what she is, used to come to the council and have a cup of coffee in the cafe. I used to talk to her and she needed her garden doing. So I said: "I will come and do it." And I did that and she put me onto her daughters. So I did their garden. I bought some machinery from my mate with whom I lived with to start with. And eventually very quickly I took a step of faith. And I walked out of my job and became a self-employed gardener. And now I have truck. I now got four men working with me today. They're all volunteers. They are all recovering addicts. I get guys from the Salvation Army who want to come along and work with me for work experience, for fellowship, for relationship. We got one lad who has just come back from another rehab called "House for Heroes." Who didn't want to go? Was kicking like stink but he wanted to save his marriage, you know. But because he spent some time with us, not me, with us, the lads who work with me as well he came to realise that if he wanted to get his life back he'd better do this rehab properly. And he did, he's come back. He's come to Christ. Not because he goes to church. But he loves going to church. He goes to prayer groups. He is a completely and utterly changed man. That's something that me and my two main lads, Carl and Dean, who are both products of the RRC, we love to see, it is in our hearts to do it. Carl and Dean are now going to get self-employed next year because there is enough business for them that we have generated. I am rushed off my feet. I am actually quite pleased to come and talk to you for a couple of hours and, you know, have the time out.

John's personal interview

It's God. He has been so phenomenally good to me. It's a word I'm reluctant to use but because of who I was, the transformation that I went through, the love and compassion I received from so many other people I am now able to pass that on and to see the ripple effect of it. And it's all because of God. It is as simple as that. And I try not to forget it. Sometimes you get wrapped up in your mind so much but knowing that he is there all the time is absolutely phenomenal. And at the moment he is really helping because my sister who is only . . . (age omitted due to confidentiality), has four kids, has been diagnosed with liver cancer and she has got about three months to live. That's a great thing to be able to drink on. My parents are in their 70s and they are in the North East of England. My sister is with them and the four kids. And their daughter is gonna die and they are having to do the funeral, organise the funeral. She's still alive, she's . . . (age omitted due to confidentiality) years old. All of that sort of thing is a wonderful excuse and reason to go out and have a drink. Which I would be doing if it wasn't for Christ. If it wasn't for the relationships I have with the guys I work with; with this place with which I have brilliant relationship. Like anywhere you have ups and downs but basically I have a fantastic relationship. So the kind of a progression from alcoholic bum through the programme to sobriety, to Christ, to marriage, to self-fulfilment basically in what I do. And if you like the manly stuff: I can earn my living now; I can pay for stuff; I've got a nice big truck; you know, I can go on holiday; the sort of the nice things in life. There aren't many . . . . There are hundreds and hundreds and hundreds of men who've been through this programme and are clean and sober and living great lives. But I have spoken to the staff here and there aren't many whose lives have being transformed so quickly, so rapidly. I feel extra blessed. I think. Is that good?

I: Thank you John. Let's go to the questions. I will read them, question by question with the sub-questions together. And then if you feel that you don't need to add anything you don't need to.

J: Okay.

I: But if you feel that you can add something please do.

J: All right.

I: So the first question is: How do you perceive your conscience? What is conscience? How did it develop? How does it function?

J: Okay. I touched on that. Conscience is the Holy Spirit. It is right from wrong. It is inbuilt. It is not something you learn. It is not quite like pleasing, thank you. It is something that is within you. We all know right from wrong. We can suppress it though with drugs, alcohol, money, sex, whatever. We have a choice. And we can choose to use our conscience, or we can choose to ignore it.

I: What about in the past when you didn't know Christ?

J: Christ can be a real pain because he will prod your conscience. If you gonna do something wrong or considering doing something and you are evaluating, is it right or is it wrong then he will prod you. He will kick my backside and say: "Ah-ha, that's not good." A very brief scenario: we have our recovery addicts group tonight. Two men left the programme three weeks ago because they used heroin. They came to the last recovery addicts group because we wanted to try and help them before it was too late. Well they didn't take our help. They didn't take anybody's help. And then now, very sadly, are on the streets in a really rough way. And I had to make a decision for other people: "Am I going to allow them in this group this evening?" And my answer is: "No." And I know that that is the right answer because I haven't been punished, I haven't been kicked in the stomach by God to say: "That's not Christ like." I have to do that because I have three or four other men coming from the SSRRP who are vulnerable men who do not need to see these guys. So that's an example of knowing the right from wrong what my conscience is telling me. These are uncomfortable things sometimes that we have to do. I don't want to ostracise these men. But in fact they ostracised themselves. That's the way. So that's the way I think the conscience can work in some respect.

I: In terms of the past you mentioned that when you were drinking, you were doing immoral things in terms of stealing and lying and things like that. At that time how did you perceive conscience?

J: I still knew, I still knew it was wrong because I've been brought up like that but the desperation, the need for alcohol overrides anything your conscience is trying to tell you. Even though actually so many times now with Christ in your life you still have those choices. You can override even what you know. Even if you know that you have that love of Christ, addiction is not more powerful than Christ at all but if you don't keep your eye on Christ then it is insidious. It will get you. It will get you, basically.

I: Thank you John. Second question: How did you develop alcohol addiction? What is alcohol addiction? When did you realise that you have been addicted to alcohol? How did you try to manage your alcohol addiction? You covered pretty much these. Do you have to add anything?

J: Most of it, I think. I don't think there is much more to add there. I think I sort of gave you that kind of story in the main.

John's personal interview

I: Okay. The next question: What were your moral views before your moral, spiritual, and/or religious transformation? What is morality? How did you deal with moral dilemmas? How much did morality matter for you?

J: If it was my own morality it didn't matter at all. All I needed was a drink. But addicts and specially alcoholics are great at writing the rest of the world. So anything sort of political that's on the news that we can talk about it etc., you know. We will expound and, you know, shout from the roof tops what's right and what's wrong. But the one thing that addicts never do until it comes to the point is look at themselves. It's all about everybody else. It's all about everybody else. Addiction is just utterly self-centred. And there is no morality. It goes out of the window because the addiction overrides the morality.

I: Next question: Did you practice spirituality before your moral, spiritual, and/or religious transformation? What is spirituality? How did you practice spirituality? How much did spirituality matter for you?

J: No, I didn't. I left it. You know. In a very bigoted way, all Catholics were screwed up loonies. The priests were paedophiles. Pope was the devil incarnate. I laughed at people who went to church especially the Church of England. It was all: "Look at my big car, my new posh frock." It's stereotyped image that, you know, we are fed almost. The Church of England does not always do itself any favours but . . . . No. I laughed at the whole situation really. That's what people do. A lot of it is fear because we think we're in control of our own lives, where in fact we're not. We are in utter chaos but we can't admit it to ourselves.

I: Thank you John. Next one: Did you practice religion before your moral, spiritual, and/or religious transformation? What is religiousness? How did you practice religion? Did you have religious affiliation? How much did religion matter for you?

J: No I didn't. And even now I'm not religious. I don't practice religion. I'm a Christian. Christians do Christianity. I like going to church because like many people I like worshipping God with other people. I like being told the Word by other people because I need it. But I'm not religious. I'm far from it. I sort of put that in the same bracket as spiritual. I'm not that kind of Christian. It's—what can I do? What physically can I do? How can I help? I leave other people to do the speaking in tongues and all that kind of things.

I: The next question: Did you experience moral, spiritual, and/or religious transformation? How did you experience this transformation?

When did you experience this transformation? May you identify anyone who played any influential role in the process? How much has this transformation changed your life?

J: I think I covered most of that basically. These are the staff here, as my peers, especially my counsellor, the process at the RRC, and Christ himself. And I helped a little bit.

I: What was the impact of your transformation on your life? Compare your morality, spirituality, and religiousness before and after the transformation. How did the transformation impact your understanding of morality, spirituality, and religion, and their role in your life? How much did morality, spirituality, and religion matter for you after your transformation?

J: I think I covered most of that. I am born again. I am a completely new creation. And if I don't keep my focus on it then I'm nothing again. So it is very important for me.

I: What was the impact of your moral, spiritual, and/or religious transformation on your conscience? Compare your conscience before and after the transformation. How did the transformation impact your conscientious behaviour? How much did the voice of your conscience matter for you after your transformation?

J: I think I covered it again but it was absolutely profound—a hundred percent change because my life did not revolve around addiction. The conscience was always there but I suppressed it. Now I let the conscience run free even if it does kick in the backside.

I: Thank you. What was the impact of your transformed conscience on your recovery from alcohol addiction? Compare your recovery before and after the transformation. How did your transformed conscience impact your recovery from alcohol addiction? What is the role of your transformed conscience in the maintenance of your abstinence? May you identify anyone who played any influential role in the process?

J: I think I covered that. Yeah. It's a little bit similar to the question before. But I think that's covered.

I: Nothing to add?

J: Yeah.

I: May you share your future plans related to your recovery? What is the role of morality, spirituality, and/or religion in them? What is the role of your transformed conscience in them? Do you plan to share your experience with others who need help in recovery from alcohol addiction?

You spoke about this pretty much. Anything else to add to this point? For the future plans?

J: I do actually want to become more involved in what we call "after-care." The RRC is amazing and everything that it does. Obviously that's the rehab I know. But it's amazing—everything it does. The SSRRP process is fantastic. And the after-care that they give is great. The RRC provides after-care. And it provides fantastic after-care but the man, the addict, the recovering addict has to be willing to partake in it. And what happens is when they leave the programme, when they leave the SSRRP, when they leave the RRC, their plans can quite often start going very loose. And later their lives become chaos again very, very quickly. And their pride kicks in. And they won't ask for help. Their thought processes get confused. I want to be involved. It's a bit like the recovery addicts group that we have. It's about keeping those relationships going. After, the project is finished. After they finish the project here to realise that you can ask for help; that staffs your pride because your pride will get you absolutely nowhere. You are not going to get lonely. If you don't get lonely you're gonna be in relationship. If you are in a relationship you got a far greater chance of staying clean. And also I like to do that. And that's beginning to happen.

I: The last question: May you formulate the main theme of your life story? What is the place of alcohol addiction in your story? What is the place of conscience in your story? What is the place of morality, spirituality, and/or religiousness in your story? What is the place of your moral, spiritual, and/or religious transformation in your story?

J: I think most of it is in there, isn't it?

I: How will you summarise the main theme?

J: What's the theme of it? I suppose it is, to use the word that I used a lot, it is just utter transformation, is the way I will put it. There was the child, the innocent child, baby, whatever. The not quite belong to the devil but the period of absolute blackness and darkness. And then the light, which is Christ basically. So, whatever it was, from birth to eight or nine years old—happy childhood. From age eight and nine when I started to sip and drink and whatever—absolute darkness until I was . . . (age omitted due to confidentiality). And then in specially one blinding moment—June the 23rd, 2007—absolute light. It's darkness to light basically. It is wonderful—absolutely wonderful. I love it.

I: Thank you John. This will be the end of our interview at 10:21 on the 15th of 11th. And thank you very much for sharing your story.

J: That's okay.

The present transcript presents the typical nature of the interviews in regards to the structure, the protocol, the participation of the interviewer, the approximate length of the material, and the main character of the story. One clarification is required in relation to the participant's reference to a copy of the short introductory guidance (see appendices) which has been given to him in the beginning of the interview (John, 2011, par 17:1). This guidance is provided to help with the identification of relevant topics in the story without interfering with its genuine character. One further clarification is needed for the interviewee's characterisation of his Christian faith not with the titles of religion and spirituality but with the application of their content in his life. The individualised approach identifies the uniqueness of the story which is further exhibited through the personal nature of the experiences and their understanding. These will be further presented through the results in the following chapter.

4.

Results

I will present the results from study of the narratives in two chapters. The first chapter will examine the general character of the stories. The second chapter will develop a close analysis of the narrative themes. The results section will be concluded with summary of the main findings.

4.1. Holistic analysis of narratives

I will conduct a holistic analysis of the narratives with the purpose of comparing their structure, plot, characters, and outcomes. The structure of the narratives is analysed for identification of their main units and their relationship. The latter is also reflected in the narrative plot which is examined for its thrust considering the development of crisis, culmination, and solution. The characters are observed in relation to the central role occupied by the narrator. The outcome of the story is viewed from the perspective of the changes manifested in the main character emerging with the completion of the plot (Howitt, 2010). The holistic analysis of all stories is guided through the research rationale (Langdridge, 2004). I will offer summaries of all 12 narratives in order to substantiate the framework of the holistic analysis and enable the reader to get acquainted with the personal nature of each individual story.

John's story

John's story begins with defining the roots of his alcohol addiction in his childhood. These are identified as eyesight problems, appearance concerns, high family expectations, and failure to rise to the father's achievements. They lead to low self-image, unmanageable emotional turbulence, and attachment to alcohol. John's work engagements in helping with the family business and as bar attendant lead him to developing further his substance misuse. The drinking is accompanied with theft leading to a vicious circle of addiction and immorality. The latter extends to envy of his brother and sister, sexual immorality, lying, and other vices. The conscience which according to John has a divine source of influence is completely suppressed through his own choice. The alcohol dependency leads to unsuccessful marital relationship, frequent relationship breakdowns, and physical ill health. John's life becomes completely controlled by his alcohol addiction leading to utter desperation. This is underlined by several detoxes resulting in short periods of abstinence followed by even more excessive drinking.

Salvation comes with a phone call to a Christian rehabilitation centre where from the very beginning John undergoes a spiritual impact with the realisation of Christ's help. This leads to the acceptance of professional help and fulfilment with peace and order. John begins a progressive spiritual transformation which reaches its culmination in the public declaration of his faith during a church service. He experiences an overwhelming moment in the presence of the Holy Spirit which empowers his conscience removing sin, guilt, and shame. John tries to explain the experience comparing it to a moment of high exuberance under the influence of a substance. The nature of this transformation is defined as a complete break from the past, rebirth, and beginning of a new life. The transformation impacts all dimensions of John's life. His empowered conscience leads to decisions which benefit recovery. John develops character strengths and virtues which support his relationships and work. Life gains a new purpose that of helping those in recovery which is done with wisdom and compassion. A new support group is started for providing healthy relationships and offering continuous help. John is completely fascinated by the positive impact of the transformation and is grateful to God who is at the centre of it. For John the life of darkness during his addiction is ended with accepting Christ who brings light which enlightens all dimensions of his life. (John, Personal interview, 15 November 2011)

Adam's story

Adam starts his story defining its most significant part with his spiritual transformation through the 12-step programme. His life before this dramatic change is dominated by the experience of 15 year drug and alcohol addiction. This time is filled with degradation even though initially alcohol and drugs are used as solution for Adam's crisis with the self and the world. The addictive substances appear to be the way to manage negative feelings and anger about self, life, and reality. Adam is trying to disconnect from the reality by practicing the addictive behaviour. The struggles with the addiction are deflected through blaming others for his failures, trying to manipulate God for help, and deceiving himself through false sense of control.

Finally, the addiction takes over leading to suppressed conscience, immorality, and suicidal attitude until the time of realisation of this degradation in the moment of spiritual illumination and transformation. This happens when Adam sees his totally destroyed internal and external image after the successive substance abuse, genuinely prays to God for help, and experiences transcendent guidance for following the 12-step programme of AA.

After joining the programme Adam's life is shaken by his lack of trust in God and his failure of practicing the spiritual disciplines which leads to a year and a half of relapses. This struggle continues until Adam realises that he has reached the bottom of his misery with addiction. Hence he starts practicing the spiritual disciplines of the 12-step programme which establishes the process of continuous transformation. Adam develops personal relationship with God through prayer and meditation. He experiences the empowerment of his conscience and feels that God is guiding him to life of spiritual growth. The spiritual transformation impacts positively every dimension of Adam's life leading to profound understanding of self, conscientious behaviour, development of character strengths and virtues, and new selfless goal of helping others. The latter is realised through Adam's new vocation as a counsellor. (Adam, Personal interview, 04 November 2011)

Alex's story

Alex begins his story with a brief description of his issues with addiction, health, religion, morality, and spirituality attempting to present his struggles in recovery. The understanding of God's work in his life is underlined by his experience of religious influences, his inner desires, and unfulfilled expectations of a more dramatic change. The latter is happening through God's work in his life in a continuous way. He has a traumatic childhood being bullied which establishes the foundation of drug and alcohol use and abuse. Alex presents the positive role of religion today underlining the support offered by the church, especially to young people comparing it with the lack of support of his parents during his childhood. He also considers the potential benefits of church affiliation for his spiritual, moral, and psychological development. The roots of alcohol addiction are found in Alex's hatred and anger to life in general and his history in particular. The substances appear to be means used to escape reality and as social lubricants of friendships and relationships.

Alex defines the spiritual character of his transformation as based on personal relationship with God. There is a religious dimension as well which he expresses through the development of friendships with believers through church attendance. This transformation appears to have a progressive character requiring the discipline of Alex's continuous participation. Alex's underlining moral principle of mutual respect is the guidance through life but has been suppressed during the addiction period. Conscience also suffers deterioration of functionality due to the alcohol related behaviour. Alex's experience of progressive transformation is underlined by the improvement of conscientious behaviour leading to considerable attempts for spiritual and religious devotion and obedience to the rules of the hostel. The spiritual example of the hostel staff influences positively the transformation process. Alex's recovery is shaken by relapses but he remains determined to overcome them through the development of his spiritual transformation. The life has received a new perspective through the transformation experience and Alex perceives that his recovery depends entirely on his willingness to commit daily to the practice of spirituality. (Alex, Personal interview, 09 November 2011)

Ben's story

Ben's story starts with the search of his addiction roots. At first sight these are found in his stressful job, home isolation, and failure to manage thoughts and emotions constructively. However, going deeper through a professional help Ben also recognises that the causes of his addiction may be linked to lack of bonding relationship with his father. The drinking behaviour is developing progressively after the change of circumstances related to Ben's job. Enduring the negative attitude of the employees Ben tries to manage the stress through alcohol. The drinking becomes an automatic response to the difficult time at work. The addiction leads to moral compromises which result in losing his driving licence and his job as well as receiving a prison sentence for drink driving while being banned. The addictive behaviour is managed after prison with a new job and marriage but its stress related causes lead to its reestablishment in a more severe form with the cancer diagnosis of Ben's sister. The alcohol driven life impacts negatively the marriage. Ben suppresses his conscience through deceitful behaviour of trying to hide his addiction from his wife, parents, and church members. This results in failure to grasp the nature of his problem and living with the burden of a guilty conscience.

Introduced by his church minister Ben decides to come to a residential rehabilitation centre for the purpose of dealing with his poor health. There through the help of a Christian counsellor he reaches the understanding of his addiction. This establishes the beginning of Ben's transformation. The latter is defined spirituality through the experiences of God's forgiveness and the power of the Holy Spirit. Ben develops through the transformative process refusing temptation to drink and dealing successfully with his stressful thoughts and emotions. The nature of Ben's transformation has also a religious character forming a new commitment to the Christian faith and the church. The transformation leads to a free conscience, a new understanding of self, lifestyle of discipline, helping in the church, rebuilding his marriage, and using his experience to help others and support his wife. The future of Ben's successful recovery is based on his spiritual and religious devotion in a world full of temptations where his relationship with Jesus leads to maintaining abstinence and life of joy and content. (Ben, Personal interview, 15 November 2011)

Jack's story

Jack's story begins with revealing his dramatic childhood filled with suffering from his abusive mother. The experience is so severe that Jack tries to commit suicide with his father's medication. This suffering marks him with anger and hatred which turns into a violent behaviour at school as soon as being provoked through the negative attitude of others. After he gains his independence Jack is not able to manage relationships and is introduced to drugs by his roommates. Soon after he starts using alcohol as means to suppress the thoughts and emotions about the past. Jack's life is shaped by anger and hatred which leads to social violence. The drinking behaviour develops but it reaches a period of temporary manageability when he is expecting the birth of his son. However, his suppressed anger takes over as soon as he sees his family. The alcohol addiction and the suppressed anger lead to immoral behaviour of drink driving, not paying a fine, and carrying a knife with the outcome of losing his driving licence and prison sentences. By that time Jack is living with a constant desire to end his life. The need to escape to England due to life threats is bringing something new to him, a life in a Christian rehabilitation centre.

Jack's life is still shaped by his anger and he resists the programme even convincing other clients against it. He is almost evicted but receives one last chance. Jack is determined to show the ineffectiveness of the programme through fulfilling its requirements. This is the time when the change happens. Within few months of doing the spiritual programme Jack realises that he is experiencing a spiritual transformation. After serious consideration of what has happened he establishes a personal relationship with God. This is the culmination of Jack's transformation. Jack experiences a resurrection of his conscience. He understands his past moral failures and makes amends wherever possible. Jack's anger and hatred against his family are transformed into love and acceptance. The spiritual transformation brings a new perspective of the past, present, and future of Jack's life. The past underlines the significance of the change and God's crucial role in it. The present is defined through the spiritual practices and filled with joy, love, peace, and help to others. The future is understood as an opportunity to fulfil the purpose in life through sharing the experience of God's transforming power with others. (Jack, Personal interview, 20 November 2011)

James's story

James's story begins with his very first use of alcohol during his childhood. The reason has been to dissociate from the context of domestic violence. James is stealing the alcohol from his father and even prays for God to provide such an opportunity which may lead to his temporary alcohol related solution. James experiences the lack of love from the father and the departure of his mother. He is trying to manage his feelings of anger, hatred, fear, and worry through the use of alcohol. The drinking progresses leading to stopping school, hanging with the wrong crowd on the streets, beating someone, and the first detention sentence. The alcohol starts dominating completely James's behaviour shaping his life with violence, crime, and frequent imprisonments. The addiction destroys two relationships and distances him from his children. James realises that the addiction has taken full control over his life and behaviour. His anger fuelled by alcohol leads to almost murdering a person. He is imprisoned for life but continues drinking even behind bars.

James's transformation begins in the prison when he is invited to go to a church meeting. He reluctantly attends but eventually likes it and continues to participate in the religious gatherings. When he sees that there might be hope for a parole he starts praying for that. His behaviour changes positively and eventually he is released to go to a Christian rehabilitation centre. For the first time James follows his conscience's guidance and takes a decision to change his life. He goes to the centre. There James experiences the culmination of his spiritual and religious transformation started in prison, devoting his life to God publically during a church service. The personal relationship with God leads to dramatic changes. James believes in Jesus, searches for God's guidance daily, prays, goes to church, establishes his life's purpose and is grateful to God for saving him. Passing through the spiritual transformation James experiences the resurrection of his conscience leading him towards new life of hope for a stable recovery and positive relationships. James undergoes complete moral reformation through the spiritual transformation. Practicing spirituality and religiousness establishes the foundation for his daily life and continuous recovery. (James, Personal interview, 20 November 2011)

Luke's story

The underlining notion of Luke's story is the impact of God's deliverance and transforming power on his life. The roots of his alcohol addiction are to be found in childhood as lack of love and healthy attachments to his parents. Luke presents in vivid details the scenery of his first alcohol consumption. The drinking behaviour is well established in his youth and eventually starts dominating Luke's life defining friendships, forming his image, and leading to loose night life. Acknowledging the attachment to alcohol appears to be very difficult for Luke. In spite of the change of context and the beginning of teaching career the drinking continues and shapes Luke's thinking and life. The behaviour leads to sexual immorality and destroys relationships. Luke perceives his attachment to alcohol and attempts to control it unsuccessfully. He moves to the United Kingdom where after a period of abstinence the addiction takes over. Luke's behaviour undergoes further moral failures of drink driving, stealing alcohol and drinking at work, sexual promiscuity, and hypocritical behaviour of protecting his social image. His conscience is challenging the immorality during the times of sobriety but it is ignored and suppressed.

Luke's transformation begins with his commitment to Christianity during a church service. There is a period of abstinence but the addiction is re-established with the stress of studies. Luke undergoes inner struggle with his conscience which is being revived through faith in God. He feels on the bottom of his resources to manage the addiction and cries for God's help. The moment of transformation comes in a time of prayer with a Christian minister. Luke experiences an inner spiritual revival by the presence of the Holy Spirit. This creates a radical shift away from all addictive behaviours stopping both drinking and smoking at the same time. Luke's transformation continues with life of spirituality through personal relationship with God, prayer, and Bible study. A new moral understanding and behaviour are achieved with the empowerment of conscience. The transformation leads to a new attitude towards others underlined by empathy and compassion. The view of the past is also transformed to serve as experiential wisdom. Luke's faith in God's transforming power and desire to help others establish his life goals and shape his Christian ministry. (Luke, Personal interview, 11 November 2011)

Mary's story

Mary's story begins with her traumatic childhood witnessing her father's alcoholic degradation and experiencing her mother's lack of love due to the loss of her three children and the subsequent depression. The family with its positive attitude towards alcohol, the related addictions of some members, and the loss of some relatives due to alcoholism establish the background of Mary's alcohol addiction. Her first drinking event underlines the predominant characteristic of addiction as the complete loss of control. Mary's life is shaken by crises with the loss of her father, separation from a heroin addicted boyfriend, death of a patient, end of nursing career, diminishing motherly role, insulting husband, and marriage breakdown. The initial interest and attachment to alcohol and drinking behaviour develop further to reach the level of addiction. The undergone treatments and hospitalisations appear to be ineffective. The alcohol addiction dominates Mary's life, striving for alcohol is her daily purpose. The damages spread from her deteriorating health to social humiliation, crawling to the shop to buy a drink and not being able to manage her clothes by coming home half naked. During this time when everyone deserts her she is helped by a vicar from the local church which leaves a significant positive impact on her. Mary is hospitalised again and eventually sectioned due to her serious condition.

The moment of spiritual transformation comes with the realisation of miraculous physical recovery unexplainable by medical knowledge. Mary's worldview undergoes a dramatic change with the perception of life as a marvellous gift and development of deep gratitude towards the giver of life. This brings her to church where she discovers her own faith in God. Mary experiences spirituality and religion in a profound personal way contrary to the negative religious connotations encountered in the self-help groups. The transformation empowers Mary's conscience in leading to the development of virtuous character underlined by love and kindness towards herself and others. Mary experiences also the moral guidance of her conscience in a novel way through the practice of prayer. Life receives a new focus to help those passing through the turmoil of addiction. Mary defines the experience of spiritual transformation from addiction to recovery as a new birth and a fresh beginning of life in relationship with God. (Mary, Personal interview, 10 November 2011)

Max's story

Max's story reveals the background of his alcohol addiction in his unmanageability of emotions and protective attitude of his self-built image of success. The emotional turmoil due to abuse leads to early attachment to alcohol. The overwhelming desire to success formed on the basis of Max's poor childhood dominates the story underlining his significant achievements in career and religious status. The hard work is even used as a means for emotional management when life crisis arrives with the loss of his sister, brother, and mother as well as the sickness of his wife. Failing to deal with his emotions Max turns to alcohol which leads him to lose his wife, ministry, and job. Max's conscience challenges his drinking behaviour underlining the conflict with his church involvement and job. The resolution is attempted through succumbing completely to the addiction. The latter destroys Max's new relationship and leads to his move to a Christian rehabilitation centre. There Max experiences the revival of his spirituality and renewal of his conscience. However, he decides to move back with his partner after the first stage of the programme. This decision is taken against the guidance of his conscience. The reunion with the partner leads to the suppression of Max's spiritualty and conscience. Hence, his alcohol addiction redevelops bringing devastating consequences on his morality and life. He is living on the streets, steeling to feed his addiction, and trying to escape reality. The only chance for help is seen as a return to the centre for his treatment. However, that seems impossible due to lack of finances.

In a moment of total despair Max turns to God for help. This is the time when he begins the spiritual transformation, dying for his old life, and receiving God's answer as a possibility for entering the programme again. Max develops personal relationship with God and practices spiritual disciplines daily. This leads to the empowerment of his conscience and realisation of the damages he has done during his addiction to himself and others. Max follows his conscience by making amends and living according to his renewed moral standards of treating others with respect. Max's spiritual transformation changes him internally reshaping his image according to his faith in God and leading to positive external behaviours. Max whole attitude towards his recovery, life, and future is shaped by his spirituality. He is taking conscientious decisions to help others in recovery and develop further his spirituality. Max's transformed life is full of joy, peace, content, and delight in nature. (Max, Personal interview, 15 November 2011)

Paul's story

Paul's story begins highlighting his special place in the family due to his father's interest to have a son. However, this attitude diminishes with the birth of his younger brother. Paul experiences a form of family rejection when he is sent to boarding school. The latter provides the context for Paul's encounter with illicit substances and their use. Nevertheless, he refuses to participate due to his negative image of the drugs' impact and positive attitude to sport. The alcohol is introduced to him by a friend in the same context and this time it triggers curiosity and desire to try. This happens when Paul being attracted by the appearance of a bottle uses for first time. The experience has very negative outcome. Nonetheless, under the influence of friends Paul starts drinking regularly. Alcohol becomes the means for Paul to change his internal and external disposition in order to gain the approval of his male friends and the fascination of his female company. Paul's morality deteriorates with the practice of sexual promiscuity. The addiction develops quickly and impacts Paul's life seriously. He is not able to continue his university education. With the help of his family he undergoes his first rehabilitation treatment but without significant success. After the second treatment Paul is able to stay abstinent for some time by keeping away from old friends. However, as soon as he is back in their company he starts drinking again and the addiction takes over his life.

The real change happens when Paul is accepted in a rehabilitation centre in England away from his home country. He experiences inner spiritual transformation through a personal relationship with God. This changes his whole life leading to reconciliation with self and acceptance of his own personality. Paul's recovery is underlined by developing his understanding of himself and his needs through his personal relationship with God. Even the brief relapse is assessed as a form of learning and contributes to his continuous transformation. Paul's empowered conscience guides his daily life to apply his inner transformation in his relationships building the appropriate boundaries, maintaining abstinence, and experiencing fulfilment and content. (Paul, Personal interview, 15 November 2011)

Sam's story

The story of Sam begins from his traumatic childhood where he first faces the difficulty to cope with various issues of bulling at school, late puberty, and overly strict father. Alcohol is tested because of curiosity and is embraced as the magical solution which makes unwanted thoughts, feelings, and experiences disappear. It becomes the means for dealing with emotional pain. Hence alcohol attachment is established and addiction developed when passing through the traumatic events of the sickness and death of his mother and wife. A rehabilitation treatment is attempted without any success. Alcohol becomes the way to disconnect from reality. God is blamed for the loss which leads to development of anger and unforgiveness. The conscience is intentionally suppressed through the use of alcohol so that its role of challenging immoral behaviour is diminished and the latter is exercised freely.

The addiction develops and extends to another addictive behaviour, namely, self-harming and suicide attempts. Sam tries to resolve the emotional pain replacing it with physical one. A second treatment leads to nine months of abstinence but the addiction takes over again due to emotional disturbances caused by the sexual advances of a member of staff and the lack of leadership support. The addiction seems to be managed when Sam moves to a hostel and stays abstinent for several months. He begins a new relationship but his unfulfilled expectations become a trigger for a new relapse. Sam attempts again to end his life unsuccessfully and then returns to drinking. This leads to hospitalisation due to serious physical danger.

The turning point of Sam's story comes with the visit of two spiritual men in the hospital. The conversation with the visitors underlines the importance of spirituality. The personal enlightenment of the destructive nature of alcohol addiction leads Sam to the experience of a transformative moment which begins his recovery. Sam's transformation continues with developing trust in God and exercising spirituality following the model of spiritual and religious people. He develops a conscientious attitude towards himself and others. The voice of conscience becomes a key to Sam's management of his daily engagements. Challenging times are approached through prayer, church attendance, attention to conscience, and compassion to others. The transformation leads to complete redefining of Sam's conscience, morality, spirituality, and religiousness. He experiences the empowerment of his conscience which leads to a new life perspective, moral behaviour, spiritual growth, and religious understanding. Sam is continuing the journey of recovery through developing his spirituality and helping people going through addiction to transform their lives. (Sam, Personal interview, 16 November 2011)

Victoria's story

Victoria's story starts in a religious family without active spiritual life. All its members appear to have some alcohol related issues. In contrast to her family Victoria is befriended by a couple who are practicing Evangelical Christians. They set for her a role model of being a loving and accepting couple. Seeing their faith in action Victoria decides to accept Christianity. She becomes a committed Christian with active spiritual life. The background of her alcohol addiction appears to be the beginning of a relationship which she develops against her conscience and Christian convictions. When the relationship suffers from the unfaithfulness of the partner with another colleague Victoria experiences emotional turmoil which she tries to resolve through alcohol. During the next five years the drinking behaviour develops taking complete control over Victoria's manageability. Victoria is living a double life compromising her Christian convictions and suppressing her conscience through the unhealthy relationship and addiction. She feels that this is unbearable and decides to commit suicide through excessive drinking of alcohol.

During the period of intense drinking when she is at her lowest point on the edge between life and death she experiences a moment of spiritual transformation feeling that God is giving her another chance. This experience establishes the beginning of her recovery which involves professional help. However, Victoria comes back to the same unhealthy relationship and attempts to manage her emotions through drinking which leads to several relapses. She decides to escape the relationship through moving to the United Kingdom. There a new unhealthy relationship leads to her longest and final relapse. The latter is ended when she experiences a second moment of spiritual transformation. During this transformation she accepts God's supremacy in her life and through her empowered conscience reaches the decision to manage the emotional turmoil by God's help and without the use of alcohol. This second moment of spiritual transformation establishes the beginning of the period of complete abstinence and long term recovery. Victoria defines two important aspects of the stability of her recovery, namely, continuous relationship with God and helping others who are going through addiction. (Victoria, Personal interview, 21 November 2011)

The narratives reveal a structural pattern consisting of two main parts, namely, addiction and recovery. The former is grounded in traumatic childhood, develops through unmanageability of emotions, and is depicted as a destructive force of self, morality, and life. The recovery is presented as a new birth, the beginning of a completely reformed life guided by clear conscience and fulfilled through spiritual devotion and selfless commitment to help others. The key point of division appears to be the experience of transformation. The latter has a spiritual nature, impacts positively on one's conscience, and in all of the narratives undergoes a process of development. Many of the stories reveal a moment of spiritual transformation which is characterised by the exceptional experience of the transcendent presence of God and deep changes of perspective and perception of self and life. The plot of all the stories is developed from the problematic experience of addiction through spiritual transformation to the solution of recovery. The thrust of this plot differs in some accounts presenting vague borders due to the insecure commitment to the spiritual transformation in the story of Alex and the experience of transformation in two stages, separated by time of relapse, in the narratives of Adam, Luke, Max, and Victoria. The main characters of the narratives are connected with the transformation and have spiritual characteristics. The most pronounced ones are God, Jesus, and the Holy Spirit. Other significant characters show a spiritual model which is attractive and leads to a desire to follow and imitate. The outcomes of the narratives depict lives completely transformed and characterised by empowered conscience, moral behaviour, virtuous character, spiritual devotion, robust recovery, and selfless dedication to helping others.

4.2. Detailed analysis of narratives

I will present analysis of all narratives guided through the research rationale and based on the topics explored through the interviews in combination with the main themes derived from the stories. The structure of the analysis follows the natural flow of the stories from problem to solution. The topics presented link the narrative themes with the research questions by providing evidential material.

Conscience's nature and functioning

Mary associates conscience with her moral standards and behaviour. "And I think I have good conscience. . . . I do believe I'm morally good person. And I mean I've done bad things." (Mary, 2011, par 28:1–2; 2–3; see also par 28:3–8; par 51:3–4) Sam considers his conscience to be very important for the way he manages day to day life. "Because my conscience is one of my biggest beliefs, you know. If you promise or if you do—is on my conscience." (Sam, 2011, par 30:9–10)

Max defines conscience as an inner voice for guidance of right and wrong. The conscience is always present but its guidance can be disregarded and its role can be suppressed. "So it actions a warning, a break and I can choose to override that if I want to." (Max, 2011, par 14:6–7) He uses an example of a pot plant to describe the relationship to his conscience. The plant's wellness is to be maintained with a good care which resembles the appropriate attitude to his conscience. If he neglects and suppresses the conscience he becomes vulnerable to addiction. ". . . and I had the choice whether I listen to it and do something about it, or I don't. And if I don't I'm vulnerable to drink. So I chose to do something about it. So listening to it and keeping it healthy just like a pot plant, you know." (Max, 2011, par 39:4–7) Victoria also understands conscience as the inner voice which interacts with her emotions leading to feeling well when the results from her assessment of the behaviour are positive and feeling guilty when they are negative. "But I think there is also that, I don't know how you call it, instinct that you have about when you're doing something that is good or bad. You have that inner voice. So I would call it an inner voice, kind of prompts you. It also plays on the feeling of guilt or feeling of okay when you're doing okay." (Victoria, 2011, par 19:3–7)

Luke defines conscience as a divine substance in the person. The conscience is a part of every human being in spite of his or her relationship with God. Its function is to guide the person in distinguishing right from wrong and towards a decision for choosing the right. The conscience is also influenced by the laws of a just society.

> Because I believe that God has given us basic conscience by breathing into us. So through this man became a living soul. Part of it is our conscience. God's nature is in us. So man failed but the conscience is with us. So it became like: so you know wrong from right. So you know that this is right and this is wrong. And conscience is also determined or mould out, either way by the laws and the norms of the justice society. Then when you are betrayed and this is bad and the law says this is bad. So when you do something that the law has said that this is bad your conscience will prick you that you have done mean thing. (Luke, 2011, par 23:1–9)

Conscience and spirituality

Adam's relationship with God is based on daily prayer and meditation. This communication involves God's response to Adam through various means for establishing a close bond. One of the essential ways God interacts with Adam is through his conscience. Adam believes that his conscience guides him to make the choice of good over bad and that God plays a significant role in the process. Hence, through the development of spirituality Adam's life has become more responsive to God's will. "You know, the conscience in a sense I guess, conscience, God's consciousness—I'm conscious of God within me; you know telling me right from wrong. . . . But, I do know that today I try to live differently. I try to live in accordance with what I believe God would want from me." (Adam, 2011, par 34:21–23; 28–30)

John defines conscience as the presence of the Holy Spirit in the person. The conscience is associated closely with one's spirituality. John also believes that conscience is an integral part of oneself and as such it is the pathway of communication received from God. Conscience is a moral guide which the person decides to follow or to suppress through the use of addictive substances and behaviours. Conscience is being suppressed during the addiction but is fully restored through the spiritual transformation.

> I mean if you look at conscience which in my mind is basically: every human being is born with the conscience, it is called the Holy Spirit—right and wrong.... And one of the things that we addicts do is suppress that conscience.... So your conscience is brought back to life again, your morality which is right—wrong, your conscience.
>
> We can suppress it though with drugs, alcohol, money, sex, whatever. We have a choice. And we can choose to use our conscience, or we can choose to ignore it. (John, 2011, par 16:2–4; 7; 10–11; par 29:4–6)

Max experiences a spiritual revival of his conscience by passing through the programme of a Christian rehabilitation centre. Hence the decision to move back with his partner after the treatment creates an internal struggle due to his conscience's role of exposing the inappropriate choice. Through the help of his conscience Max perceives that the relationship will lead to his spiritual decline, moral failure, and re-establishment of the addictive behaviour. However, he decides against the warning of his conscience which leads to his most destructive period of his addicted life. "But also from a spiritual point of view I knew I was doing wrong. You know, after living abstinent and being in the church for 18 years you kind of...; there are, you know, obvious links of what's right and what's wrong, that kind of moral perspective." (Max, 2011, par 8:19–22)

Conscience and consciousness

Paul understands conscience as being in a close relationship with his consciousness. This shapes conscience as a guide for his responses to life issues. "And I understand it to be the inner thought of myself, being, you know, what goes in my mind. And how I react towards issues that come across my way in life and everything." (Paul, 2011, par 19:2–4) Paul defines the decision to move away from his spiritual and moral framework as being based on his personal choice to go against his conscience. The latter exposes his conflicting choice leading to amplified awareness of his decision and actions. His perception of conscience in this light is closely linked with consciousness, underlining the aspect of conscious personal responsibility for his own choice, decision, and actions. "But I decided, I took a conscious step; to link it with my conscience again; I took a conscious step to drift from what I've grown up learning." (Paul, 2011, par 23:6–8)

The spiritual transformation promotes a close relationship between Adam's conscience and consciousness. He understands that going against his conscience through acting immorally would lead him back into addiction since he would not be able to deal with the voice of his conscience without spirituality and would need the influence of the substances to manage his condition. However, through his relationship with God practicing the spiritual principles he becomes in tune with the voice of his conscience. Adam knows that he needs to make the moral choice on daily basis. After his spiritual transformation he has developed an understanding of how to stay in line with his conscience in all matters of life.

> So what I have today through (with) God in my life or perhaps God talking to me through my conscience or perhaps my conscience is God. I think that's probably what it is. I think really God is my conscience. Or that's how I can really; for me really access God in my conscience. And I know when I am doing things that I shouldn't be doing.... So that's how my conscience has grown, is developed over time, or my awareness of how to work with my conscience not against it. So really what I am doing is working with God not against God. I'm choosing to try to live in accordance with God, God's principles today. (Adam, 2011, par 41:22–26; 29–33)

Jack's conscience experiences a positive spiritual influence and becomes more active. He understands that manipulating people's attitudes about the treatment programme is wrong. "You know that we have been doing a negative group. I was beginning to see how wrong that was." (Jack, 2011, par 15:19–20) Jack's transformation influences his conscience radically to redefine his whole understanding of himself, others, and life. He manages abstinence successfully through the use of his conscience. His life receives purpose and his attitude towards others is that of love, joy, and acceptance.

> When my morals changed everything changed. You know, my need for a drink, my desire to drink, everything, you know, had left. It definitely prevents me from going back to that way of life. Because I see, life today is much more valuable, today. Life for me before was with no purpose.... It just makes me appreciate life today more and people and the importance of people. (Jack, 2011, par 45:1–4; 15–16)

James's conscience plays a significant role in shaping the contrast in the understanding of his behaviour during the period of addiction and after the transformation. Formerly, the inactive conscience leads to shifted responsibility of his behaviour to others. He does not acknowledge his addiction and blames others for the consequences of his alcohol driven behaviour. However, after James's spiritual transformation his revived conscience guides his consciousness and he is able to take responsibility for his actions. He accepts that his behaviour during the period of addiction has been wrong and assesses that presently he is acting correctly. "I was a typical alcoholic. I haven't got a problem. It's other people that have got the problem. It's other people that are picking things. It's other people. But now I can take responsibility. And I can take responsibility for my own actions . . . ." (James, 2011, par 35:1–4)

Negative impact on conscience before addiction

For Victoria religiousness, spirituality, morality, and conscience are closely connected. Hence when she develops a relationship with a guy and the dynamics go against her spiritual, religious, and moral convictions she considers it as going against her conscience. This establishes the foundation for her alcohol addiction. "So it was something that in a way I was going against my conscience." (Victoria, 2011, par 4:2–3)

Max acknowledges that the absence of his parents and the immature role of his sister in his upbringing had a negative influence on his conscience. "I guess some of that development was flawed." (Max, 2011, par 14:15) The extreme strictness of Sam's father also imposes unhealthy influence on his conscience. "I always had a conscience; a forced upon conscience by my dad, you know." (Sam, 2011, par 62:3–4) "So you know my dad also brought me up very disciplinarian." (Sam, 2011, par 4:12)

Negative impact on conscience during addiction

Luke experiences his conscience through fear about his behaviour during the drinking event which is difficult to recall. Conscience is still functional and triggers cognitive assessment of the drinking behaviour. The impact is positive with the reduction of drinking. "Then I came down with the drinking; it subsided." (Luke, 2011, par 12:19) This is followed by a religious action of going to church. Attempts are made to resolve the drinking but are unsuccessful. The development of Luke's addiction leads to complete deterioration of his conscience's functioning. Conscience appears to be subdued by the addiction and unable to influence his behaviour.

> But in terms of when you are under alcohol you throw everything overboard. You don't consider anything until after the event. You probably become moral, you become sorry but because of the addiction you would do it next time again when you have a drink. Because what you did for your conscience to prick on you was fuelled by alcohol. And you're controlled by the need to drink. (Luke, 2011, par 23:9–14)

Sam silences his conscience through a way of escaping reality. "Because the devil played the biggest part in my life is that: 'If you go gambling you don't have to worry.'" (Sam, 2011, par 12:16–18) In addition, Sam's anger and lack of forgiveness to God because of the belief that he has taken away those loved ones, interfere with the guidance of his conscience. It is this attitude which leads him to do the opposite of what his conscience indicates as right. "I get taught; little sort of voices in my head that would say: 'This is the right thing to do and that's the wrong thing to do.' And I didn't know that was God telling me or whoever but I will always do the opposite. I would go with the bad." (Sam, 2011, par 12:13–16) Sam also intensifies the drinking intentionally to suppress the voice of his conscience. Hence, its functionality and ability to challenge the behaviour are completely diminished. "Because you don't have any feelings; so—no conscience when I'm drinking, not at all. And if you do you just drink a bit more and it goes away." (Sam, 2011, par 30:20–22)

Alex's conscience is manipulated by his use of alcohol. The addictive behaviour dominates his decisions and actions. ". . . my addiction to alcohol; it outweigh my conscience." (Alex, 2011, par 27:3–4) During the moments of sobriety and realisation of the unlawful actions the conscience's impact is strong and leads to moral determination and subsequent behaviour. "And every time I would go to court for drink driving then my conscience kicks in even more. And then I've never broke the law while I was under a ban. So my conscience comes through." (Alex, 2011, par 28:2–3) However, the addiction overpowers conscience and leads to immoral behaviour. "So there is no point of me having a licence because my conscience wouldn't stop me from drink driving." (Alex, 2011, par 27:12–14) Conscience becomes inadequate in influencing Alex's behaviour during addiction. ". . . if my conscience has worked properly in the first place I would have never drunk and drove." (Alex, 2011, par 27:9–10) The insufficient influential power of the conscience to prevent moral failures during addiction may also be attributed to the lack of spiritual and religious input towards its development in Alex's life. "And I wish that church was more like it is now when I was younger. . . . . . . church is a good place. It's where you learn morality. It's where you learn how to be sort of like conscientious, conscious in the way that you live your life." (Alex, 2011, par 15:8–9; 25–27) "So really if I had God in my life, earlier on in my life, then it would have made my life better." (Alex, 2011, par 22:1–2)

Conscience becomes a burden during addiction

Luke realises the negative consequences of the addiction through the input of his conscience. After drinking he is prompted to think about the moral nature of his behaviour during the events which he finds difficult to recall.

> It hit me a bit. Because what did I do? What did I say to my friends? What conversations did they have? And to make it worse at that moment, that is conscience which moved, that I could have behaved badly to drink. What has happened? So I just was the guy who was drinking near. Why? Why was somebody knocking on my door to sell me drink? But one thing is to be assuming—you should not behave like that, you see. (Luke, 2011, par 12:9–15)

Luke feels the burden of his conscience and wants to overcome the addiction but does not find the resources within him to manage it.

> Because my drinking became worse and I decided I'm not going to drink. So that's really helped a bit. But I went back into drinking again. So I believe that about six or seven times I stopped it and came in, stopped it and came in. Because I wanted to stop. Because when it gets very bad I think: 'Did I do the right thing? Is that the proper way to behave? I should stop.' (Luke, 2011, par 20:5–10)

The conscience brings feelings of sadness, discomfort, and guilt once the effect of alcohol has diminished.

> All the time you are watching yourself and you're saying that you should stop; you don't feel happy after you smoke, or you've been drinking, you feel bad. Because you know, something in you tells you that this is not what it should be. So that's where the conscience would come in. And the conscience is the level of God's consciousness in us. (Luke, 2011, par 35:15–19)

Luke identifies God's role in influencing his conscience to challenge the addictive behaviours.

Mary experiences her conscience as a continuous preoccupation with her behaviour towards others. The absence of active spirituality leads to overwhelming conscientiousness which is considered contributory to her addiction. "I think my conscience is too much, I would say. . . . I've always been one of these people, I sat down, and I ponder about stuff, and I think about stuff. . . . And I think that has contributed to my alcohol problem." (Mary, 2011, par 26:1–2; 4–5; 8–9) With the spiritual transformation conscience is empowered and results in morally stable attitude towards self and others. ". . . when I was drinking alcohol, yeah, you become very selfish and disregard the other people but mostly you're disregarding yourself. But now I have more conscience not only towards other people but towards how I deal, treat myself as well as other people." (Mary, 2011, par 51:1–4)

Ben encounters the role of his suppressed conscience during the time of addiction. The experience is negative showing a heavy burden being carried around and a dark cloud always hanging above him. The spiritual transformation removes this negative affect from Ben's life providing freedom for a new life and brighter future.

> Before I didn't realise but I was walking around with a huge burden, like a huge sack on my back. And I was carrying that around everywhere I went. And it was like having a dark cloud over my head. And now after this transformation, now the sun is shining and the burden, the load has been lifted from me. So now actually I am able to concentrate just on the future way ahead. I'm free to look up instead of struggling, looking down, trudging along. (Ben, 2011, par 42:1–7)

Conscience is suppressed—silenced during addiction

Luke passes through an event during which he seriously breaks the law by driving a borrowed vehicle under the influence of alcohol and also without proper documentation. His purpose is to go to another party and drink more. After the event when he sobers up his conscience is challenging his behaviour and he feels guilty, ashamed, and sorry for what he has done but suppresses the conscience's guidance and continues drinking. "But why do you go and take it to go to another place to drink more? That's what addiction can drive you into. But all I believe that as soon as you start thinking your conscience will pull up on you. I believe that the conscience is something you know that is right but you are not able to do. Your conscience will prick you." (Luke, 2011, par 22:10–14)

Sam believes that his moral understanding and conscience are not lost but suppressed during the addiction. The conscience appears to be challenging the immoral behaviour only in rare moments of sobriety. "And my mum told me all these morals and I didn't lose them through alcohol. They were as I say 'squashed,' 'squashed.' They were still there because there would be times during my drinking that I would sober up for a while and I think: 'Gee, I'm doing the wrong things,' you know." (Sam, 2011, par 60:11–15) Victoria confirms that she has a sensitive conscience. However, during the addiction she suppresses it, neglecting its influence towards a positive change. ". . . when caught in the addiction I didn't have the strength to follow my conscience. So the addiction kind of overruled the voice of conscience." (Victoria, 2011, par 19:10–12) John also states that contrary to the challenges of his conscience about his immoral and addictive behaviours he decides to ignore and suppress it. He maintains that his addictive cognitive impulse shapes his personal choice to refuse the conscience. ". . . I still knew it was wrong because I've been brought up like that but the desperation, the need for alcohol overrides anything your conscience is trying to tell you." (John, 2011, par 33:1–3)

Adam acknowledges the presence of his conscience during the time of his addiction as providing him with the understanding that the addictive behaviour is wrong, but he defines the latter as more powerful in influencing his decisions and actions. In addition, the need for the substance, the peer pressure of friends, and his curiosity influence him to suppress his conscience and continue with the addiction. Adam experiences the affect of his conscience during the episodes of sobriety. Even though the feeling of guilt is overwhelming, the power of the addiction is stronger leading him to continue using alcohol. "So I don't know, in that moment I guess I knew that perhaps I was going against my morals or what my conscience told me but my need to be part of was greater." (Adam, 2011, par 40:8–10)

Ben describes the role of his conscience during addiction as informative but inactive. The conscience identifies the addictive behaviour as wrong but cannot influence its positive modification. The behaviour is based on his choice to use alcohol for a temporary support and as a result ignore and suppress the conscience's input towards its cessation. "My conscience really was about: I knew what's wrong and I hid it from people but it didn't stop me drinking. It was my form of support in that." (Ben, 2011, par 15:1–3) Ben's deceitful behaviour to cover his addiction does not only manipulate other's perceptions about him but also his own understanding of his condition. This clearly shows the lack of proper functionality of his conscience which appears to be manipulated and suppressed. "I've realised I've deceived a lot of people. And also deceived myself on that of hiding the drink . . . ." (Ben, 2011, par 28:1–3)

Max's decision to go back to his partner taken against his conscience leads to devastating results. He suppresses his conscience and the drinking and immoral behaviours materialise quickly and firmly in his life. The relationship ends with Max being expelled from home. He is going through the worst stages of his addiction trying to disconnect from reality. His immorality takes control by stealing to feed his alcohol dependency. "Morally I became; well I didn't have any morals as long as I drank. Spiritually I was totally divorced. All I needed, all I wanted was to drink myself into oblivion really because of this situation I've got myself into; nobody else's responsibility but mine." (Max, 2011, par 8:33–36)

Conscience is deadened during addiction

James explains that he did not have conscience during his addiction. He does not feel either its presence or the associated emotions of guilt and shame. "My conscience, I mean while I was drinking I didn't use to have any conscience. Yeah. I didn't use to have any conscience, guilty conscience, shame, anything." (James, 2011, par 31:1–3)

Jack believes in the absence of his conscience during the addiction. He feels no remorse for behaving immorally and justifies his actions on the grounds of his past suffering. "Before I knew the Lord I don't think I really had a conscience. You know I . . . ; it was normal or what seemed to be normal: to think and act and behave the way I did. And because of the way I was mistreated, you know, I thought I could justify my behaviour." (Jack, 2011, par 21:1–4)

Conscience avoidance leads to immorality

Sam's morality is deteriorating during his addiction. ". . . my moralities were always there until I had a drink. So I don't believe I've lost them. As I said, they were just overpowered by alcohol." (Sam, 2011, par 81:1–3) The same is true for Alex. "Morals go out of the window when you're drinking because the alcohol overtakes the way that you feel; the way that you act towards people. . . . It's sort of like, you treat people terribly." (Alex, 2011, par 37:1–2; 9) Taking the road of alcohol addiction meant for Paul complete disregard of his Christian moral values. "And I totally ignored the moral values of Christianity and everything I grew up learning." (Paul, 2011, par 8:7–9) Driven by the addictive behaviour Adam also experiences complete moral degradation. "My morals at that point obviously were fallen back from what they would have been." (Adam, 2011, par 47:26–27) Ben's alcohol addiction leads to moral compromises as well. "And I was disqualified from driving. And I did receive two months prison sentence for that. That was okay. That was correct." (Ben, 2011, par 6:6–8)

Luke believes that addictive behaviour cannot coexist with moral behaviour. "So I believe that morality; when people are addicted morals are thrown through the window. Because their primary purpose, everybody alike, is to feed their addiction." (Luke, 2011, par 33:5–7) John describes the absence of morality during addiction as the result of total selfishness of the person. "Addiction is just utterly self-centred. And there is no morality. It goes out of the window because the addiction overrides the morality." (John, 2011, par 37:7–9) Finally, Max observes a clear link between the decline of his spirituality, morality, and the development of his alcohol addiction. "So the link between all three for me is, you know, spiritually if I'm not well then for me morally I'm making impaired decisions; the more impaired decisions that I make the more likely I am to drink, you know." (Max, 2011, par 9:33–35)

The disregarded and suppressed conscience through the addictive behaviour leads to immorality, which is then manifested through vices. All seven vices defined in the introduction are revealed in various narratives as the driving forces of immorality during the addiction.

- Anger is clearly present in the stories of Sam ("But at the time I was angry with God. . . . And I didn't know that was God telling me or whoever but I will always do the opposite. I would go with the bad." Sam, 2011, par 12:2–3; 15–16), Adam ("And in a fit of rage I smashed my flat up, totally. . . . like an animal which has been caged and somehow it got out and running. . . . I was like a savage. That's where my addictions led me." Adam, 2011, par 48:5–6; 9–10; 11–12), Jack ("Soon after the drink problem begun to become more of a problem and so was my attitude. Any people that I had around me were starting to drift away from me. Because I was becoming somebody that they didn't like." Jack, 2011, par 10:11–14), and James ("Same old story: go in prison; do the sentence; come out; get drunk; go back into prison; get arrested. But the violence was escalating. I started stabbing somebody. Hitting someone with armours, bats." James, 2011, par 8:18–21).

- Envy occurs in the stories of Paul (". . . I had kind of a low self-esteem. . . . it was inbuilt in my mind. And I always wanted to be more than what I was. And I was extremely shy. And this was where alcohol formed an incredible partnership with me." Paul, 2011, par 6:4; 6–8) and John ("When my dad took over the tennis club as a manager and he stopped teaching they were at the right age so it was all falling into place for them. . . . But there was a degree of envy there as well and I felt rather useless with it." John, 2011, par 9:15–17; 18–19).

- All narratives expose gluttony as a characteristic of the addictive behaviour with the most extreme examples being found in the stories of Alex ("I've never stole alcohol. I begged for alcohol. I begged on the streets to get alcohol, to get drugs." Alex, 2011, par 25:11–12), James ("I started drinking heavily then, heavily, heavily every day, every week where I could bother. Every week when I could get a drink I would get one, yes." James, 2011, par 8:14–16), John ("I was a good barman as in the service and the communication, all like that, I think. I was terrible with the stock control because I was drinking most of it." John, 2011, par 10:7–9), Max ("So the more I drank the more I stole. Spiritually, my awareness or my willingness to be accountable spiritually diminished." Max, 2011, par 9:21–22), and Luke ("That's where the drinking was but you are always looking forward to, you are looking forward to go and drink. So that is a little that pushes you." Luke, 2011, par 19:10–12).

- Greed is clearly displayed in the stories of Adam ("I do not give a damn about anybody. I can't care about anything apart from me and where I am going to get my next lot of drugs." Adam, 2011, par 25:16–18), John ("I would steal from the tennis club. I would open up the fruit machines and steal money from there; steal from my dad; steal from the tills; steal from the bar. And I didn't think anything about it. . . . And with alcohol it sort of became the norm, I suppose." John, 2011, par 9:3–6; 9), and Luke (". . . but it might go beyond stealing to feed your addiction; and commit criminal offence because then you develop other character which is because of the addiction." Luke, 2011, par 37:13–15).

- Lust is observed in the accounts of Paul ("And it was just about women and alcohol every single day." Paul, 2011, par 11:11–12) and Luke

("Because of the drink, I would buy drink and would have an affair in the afternoon and come and continue my work which is highly unethical." Luke, 2011, par 29:4–6).

- Pride is visible in the stories of Adam (". . . I had the first seep of a drink or the first line of cocaine or the first pill, or whatever it was I was taking, I would continue until all the drugs and all the alcohol run out. . . . So the delusion for me was that I'm in control." Adam, 2011, par 5:5–7; 14), Mary ("And I was put into detox. And I spent two weeks there. And I came out, and I was under the false impression—I could control alcohol, which was a mistake. And I started drinking again." Mary, 2011, par 9:3–6), Jack ("People quite often told me that I had a problem. I didn't believe them. I believed that I had everything under control." Jack, 2011, par 23:5–7), and John ("I laughed at the whole situation really. That's what people do. A lot of it is fear because we think we're in control of our own lives, where in fact we're not. We are in utter chaos but we can't admit it to ourselves." John, 2011, par 39:6–9).

- Sloth is found in the stories of Mary ("And anyway my drinking got worse and worse. . . . There was no need for me to go to work. There was no need for me to do, there was . . . . I had no purpose basically. And so I stayed at home. Yeah, I started picking up earlier and earlier each day and every day. And as the days go on each day earlier and earlier." Mary, 2011, par 9:1; 11–12; 12–14), John ("My whole life just evolved around alcohol. . . . And the days I didn't have alcohol, cigarettes, or food I would just sit in my grotty flat shivering, shaking, retching, and vomiting, and feeling sorry for myself basically." John, 2011, par 12:27; 30–33), and Jack ("Life for me before was with no purpose. I didn't want to be a part of it. And definitely I didn't appreciate it." Jack, 2011, par 45:4–5).

Conscience exposes conflict during addiction

Victoria experiences the challenges of conscience about her double life of addiction and work. "I knew all the time deep down in my conscience that it's not good, what I'm doing." (Victoria, 2011, par 7:12–13) When she attempts to commit suicide through drinking the conflict with her conscience is experienced in the spiritual realm as a battle for her existence and belonging to God. "So when I had those six days of drinking, and I said that I felt suspended between two realities, I felt that there was a kind of struggle for me. If kind of I'm to die or if I'm to live; if I'm to be with God; if I am to be separated." (Victoria, 2011, par 10:10–13)

Max's conscience exposes the conflict between his spirituality and drinking behaviour as well as between the nature of his work and addiction. Max responds to the challenge of conscience negatively by embracing addiction rather than abstinence. This leads to the failure to resolve the conflict successfully and quitting both church ministry and work in order to continue with the alcohol addiction. "Conscience-wise I resigned from work because I knew I couldn't work with people with drug and alcohol problems and actually be drinking or manage simply outside of that. . . . And I ended up really from October . . . (year omitted due to confidentiality) just bumping along, just drinking myself into oblivion." (Max, 2011, par 7:3–5; 7–9)

Luke experiences the admonitions of his conscience, but does not follow them to reform his behaviour (Luke, 2011, par 22:11–15). Paul believes that his conscience challenged the addictive behaviour and guided him to take a decision for recovery leading him to spiritual transformation. "The voice of my conscience told me what I was doing wasn't right. And the people that were around me, I was hurting them. And they don't deserve it. So I had to use my conscience to come here and make up my mind to do the programme and get the best out of it." (Paul, 2011, par 33:1–4)

Spiritual transformative moment and process

Transformation occurs in all of the narratives. Its nature is defined as spiritual and/or religious and its character as a momentous experience and a progressive development. Transformation as a transformative moment appears in the following stories:

- Sam: "That man coming from church; reading me scriptures from the Bible; that night was my defining moment." (Sam, 2011, par 56:6–7); "You know, that was God's hand reaching out pulling me from the gutter and helping me." (Sam, 2011, par 60:3–4);

- Paul:

    But the spiritual awakening came for me when there was a time I drank so much, and I was withdrawing, and I was really vomiting blood. I passed out. And there was a dark path I saw. And it was later revealed to me that that path was hell because of the life I was living. So yeah, I do believe in the afterlife, and God has given me this opportunity to come here and build my identity, build myself, build my spirituality, you know to be a better man. (Paul, 2011, par 29:3–9);

- Victoria: "And I prayed at that moment, and I said: 'God please give me another chance.' And I felt like God was saying: 'You have another chance but it's a matter of life and death. You better take it seriously.'" (Victoria, 2011, par 12:12–14); another moment after the relapse: "And it was that moment of complete surrender, and I said: 'God, if you don't help me I cannot do it.' And that happened on the 8th of the 8th of the 8th. And I have never drunk since. So that seemed to me to be a moment of probably deep reconnection with God and reconciliation with God." (Victoria, 2011, par 17:11–15);

- Mary: "And I suddenly realised. I suddenly put everything into perspective. And I felt a huge appreciation for my life for the first time. That's it basically." (Mary, 2011, par 18:5–7);

- Adam: "In that moment of clarity I did something different. I asked for God's help properly, sincerely, you know." (Adam, 2011, par 8:1–2);

- Jack: "After a while I decided to, you know, thinking a lot, I'm gonna hand my life over to the Lord, which I did." (Jack, 2011, par 16:7–8);

- James:

    And all of a sudden I started to sweat. I felt dizzy. I went downstairs to get blessed and everything. Whilst there I was swaying with, and the Holy Spirit was swaying with me. It was a very, very nice experience. Since then, since then I cannot get enough of church. I cannot get enough of praying, meetings etc. Do you know what I mean? I mean the transformation in myself; I mean even my peers and even people here, counsellors, staff have even noticed the transformation in me. I mean every time I go to church now and I pray I know the Holy Spirit is in me. He's overwhelming the spirit that I have in me. I'm singing. I'm praying. I am at the front. I am there for everything. That to me is one transformation that at times I cannot believe myself. The transformation that I've changed in myself. I mean I have. (James, 2011, par 21:6–17);

- John:

  And as soon as I walked through the doors I knew this is where I needed to be, where I wanted to be. And I felt something at that point: a real buzz, a real high, a real sense of comfort, a real sense of peace. All sorts of different adjectives I can use here. I know now it was Christ. And I can look back that whoever gave me that telephone number that's when Christ had come into my life. (John, 2011, par 13:1–6);

- Max:

  The transformation took place, as I said earlier, on . . . (month and date omitted due to confidentiality) when I prayed in the woods: 'God if you are there open the door or take my life.' And the fact that I was there the next morning and I was able to come in because it was never certain I guess was God saying: 'Yeah, I am there. And I've opened the door.' (Max, 2011, par 27:1–5);

- Luke: "I received the baptism of the Holy Spirit and that was it. . . . It didn't take much time. It didn't take long on the deliverance from addiction. We were just praying. We started speaking in tongues. The man prayed breaking the addiction with that prayer and that was it." (Luke, 2011, par 29:8–9; 13–15)

Transformation as a transformative process is evidenced through examples from the following narratives:

- Alex: "The spiritual transformation is still happening." (Alex, 2011, par 33);

- Paul: Paul's analogy depicting life before and after the transformation (Paul, 2011, par 15) defines the solution of his main issue to be the person who is liked by everyone. The analogy of the beautiful but uncomfortable shoes and the ugly but comfortable pair shows that he found himself through the spiritual transformation. The process of self-realisation is accomplished through spiritual edification based on Paul's personal relationship with God. "And I've really grown spiritually knowing God." (Paul, 2011, par 16:3–4);

- Adam: "To continue to pass on the message; keep on growing spiritually; to keep on developing my relationship with God, which really, really, I am just on the start of my journey." (Adam, 2011, par 65:1–3);

- Ben: "And so coming back into God's presence for guidance and to cleanse my body of my past which I am not happy with but I cannot change my past. But we can change our future, or we can shape our future. So spirituality now is paramount for me. And into that comes morality . . . ." (Ben, 2011, par 40:3–7);

- Jack: "My conversion wasn't anything spectacular. I just found myself one day in a place where everything was different. All the anger had gone. I was no longer thinking about alcohol. I was no longer thinking about drugs. I was no longer alone. I was no longer seeking revenge." (Jack, 2011, par 17:1–4);

- James:

  There's only one thing I can say about my story. I've got God on my side and God is the man who keeps me on the straight and narrow every day. I pray, I pray to God. I pray to God: 'God please send me through this day.' Right! 'Alcohol free and another day clean and sober.' And God has planted the seed. And the Holy Spirit says: 'Well no more, no more, no more alcohol.' (James, 2011, par 53:1–6);

- John:

  It's God. He has been so phenomenally good to me. It's a word I'm reluctant to use but because of who I was, the transformation that I went through, the love and compassion I received from so many other people I am now able to pass that on and to see the ripple effect of it. And it's all because of God. It is as simple as that. And I try not to forget it. . . . So the kind of a progression from alcoholic bum through the programme to sobriety, to Christ, to marriage, to self-fulfilment basically in what I do. (John, 2011, par 23:1–5; 19–21);

- Max:

  So that spiritual transformation has taken place. Morally, the fact I'm physically well and spiritually I'm vulnerable is really improved my moral decisions, you know. I'm clearheaded; spiritually I have a good understanding of what's right and what's wrong, what's right for me at the minute. Therefore, my moral decisions are moral, you know, they are sounder. And therefore, my conscience is clear. . . . And therefore, having a clear conscience is enabled and morally being refreshed, spiritually being, you know, transformed as you got here and alcohol free,

I'm able to relate back to people as people. And that's critical I think for my on-going wellbeing really. So that's what I can say. (Max, 2011, par 12:7–12; 17–21)

The impact of spiritual transformation on conscience

Victoria understands the input of her conscience in resolving her moral conflict. She identifies the transformation as a crucial point for re-establishing the role of her conscience. During the addiction the voice of conscience is suppressed intentionally through a combination of immoral and addictive behaviours. However, conscience creates an unbearable conflict which leads to the spiritual experiences and transformation.

> I feel that my conscience impacted my moral, spiritual, and . . . . The conscience was the bit that in a way forced me to address this contradiction, this moral contradiction I was living in. And kind of settled, settled it, reconciled it. Before the transformation I would say the conscience, I was putting my fist in its month, to be very graphic. And now, now I'm listening to it. I'm kind of sensitive to it. I'm trying to pick up on its voice. So now it's in a way the opposite. (Victoria, 2011, par 45:1–8)

Jack's negative thinking during the addiction based on suppressed emotions and silenced conscience defines his immoral behaviour of trying to hurt himself and others. The spiritual transformation establishes a new perspective defined through the empowered conscience and managed emotions leading to a behaviour of love towards self and others. "You know, my thinking today is totally different. From being so disturbed, so wicked, so violent to just, I just want to love people today, you know, and just to encourage people in that." (Jack, 2011, par 18:30–33)

During the culminative moment of John's transformation he experiences the revival of his conscience through the public acknowledgement of his faith in Christ and the encounter with his presence and the Holy Spirit. This is an overwhelming emotional time for John. He uses a terminology which may describe the effects of addictive substances in his attempt to depict the event. John's conscience is transformed resulting in the experience of complete freedom from sin, shame, and guilt. This feels like a total break from the past for an entirely new beginning. "And at that one moment quite literally all of my angst, all of my sin, all my shame, all of my guilt were lifted off my shoulders, there and then. Done." (John, 2011, par 15:30–32)

Conscience's freedom

Since his spiritual transformation James experiences the freedom of his conscience. He believes that God is guiding and directing him in the process of assessing and revising his behaviour. "I have no worries. I have no fears. I've got the man at the side of me. . . . If there is anything that I was gonna do wrong he kind of says: 'Hold on a minute.' Yeah." (James, 2011, par 49:5–6; 6–7) John's transformation also frees his conscience. He is able to allow his conscience to function in its full capacity even when difficult moral decisions are to be made. "The conscience was always there but I suppressed it. Now I let the conscience run free even if it does kick in the backside." (John, 2011, par 47:2–4)

Jack's transformation has freed his conscience. He is able to understand his former immoral behaviour. Conscience leads him to make amends wherever possible. Even where amends are not possible the outcome is peace since conscience's role is shaped through his spiritual outlook.

> And then after my transformation, the conversion, I began to get convicted a lot. You know, I was very ashamed of a lot of stuff that I've done. Some of those things I've been able to put right. But there are other things I can't. . . . But today even in not being able to see my father's grave and not being able to see my family, all of those things, I've still got peace. (Jack, 2011, par 43:1–4; 12–14)

Conscience's resurrection

Jack explains the total contrast in experiencing his conscience during the addiction and after the transformation. He did not feel the presence of conscience before his spiritual transformation. Jack even felt justified to do the immoral, evil deeds without any trace of guilt or shame. However, after the transformation he starts experiencing his conscience in regards to both understanding his past actions and present behaviour. He feels how his conscience convicts him of his past immorality through reading the Bible. Jack acknowledges his past immoral behaviour and asks the Lord for forgiveness. He experiences the role of his conscience for guidance of his everyday behaviour. Following his conscience's lead Jack achieves peace. "Before I knew the Lord I don't think I really had a conscience.... Because to me my conscience is very alive at the moment, you know. And, yeah, I am aware on a daily basis of the things that I do that are right or wrong." (Jack, 2011, par 21:1–2; 20–22)

James experiences the resurrection of his conscience being regenerated through the spiritual transformation. The present guidance of his conscience leads to the understanding of the past as being left behind and the future as full of hope. The conscience is experienced as in a state of cleanness. It provides support for a decisive resolution of continuous abstinence and spiritual life. James believes that with the resurrected conscience comes a resurrected social life of new trustworthy relationships.

> Now the conscience I have got, yeah, is all right. You cannot change the past. The past is gone. The past is gone. The conscience is on the future. And the conscience that I have got now is: I will live alcohol free; I will live with friends, proper, proper friends; I will live with friends who believe in me. I have people that will believe that I will succeed. And I have got people who do believe that I am a gentleman. So my conscience is clear. And my conscience is good now. (James, 2011, par 31:3–9)

Conscience's cleanness

Adam experiences the cleanness of his conscience through the spiritual practice of repentance and confession of his moral failures.

> I started to realise how selfish I was. And I started to realise who I was. It was the first time I ever really looked at myself and actually realised and actually could admit to God: 'Yeah, this is what I've done.' And that for me was massive, like an internal cleanse; like somebody is taken out my insides and put it through a human wash, like a car wash but human, and put it back in. (Adam, 2011, par 26:21–26)

The progressive transformation of Max which involved spiritual and religious practices leads him to sound moral decisions and clear conscience. As a consequence he feels peace which contributes to his overall wellbeing. "So that spiritual transformation has taken place.... I'm clear-headed; spiritually I have a good understanding of what's right and what's wrong, what's right for me at the minute. Therefore, my moral decisions are moral, you know, they are sounder. And therefore, my conscience is clear. I sleep better." (Max, 2011, par 12:7–8; 9–13)

Paul's experience of spiritual transformation leads to a renewal of his life, relationships, and conscience. Paul's clear conscience provides the effective management of emotions in relationships even during difficult situations. "And it thus has made a complete transformation for me; and me having a clear conscience. Even when I'm going through confrontations and I knew it is not my fault I don't get the hump about it because my conscience is clear." (Paul, 2011, par 39:8–11)

Conscience's peace

Victoria recognises that during the addiction her conscience has been challenging her behaviour in spite of her efforts to suppress it. The conflict between belief and behaviour is exposed by the conscience and leads to a spiritual transformation and congruence between these two. "So now my conscience is not nagging me for going against what I believe. It's congruence between what I believe and how I behave." (Victoria, 2011, par 47:1–3) The transformation brings Victoria to a state of freedom and peace. Her conscience experiences spiritual empowerment leading to a positive behavioural change and reconciliation between her belief and way of life and between her moral, religious, and spiritual convictions and her behaviour. "So I feel like I have that freedom because I know I'm living what I believe." (Victoria, 2011, par 41:4–5)

Max also experiences the peace of his conscience through the spiritual transformation. This is a process and requires a continuous attention to the voice of conscience. It also depends on his personal choice to follow or neglect his conscience. The decision results in corresponding consequences. When the voice of conscience is followed the experience is that of peace and freedom. If it is ignored or suppressed there is a conflict within oneself which requires resolution.

> . . . my conscience was totally revoked when I was drinking . . . . Afterwards it was a painful process of choosing to listen to my conscience in respect to what I did and how I treated people. And that's still an on-going process. . . . actually my conscience is a warning sign that things are not well. And if I override that I reap the consequences of that. My conscience really; if I can go to bed at night and realise that actually today I had a good day I sleep better. If I go to bed at night and I realise that there

is a conflict between me and somebody else or in something that I've done then I make amends the next day. So it's a way of keeping me well. (Max, 2011, par 37:1–2; 2–4; 5–10)

John's conscience guides him to respond to a difficult situation according to his spiritual convictions. He takes even an uncomfortable decision which provides continuity between belief and action. John experiences the peace of his conscience since the behaviour corresponds to his belief of God's will. "And I know that that is the right answer because I haven't been punished, I haven't been kicked in the stomach by God to say: 'That's not Christ like.'" (John, 2011, par 31:11–13)

Conscience's empowerment

After the moment of spiritual transformation Victoria starts receiving professional help by a psychiatrist. The main role in the treatment is played by Victoria's empowered conscience. The latter is used through reflective journal writing and accountability to maintain abstinence and to deter her from drinking. "And that for me, because I have sensitive conscience despite the way I went against it, the fact that I knew I needed to be accountable to someone, and that I needed to be honest, for me it was good enough to hold me from drinking." (Victoria, 2011, par 14:8–11) Victoria's empowered conscience leads to realisation, acknowledgement, and modification of her immoral behaviour. "I was coming to terms that what I was doing was wrong. And then, kind of taking practical steps into changing my behaviour. So, as I said, the fact that I was going to this lady with my diary once a week and having that accountability and knowing that I needed to be honest, that was good enough for me." (Victoria, 2011, par 51:3–7) The process of spiritual transformation with its culmination in Victoria's recommitment to God after the relapse leads to the re-empowerment of Victoria's conscience which becomes a guiding tool for her. "How much the voice of the conscience matter? I said: 'Very much.' I'm trying to be sensitive to it. And now it's a good guiding tool." (Victoria, 2011, par 49:2–4)

James experiences his active conscience after the beginning of his spiritual and religious transformation. He is released from prison to go to a Christian rehabilitation centre and handed back large sum of money. He vividly depicts this in the story as a moment when he feels his strong spiritual connection with God through the Holy Spirit which empowers his conscience and leads to his decision to continue his change outside the prison.

> ... I was handed £1,000 in my pocket, which was my money. Yeah. Now the gentleman, the Holy Spirit says: 'Well.' Right—was with me. Because I come from this south Yorkshire town (TSYT, name substituted due to confidentiality) on my own, hundred and seventy miles away with £1,000 in my pocket, an alcoholic. Yeah. And I knew myself that I had a .... I hit, I hit rock bottom and the time for change had come. Yeah. The time for change had come for myself that I was very, very, very focused. Well, very focused to the case of: 'I need to change.' (James, 2011, par 18:17–25)

The impact of the transformation on Sam's conscience is significant. It is viewed in terms of empowerment which source may be considered as divine. "... 'When God pays you back is tenfold.' My conscience now is tenfold in a way. I have the same morality and the same beliefs and the same conscience but they have become stronger. Because of what I did when I was drinking now I try hundred times more consciously to make sure I don't let people down, not through drink." (Sam, 2011, par 70:2–6) Adam also defines the new state of his conscience as being empowered by his spiritual transformation.

> But, the thing is about the conscience is that as I was coming to recovery my awareness of my conscience is become as I said, is like the pilot light turning up. It's like my conscience is become; I've become much more aware of my conscience; or I'm choosing. I guess what I'm doing is I'm choosing to listen to my conscience. I'm choosing today to go in accordance with what my conscience says .... (Adam, 2011, par 41:1–6)

Conscience in recovery

After the religious experience Luke is managing well without drinking. However, with the increase of pressure during his studies he starts drinking again and it seems that this period is even worse than before. Nevertheless, Luke's conscience is empowered through the religious experience and its function of cognitive assessment is strengthened. He realises that he cannot overcome the addiction by his own strength and turns in prayer for God's help.

> ... because I've been born again the spirit of God was fighting against drinking in my conscience. ... The spirit of God came; God's conscience came; put into your life and working. So in another way previously where you don't feel that guilty when the spirit of God comes in your life, as it says, the spirit of God convicts us. So there is a serious conviction not by my own assessment or what is written or societies have said but the consciousness. The conviction comes with the Holy Spirit in my life. So I was even calling when I was alone: 'Oh, Lord come and help me.' (Luke, 2011, par 28:7–8; 8–15)

Paul believes that the transformation underlined by his practice of spirituality leads to clearance and empowerment of his conscience as well as conscious openness for its functionality. Conscience plays a significant part in recovery promoting discipline, spiritual devotion, and personal growth.

> So I had to use my conscience to come here and make up my mind to do the programme and get the best out of it. Because the programme is workable if you only put an effort in on your own. And that is what I've done here. ... And I always pray to God and he helps me and shows me a path that I can follow.
>
> So it has cleared my conscience in terms of impact; it has cleared my conscience a lot. And I have a clean slate in my heart. And whatever I'm doing wrong my conscience always tells me: 'You know where this will end up if you follow this path.' So I'm more self-aware of my conscience, the power of my conscience. I am more self-aware about it. And you can either use your conscience to build you or destroy you. But mine has actually been building me. That's my view. (Paul, 2011, par 33:3–6; 7–8; par 35:4–10)

Victoria defines life during the addiction and after the transformation as a movement from dualism and duplicity to wholeness and integrity. The conflict between her conscience and way of life leads to this duplicity which is resolved through the spiritual transformation. The latter empowers the conscience bringing reconciliation of these two disintegrated parts and wholeness of life and self. "While drinking and being in this relationship it was this duplicity that I mentioned. It was this dualism, this double life which was quite hard to live. While now I feel like I am a whole person. And I am an integer person. So I can live with integrity which is one of the things I value very much being able to be 'what it says on the tin.'" (Victoria, 2011, par 43:1–6)

Mary defines the crucial place of her transformed conscience in her recovery as providing her with purpose in life to help others. Her conscience is working in combination with prayer to find the guidance for doing the right things in life. "I just hope I am doing the right thing. When I pray, I pray for guidance. I want to know if I'm going wrong, if I'm doing things wrong. It is important to me. I want to know." (Mary, 2011, par 65:3–5)

Max experiences the role of his renewed conscience in the process of reconciliation with the people he has hurt during his addiction. He suffers the pain of hurting others brought to his cognitive and emotional perception by his conscience. He also understands that he cannot excuse himself of being under the influence of alcohol but should take the responsibility for his actions. Hence, following the guidance of his conscience he is trying to make amends with the people who suffered from his behaviour in the past.

> And as I look back now, you know, it breaks my heart, when you talk about conscience, it breaks my heart; the people that I've hurt and damaged. . . . But during the seventh—eight months I've been here now, seven months, part of the recovery process for me is not just walking away from those people, an element of conscious, conscience really of who I've hurt, who I've damaged, who I've stole from; it would be very easy to say: 'Well that's in the past. I know I can't help that. You know I was drinking, tha, tha, tha.' But an important part of my recovery is been trying and then endeavouring to make contact with those people. . . . And I know, I look at my partner when she kicked me out in February. I had contact with her, you know. And she wrote a very open and honest letter two weeks ago. And some of the things that she wrote were really quite hurtful. But that was because in my conscience as it were, you know, that right and wrong, the morality side of things, I realised she was right. There is no hiding from it. I wish I could have said: 'Yeah that was because I was an alcoholic.' No! I chose to drink. And because I chose to drink that behaviour came with it. (Max, 2011, par 10:1–3; 4–11; 18–25)

Adam summaries his story in three main parts. First, he identifies the time of his addiction as the time of "spiritual maladjustment," when his life is dominated by the addictive behaviour causing destruction and leading to suicide attempt. "I was like a wild wind of chaos." (Adam, 2011, par 68:3) Second is the role of spirituality in general and God in particular as the transforming power of him and his life. "Because of that I've had, what I would call a 'spiritual awakening,' 'a psychic change.' You know my whole psyche is changed; my whole thinking; my behaviour. I am in touch with my conscience today. I am in touch with other people, you know." (Adam, 2011, par 68:11–14) Finally, the spiritual transformation defines Adam's new experience of self closely connected with his conscience, emotions, and perception of life with purpose and hope.

> That's what it comes down to; comes down to God at the end of the day. Everything that I do, everything that I think; everything I do, think, do and feel and breath, my conscience, my every single muscle fibre, every single part of me today is about my relationship with God. And that's it, that's it. And I will continue with that. (Adam, 2011, par 69:35–39)

Conscience and the principle of mutual respect (Golden Rule)

Max identifies the importance of his morality before the addiction. His desire to be successful shapes the moral values and their extreme applications. The morality appears to be an external facade to supplement the self-built image of success. Internally Max recognises his fear of being immoral. The addiction completely destroys the moral framework of life bringing the fears of immorality into reality. The spiritual transformation leads to complete inner change activating Max's conscience from within, establishing the key element of the moral framework as proper treatment of others. Hence Max strives to make amends with people from his past that he has hurt and follows his empowered conscience behaving appropriately towards others.

> Before I was probably very legalistic, moralistic. . . . Making sure that; is part of that drivenness, that performance, you know, that sense of being in the right place, being dressed right, saying the right thing, behaving in the right way. And in a sense it probably; it was a mask that I wore and deep down I guess I've always feared that morally I was, you know, vulnerable or, you know, corrupted in some ways. And I guess when I started drinking again morally I just became inert. I just became; it became a passive part of my life. You know, drink was the most important thing. And, as I said before, the spiritual transformation woke me up to the fact that actually I damaged so many people over the last three years. . . . So the spiritual transformation; that's probably morally made me look at the damage and the responsibility aspects of my life.

Conscience in Recovery from Alcohol Addiction

> I found that early on in my addiction that actually I related to people not because of the person but because of what I can get from them; and what are they for me—to drink. If that makes any sense. And therefore, having a clear conscience . . . I'm able to relate back to people as people. (Max, 2011, par 20:1; 6–15; 24–26; par 12:14–17; 19–20)

Mary experiences the changes of her character after the empowerment of her conscience through the spiritual transformation. The empowered conscience leads to loving herself and others. The principle of mutual respect becomes a basic guiding tool in life after Mary's conscience gains its functionality and important place in her life.

> Yeah. Because suddenly I love myself. While before I didn't love myself. So I think if you don't love yourself you can't really love others. I don't know. I think with alcoholism you don't have love for anybody, do you? You don't, you don't have, you don't think about anybody, you just think about that bottle. But now, yeah. I mean: How other people are feeling? How much more I am aware of other people's feelings and my own. And I just want to treat everybody and myself as they should be treated. (Mary, 2011, par 53)

Conscience in future plans

For Max the role of conscience is very important in relation to his decisions about the future. Presently his choice to do volunteer work is based on giving back freely to others. His future plan is also to develop further his spirituality through enrolment to Bible college and help others in recovery.

> So at the minute I am doing voluntary work and I'm loving every minute of it, you know. So it's giving without receiving. Because I've taken a lot from people with or without their permission; so giving back. And then, probably I'll end up, hopefully going to Bible college from October next year. I can only do that, as I said before, as long as I haven't anything lurking in my conscience or in the moral decisions that I've made. So they play a critical role again in my future plans. (Max, 2011, par 41:4–11)

Luke considers essential the role of spirituality and conscience in his future plans to help others. He believes that through God's help people's addictive behaviour can be challenged and they may be led to transformation.

"So, therefore, when I'm dealing with people now I have to know that people can change. And God's Word for people refers well that we change. . . . get the person to sit down and think: 'Oh, this is wrong and I need to . . . all being that I cannot help myself.' . . . And God will help us . . . ." (Luke, 2011, par 69:12–14; 21–22; 25)

Paul sees the role of his conscience in his present and future recovery as giving him a better understanding of addiction, providing guidance for helping others, and helping him to manage relationships. "I plan on being along with them. We are all brothers of the same struggle. And we need to be there for each other. . . . And honestly since this cleansing of my . . . conscience—that's helped me a lot to just understand my addiction better." (Paul, 2011, par 37:1–2; 7–9)

Conscience, morality, character, and virtue

The positive impact of spiritual transformation on morality through the empowerment of one's conscience is testified throughout the narratives as development of moral perspective, relationships, and behaviour. The following examples demonstrate this moral change.

Morality as in the case of conscience is overpowered by the addiction. The immoral acts shape Sam's behaviour driven by the desire to feed his alcohol addiction. When he thinks about his immoral behaviour in retrospect especially of misusing the death of his mother he hears the challenge of his spiritually empowered conscience as a divine voice. This leads to the understanding of the former moral failure in light of the addiction and underlines the maintaining of abstinence as a morally sound decision. "I look back at that and I think: 'I don't really want to say God but you know—How could you stoop that low?' But now I've realised that's the power of alcoholism. You know you would tell a lie as big as that one to get money for gambling and drink. And that doesn't hold me now because I understand that that's not an excuse but that's the power of addiction." (Sam, 2011, par 38:18–23)

Adam defines the dramatic change of his morality after the transformation. His approach to life is changed completely through his spirituality. His conscience is empowered through his relationship with God and he is living according to the spiritual principals applying them in his moral stand and behaviour. As part of his moral understanding Adam develops love towards God, himself, his family, and others. His life gains a strong purpose to help others in recovery. The understanding of the moral principles and spiritual practices encourages their disciplined application in day to day life. "I believe I've regained my sense of good values and trying to do the right thing. . . . I'm just trying to do the best that I can today because I think I owe it to myself, for first and foremost. I owe it to my family. . . . But also today I've got a duty towards God. . . . God has come and transformed my life, you know." (Adam, 2011, par 49:3–4; 6–8; 15–16; 16–17)

The immoral behaviour defined through the addiction and dominated by vice is transformed to a moral framework shaped through one's conscience and embodied in one's virtuous character. The evidence coming from the stories demonstrates the development of virtues and character strengths (Peterson and Seligman, 2004).

- Integrity is present in the stories of Adam ("So the first one is being: honesty, you know, honest with myself. The one needs to stop taking cocaine. If I don't stop drinking alcohol will it take me back to cocaine—so honesty." Adam, 2011, par 27:11–13) and John ("I was proved to be trustworthy. For somebody to give you trust when you don't even trust yourself makes, you know, makes a huge difference." John, 2011, par 15:4–6).

- Humanity is shown in the narratives of Sam ("I've never had a passion for something so much as helping other people in recovery." Sam, 2011, par 76:2–3), Mary ("So I treat people a lot better. I'm kind of a lot more thoughtful. And I do have compassion for people. . . . And I do feel for them. And I can show them empathy because I know the misery of it [*the bottle*]." Mary, 2011, par 55:8–9; 11–12), and Max ("And making sure that I don't do anything that would destabilise social relationships really." Max, 2011, par 11:24–25).

- Leadership is displayed in the story of John ("And I walked out of my job and became a self-employed gardener. And now I have truck. I now got four men working with me today. They're all volunteers. They are all recovering addicts. . . . We got one lad who has just come back from another rehab . . . . He's come to Christ. . . . He is a completely and utterly changed man. That's something that me and my two main lads, . . . we love to see, it is in our hearts to do it." John, 2011, par 22:12–15; 16–17; 22; 23–24; 25–26).

- Humility and modesty appear in the narrative of Adam (". . . another spiritual principle I've really had to learn is humility and humbleness. . . . So I had to realise I was powerless over certain elements of myself, my shortcomings, my defects. So I had to ask God humbly to remove these shortcomings, these defects as well. . . . And overtime again I've changed further because I am learning more now to use spiritual principles." Adam, 2011, par 28:1–2; 6–8; 11–12).

- Forgiveness and mercy are demonstrated in Ben's story ("And something that my father still doesn't accept. I thought he would do as a medical man but no, he doesn't. So I don't go down that line anymore. But I'm going through forgiveness to cleanse myself of that." Ben, 2011, par 13:10–12).

- Transcendence is visible in the stories of Mary ("This is probably wishful thinking but I almost feel as if divine intervention. There have been a few things like that." Mary, 2011, par 45:10–11; pars 42 and 44) and Adam ("It has filled me with excitement, and wonderment, and hope, faith, courage. I never had that. I never had that. Today, I have that. My life is transformed without doubt, without a question." Adam, 2011, par 65:9–11).

- Spirituality is part of all the narratives and a specific example may be given with the story of Paul ("And there is a lot of joy each day I derive from communication with God and telling him about my problems." Paul, 2011, par 31:2–4).

- Gratitude is expressed in the stories of Adam ("Gratitude ultimately goes to God because that is what has turned my life around." Adam, 2011, par 49:43–44) and James ("He [*God*] saved my life. He saved my life because if he hasn't taken me as I was I would be dead now. I would be dead. I would be dead cause I would have either drunk myself to death, or I would have killed somebody with the alcohol in me. And he's . . . ; he guided me. He guided me for a reason. He's got a purpose for me. And I am forever grateful for that." James, 2011, par 22:8–13).

- Wisdom and knowledge are clearly observed in Sam's story ("And then you get four out of the twenty people leave the room because the word 'God' is there. And I would say: 'No'; I would say; I convinced people in the community rehabilitation centre [CRC] to go to that. I would say: 'Look at it; break the 'god' down. The 'g' is a 'group.' And the 'o' is 'of.' And 'd' is 'drunks.' 'A group of drunks.' And we hand our will and our lives over to 'a group of drunks.'' First of all we've had experiences. And as you go further and get that person, you know, not fearful of the word 'god' then you bring it in, or I would bring it in then. And now they may say: 'And then I started realising it; they weren't group of drunks really, you know, is God without us knowing.' And they say: 'Yeah it is.' 'You know, it is,' I think. You know, that's the way I want to use my recovery." Sam, 2011, par 77:22–33).

- Open-mindedness is demonstrated in Adam's story ("Open-mindedness: I need to start to think: 'Well if these guys that related the story got solution and they are telling me about the solution do I need to follow what they say.' Do I need to be open-minded enough to say: 'Would that can work for me as well.' . . . They just said: 'Adam, you just need to be willing to come along; be willing to get on your knees in the morning and pray; be willing to ask God for God's help, you know.' And I started to do that stuff and over time the denial started to break down. . . . I started; it was almost like I melted; I came back to life, you know. I believe I was reborn at that point. I believe that I suddenly had a second chance in life, you know." Adam, 2011, par 27:13–16; 19–23; 26–28).

The analysis of narratives from the perspective of the research rationale reveals themes which shape the understanding of conscience and its role in the life of the participants. The latter present a comprehension of conscience as an internal moral guide which is spiritually resourced. Conscience suffers from inadequate moral input and spiritual conflict, which establishes the grounds for the development of alcohol attachments. During active addiction conscience endures the overwhelming negative impact of the addictive behaviour. It challenges the behaviour during times of sobriety but its role is subdued by the addiction. The diminished function of conscience allows the proliferation of immorality and vice. The spiritual transformation revives the conscience completely leading to its key presence in the life of recovery. The empowered conscience shapes all dimensions of life providing constructive evaluation of the past, guidance for the present, and purpose for the future. The role of conscience in recovery leads to a moral development of character strengths and virtues. I will continue developing these summaries through the discussion in light of the relevant studies.

5.

Discussion

THE CHAPTER DEVELOPS THE results from the study in light of the scholarly debates presented in the introduction with the purpose of answering the research questions. Hence three main dimensions are to be considered, namely, the nature and function of conscience, its state during the addiction, and its actualisation after the transformation.

5.1. Conscience's nature and functioning: spiritually defined realisation and integration of conscience's elements

The results show that conscience is closely related to consciousness (Koops, Brugman, and Ferguson, 2010). Conscience provides a guide to moral conduct which application depends on personal choice (Max, 2011, par 14:6-7; par 39:4-7; John, 2011, par 29:4-6). The manipulated conscience during addiction leads to shifting the failure of one's responsibilities to others (James, 2011, par 35:1-4; also Schimmel, 1997). Spiritually renewed conscience brings enlightenment of one's consciousness related to one's moral decisions (Adam, 2011, par 34:21-23; 28-30; also McCosh, 1887; Wall, 1996). The latter are actualised through the input of one's empowered conscience leading to the activation of one's wilful choice which breaks the cycle of automaticity (Bargh, 1997) and interferes with one's addiction related attentional bias (Albery, Sharma, Niazi, and Moss, 2006). The continuity in the interaction between conscience and consciousness enables the formation of morally sound automaticity (Martin, 2006) and promotes personal character edification (Xavier, 2010). The fourfold conscientious process of evaluation, decision, application, and re-evaluation of consequences is made automatic and habitual through the practice of routine moral inventories. An example of the latter is found in the 12-step programme which is spiritually defined and operates on the basis of spiritual discipline (Xavier, 2010).

Spirituality is identified in the stories as part of the very nature of conscience (Adam, 2011, par 34:21-23; 28-30; John, 2011, par 16:2-4; 7; 10-11). This establishes the conative dimension of conscience as being fulfilled by its relationship to the transcendent. Piedmont's (2004) study of spiritual transcendence presents evidence of the crucial place of spirituality in a person's psychology and personality. Spirituality establishes the core of an individual's worldview providing sustainable structures in life even during crises and positively influencing recovery from substance addiction (Piedmont, 2004). Spirituality consisting of a personal relationship with God through the involvement of conscience facilitates life manageability and moral choice (Adam, 2011, par 34:21-23; 28-30). Conscience is understood as spiritually resourced from a divine guidance for distinguishing right and wrong (Luke, 2011, par 23:9-14; Adam, 2011, par 41:22-26; 29-33; also McCosh, 1887; Wall, 1996).

Finally, the emotive dimension of conscience is perceived as the affective impact from one's behaviour which results in guilt or fulfilment (Victoria, 2011, par 19:3-7). The process involves conscious ethical perception (Koops, Brugman, and Ferguson, 2010) and may lead to internal and external moral adjustments (McCosh, 1887). Conscience is presented in the narratives as a guide to behaviour which when not followed may lead to emotionally overwhelming and addictive desires (Max, 2011, par 8:19-22; 33-36; par 39:4-7; Victoria, 2011, par 4:2-3). This is resolved through the conative conscience which is shaped by active spirituality (Jack, 2011, par 45:1-4; 15-16; also Canda, 2009; Maton, 2004). On the other hand, spiritual deficiency leads to the development of the addictive behaviour (Delaney, Forcehimes, Campbell, and Smith, 2009) and overpowering of conscience (Miller and Jackson, 1995).

5.2. Conscience in addiction: conscientious deterioration, immoral escalation, character degradation, conflict intensification, and addictive expansion

The development of addiction is underlined by the negative influences upon conscience. Going against one's spiritual convictions demoralises conscience (Victoria, 2011, par 4:2-3). Green, Fullilove, and Fullilove (1998) identify, in the context of alcohol addiction, a strong dependent relationship between conscience and spirituality in which the absence of

Discussion

the latter leads to the inadequacy of the former. Furthermore, conscience is adversely impacted by overly strict or weak parental role (Sam, 2011, par 4:12; par 62:3-4; Max, 2011, par 14:15). The characteristics of strictness and demands may be linked with weak conscience in the light of psychopaths' view of parents (Stephenson, 1998).

The evidence from the narratives shows that conscience is being suppressed during addiction (Luke, 2011, par 23:9-14). This may be manifested through behaviour contrary to one's conscience guidance due to anger against God (Sam, 2011, par 12:13-16). The addiction processes overpower the conscience's functions leading to unlawful actions (Alex, 2011, par 27:3-4; 12-14). Kingery-McCabe and Campbell (1991) argue that criminal behaviour is directly related to influence from the addictive substance. Antisocial behaviour is viewed as a dominant factor in addiction (Kingery-McCabe and Campbell, 1991).

Some of the interviewees experience conscience during addiction as a burden (Ben, 2011, par 42:1-7; Luke, 2011, par 20:5-10) accompanied with feelings of sadness, discomfort, and guilt (Luke, 2011, par 35:15-19). This experience is underlined by the study of conscience in a health care context as based on the discontinuity between moral convictions and subsequent behaviour (Dahlqvist et al., 2007). According to McCosh (1887) conscience generates an obligation for continuity between moral assessment and subsequent actions. When this is violated character and conscience are impacted negatively.

The predominant description of conscience during addiction in the narratives is the state of being suppressed—silenced (Victoria, 2011, par 19:10-12; John, 2011, par 33:1-3). When the influence of alcohol is diminishing and sobriety takes control, conscience is experienced through cognitive perception and emotional turbulence, related to the addiction failures and immoral behaviours (Sam, 2011, par 60:11-15; Max, 2011, par 8:33-36; Ben, 2011, par 15:1-3). The addictive drive shapes one's decision to go against conscience and suppresses its guidance to avoid dissonance (Luke, 2011, par 22:10-14; Adam, 2011, par 40:8-10). Hence conscience is activated during periods of sobriety but with the intensification of the addictive behaviour it is completely suppressed (Luke, 2011, par 23:9-14). Conscience's guidance may be disregarded or followed according to the individual choice (Dahlqvist et al., 2007). The addictive cognitive processes underlined by attentional bias and inadequate nonautomatic responses to the addiction salient contextual cues shape one's choice against abstinence promoted by conscience's guidance (Albery, Sharma, Niazi, and Moss, 2006).

Conscience in Recovery from Alcohol Addiction

Conscience in the accounts of the most pronounced criminal behaviours appears to be deadened during addiction. There are no emotions of guilt and shame associated with the immoral actions (James, 2011, par 31:1–3; Jack, 2011, par 21:1–4). Results from studying psychopaths demonstrate a clear connection between inactive conscience and devaluing of personal morality, disregard of obligations to others, selfish attitude, and diminished remorseful emotional response to immoral behaviour (Stephenson, 1998). Raskin and Daley (1991) report a strong link between immorality among family members and alcohol dependency. The latter is also seen as the cause of behaviour against oneself (e.g. suicide) and society (e.g. drink driving) (Raskin and Daley, 1991).

Conscience avoidance leads to immorality which is testified by the narrators. The dominance of the addictive behaviour is associated with the rejection of conscience's guidance, disregard of spirituality, and increase of immorality (Paul, 2011, par 8:7–9; Max, 2011, par 9:33–35). The latter is exhibited throughout various accounts with the existence of all seven core vices, namely, anger Jack, 2011, par 10:11–14), envy (Paul, 2011, par 6:4; 6–8), gluttony (Alex, 2011, par 25:11–12), greed (Luke, 2011, par 37:13–15), lust (Luke, 2011, par 29:4–6), pride (Mary, 2011, par 9:3–6), and sloth (John, 2011, par 12:27; 30–33). Miller and Jackson (1995) identify parallels in attitudes to sin and addiction related to surrendering to the temptation in knowledge of the negative consequences instead of surrendering to spiritual fulfilment in relationship with God. Xavier (2010) formulates the development of vices in the context of alcohol addiction as the excessive supply of needs in contradiction with conscience. Steps four and six from the 12-step programme underline the problem of character vices linked to suppression of conscience and their solution through spiritual transformation of character leading to healthy guilt and moral behaviour (Xavier, 2010).

Conscience exposes the conflict between addiction driven behaviour and spiritual, religious, and social responsibilities. This calls for a decision and may lead to deepening the addiction and ignoring the responsibilities (Max, 2011, par 7:3–5; 7–9) or to spiritual transformation (Paul, 2011, par 33:1–4). Kingery-McCabe and Campbell (1991) identify the decay of spirituality as a result of addiction manifesting in hopelessness, loss of faith in God, religious withdrawal, and immorality. Orford (2006) defines the goal of addiction treatment as behaviour modification which is successfully achieved through dramatic spiritual-moral transformation that involves conscientious decision.

5.3. Conscience after transformation: spiritual empowerment, moral enhancement, virtuous character edification, and robust recovery advancement

Transformation is presented by the narratives as a spiritual transcendental experience with momentous and progressive character defined by a dramatic nature leading to internal and external positive changes. The progressive character of transformation is depicted as a characteristic of the complete experience (Alex, 2011, par 33; Ben, 2011, par 40:3-7; Jack, 2011, par 17:1-4; John, 2011, par 23:1-5; 19-21). The transformative moment is described by most of the narrators as a single experience of divine encounter with profound cognitive enlightenment and deep emotional involvement leading to substantial moral behaviour changes. The person experiences divine salvation from a condition of complete physical, psychological, and moral deterioration (Sam, 2011, par 60:3-4; Victoria, 2011, par 12:12-14; Max, 2011, par 27:1-5). The result is a total internal renewal for a new beginning (Victoria, 2011, par 12:12-14; Max, 2011, par 27:1-5). The divine presence is narrated primarily in Christian terms as God, Jesus, and the Holy Spirit (Paul, 2011, par 29:3-9; John, 2011, par 13:1-6; Luke, 2011, par 29:8-9; 13-15). The transformative moment leads to a process of continuous spiritual growth based on a personal relationship with God shaping one's moral standards, stable recovery, and positive attitude to self, life, and others (Adam, 2011, par 65:1-3; James, 2011, par 53:1-6; Max, 2011, par 12:7-12; 17-21).

Miller and Baca (2001) define quantum change as a dramatic personal transformation characterised by cognitive enlightenment, transcendental external influence, and affective transition from guilt to forgiveness bringing a holistic positive reformulation of one's life. The temporal nature of the experience is momentous which may be characterised as a culmination of continuous contemplation on life engagements (Miller and Baca, 2001). The post culmination period may be described as a process of continuous personal growth (Baca and Wilbourne, 2004). The experience establishes an enduring positive change of cognition and behaviour (Baca and Wilbourne, 2004). One of the perspectives of quantum change is the salvific divine intervention inaugurating a personal relationship with God (Miller and Baca, 2001). The latter is viewed by Mahoney and Pargament (2004) as a spiritual conversion defined as internal reorganisation of priorities from self to God leading to complete positive reformulation of one's moral, value, and belief system. The experience's nature may be progressive or a single time-focused event both underlining the significant outcomes of the transformation (Mahoney and Pargament, 2004). Christian conversion is understood to be a complete spiritual and moral reorientation of one's life to God by faith in Christ (Conn, 1983). Protestant theology underlines the significance of Christian conversion for enlightening conscience through the will of God and the work of the Spirit for divinely shaped moral life (Billy and Keating, 2001). Mahoney and Pargament (2004) emphasise the contribution of spiritual transformation to one's recovery from addiction. The essential role of spiritual and moral transformation for one's successful recovery from addiction is also argued by Orford (2006). He identifies the nature of this transformation in light of an AA study as twofold, namely, a dramatic instantaneous event resembling religious conversion and a long progressive personal growth. The process undergoes three key stages from complete deterioration of self depicted as death through total submission to a modelling entity, group, or system to entirely renewed self with dramatically reorganised morality and redefined perspective on life (Orford, 2006).

The impact of spiritual transformation on conscience is emphatic and holistic. Green, Fullilove and Fullilove (1998) study the role of spiritual awakening in recovery from alcohol addiction providing clear evidence for the positive impact of spirituality on one's conscience and recovery. Through the experience of spiritual transformation conscience is reinstituted to its place as a cognitive, emotive, and behavioural guide. The internal cognitive conflict is resolved (Victoria, 2011, par 45:1–8). The feelings of guilt and shame are satisfied through Christ's salvific encounter (John, 2011, par 15:30–32). The behaviour is morally reshaped formulating one's relationship to self and others based on love (Jack, 2011, par 18:30–33). The narratives testify to the influence of spiritual transformation on conscience in defining its characteristics of resurrection, cleanness, freedom, peace, and empowerment.

Conscience's resurrection is accounted for as the deadened conscience, followed by immoral behaviour during the addiction, is brought to a state of full awakening by the spiritual transformation, generating understanding of behaviour, guiding daily abstinence, and providing new moral fulfilment in life (Jack, 2011, par 21:1–2; 20–22; James, 2011, par 31:3–9). Conscience is brought to a state of cleanness through one's encounter with God which is underlined by confession and repentance (Adam, 2011, par 26:21–26) leading to redefining moral decisions and impacting positively on emotional and physical wellbeing (Paul, 2011, par 39:8–11; Max, 2011, par 12:7–8; 9–13). Conscience experiences freedom defined through the capacity to assess and modify behaviour according to spiritually formulated moral standards (John, 2011, par 47:2–4) not only related to the present but also in connection to the past making the necessary restitutions where possible (Jack, 2011, par 43:1–4; 12–14). The revived state of conscience with its exceptional qualities and spiritual nature facilitates the communication of divine perfection into one's existence. Conscience is considered as a reflection of God's will guiding for the application of the latter in one's life (Wall, 1996). Relationship with God through practicing spirituality and having an edifying religious affiliation defines a healthy conscience and develops conscientious responsibility to oneself, others, the world, and the divine being and realm (Xavier, 2010). The spiritual source of defining one's conscientious moral framework is viewed by McCosh (1887) as perfect divine law with absolute qualities resembling the character of the law-giver, God. One's personal experience of the divine presence is understood as a process involving consciousness and leading to significant cognitive, emotive, and behavioural changes due to the perceived divine interaction (Natsoulas, 2005. *The varieties of religious experience*).

Some of the narratives testify for the experience of conscience's peace reached through the reconciliation of beliefs, morals, and behaviour (Victoria, 2011, par 41:4–5; par 47:1–3). The conscience's guidance to cognitive assessment, decision, and consecutive actions involves choice and being synchronised with spiritual convictions facilitates peace in personal and social interactions (Max, 2011, par 37:1–2; 2–4; 5–10; John, 2011, par 31:11–13). Green, Fullilove, and Fullilove (1998) maintain that after the experience of spiritual awakening the person identifies the input from conscience as a gut feeling related to moral choices. Xavier (2010) argues that conscience plays a crucial role in providing inner peace through shaping internal resources towards their external utilisation guided through character strengths and virtues. Conscience provides balance in managing cognition, emotion, and behaviour leading to healthy choices which positively impact on psychological, physical, and social life.

Conscience is empowered through the experience of spiritual transformation. This elevates cognitive and emotive susceptibility to conscience's role and supports accountability for actions, behaviour modifications, and progressive recovery (Victoria, 2011, par 14:8–11; par 51:3–7). The empowered conscience, being resourced through divine spiritual relationship, encourages the decision to abstain (James, 2011, par 18:17–25) and the will to maintain recovery (Sam, 2011, par 70:2–6). Green, Fullilove, and Fullilove (1998) view the spiritually empowered conscience as providing altogether a new way of life which counterbalances the destructive way of life defined by the addiction. The spiritual and moral dimensions of the new lifestyle shape cognition and behaviours and resolve their former addictive nature. According to Xavier (2010) addiction leads to false empowerment while the empowered conscience leads to appropriate use of power and exercise of freedom in life through the employment of wisdom, love, and open-mindedness in realistic outlook and decision-making. The developing of conscience through spirituality is considered to be of significant importance for maintaining abstinence and progressive recovery.

The empowered conscience through spiritual transformation plays a crucial role in recovery from alcohol addiction. It is challenging relapse through rising affective remorse leading to a spiritual reassessment and commitment (Luke, 2011, par 28:7–8; 8–15). The embrace of one's empowered conscience strengthens the practice of spirituality, facilitates personal growth, and underlines substantial recovery (Paul, 2011, par 33:3–6; 7–8; par 35:4–10; Adam, 2011, par 69:35–39). This state of conscience leads to a life of integrity and wholeness which shapes recovery with stability (Victoria, 2011, par 43:1–6). Recovery is further benefited by a redefined purpose in life achieved through conscience's guidance supported by prayer (Mary, 2011, par 65:3–5). The accepted guidance not only reformulates one's approach to the future but also shapes one's attitude to the past leading to reconciliation with those who suffered the damages resulting from one's addiction related immoralities (Max, 2011, par 10:1–3; 4–11; 18–25). Billy and Keating (2001) underline the important place of prayer in reflecting one's relationship with God onto one's morality through conscience. Prayer is considered essential for spirituality and recovery from alcohol addiction (Delaney et al., 2009; Seppala, 2001).

Xavier (2009) states that the most effective outcomes in recovery from addiction are reached by people using their conscience continuously. Personal spiritual commitment underlines the use of conscience and may be considered in the practice of the 12-step programme. Conscience guides the process of managing failure and guilt through forgiveness and reconciliation. It reshapes character rebuilding relationships and promotes social integration defined through open-mindedness and high moral values. It leads to self-assessment of behaviour and more conscientious choices and decisions. Finally, it supports spirituality and psychological wellbeing (Xavier, 2009).

The empowered conscience shapes one's attitude to self and others with the principle of mutual respect, namely, to treat others as one expects to be treated (Mary, 2011, par 53). This moral responsibility is facilitated through the role of one's conscience being resourced by spirituality (Max, 2011, par 20:1; 6–15; 24–26; par 12:14–17; 19–20). Klass (1978) maintains that morality is a holistic dimension of life which forms an attitude of responsibility for behaviour towards oneself and others. This moral responsibility is viewed by Xavier (2010) as the principle of mutual respect or "Golden Rule" which is an essential attribute of conscience. The content of the rule for reciprocal attitude of love, justice, and fairness to others is operational for one's conscience in combination with the cognitive assessment of right and wrong. When it relates to others' needs Xavier (2010) advises that the rule is not to be interpreted literally, due to different people's tastes and priorities, but in its spirit of mutual respect. The rule is upheld by various religions and may be considered as spiritually defined (Xavier, 2010).

Conscience plays important part in taking decisions for future plans. The latter are shaped through altruistic and spiritual intentions (Max, 2011, par 41:4–11). The underlying result from the guidance of the spirituality empowered conscience is the embodiment of one's desire to help those addicted to alcohol. The personal knowledge and wisdom gained through spiritual and conscientious transformation are shaping one's attitude to guide others towards the same experience and outcome (Luke, 2011, par 69:12–14; 21–22; 25). The renewed conscience also enlightens the understanding of addiction and provides guidance for healthy relationships (Paul, 2011, par 37:1–2; 7–9). Xavier (2010) underlines the importance of conscience in managing one's approach to past, present, and future. Affective impact of conscience through guilt and shame encourages decisions for positive present changes in regards to past failures. The latter are also conscientiously balanced through forgiveness and reconciliation. The past experiences are also used by one's conscience to derive wisdom for present actions. Conscience provides a hopeful outlook for the future through the assessment of present realities leading to decisions with spiritual and psychological value (Xavier, 2010).

The impact of spiritual transformation on conscience encompasses morality and character. The renewed conscience shapes moral cognition, affect, and behaviour leading to the development of virtuous character. The new moral stand and edified character support abstinence and progressive recovery. The latter is identified as a morally sound choice for appropriate behaviour through the renewed conscience and in light of the immorality practiced during the time of addiction (Sam, 2011, par 38:18–23). The new moral stand defined through spirituality is conscientiously undertaken to shape everyday life leading to an attitude of love towards God, oneself, family, and others. The transformative power is kept on-going in life through practicing spiritual disciplines and being attentive to the voice of conscience (Adam, 2011, par 49:3–4; 6–8; 15–16; 16–17).

The acceptance and application of the guidance from one's spiritually empowered conscience contributes significantly to the elevation of character. The nature of the latter has undergone a dramatic moral edification from being defined by vice during the addiction to being characterised by strengths and virtues after the spiritual transformation. Conscience plays a crucial role in this process. The narratives testify to the development of one's virtuous character by giving accounts for various strengths and virtues. The following are some of the most explicit examples identified in the stories: integrity (Adam, 2011, par 27:11–13; John, 2011, par 15:4–6), humanity (Sam, 2011, par 76:2–3; Mary, 2011, par 55:8–9; 11–12; Max, 2011, par 11:24–25), leadership (John, 2011, par 22:12–15; 16–17; 22; 23–24; 25–26), humility and modesty (Adam, 2011, par 28:1–2; 6–8; 11–12), forgiveness and mercy (Ben, 2011, par 13:10–12), transcendence (present in all narratives; some of the most obvious references are found in Mary, 2011, par 45:10–11; see also pars 42 and 44 and Adam, 2011, par 65:9–11), spirituality (present in all narratives; example is given with Paul, 2011, par 31:2–4), gratitude (Adam, 2011, par 49:43–44; James, 2011, par 22:8–13), wisdom and knowledge (Sam, 2011, par 77:22–33), and open-mindedness (Adam, 2011, par 27:13–16; 19–23; 26–28).

Schimmel (1997) argues that vices are part of human nature and their remedy through development of virtuous character should not be only in the focus of morality and religion but also of psychology. The solution for all vices is found in the formation of virtues through spiritual edification (Schimmel, 1997; DeYoung, 2009). Billy and Keating (2001) maintain that divinely resourced conscience through spiritual devotion leads to an ethical and virtuous life. Canda (2009) identifies relational dependency between religious narratives, spiritual edification, moral formation, virtuous character, and progressive wellbeing. The latter is clearly linked with the development of character strengths and virtues (Peterson and Seligman, 2004). These are crucial for overcoming times of crisis and physical illness (Park, 2009).

The present chapter discusses the results from NA in light of the academic research supporting the theories presented in the introduction and requires consideration of any possible limitations. Hence, I would like to consider the issue of my interpretive bias in the process of interrelation between results and theories. The latter may have influenced a selective treatment of the material underlining its aspects which provide close relationship to the theories supporting the main argument. In addition, my own understanding of the research topics may have contributed to my interpretive bias. The solution is found in the holistic nature of NA which balances the influences of my bias. The structure of the narratives underlines the key point of spiritual transformation which divides the stories in two contrasting main parts in relation to the place and role of conscience in one's life. This is also defined through the thrust of the plots from problem to solution and the divine nature of the main characters. The demoralised conscience during addiction experiences dramatic positive changes through the spiritual transformation leading to morally stable life of abstinence and progressive recovery.

The three main dimensions considered in the discussion reveal the continuity between the results and the scholarly findings. First, conscience's nature and functioning underline the role of its three elements in the stories. The conative conscience is defined by one's spirituality and plays significant role in relation to the other two elements. Cognitively conscience formulates one's moral choices the impairment of which in addiction due to automaticity and attentional bias requires spiritual resolution. The emotive conscience defines affective morality and requires spiritual input for healthy actualisation in life.

Second, the state of conscience during addiction shows clear degradation of all its elements to the point of complete suppression of conscience's functionality. The latter results in criminal activity without affective consequences. The suppressed conscience leads to development of immorality, vice, and entrenched addiction. The short outbursts of conscience's functionality during times of sobriety challenge one's immorality and addiction. These underline the upcoming spiritual transformation in some cases.

Third, the experience of spiritual transformation leads to dramatic positive changes on conscience. The transformation's transcendent nature is defined through a personal divine encounter followed by a relationship with God. The time frame is momentous and progressive. The impact on one's conscience is characterised by resurrection, freedom, cleanness, peace, and empowerment. These formulate relationships with an attitude of mutual respect, define a new altruistic purpose in life, facilitate a solid moral stand, and develop virtuous character. The regenerated conscience shapes continuous abstinence and stable progressive recovery from alcohol addiction.

6.

Conclusion

THE PRESENT RESEARCH ATTEMPTS to provide methodological unity and pragmatic actualisation of the diverse academic perspective on alcohol addiction and recovery through the concept of spiritually empowered conscience. On the one hand, the scientific conceptualisation of addiction underlines a multiplicity of theories which in some cases stay in tension, i.e. the moral versus disease models. On the other hand, the subjects of conscience, morality, and spirituality appear to be under-researched in the context of addiction in general and alcohol treatment in particular. Hence, the present study engages in developing the understanding of conscience in the context of alcohol addiction and spiritual transformation endeavouring to advance academic research, provide unity among its theories, and formulate applications for successful recovery.

The present methodological framework focusing on personal narrative is attested as appropriate for the study of conscience, spirituality, and morality in the context of recovery from alcohol addiction through previous academic research. NA is used to examine the personal stories and reveal the changes to one's conscience during addiction and spiritual transformation and its impact on one's recovery. The method provides a detailed analysis of the alterations to conscience within a holistic treatment of the narratives considering their structure, plot, characters, and outcomes. The twelve narrative accounts are collected through the means of semi-structured interview from a self-selected group of participants homogeneous in relation to their experiences in addiction, spirituality, morality, and recovery and diverse in relation to their demographic characteristics. The main purpose of the study is to provide an answer to the question: Does the relationship between spirituality and conscience lead to positive impact on recovery from alcohol addiction?

Conclusion

The analysis of the results in light of the relevant scholarly theories substantiates a threefold answer. First, conscience's nature and functioning are underlined by spirituality through the communication between its conative, cognitive, and emotive elements for actualisation and application of a moral system in life. Second, all conscience's elements and their functions are compromised during the active phase of addiction establishing conscience's inadequacy and leading to immorality, vice, and intensification of the addictive behaviour. Third, conscience with all its elements and functions experiences complete rejuvenation through spiritual transformation leading to moral actualisation, positive life reformulation, virtuous character edification, and robust recovery from alcohol addiction.

The future of the research is envisaged in a direction to expand the trial group and explore the possibilities of formulating a new model of treatment. The present group of participants is defined by the experience of alcohol addiction. The most natural expansion of the group is to involve people who have experienced drug addictions and in this way to address generally the field of substance misuse. Hence, by using the same methodology and means for obtaining data 12 stories will be collected from interviewees with history of drug addiction, who have achieved abstinence through the experience of moral, spiritual, and/or religious transformation, and maintain successfully their spirituality and recovery. Some of the present stories involve the use of illegal substances together with the alcohol which suggests continuity with the outcomes from the analysis of the drug addiction narratives. The results from both studies will establish the grounds for the formulation of a new theoretical model of treatment, conscience therapy. The latter will provide therapeutic guidance for integrating spirituality in the process of conscientious transformation and development of robust progressive recovery from substance misuse. The relevance of the new treatment model may be underlined by its holistic nature dealing with cognition, affect, behaviour, character, spirituality, and morality in the context of recovery and providing references to acknowledged contemporary treatments such as 12-step facilitation, cognitive behaviour therapy, and motivational interviewing. The continuation of the present study and its development into conscience therapy is supported by my acceptance on the Doctorate in Professional Studies programme at Middlesex University in London, United Kingdom.

References

Adam (2011). Personal interview (Conscience in recovery from alcohol addiction), 04 November.
Albery, I. P., Sharma, D., Niazi, A., and Moss, A. C. (2006). Theoretical perspectives and approaches. In M. R. Munafo and I. P. Albery (Eds.), *Cognition and addiction* (pp. 1–29). Oxford: Oxford University Press.
Alex (2011). Personal interview (Conscience in recovery from alcohol addiction), 09 November.
Baca, J. C. and Wilbourne, P. (2004). Quantum change: Ten years later. *Journal of Clinical Psychology* 60, 531–541.
Bargh, J. A. (1997). The automaticity of everyday life. In R. S. Wyer (Ed.), *Advances in social cognition* (Vol. X, pp. 1–61). New Jersey: Lawrence Erlbaum.
Ben (2011). Personal interview (Conscience in recovery from alcohol addiction), 15 November.
Billy, D. J. and Keating, J. F. (2001). *Conscience and prayer: The spirit of Catholic moral theology*. Collegeville: The Liturgical Press.
Canda, E. R. (2009). Spiritual well-being. In S. J. Lopez (Ed.), *The encyclopedia of positive psychology* (pp. 924–927). Oxford: Blackwell Publishing.
Carter, T. M. (1998). The effects of spiritual practices on recovery from substance abuse. *Journal of Psychiatric and Mental Health Nursing* 5, 409–413.
Chau, L. L., Johnson, R. C., Bowers, J. K., Darvill, T. J., and Danko, G. P. (1990). Intrinsic and extrinsic religiosity as related to conscience, adjustment, and altruism. *Personal and Individual Differences* 11, 397–400.
Conn, W. E. (1983). Conversion. In G. S. Wakefield (Ed.), *The Westminster dictionary of Christian spirituality* (pp. 96–97). Philadelphia: The Westminster Press.
Cook, D. E. (2007). Always let your conscience be your guide. *The American Journal of Bioethics* 7, 16–18.
Dahlqvist, V., Eriksson, S. Glasberg, A-L., Lindahl, E., Lutzen, K., Strandberg, G., Soderberg, A., Sørlie, V., and Norberg, A. (2007). Development of the perceptions of conscience questionnaire. *Nursing Ethics* 14, 181–193.
Delaney, H. D., Forcehimes, A. A., Campbell, W. P., and Smith, B. W. (2009). Integrating spirituality into alcohol treatment. *Journal of Clinical Psychology*: In session 65, 185–198.
DeYoung, R. K. (2009). *Glittering vices: A new look at the seven deadly sins and their remedies*. Baker Publishing Group: Brazos Press.
Dragon Naturally Speaking (Version 11) [Computer software]. Burlington, MA: Nuance Communications.
Edwards, L. M. (2009). Hope. In S. J. Lopez (Ed.), *The encyclopedia of positive psychology* (pp. 487–491). Oxford: Blackwell Publishing.

References

Emmons, R. (2009). Gratitude. In S. J. Lopez (Ed.), *The encyclopedia of positive psychology* (pp. 442–447). Oxford: Blackwell Publishing.

Emmons, R. A. (2003). *The psychology of ultimate concerns: Motivation and spirituality in personality*. London: Guilford Press.

Express Scribe Pro (Version 5.43) [Computer software]. Greenwood Village, CO: NCH Software.

Fairlie, H. (1979). *The seven deadly sins today*. Notre Dame: University of Notre Dame Press.

Forcehimes, A. A. (2004). De Profundis: Spiritual transformations in Alcoholics Anonymous. *Journal of Clinical Psychology* 60, 503–517.

Fowers, B. J. (2009). Virtues. In S. J. Lopez (Ed.), *The encyclopedia of positive psychology* (pp. 1016–1022). Oxford: Blackwell Publishing.

Glasberg, A. L. Eriksson, S., Dahlqvist, V., Lindahl, E., Strandberg, G., Soderberg, A., Sørlie, V., and Norberg, A. (2006). Development and initial validation of the stress of conscience questionnaire. *Nursing Ethics* 13, 633–648.

Green, L. L., Fullilove, M. T., and Fullilove, R. E. (1998). Stories of spiritual awakening: The nature of spirituality in recovery. *Journal of Substance Abuse Treatment* 15, 325–331.

Hobbs, D. (2005). Gluttony: 'Binge drinking' and the binge economy. In I. Stewart and R. Vaitilingam (Eds.), *Seven deadly sins: A new look at society through an old lens* (pp. 24–27). Swindon: Economic and Social Research Council (ESRC). Retrieved from http://www.esrc.ac.uk/_images/seven_deadly_sins_tcm8-13545.pdf

Hodge, D. R. (2011). Alcohol treatment and cognitive-behavioral therapy: Enhancing effectiveness by incorporating spirituality and religion. *Social Work* 56, 21–31.

Howitt, D. (2010). *Introduction to qualitative methods in psychology*. Harlow: Pearson Education Limited.

Jack (2011). Personal interview (Conscience in recovery from alcohol addiction), 20 November.

Jaffe, J. H. and Meyer, R. E. (2001). Disease concept of alcoholism and drug abuse. In Rosalyn Carson-De Witt (Ed.), *Encyclopedia of drugs, alcohol, and addictive behavior* (2nd ed., Vol. 1, pp. 398–405). New York: Macmillan Reference USA.

James (2011). Personal interview (Conscience in recovery from alcohol addiction), 15 November.

John (2011). Personal interview (Conscience in recovery from alcohol addiction), 15 November.

Johnson, R. C., Danko, G. P., Huang, Y-H., Park, J. Y., Johnson, S. B., and Nagoshi, C. T. (1987). Guilt, shame, and adjustment in three cultures. *Personality and Individual Differences* 8, 357–364.

Kingery-McCabe, L. G. and Campbell, F. A. (1991). Effects of addiction on the addict. In D. C. Daley and M. S. Raskin (Eds.), *Treating the chemically dependent and their families* (pp. 57–78). London: SAGE Publications Ltd.

Klass, E. (1978). Psychological effects of immoral actions: the experimental evidence. *Psychological Bulletin* 85, 756–771.

Koops, W., Brugman, D., and Ferguson, T. J. (2010). The development of conscience: Concepts and theoretical and empirical approaches. An introduction. In A. F. Sanders, W. Koops, D. Brugman, and T. J. Ferguson (Eds.), *The development and structure of conscience* (pp. 1–22). New York: Psychology Press.

References

Kurtz, E. (2001). Afterword. In W. R. Miller and J. C. Baca. *Quantum change: When Epiphanies and sudden insights transform ordinary lives* (pp. 193–195). London: The Guilford Press.

Ladd, R. E. (2007). Some reflections on conscience. *The American Journal of Bioethics* 7, 32.

Langdridge, D. (2004). *Introduction to research methods and data analysis in psychology*. Harlow: Pearson Education Limited.

Langston, D. C. (2001). *Conscience and other virtues: From Bonaventure to Macintyre*. University Park, Pennsylvania: The Pennsylvania State University Press.

Lewins, A. and Silver, C. (2009). Choosing a CAQDAS package. *CAQDAS Network Project and Qualitative Innovations in CAQDAS Project (QUIC)*. Retrieved from http://www.surrey.ac.uk/sociology/research/researchcentres/caqdas/files/2009ChoosingaCAQDASPackage.pdf

Luke (2011). Personal interview (Conscience in recovery from alcohol addiction), 11 November.

Maddux, J. E. (2009). Self-regulation. In S. J. Lopez (Ed.), *The encyclopedia of positive psychology* (pp. 889–893). Oxford: Blackwell Publishing.

Mahoney, A. and Pargament, K. I. (2004). Sacred changes: Spiritual conversion and transformation. *Journal of Clinical Psychology* 60, 481–492.

Martin, R. A. (2009). Humor. In S. J. Lopez (Ed.), *The encyclopedia of positive psychology* (pp. 503–508). Oxford: Blackwell Publishing.

Martin, W. (2006). *Conscience and consciousness: Rousseau's contribution to the Stoic theory of Oikeiosis*. Paper presented at the Research Seminar on Mind and Language, Consciousness and Self-Consciousness in Modern Philosophy, New York University, New York, NY. Retrieved from http://philosophy.fas.nyu.edu/docs/IO/2575/martin.pdf

Mary (2011). Personal interview (Conscience in recovery from alcohol addiction), 10 November.

Maton, K. I. (2004). Community psychology. In C. Spielberger (Ed.), *Encyclopedia of applied psychology* (Vol. 1, pp. 421–428). New York: Elsevier Academic Press.

Max (2011). Personal interview (Conscience in recovery from alcohol addiction), 15 November.

MAXQDAplus (Version 10) [Computer software]. Berlin: VERBI GmbH.

McCosh, J. (1887). *Psychology. The motive powers: Emotions, conscience, will*. New York: Charles Scribner's Sons.

Microsoft Word (Version 2010) [Computer software]. Reading: Microsoft.

Miller, W. R. and Baca, J. C. (2001). *Quantum change: When epiphanies and sudden insights transform ordinary lives*. London: The Guilford Press.

Miller, W. R. and Jackson, K. A. (1995). *Practical psychology for pastors* (2nd ed.). New Jersey: Prentice-Hall.

Miller, W. R. and Thoresen, C. E. (1999). Spirituality and health. In W. R. Miller (Ed.), *Integrating spirituality into treatment* (pp. 3–18). Washington, DC: American Psychological Association.

Moberg, D. O. (2010). Spirituality research: Measuring the immeasurable? *Journal of the American Scientific Affiliation* 62, 99–114.

Natsoulas, T. (2005). Freud's phenomenology of the emotions. In R. D. Ellis and N. Newton (Eds.), *Consciousness and emotion: Agency, conscious choice, and selective perception* (pp. 217–242). Amsterdam: John Benjamin's Publishing Company.

References

Natsoulas, T. (2005). The varieties of religious experience considered from the perspective of James's account of the stream of consciousness. In R. D. Ellis and N. Newton (Eds.), *Consciousness and emotion: Agency, conscious choice, and selective perception* (pp. 303–326). Amsterdam: John Benjamin's Publishing Company.

The New International Version (1984). International Bible Society. Zondervan Publishing House. Bible Works for Windows, version 7.

Orford, J. (2001). Conceptualising addiction: Addiction as excessive appetite. *Addiction* 96, 15–31.

Orford, J. (2006). *Excessive appetites: A psychological view of addictions* (2nd ed. Reprint of original work published 2001). Chichester: Wiley.

Pargament, K. I. (2009). Spirituality. In S. J. Lopez (Ed.). *The encyclopedia of positive psychology* (pp. 928–932). Oxford: Blackwell Publishing.

Pargament, K. I. and Mahoney, A. (2002). Spirituality: Discovering and conserving. In C. R. Snyder and S. J. Lopez (Eds.), *Handbook of positive psychology* (pp. 646–662). Oxford: Oxford University Press.

Park, N. (2009). Character strengths (VIA). In S. J. Lopez (Ed.), *The encyclopedia of positive psychology* (pp. 135–141). Oxford: Blackwell Publishing.

Patock-Peckham, J. A., Hutchinson, G. T., Cheong, J., and Nagoshi, C. T. (1998). Effect of religion and religiosity on alcohol use in a college student sample. *Drug and Alcohol Dependence* 49, 81–88.

Paul (2011). Personal interview (Conscience in recovery from alcohol addiction), 15 November.

Peterson, C. and Seligman, M. E. P. (2004). *Character strengths and virtues: A handbook and classification*. Oxford: Oxford University Press.

Piderman, K. M., Schneekloth, T. D., Pankratz, V. S., Maloney, S. D., and Altchuler, S. I. (2007). Spirituality in alcoholics during treatment. *The American Journal on Addictions* 16, 232–237.

Piedmont, R. L. (2004). Spiritual transcendence as a predictor of psychosocial outcome from an outpatient substance abuse program. *Psychology of Addictive Behaviors* 18, 213–222.

Pury, C. L. S. and Woodard, C. (2009). Courage. In S. J. Lopez (Ed.), *The encyclopedia of positive psychology* (pp. 247–254). Oxford: Blackwell Publishing.

Raskin, M. S. and Daley, D. C. (1991). Introduction and overview of addiction. In D. C. Daley and M. S. Raskin (Eds.), *Treating the chemically dependent and their families* (pp. 1–21). London: SAGE Publications Ltd.

Saillard, E. K. (2011). Systematic versus interpretive analysis with two CAQDAS packages: NVivo and MAXQDA. *Forum: Qualitative Social Research 12*. Retrieved from http://www.qualitative-research.net/index.php/fqs/article/view/1518/3133

Sam (2011). Personal interview (Conscience in recovery from alcohol addiction), 16 November.

Sanderson, C. and Linehan, M. M. (1999). Acceptance and forgiveness. In W. R. Miller (Ed.), *Integrating spirituality into treatment: Resources for practitioners* (6th ed., pp. 199–216). Washington: American Psychological Association.

Schimmel, S. (1997). *The seven deadly sins: Jewish, Christian, and classical reflections on human psychology*. Oxford: Oxford University Press.

Schönfelder, W. (2011). CAQDAS and qualitative syllogism logic—NVivo 8 and MAXQDA 10 Compared. *Forum: Qualitative Social Research 12*. Retrieved from http://www.qualitative-research.net/index.php/fqs/article/view/1514/3134

References

Seppala, M. D. (2001). *The clinician's guide to the 12-step principles*. London: McGraw-Hill.

Sharma, D., Albery, I. P., and Cook, C. (2001). Selective attentional bias to alcohol related stimuli in problem drinkers and non-problem drinkers. *Addiction* 96, 285–295.

Stephenson, G. M. (1998). *The development of conscience*. London: Routledge.

Sundararajan, L. (2009). Awe. In S. J. Lopez (Ed.), *The encyclopedia of positive psychology* (pp. 86–92). Oxford: Blackwell Publishing.

Tangney, J. P. (2009). Humility. In S. J. Lopez (Ed.), *The encyclopedia of positive psychology* (pp. 496–502). Oxford: Blackwell Publishing.

The top 10 changes in MAXQDA 10. (2010). *Installations- und Aktivierungsanleitung*. Seite 5 von 5.

Underwood, L. G. (2006). Ordinary spiritual experience: Qualitative research, interpretive guidelines, and population distribution for the Daily Spiritual Experience Scale. *Archive for the Psychology of Religion/ Archiv für Religionspsychologie* 28, 181–218.

VERBI GmbH. (2011). *MAXQDA: The art of text analysis* (Version 10). Berlin: VERBI software. Consult. Sozialforschung. GmbH. Retrieved from http://www.maxqda.com

Victoria (2011). Personal interview (Conscience in recovery from alcohol addiction), 21 November.

Wall, R. W. (1996). Conscience. In D. N. Freedman (Ed.), *The Anchor Bible dictionary* (Vol. 1, pp. 1128–1130). New York: Doubleday.

Waltke, B. (1988). Evangelical spirituality: A biblical scholar's perspective. *Journal of the Evangelical Theological Society* 31, 9–24.

Watts, F., Dutton, K., and Gulliford, L. (2006). Human spiritual qualities: Integrating psychology and religion. *Mental Health, Religion & Culture* 9, 277–289.

West, R. (2001). Theories of addiction. *Addiction* 96, 3–13.

Wiersbe, W. W. (1989). *The Bible exposition commentary: An exposition of the New Testament comprising the entire 'BE' series*. Wheaton, Ill.: Victor Books, 1996, c1989. (Libronix Digital Library System 3.0c, 2000–6, Libronix Corporation).

Witvliet, C. O. (2009). Forgiveness. In S. J. Lopez (Ed.), *The encyclopedia of positive psychology* (pp. 403–410). Oxford: Blackwell Publishing.

World Health Organization (1993). *The ICD-10 classification of mental and behavioural disorders: Diagnostic criteria for research*. Geneva: World Health Organization.

Xavier, N. S. (2010). *Fulfillment using real conscience: Practical guide for psychological and spiritual wellness*. Bloomington: Author House.

Zhekov, Y. K. (2011). *Conscience therapy*. [website]. Retrieved from http://www.consciencetherapy.com

Appendices

Appendices

Interviewees' Personal Data

(Note: Some of the information presented in the table has been obtained from the interviewees and it has been sensibly modified and organised for preserving their confidentiality)

Fictional name	Interview date	Interview time (min)	Age group	Gender	Education	Occupation	Ethnic origin
Adam	04/11/11	100:23	35–40	M	Counselling diploma	The following list represents randomly the interviewees' occupations to avoid association with their fictional names: Former Carpenter, Gardener, Former Council Worker, Employee in the Housing Industry, Worker in a Residential Rehabilitation Centre, Substance Misuse Counsellor, Managerial Position in a Homeless Hostel, Support Worker, Former Nurse, Former Hotel Manager, Former Team Manager in the Substance Misuse Field, Worker in the Furniture Industry.	The following representation of the ethnic origin of the interviewees intends to avoid association with their fictional names: seven white British, two black Africans, and three white Europeans.
Alex	9/11/11	56:05	40–45	M	College		
Ben	15/11/11	73:00	50–55	M	College		
Jack	20/11/11	76:05	35–40	M	NVQ-2		
James	15/11/11	51:05	45–50	M	College courses		
John	15/11/11	47:22	40–45	M	O level		
Luke	11/11/11	77:46	55–60	M	BA (Hons) MCIH		
Mary	10/11/11	47:35	45–50	F	RGN		
Max	15/11/11	51:20	45–50	M	PGCE		
Paul	15/11/11	28:26	35–40	M	Unfinished Undergraduate Degree		
Sam	16/11/11	97:08	40–45	M	City and Guilds		
Victoria	21/11/11	58:45	35–40	F	Sociology degree (BSc)		

Interview Schedule

Narrative Analysis Interview Protocol
Questions and Sub-questions for an Episodic Interview

The following is a short introductory guidance.

1. Structure your life story in chapters. Think about their names, summaries, and progressive links.

    a) Without interfering with the genuine character of the story can you identify the role of the following topics in your life narrative: conscience; alcohol addiction; morality; spirituality; religiousness; moral reformation; spiritual transformation; religious conversion and/or affiliation; the relationship between morality, spirituality, religiousness, and conscience, and recovery from alcohol addiction.

    b) How will you summarise each of these chapters?

    c) What progressive links will you make between these chapters?

The following questions and sub-questions will be asked for further clarification of the research topics as part of the individual story after the narrative has been developed.

2. How do you perceive your conscience?

    a) What is conscience?

    b) How did it develop?

    c) How does it function?

3. How did you develop alcohol addiction?

    a) What is alcohol addiction?

    b) When did you realise that you have been addicted to alcohol?

    c) How did you try to manage your alcohol addiction?

4. What were your moral views before your moral, spiritual, and/or religious transformation?

    a) What is morality?

    b) How did you deal with moral dilemmas?

    c) How much did morality matter for you?

Appendices

5. Did you practice spirituality before your moral, spiritual, and/or religious transformation?

    a) What is spirituality?

    b) How did you practice spirituality?

    c) How much did spirituality matter for you?

6. Did you practice religion before your moral, spiritual, and/or religious transformation?

    a) What is religiousness?

    b) How did you practice religion?

    c) Did you have religious affiliation?

    d) How much did religion matter for you?

7. Did you experience moral, spiritual, and/or religious transformation?

    a) How did you experience this transformation?

    b) When did you experience this transformation?

    c) May you identify anyone who played any influential role in the process?

    d) How much has this transformation changed your life?

8. What was the impact of your transformation on your life?

    a) Compare your morality, spirituality, and religiousness before and after the transformation.

    b) How did the transformation impact your understanding of morality, spirituality, and religion, and their role in your life?

    c) How much did morality, spirituality, and religion matter for you after your transformation?

9. What was the impact of your moral, spiritual, and/or religious transformation on your conscience?

    a) Compare your conscience before and after the transformation.

    b) How did the transformation impact your conscientious behaviour?

    c) How much did the voice of your conscience matter for you after your transformation?

Appendices

10. What was the impact of your transformed conscience on your recovery from alcohol addiction?

    a) Compare your recovery before and after the transformation.

    b) How did your transformed conscience impact your recovery from alcohol addiction?

    c) What is the role of your transformed conscience in the maintenance of your abstinence?

    d) May you identify anyone who played any influential role in the process?

11. May you share your future plans related to your recovery?

    a) What is the role of morality, spirituality, and/or religion in them?

    b) What is the role of your transformed conscience in them?

    c) Do you plan to share your experience with others who need help in recovery from alcohol addiction?

12. May you formulate the main theme of your life story?

    a) What is the place of alcohol addiction in your story?

    b) What is the place of conscience in your story?

    c) What is the place of morality, spirituality, and/or religiousness in your story?

    d) What is the place of your moral, spiritual, and/or religious transformation in your story?

Appendices

A Short Introductory Guidance for the Interviewee—Interviewee's Copy

1. Structure your life story in chapters.

2. Think about:
   - Chapters' names;
   - Chapters' summaries;
   - Chapters' progressive links.

3. Without interfering with the genuine character of the story can you identify the role of the following topics in your life narrative:
   - Conscience;
   - Alcohol addiction;
   - Morality;
   - Spirituality;
   - Religiousness;
   - Moral reformation;
   - Spiritual transformation;
   - Religious conversion and/or affiliation;
   - The relationship between morality, spirituality, religiousness, and conscience, and recovery from alcohol addiction.

4. How will you summarise each of these chapters?

5. What progressive links will you make between these chapters?

Appendices

Debriefing Information

Organisations Providing Counselling and Other Type of Support

(Note: The local contact details of the organisations below have been substituted with their national ones to preserve the confidentiality of the interviewees in a better way)

1. **Research project:** The researcher offers an email support through the website dedicated to the project; website address: http://www.consciencetherapy.com

2. **Turning Point:** A national health care provider offering counselling and other type of support in the area of substance misuse. Head Office: Standon House, 21 Mansell Street, London E1 8AA; phone number: 020 7481 7600; email address: info@turning-point.co.uk; website address: http://www.turning-point.co.uk

3. **Community Drug and Alcohol Team (CDAT):** A community based team of professionals who provide variety of support and treatment services, including counselling, in the area of substance misuse. Local contact information may be obtained through the following local authorities: Mental Health Trust (MHT), Council, General Practitioner (GP) Practice, and Citizens Advice Bureau (CAB).

    - Local MHT contact information is accessible via the National Health Service website; website address: http://www.nhs.uk/ServiceDirectories/Pages/MentalHealthTrustListing.aspx;
    - Local Councils contact information is accessible via GOV.UK (the UK government's information service) website; website address: https://www.gov.uk/find-your-local-council;
    - Local GP Practices contact information is accessible via NHS website; website address: http://www.nhs.uk/servicedirectories/Pages/ServiceSearch.aspx?ServiceType=GP;
    - Local CAB contact information is accessible via Citizen's Advice website; website address: http://www.citizensadvice.org.uk/index/getadvice.

Appendices

4. **Community Mental Health Team (CMHT):** A community based team of professionals who provide variety of support and treatment services, including counselling, in the area of mental health. More information about the CMHT is available via the Royal College of Psychiatrists website; website address: http://www.rcpsych.ac.uk/mentalhealthinfo/communityteam.aspx. Local contact information may be obtained through the following local authorities: Mental Health Trust (MHT), Council, General Practitioner (GP) Practice, and Citizens Advice Bureau (CAB).

    - Local MHT contact information is accessible via the National Health Service website; website address: http://www.nhs.uk/ServiceDirectories/Pages/MentalHealthTrustListing.aspx;
    - Local Councils contact information is accessible via GOV.UK (the UK government's information service) website; website address: https://www.gov.uk/find-your-local-council;
    - Local GP Practices contact information is accessible via NHS website; website address: http://www.nhs.uk/servicedirectories/Pages/ServiceSearch.aspx?ServiceType=GP;
    - Local CAB contact information is accessible via Citizen's Advice website; website address: http://www.citizensadvice.org.uk/index/getadvice

5. **Mind:** An organisation which works in the field of mental health providing variety of support, including counselling, through its local branches. Head Office: 15-19 Broadway, Stratford, London E15 4BQ; phone number: 020 8519 2122; email address: contact@mind.org.uk; website address: http://www.mind.org.uk

6. **Samaritans:** An organisation which provides 24 hour help line for emotional support in the context of complete confidentiality. Contact may be established via phone: 0845 790 9090, email: jo@samaritans.org, letter: Chris, PO Box 9090, Stirling FK8 2SA. One to one session is possible in the local Samaritans branch. Head Office: The Upper Mill, Kingston Road, Ewell, Surrey KT17 2AF; phone number: 020 8394 8300; email address: admin@samaritans.org; website address: http://www.samaritans.org

7. **Women's Centres:** Local centres which provide support exclusively for women offering variety of services among which counselling with a female professional for adequate number of sessions. Local

Appendices

contact information is accessible in Berman, K. (2004). *National Directory of Women's Centres*. Keighley: Keighley Women's Centre. Retrieved from http://www.equal-works.com/resources/content-files/430.pdf

8. **Alcoholics Anonymous (AA):** AA is a mixed gender fellowship which operates on the basis of 12-step programme and provides an environment for sharing and support in a group setting. General Service Office: Alcoholics Anonymous, PO Box 1, 10 Toft Green, York YO1 7NJ; phone number: 01904 644026; email address: gso@alcoholics-anonymous.org.uk. Helpline phone number: 0854 769 7555; email address: help@alcoholics-anonymous.org.uk; website address: http://www.alcoholics-anonymous.org.uk. Locations of local group meetings are accessible via the AA website.

Appendices

Table of Substitution Phrases and their Acronyms Used Throughout the Interview Transcripts due to Confidentiality

Substitution phrase	Acronym	Interview transcript	Number of occurrences
This South Coast English City	TSCEC	John	1
Residential Rehabilitation Centre	RRC	Ben	12
		Jack	3
		James	11
		John	10
		Max	4
		Paul	1
This South East English City	TSEEC	Ben	2
		Mary	1
		Sam	1
This South West English City	TSWEC	Paul	1
Second Stage of the Residential Rehabilitation Programme	SSRRP	John	7
		Ben	1
		James	1
		Max	1
This North East English City	TNEEC	John	6
Homeless Charity	HC	Alex	7
		Sam	3
The Local Church	LC	Alex	4
		Sam	1
Community Centre for Homeless	CCH	Alex	1
Short Term Hostel for Homeless	STHH	Alex	3
		Sam	3
Small Town	ST	Alex	2

Other Hostel for Homeless	OHH	Alex	4
Hostel for Homeless	HH	Alex	1
		Sam	1
This South Coast English Town	TSCET	Ben	2
West Africa	WA	Luke	1
My Home Country	MHC	Jack	6
		Luke	6
		Victoria	5
One Religious Group	ORG	Jack	9
Another Religious Group	ARG	Jack	7
Particular Political Party	PPP	Jack	2
My Home Town	MHT	James	1
This North West English Town	TNWET	James	4
Another North West English Town	ANWET	James	5
This North West English River	TNWER	James	3
This Town on the English Coast	TTEC	James	1
This North West English City	TNWEC	James	1
This South Yorkshire Town	TSYT	James	1
This West African Country	TWAC	Luke	18
My Own Nationals	MON	Luke	3
Employee in the Housing Industry	EIHI	Luke	6
European Country	EC	Mary	1
This English County	TEC	Mary	3
This Detox Facility	TDF	Mary	2
This Large English Village	TLEV	Mary	2

Appendices

This General Hospital	TGH	Mary	1
Mental Health Hospital Unit	MHHU	Mary	6
Accommodation for Homeless	AH	Sam	4
This South East English Town	TSEET	Sam	2
Another Town	AT	Sam	3
Independent Accommodation With Support	IAWS	Sam	3
Community Rehabilitation Centre	CRC	Sam	5

Appendices

Complete Interview Transcripts

Adam (2011). Personal interview (Conscience in recovery from alcohol addiction), 04 November.

Interviewer (I): So in regards to the story the following instructions are: Structure your life story in chapters. Think about their names, summaries, and progressive links. Without interfering with the genuine character of the story can you identify the role of the following topics in your life narrative: conscience; alcohol addiction; morality; spirituality; religiousness; moral reformation; spiritual transformation; religious conversion and/or affiliation; the relationship between morality, spirituality, religiousness, and conscience, and recovery from alcohol addiction. How will you summarise each of these chapters? What progressive links will you make between these chapters? So these instructions are there to remind you. And, yeah, it's your time and develop your story.

Adam (A): Okay. Hi, my name is Adam. And I am a recovering addict and alcoholic. I have absolutely no doubt in my mind today that I, my life, walking, breathing, working, living free of alcohol and drugs one day at the time on a daily basis is because of a connection and understanding, rebirth, a development of spirituality, and a conscious contact most importantly with God of my understanding, my own understanding. This development has come about as a result of working a 12-step programme that has come from the programme of Alcoholics Anonymous which was developed originally from, I believe, a Christian movement called "the Oxfords groups." And I followed the 12-step programme through AA, Alcoholics Anonymous, through Cocaine Anonymous and through Narcotics Anonymous. And like I said that for me, the programme itself has developed for me an understanding of God in my life which has removed from me the compulsion to drink alcohol and use other substances.

So how that come about? I certainly didn't go into 12-step recovery to try to find God. In fact that's was not really at all what I expected when I first started going to the 12-step recovery. I went to my first CA meeting, Cocaine Anonymous meeting, because of a 15 year addiction with drugs and alcohol. Although I didn't think that alcohol is part of my problem. I went because I was unable to stop taking cocaine. And I realised that; I realised one day after having sworn on my life and my mother's live and on all the members of my family that I would never ever use again. The following day I went out to go and buy a newspaper. Saw that there was a

Appendices

football match on; decided to go and watch the first half of the football in the pub and thought that I would be okay to have one pint which led to eight pints; which led me calling a dealer; which—so I picked up cocaine; went home by the off-licence; went home and two days later I woke up in my own, covered in my own vomit. When I looked in the mirror my eyes were black. I hardly recognise myself. And this was a pattern really that developed over many years of using.

But that's where I ended up and in that moment, what I would call a moment of clarity, I realised that no matter how much I never wanted to use drugs or alcohol, well at that point drugs again, I realised I had no choice in the matter. I understood at that moment of understanding of what we would call in 12-step recovery "powerlessness." And it's absolutely scared me like I can't find words to describe the fear that ripped through my body as I realised in my mind that although I never wanted to use again I had no choice because I tried and tried many, many times to swear off; I moved countries; I moved towns; I changed partners, girlfriends; bought a flat; moved home with my mum; moved out back into another flat. And I tried many, many different methods of changing different types of alcohol; changing drug dealers; changing my surroundings. And everything that I tried to try to stop using drugs and alcohol didn't work. I tried counselling. I tried acupuncture. I tried social workers. And all those things would help at times. For example, I may have lessened the using. The using may slow down or in periods stop for brief moments. When I am talking about 15 year drug and alcohol addiction when I say brief moments I mean a few days. And literary I don't mean, you know, not like months, years we're talking about few days which for me would give me a feeling of: "There you go it wasn't so bad, or I'm better now."

And then I would have fell under the delusion that I would be okay to have that first drink. Which I am led to understand now is insanity, it's insane. If I once pick up a drink or a drug and I can't stop till I pick up that drink or drug again. Well back then at those days I was, my mind was insane. I had no concepts that once I'd pick to use, I had the first seep of a drink or the first line of cocaine or the first pill, or whatever it was I was taking, I would continue until all the drugs and all the alcohol run out. So at that point of clarity I realised this. I realised, you know, whatever I do, I cannot stop taking drugs because I guess at the end of the day the point is, I am trying to control something that I can't control. Now I used to say to so many people: "It's all right, I'm in control." Well the fact is this, if I needed to control something, if I tried to control something that is going to be a problem because the people that don't need to control something obviously have no problem. So the delusion for me was that I'm in control. So that simple fact—I am trying to control something shows that at some level there is an issue.

But it took me a long time to really, to really have that moment of clarity and actually thought: "Do you know what? I need help. And I don't know where to get this help." And this is where for me God comes in because there were many, many times when I would lie there at four o'clock in the morning after having my last line of cocaine and drank my last beer and finished my last bit of skunk. And I would lie there and I would have a couple of hours till I have to get up for work. And I would lie there and I would be panicking and having panic attacks; physically shaking; my heart pumping in my chest from the cocaine and panic attacks; and lying there absolutely so fearful that I had to, you know, get up and go to work. And I would say to myself: "Why have I done this?" I would be self-loading, hating myself, in absolute bits, crying. And in those times I would say: "God why is this happening? Why are you allowing this to happen? Help! Stop! Stop it! I promise you God if you stop me using or you take away this pain I would never do it again, I would never do it again." But the thing was I would do it again, you know.

And then I'd blame everybody apart from myself, you know. I'd blame my childhood situation. I'd blame my dad for leaving when I was 10. I'd blame the bullying I received at school. I'd blame the teacher that told me that I was useless when I was six. And I'd blame all these external situations. I'd blame my girlfriend because she was just easy to blame. I'd blame my parents. I'd blame my sister. I'd blame my friends. I'd blame everybody. But the last person I didn't really blame a part from when I was in those moments of coming down heavily from drugs was myself, you know; and in those moments the realisation that: what a sad, desperate person I was. You know, so I even blamed God. I would say: "It is your fault, you know."

In that moment of clarity I did something different. I asked for God's help properly, sincerely, you know. I actually sat on the edge of my bed and I put my hands together and I said: "God I'm in trouble here and I don't know what to do. I really don't know what to do. And I need your help." Which was different from saying: "God if you take away this pain I would never use again." Because that's trying to bargain with God not asking for God's help. And in this instance I asked for God's help. And then there was a series of events that follows. Some people might call this coincidence. I have in what we call between us in recovery "our sponsor," who is somebody who's taken me through the 12-step programme, who would call it not coincidence but God-incidence. It is a God moment which was: I've spoken with a friend, very, very, within an hour after this waking up in my own vomit and praying to God. And I've had a consultation with a friend who expressed his concern for me. And I expressed my concern back and I said: "Yeah mate." I said: "I'm scared." I said: "I've got to realise that no matter how much I don't want to use drugs and alcohol again I don't think I can stop." And he said the same thing: "I'm really worried about you, mate." He said: "Okay. You're worse and worse of using daily. Every time I see you are on it, you know." And I thought back all the things I tried to do to try to stop, and all the things that have failed. And again I said: "God what can I do? What can I do?"

And why did I do that? Why did I pray to God? Where did that come from? I've had to think about where that comes from because I was brought up to believe in Christian values. I went to Sunday school as a child. These occasions I've been to church when I was younger. I had to be honest and say that I've never really got into any kind of religious rule practice, you know. I'm not gonna sit here and say that I consider myself religious. But I did have a conception of what I believed God was. And to start with it was the Christian God. If I could visualise God he would be the bloke on the cloud with the beard and a stick or something, you know. Perhaps looking down at me and, you know, not happy with what I was doing but may be wanting to help me. And so that's why I did that. That's why I did pray to God on occasions. But it was always only whenever I was in trouble. That's the thing. I've never asked God to; I've never said in the morning: "Hello God, how are you today?" Or I've never really thought of speaking to God. It was only when I was in absolute mess, or I owed money to people, you know, there you go.

I believe in that moment I really reached out and said: "God I really need your help. I really need your help." I believe in that moment God did help me. Because, as I said, I had this conversation with a friend and when I came off the phone I sat there thinking about what I could do. Into my mind came this thought which was: "Adam, in your jacket pocket there is a flyer with a telephone number on it" (that I picked up from the Community Drug and Alcohol Team about four months previous and I left in my jacket pocket and I've forgotten about). "And go get that flyer and go ring the number." And this thought has come into my mind. And I walked straight to my wardrobe, straight to the jacket were it was, straight to the pocket where it was, and there it was. I got it out. And there is this paper.

And on the top it said: "Cocaine Anonymous." It had a telephone number and guy's name. And I rang the number. And the guy said: "How can I help you?" And I said: "I've got a really bad cocaine problem." And I said: "This is what has been happening." I explained my story. And he said: "I would relate to everything you've just said," he said. And he told me a bit about his story. And I sat there and I thought: "Well. You know there is a guy that I can relate to. He told me his background, what led up to him going into Cocaine Anonymous." And he said: "Adam, there is a meeting tonight. Come along."

And I went to that first meeting and that meeting changed my life. That meeting absolutely turned my life around. Because what I discovered was, to cut the long story short really, I discovered I suffer of an illness, a spiritual maladjustment, myself with the disease of negativity. I am; in my understanding I was separated from God. I was cut off from God. God was there but I was full of fear. I was full of resentment. I was full of self-pity. I was full of self-consciousness, low self-esteem, selfishness, self-centredness. And all those things for whatever reason blocked me from God. So in my understanding that's where in the first step of the 12-step recovery programme they say: "We admit we're powerless over cocaine, alcohol, your addiction, whatever: for some people gambling; for some people sex; for some people chocolate cake; for some people shopping." For me I think I can qualify for any of those things. Because I suffer with a disease where without God in my life I feel that fear and that self-centredness, and the negativity that it creates fills me with such a deep self-loading and hatred for myself and for life. Even though I really tried, I really tried to manage well and to try to get on and try to work and to try to get on in life.

I found life so difficult. I always found so, right from when I was .... I mean, I have a running joke with my mum which is: when I was born, I was born as a breech. I was a breech birth. I came out with my feet first. And the joke with my mum is: I was difficult coming out and I've been difficult ever since. That's kind of a joke. But the joke has an element of realness and truth to it. It's a kind of a joke but it is not really a joke because really from when I was born I was born a breech. I was born exactly at midnight. And for whatever reason these days because it was midnight they took me. My mum had me for two minutes and they said: "He's going to go upstairs now into the cot." Which I don't know how they can do this these days but .... I was cut off of my mum and put up in a cot upstairs and by the time I came down I've already been given a bottle of milk. So I wouldn't go to my mum's breasts. So although me and my mum are getting very well we didn't have that connection. Whether any of that has anything to do with it I don't know. However, all what I know is, from my earliest, from my very first moments, my life seemed to be difficult. My first experience was of a difficult, uncertain world where I believe having studied counselling that I fear abandonment. I fear not being good enough. I fear of what people think of me.

When six years old I was told by a schoolteacher that I was useless, or I took it that she was saying that I was useless but she was actually saying that my work was useless. And I took it that she was saying that I was useless. And I carried that resentment for 30 odd years. It was the biggest resentment. It was my . . . . That resentment for somebody that is an alcoholic and an addict . . . , well I believe I was, I mean.

Okay, what makes me an alcoholic and an addict? I have no idea really if I am honest. I have no idea. Certain factors could be: life events; I was born that way; it runs in my family; I have great-grandparents that both died from alcoholism; uncles and aunts who have died of alcoholism. Neither of my parents are alcoholics or addicts nor my sister. I am for whatever reason. I believe those childhood events may have some kind of bearing on perhaps the reasons why I'd turn out the way I did. My old, my dad had an affair with my next-door neighbour when I was 10 years old and walked out and left. And I used to see my dad coming home from work and instead of coming home he is going next door. And he waved for me from the window which was quite a disturbing thing to go through. But do I blame any of that on why I am an addict? I don't know because I could have perhaps from what I know from other addicts and alcoholics in recovery or recovering in 12-step recovery it doesn't matter where are you from, what your background is or whatever happens if you're an addict you are an addict. You know to be honest I still don't really know the answer.

But the point is this, you know, to bring it back to the meeting. I discovered what for me is, what makes me an addict. And really, ultimately it comes down to the fact that I'm powerless over drugs and alcohol. I am powerless over them. I don't have the power within me. I lack power. We have a book in AA that we call it the Big Book of Alcoholics Anonymous. And that book says that lack of power is our dilemma, is my dilemma. I'm bodily and mentally different from my fellows. I suffer from lack of power when it comes to alcohol, drugs or anything which is potentially addictive. And it all comes from the elements of an illness. Or we will call that threefold illness. The first element is, what we call "an obsession of the mind," which is: obsessed about anything that makes the changes the way I feel. Because ultimately I don't like the way I feel because of all those characteristics: the low self-esteem, the self-loading, the fear, the self-consciousness, the self-centredness. So I'm obsessed about things I've tried in the past. That changes the way I feel. And for me when I first drank alcohol, seven or eight years old, it gave me exactly what I never had before. It gave me a sense of belonging. It gave me a sense of esteem. It made me feel good about myself. I could talk to people. I felt part of, not in the outside. And I never felt like that before. So instantly after I liked this I would obsess about the next time I can take alcohol. And when I first took my ecstasy tablet again bang, straightaway I got this wish of and the rush of: "This is what I've been looking for all my life." You know, for me was like this: somebody would have flicked the switch inside me and I was able to talk to girls; I was able to dance; I was able to . . . . You know, that's the effect of ecstasy but for me I can't leave the stuff alone because I always wanted to feel like that. When I stopped, when I didn't take drugs and in between and when one of the drugs has come down and I would go back to work I would feel depressed. And then slowly I would slip back into the self-consciousness and all that. I was obsessed about the next weekend when I would again take this ecstasy tablet, you know.

And then, the next element of the disease for me is what we call "the phenomenal of craving," which for me is when I, when I as an alcoholic and an addict is what makes me an addict and alcoholic is: I can't have one of something whether it would be a drink, a line of cocaine and ecstasy tablet. I've never done heroin but if it was a heroin once I had one it sets up a craving in me that screams out for more that I have no control over. So if I buy a packet of cocaine and I do one line I would do the whole lot. Somebody that is not an addict will do one line, maybe two lines, maybe five lines but then they would put the rest back in the drawer for another day because they've to go to work the next day. I have to go to work the next day but I would sit and I would do whether is one packet of cocaine, five packets of cocaine, if there were twenty packets of cocaine, I would sit there until the lot was gone; and that the same with alcohol with any other substance, you know. For some people with addiction it could be a packet of chocolate biscuits. Once they have the first one they would sit and eat the whole lot. Luckily for me chocolate biscuits are not really my thing but cocaine and alcohol is. Because for me it gives me that, it gives me the ultimate, when I drink and use drugs I don't just have a little bit I do it to

Appendices

get smashed. I do it to go to oblivion because that's where my alcoholism and drug addiction led me.

It led me from having a little bit here and there but always, always right from the first time I drank alcohol I was sick; I blacked out; I couldn't remember what I've done the next day. My mum was horrified and ashamed of me and told me off. "You know, what are you doing? Why did you drink so much?" And to be honest I didn't know. I had no idea. All that I know is that I liked it. Now really any normal person that has experienced that and drank like I did and was sick and fell ill they probably wouldn't touched it again. But I obsessed about the next time I could drink alcohol. And the thing is that I got to know where my mum kept her bottles of alcohol for family occasions, Christmas and that. My mum wasn't a drinker. And I would go sometimes before school and I would have a neck of brandy or whiskey or whatever is in there. And that is not normal behaviour, I believe. But I believe right from my first drink of alcohol that I was an alcoholic. Because I believe I was an alcoholic anyway. I believe is in me.

So I found out my truth when I went to these meetings. I found out that I have an obsession with anything that it changes the way I feel because I don't like the way I feel. And once I ingested one of anything it sets up a craving that's far beyond my mental or physical control—powerlessness. So that on paper is one hell of a problem. But not only on paper it was my experience because what these guys told me in the meeting was: "Adam, that's what's wrong with you—do you relate." And somebody said: "Here take this book, the big book of Alcoholics Anonymous. Read it. Read the first few chapters." Which I did. So I read about what it is to be an alcoholic. I read more about alcoholism. And I identified with that problem. And then I said: "So if that's the problem, you know. And you guys are all clean and sober. What is the solution? What is the solution to that? How, what do I do?" And they said: "Adam, there is a 12-step programme. If you follow the 12-step programme you can be clean and sober as well, you know." And that's when for me the hard work begun. Because I left to discuss this programme. I saw the word "God." And even though I had the experience when I first got into my first meeting I thought: "How would God help me?" And what they said was: "Adam, what you need to do is, you need to work this programme. And what it would do is the elements of the programme—clear your resentment, clear your fear. It starts to change the way you think. It would start to change the way you act, you know." And they said: "It won't happen overnight." Because I said: "Adam, you know . . . ." When I went into CA and AA I was . . . (age omitted due to confidentiality)." I am now . . . (age omitted due to confidentiality). It took me a year and a half to get properly clean and sober. I am just coming up to three years clean and sober. On the 13th of December 2011 I would be three years clean and sober. When I couldn't get a day clean and sober. So for a year and a half I struggled. And the reason I struggled was because I didn't do exactly what they suggested at the meetings. They said: "Adam, you need to go to a lot of meetings. You need to: in the morning you need to pray to God of your understanding." The second step for recovery in the 12-step programme is: "we came to believe in the power greater than ourselves to restore us to sanity." A power greater than myself is anything that isn't me. There is a power greater than me. And they said: "If you believe in any kind of god or anything spiritual use that. If you don't then;" they said: "Just press believe that I believe." Somebody said to me: "Adam, do you make the sun come up in the morning and go down in the evening?" I said: "No." They said: "All right. Then use that." So, you know, like I said because I already had a bit of a conception of God in my life anyway it wasn't too hard for me to actually get my head around that but to actually, to take up the suggestions which were: to pray in the morning; to ask God daily to help or relieve me of my addiction; I didn't really think that that would work. So when I didn't practice it I kept on relapsing.

So I was absolutely smashed when I've come into Cocaine Anonymous; and I mean properly smashed. I was in a seriously bad way. I mean, I was just about holding my job down, I don't know how. My health was terrible. My financial situation was terrible. I owed a lot of money to dealers, you know, to banks, credit card loans, that sort of stuff. I've thrown my girlfriend out. I was really alone. A lot of my friends weren't really talking to me. My work was suffering. I was getting sent home on occasions because I would become very aggressive when I've been using cocaine. I was going to work under the influence of drugs and alcohol constantly using and drinking. I was a chef for years, so I could get away with it, or I thought that I could get away with it.

So ultimately what recovery I do is really ultimately about getting God into my life. Because as I said that this disease I suffer is a threefold illness. The first part is the obsession. The second part is the phenomenon of craving. The third part, what they say is a spiritual maladjustment. I am maladjusted to life, to spirituality. One of the questions in the questionnaire* I've just completed, I can't remember exactly what it was but it is something along the lines of, you know: "Do you see life as being spiritual or, you know . . . ." And the thing was I didn't. I had no reason. Well I had reasons. I just had no concept in spiritual stuff or doing things to other people or looking at lovely countryside or flower or animals, you know. I was so self-centred in my own world of self-hatred and loading and struggling with life that I was wearing almost like glasses just black-and-white. All I could see was black-and-white, nothing gloats, healthy, no colour. So I lacked anything spiritual. I was cut off spiritually. I was maladjusted, maladjusted to life and maladjusted to spirituality. I don't know, I mean I have my own kind of concepts that are okay for me to believe in to kind of get this stuff—to get the stuff that I need to stay clean and sober. Now, one thing that I, one simple thing I think about is this, all right. I don't really know much about the Bible, really, but I do know the story about Adam and Eve, and probably in a very simple way which was: they were told not to eat the apple, otherwise . . . . And they lived in the Garden of Eden I believe in God's will. And they were told: "Don't eat the apple." And when they ate the apple God gave them their own will. And from that moment they went out and they lived not under God's will. I'm not quite sure but they basically had to run free will then. Now, my thought on this is whether that's a true story or not I have no idea. Let's say it is or there is something like that. Now, over the years, we're talking about thousands, I don't know if it is or millions probably thousands of years of evolution and the growth of men that we've got further and further removed from God, you know. And really what I believe is: all God wanted us to do was to say: "I need help." Like I did that day when I was suicidal, in bids, lying in my own vomit, unable to stop using drink and drugs. For me that's my story, that's my belief. I believe that for me is the simple way of . . . . You know, when I was told: "What you need Adam is, you need God in your life. It is not actually the drink and the drugs the problem."

You see the thing was for me that alcohol and drugs were my solution. It wasn't the problem. It would become a problem but to start with it wasn't because like I said when I first took alcohol, when I first took drugs they gave me everything I needed. They gave me a sense of belonging and power and calm. And when I take a drink and a drug I get a sense of "hooooo," which for the purpose of the recording is ease and comfort. I get a sense of ease and comfort when I take a drink or a drug. You know it gives me a sense of well-being, of peace, you know. And when I'm taking drink and drugs fair enough for long time, for many years it was fantastic. But at the end of my using it stopped working. I believe the drink, alcohol, drugs have shelf life. I used enough of it and at the end it stopped working. It's like taking a medication. You need to take more and more to get the same effect. At the end I just wasn't getting any effect really, just the negative side, just the consequences. And that's what my life was at the end—of consequences, consequence after consequence; the consequences of my actions, of the using played out in my relationships, my career, in my financial situation, in my health. Every element of my life was affected by my continual, habitual using which I could not stop doing, powerlessness, you know.

So when I was told: "What you need Adam is God in your life." To start with I thought, I don't know what I thought. I thought: "Okay. I hear what you're saying but I don't know whether I need to put down cocaine. Or do I just need to learn how to use it sensibly? I just need to learn how to control." And they said: "Adam if you need to control something is a problem. You have to get it into your head that you can never take cocaine again." I said: "All right, fair enough I'm prepared because I know cocaine is a problem. I'm prepared to put down cocaine but I am not prepared to stop drinking alcohol or taking other drugs." They said: "Adam, if you do that you will always go back to cocaine." And they were right because for a year and a half I continually tried to drink sensibly and what I found was, I found out I was an alcoholic as well. And then I found out that I had multitude of addictions, really. You know I suffer with a disease of addiction, you know. And alcohol is a substance. Cocaine is a substance. And really they were the solution. They were my medication. They were the things that worked for me. But, as I said, they stopped working. And at the end I got my head around the fact that I need to be abstinent. You know the only, the only real solution to my problem, my drug and alcohol problem, was complete abstinence.

But for me to be completely abstinent, if I am powerless, it means I need a power in my life. Now where I get that power? Simply I get that power from God. That is fact. I can sit here inside and I can lay everything I have on it. I don't have to. The evidence is clear, is that: I am coming up three years clean and sober when I tried everything imaginable to get clean a part from the God thing. Now that God thing works. The God thing has worked for me. So how did I get that power in my life? Simple! I work the rest of the 12-step programme. Me, I was powerless in my life. I was unmanageable, which it was. Like I said, my life wasn't organised. I could not stop using. My whole life was a mess. When I came to believe in a power greater than myself that could restore me to sanity, I said: "Well if I need to be restored to sanity does that mean that I am insane?" And I said: "Yes man, you are insane because if you kept repeating the same thing over and over and over again you must have been insane." So I said: "God will restore that sanity if you come to believe in a power, any power." So for me first of all it was my Christian concept of God. Over time it developed. So I believe today in the spirit of universe. I believe that God is everybody's God. I believe it's probably one God but we all have our own conceptions, the Christians, the Muslims, the Jews, the Hindus, the Hare Krishna's, the Buddhists, whoever. I believe for me in my own understanding it is perhaps one God, and we all believe in that one God, and still all have different conceptions of it. That's my understanding. So they said: "Adam, what you need to do, you need to make a decision to turn your life to the care of that God." And I said: "What's that? What do I do?" And they said: "At this stage it is just a decision. All this is, you are just deciding at this point. At this point it's either you crack on and do this stuff, or you go back and use drink and drugs and die."

Because really for me to use alcohol and to use drugs is to die. That's for me how serious it is. I am an addict. I am an alcoholic. There is no question about that. If I drink alcohol, you know what, I can end up in an institution, you know. I can end up in a mental home. I can get locked away. You know I could go to prison. You know and perhaps be removed from alcohol but I would be insane because, as I said, alcohol is my solution, was my solution. And it stopped working so I needed a different solution. So I can end up in an institution. I can end up in a jail or more likely I would end up dead at some point because to me alcoholism is a killer, illness, disease. One thing is for sure if I keep on drink and using drugs I will be bloody miserable, not just miserable, I mean. On a daily basis when I drank alcohol and I used cocaine in particular I was suicidal, suicidal. Every time I used and I was coming down, and I was lying there having panic attacks about the fact that I have to go to work, and I felt so terrible, you know. The thought was, you know, I guess likely for me I didn't have the guts to do it, to kill myself, was to take a lot of tablets, was to grab a knife, to jump out of the window. These thoughts would go through my head because I believe the illness part, I believe, wanted me dead, you know. And the insidious part of it is that through the drugs and alcohol I was slowly committing suicide anyway. And the loneliness it created because in the end of my drinking and using I was alone in my flat by myself, using by myself, using mountains of cocaine and drinking ridiculous quantities of alcohol and smoking ridiculous amounts of skunk, and taking any pill I can get my hands on. In the early days it wasn't like that. In the early days was clubs, parties, girls. I had a great time. Slowly over time, over a 15 year period it got from parties to me being by myself, you know. So I believe I suffer with an illness that wants me dead.

And today I know that God doesn't want me to die like that. That's not what God wants for me because this is all about the step three part, about turning my will and my life over. Somebody said to me: "Your will and your life are your thinking and your actions." Because what the problem for me is, is my thinking. It is actually my thinking that's the problem. So what needed to be restored to sanity was my thinking. And I discovered that only God can do that for me. You know, I can try to work through, I can try to think through my own problem. But if my thinking is the problem I could never think my way out of my addiction, my alcoholism. So what do I do to recover, to stay recovered, to be in a recovery process? I go to 12-step fellowship meetings. I pray sincerely to the God of my understanding every morning. And I say: "God help me to stay clean and sober today." I ask for a direction. I ask how can I be of a maximum service and benefit for people around me. For me it's about getting it out of self. I am selfish to the core. I am a selfish person. Me by myself and without God in my life I am full of self. I do not give a damn about anybody. I can't care about anything apart from me and where I am going to get my next lot of drugs. That's what I do.

So the 12-step programme has a process of; there is a process which would be like confession, where I write. Step four is, I write my whole moral inventory of myself. That's everything that happened in my past, all my resentments, my fears, my sex conduct, my harms towards other people, money that I owe other people, everything I've done in my life. And I look for my part in it. Because I didn't realise that I had a part in all these things. I thought, therefore, it's his fault, it's her fault, is the teacher's fault, is my dad's fault, is the nurses' fault, is everybody's fault. But when I looked at it I always had a part. Not always, sometimes I just happened to be there. But generally I always had a part in a way I felt resentful over somebody. It tends to be because is affected a part of me which is either my security instincts, my social instincts, my sex instinct which gets deeply affected and I lash out, I hurt and I wanna hurt people. I wanna protect myself and I lash out. You know, I do things manipulatively or dishonestly, or I am insidious. I can do things for retaliation. And maybe that people don't realise at the time. So I had to look at that stuff and I had to share it with somebody. The thing about sharing it with somebody is when I sit and I talk with somebody I share this stuff and I invite God to listen. And I know God is listening. And for me that was a massive part of my recovery.

It was to share everything I've done with God; and say: "God this is what I've done. And confess: this is me." And by that I grew. I started to realise how selfish I was. And I started to realise who I was. It was the first time I ever really looked at myself and actually realised and actually could admit to God: "Yeah, this is what I've done." And that for me was massive, like an internal cleanse; like somebody is taken out my insides and put it through a human wash, like a car wash but human, and put it back in.

But the thing is, you know, what I realised as well is that, what I've come to realise is as human, and I am human, is that I am full of defects and shortcomings. The things that make me human, you know, the things that I've picked up all the way from being a child, all the way through, that developed me into my humanness, you know, which is dishonesty and manipulation and selfishness and inconsideration and the low self-esteem, all those negative parts of self. And what I had to learn to do is to be really willing to not be like that, to try to be different, and to try to use spiritual principles. All the way from my first coming to my first meeting I started to pick up spiritual principles, to learn what spiritual principles were. So the first one is being: honesty, you know, honest with myself. The one needs to stop taking cocaine. If I don't stop drinking alcohol will it take me back to cocaine—so honesty. Open-mindedness: I need to start to think: "Well if these guys that related the story got solution and they are telling me about the solution do I need to follow what they say." Do I need to be open-minded enough to say: "Would that can work for me as well." I need to be willing. I need to learn to be willing. Because I was never willing to do anything unless it would, it could get me something. And things were that I didn't need to get something and I needed to get recovery. They just said: "Adam, you just need to be willing to come along; be willing to get on your knees in the morning and pray; be willing to ask God for God's help, you know." And I started to do that stuff and over time the denial started to break down. It started to break me down from the outside, this core exterior that I had. I'm sorry this external exterior. What would I put up for defence? I started to break down and sharing all that stuff in step five. And then being aware of my defects because of that. I started; it was almost like I melted; I came back to life, you know. I believe I was reborn at that point. I believe that I suddenly had a second chance in life, you know.

You know the next part is, you know, another spiritual principle I've really had to learn is humility and humbleness. You know to actually realise that, you know, if I'm powerless over my addiction there is another element that I believe is more personal because as I've said the substances, there are just one point of solution. They are not really the problem, it's me that's the problem. So I had to realise I was powerless over certain elements of myself, my shortcomings, my defects. So I had to ask God humbly to remove these shortcomings, these defects as well. So I do that on a daily basis. I asked God: "God please remove from me anything undesirable, my selfishness, my inconsideration, my self-pity." And overtime again I've changed further because I am learning more now to use spiritual principles. There is a lovely prayer. I don't know it by heart but it's St Francis's prayer. I think St Francis of Assisi. There is a prayer and it starts: "Lord make me channel thy peace." And then it goes to say things like: "Where there is discord may I bring a sense of harmony. And where there is error can I bring truth. Where there is hate can I bring love. Where there is darkness can I bring lights. Where there are shadows can I . . . ." And all these things, you know, helped me to understand rather than to be understood and to listen rather than to be listened to and to love and to be loved and to be patient, and you know.

So what these 12-steps have done for me, the programme has done for me, it's changed me. But what it's done really is cleared the way to invite God's power into me. And that's what the change is. And that's where the change is for me. It's like turning up a pilot light inside me that was miniscule before, you know. I believe that; for me I believe that God is within me, you know, deep down inside. I believe the reality of God is all around me. I can't see it. I can't touch it. But I know is there. I guess it's like the wind and the trees. You can't see that wind but you know the wind is there because you can see it in trees. I believe is like that with God for me. I believe that I can't see God but the evidence of God is there. Because you know, I was a hopeless drug addict and a hopeless alcoholic. Now I am living differently, you know. You know, the changes he's brought about for me are . . . . You know, without a question, God is working in my life today. I had school without any qualifications but today, recently finished a five-year counselling diploma. And I am now a qualified counsellor. I changed my career from being a chef to a drug and alcohol counsellor. I know that I couldn't have done that. I couldn't have gone through that course. I know that I couldn't have done any of that stuff without God's guidance. And how I know that is because in my key decision to give my life over to the care of God I asked for God's guidance. I asked God, you know. Okay, I was told that God will only do for me what I can't do for myself. God won't do the things I can do. So if I want to get a new job or if I want to get an education, if I want to find a partner, if I want to do most normal human things then I have to get up and do those things. But what I can do is to turn my thinking, my actions, my will, and my life over. I can ask for God's direction. I can say: "God, I'm gonna go and do this. What do you think? I'm turning it over to the care of you. I'm going to do it, you decide on the outcome." For me to change my career was a massive decision, you know. A lot of fear evolved for me with that. So you know I turned it over. Now I don't know again it's one of those things, I did the ground work, I changed my career. Now a lot of people may just say: "Well actually you've just, you've done that. You've done that." And there was an element that I did that but I believe that there was God's influence in there. I believe that what the difference in my life today is that where I had no direction I believe that God is directing me. I believe that God is directing my life.

You know I suffered and I still suffer with, really, the delusion that I can gain satisfaction out of this world if I manage well; if I can get the right woman; if I can get the right flat; if I can get the right salary; if I can get the right cloths; if I can look good; if I can do; if I can treat people well. Because another part is, the flipside of the selfishness and inconsideration, really it stems from that, I'm a people pleaser. I want people to like me. You know I want everybody to love me. I want to walk into a room and I want people to go: "Look! Here is Adam. What a great bloke." Because, you know, my core is fear, still. But what the programme does for me and having God in my life does. He fills that. He fills the void that I feel inside. You know it allows me to live in unison and harmony with the world around me not against it. You know I'm not constantly trying to see what I can take from the world today. Today I feel I try to be more giving, more considerate and, you know, have more compassion for the world around me. You know, today those dark glasses are off. And today I have just normal vision. I can see, you know, I can acknowledge the seasons. I used to hate winter. I used to disgust it, dread it. You know I used to think that it only affected me when it was dark and cold and icy or, you know. And I used to think: "Oh, yeah, you know, it is so unfair, you know." I didn't realise that everybody else had that—get through the cold and the dark. And today, you know, when it's dark and cold I accept this because it is winter. As much in the summer I can appreciate lovely flowers, the nature, you know. In the autumn there are lovely colours because of trees' change. Because what I've got today in my life is: I've got spirituality. I am alive with spirituality. What I've got today is that I'm living as a normal human being. I don't think that before, I think before I just survived. Now I'm living, you know. And really what I've got with that really is just a normal life. That's the thing and that's the key for me. Today really I'm no different from anybody now. Where is before I felt so different, you know. I mean really I wasn't any different, I just felt I was different. So I tried to act differently to try to change everything around me to try to fit in. But really what I needed, really what I didn't realise was that I needed God in my life. Because of my, you know, normal humanness I will grow old, I will live as, you know, as long as . . . .

For me, the key is to continue to work my 12-step programme; continue to invite God into my life on daily basis; pray to God in the morning and ask for clean and sober day and thank him at night. I say: "Thank you for that today." Ask him how I can be of service to him and to other people. Try to carry the message that was given to me to other people. Because somebody said to me: "Adam, you can only keep what you got by giving it away." The message I've got is that it is possible to recover from alcoholism through working a programme which gets a power greater than yourself in your life, spirituality, for me God. For me, today I have no problem with God whatsoever, no problem whatsoever. There is a nice little story about; it's kind of an AA story and it's one that I can relate to, which was: when I was young I used to go to Sunday school. And I used to sit there and I used to daydream about of riding my bike or swimming or fishing, you know. And not really thinking, worrying; not really wanting to know about God and what they were teaching. And today the difference is; that's the difference for me between religion and spirituality. The difference for me is, today I can go riding my bike, fishing or swimming or whatever and I can be thinking about God. You know, for me it's my own interpretation. I don't know, I hear a lot of different stories. Sometimes I hear things and I think, you know, I really don't understand that. And I have to sometimes sorts of sit back and reflect, reflect and think: "Do I like this because I think it sounds good, or do I like that because it applies to me? Do you know what I mean?" Somebody said to me: "The difference between religion and spirituality is that religion is for people that don't want to go to hell. And spirituality is for people that have been to hell and don't want to go back, you know." I don't know about that. I certainly know that I lived in my own personal hell without a doubt. I know today that I don't. I just leave in the normal world as a normal person. Today I am, you know, I am a better son, not perfect son but I go visit my mum quite regularly. Today I am an uncle and a godfather to my nephew, you know, which has happened in my recovery. I believe that if I was still drinking and using drugs my sister wouldn't ask me to be the godfather, you know. There are times

Appendices

when I do go to church. A lot of the meetings I go are in churches. And quite often I would go to the meeting early. And I would go and sit in the church and pray. I can do that. I can also go to Buddhist temples. And I can go and sit there and meditate. You know I can sit on a beach and look at the waves coming in and out and think: "That's not me that is doing that, you know." That's the thing; it's not about me today, it's about other people. And really the most important thing in my life today is my developing understanding of God that is personal to me and my spiritual growth. I know that if I don't continue to grow spiritually possibly I would stay stagnant and maybe even slip back. I hear of many recovering alcoholics and addicts that have done 12-step recovery who stopped doing the stuff; who stopped praying to God; who stopped going to meetings; who stopped developing spiritually. And ultimately I suffer, you know. I hear people say: "I am a recovered alcoholic. I am a recovered addict." For me I don't think I would ever be recovered. I will always be recovering because if I stop doing the stuff that has got me well then ultimately I'd still suffer from the same disease. And I know that that disease can still play out. If I don't go to meetings or if I don't pray enough then my head very quickly starts to go negative again and that's when the thought off; and that's when I may start overeating, or I may start trying to chat to too many women because I'm still trying to change the way I feel, you know. Ultimately that would lead back to alcohol, to cocaine, to other drugs, to jail, institutions, death. Do I want that in my life? No! I don't want that in my life. Why would I? I've got everything that I need in my life today, you know.

And something I'm told is that God will give me what I need not what I want. I live by myself today. I don't have a partner at the moment. I would like to get married. I would like to have kids. But at the moment I don't. I don't have a car at the moment. I get around on a pushbike. But I live close to where I work. You know, I got the job that I am happy to do and I try to do my best there. I have my family close by. And I would say that I get well with. My relationships have got better. You know, I have a bit of money in the bank and food in my fridge. You know, I don't worry about how I'm going to put food in the fridge because I'm not worried about paying off dealers. I'm not worried about lying awake all night and having panic attacks cause I have been using drugs again. You know, I just have normal worries today but I've got everything that I need. At this moment, you know, what I'm told is that when I grow spiritually God will reveal more to me. He will reveal more himself, and he will reveal more about life and the things that I need to do to stay in recovery. Because, you know, what I've got today, I've got a change in my life. The changes are brought around by having God in my life. God is doing for me what I can't do for myself. I have no doubt about that. I have no doubt about that, the evidence is there. You know, I don't question it, I don't need to, that's my experience. A lot of people that I talk to about 12-step recovery . . . . You know, where I work is a substance misuse agency and there are people that are not addicts, not alcoholics. There are some people that are and they practice other stuff which is fine, which is okay. Not everybody believes or agrees with what I do for my recovery. A lot of people think that it's me that's doing it. "Adam, you should give yourself credit because it's you just doing it." And yes, to a degree is my choice to do it. But is God that's doing the stuff for me. I am powerless. I was cut off from God and now I have God's power in my life. You know, it is not so much God that I needed in my life because God was there anyway. It's God's power that I need. But within that I've come to believe more in God, you know. And it's without doubt the most important thing that they have and that I do in my life today, you know.

I understand that I will grow older; that life is at times difficult; life can be very difficult, you know. I've had a relative who died of cancer a few years ago. I've had other relatives that passed on. I've had, you know, financial difficulties. I've had some health implications that I had to look after. You know that is normal life stuff. You know, one day I know that I would die. You know that's reality. But I don't fear death anymore like I used to. I used to fear death. I used to fear my mum dying. I used to fear what would happen to me when I go, you know. Now, today I have sincere belief that, you know, if this is the length I have to go through to get off drugs and alcohol then when I die that can't just be it. It's got to be more after that. That have to be something to go on to, something better, you know. But I don't know what. I don't really have a conception of what that is. I mean I like the thought of heaven, but I don't know what heaven is. I imagine a beautiful; perhaps this planet but a brand-new where people walk happy and free and joyous. Perhaps reincarnation, maybe I believe in some level perhaps it could be that I come back again and have another go of learning what I've learned in this part of my life that hopefully I can carry on until I die. And perhaps use that understanding in some level as a child or an animal or whatever. I really have no idea but I do know this: I do know that I've got God's work in my life today; that I won't wanna change that for anything; that I know that God loves me; I know that God doesn't ever punish me; I know that God gives me opportunities to try again; I've learned to not take the piss out of God and go; I also know that God would forgive me because that what God does and not worry about it; I learned that I have to have a sincere desire; I've learned that prayer and meditation is very important to me.

I pray to talk to God and tell him my worries or ask him what I can do and then I meditate to listen. Obviously I would get quiet and I would sit; and I am usually here in the morning, half an hour in the morning; I would sit and I would listen to what God . . . . And I don't necessary hear anything but I would get intuitive thoughts and decisions. I may read something that springs out of me. And I would go: "There you go, that's what I was thinking about. And that's the answer." I may bump into somebody and somebody say: "Adam, blah, blah and so and so, you know on Friday." And I think: "There you go again." I don't know, God is working through people. That's what I believe. I believe that God works through people. I believe that God talks to me through people. I don't directly hear God talking to me. I've never heard God's voice in my head. But what I believe is, I believe that God would talk to me through somebody else. The first questionnaire* that I did talked about your conscience. I believe that for me is where I hear God as well. I believe that really, really, I mean, ultimately I know right from wrong. I was brought up to know right from wrong. I was brought up to know that, you know, the stealing is bad; to hurt somebody is bad; you know to murder would be bad. You know and I know that. And I know that my conscience would tell me that that is bad. I believe that if I was to do stuff against my conscience then I believe that it's . . . . You know, the conscience in a sense I guess, conscience, God's consciousness—I'm conscious of God within me; you know telling me right from wrong. Because, I believe ultimately I'm a good person. I wasn't born to be a drug addict and an alcoholic. I just think that perhaps it was in me, perhaps it just happened. Perhaps it was a result of my difficult birth. Perhaps it was a result of the nurses taking me away, and my dad walking away, and being told that I was useless, the bullying I had at school. Perhaps they are all factors, I don't know. But, I do know that today I try to live differently. I try to live in accordance with what I believe God would want from me. And the thing I need to acknowledge on a daily basis is that I'm just learning. You know, this for me is about learning. You know, as I said before that I was reborn; you know to be reborn really. I'm coming up three years clean and sober. I'm still a child really, which really I am because I know my thinking sometimes is childish. And I know that sometimes I make the wrong decisions, you know. I have the process through 12 steps of being able to document what I do on a daily basis and share it with my sponsor and to ask for help and for guidance. And then, I ask for God to remove the defects that are gone in a way of my humanness today or make me human. You know and over time I'm changing. I'm changing more and more as long as I do the stuff. It doesn't mean that I don't have fear. It doesn't mean that I don't get resentful. It doesn't mean that I don't hurt people at times. It doesn't mean that I can't be a real selfish prick sometimes. However, I have the opportunity to look that stuff and go: "I don't want to be like that. I don't want to be like that today. I want to be different. I want to try to live in accordance with what God would want from me." I don't really know if that's enough.

I: Do you want to go to the questions?

A: We can go to the questions, yeah.

I: We can see whether you can put more light to the actual concepts thinking about your story which you already nicely developed.

A: Yeah.

I: You mentioned conscience towards the end. And the first question here is about: How do you perceive your conscience? Talking about: What is conscience? How did it develop? How does it function?

A: So I mean, I guess in that respect I've never really had much of a conscience. I guess I did. I don't want to paint this picture that I was an absolutely evil or like terrible person. I don't think I was. I just think that life experience took me on the path where I became really destructive, you know, in my addiction and in my alcoholism. I became a destructive person. But like I said, I always knew right from wrong. Now for me to take drugs to start with was; I knew it was wrong, however, I guess the need to be part of was greater. So I don't know, in that moment I guess I knew that perhaps I was going against my morals or what my conscience told me but my need to be part of was greater. So when with may be a bit of peer pressure, my friend tells me: "Do you want to try one of this?" and curiosity, the two together; what an awful; and it's a danger; and it's a silly but for that moment so . . . . And that's just one example. At the end of my drinking and using I was very nasty person really. You know, I would thieve money, you know, from my mother. You know I would ask, I would lie not directly go to steal money from her purse but I would say: "I've got bills to pay mum can I borrow 40 quid. I would give it to you next month." And I would go and take £40 and spend it on a gram of cocaine. Now I know in there I was wrong but my powerlessness of my addiction was greater. It wasn't just the need to use, it was my inability to not use which was far greater. So at that moment although I was, especially when I was coming down of drugs, I would think about that and it would fill me with absolute, you know, remorse and detest from myself. You know, I guess I had no choice over it.

But, the thing is about the conscience is that as I was coming to recovery my awareness of my conscience is become as I said, is like the pilot light turning up. It's like my conscience is become; I've become much more aware of my conscience; or I'm choosing. I guess what I'm doing is I'm choosing to listen to my conscience. I'm choosing today to go in accordance with what my conscience says and not to . . . . You know, like I said I am human. I still do things sometimes. I mean my track record with women is quite . . . . I have a habit of meeting a woman and pretending, not pretending but sort of to get what I want making as things were though, you know: "I really like you." And then getting what I want and then sort of finishing it because I get bored. Now my conscience tells me that that's not good. But there is still a part of me, the addict's part of me that it still wants to change the way I feel; it's still selfish. Now as time has gone on I had to learn to not do that. You know, because it doesn't sit right with me. Ultimately, if I continue to do that behaviour it will destroy my recovery. Because, if I keep going against my conscience, sooner or later I would pick up a drink or a drug. Because, I wouldn't be able to handle it. I wouldn't be able to handle the torture that I feel. I don't think, I think it's a difference between feeling heartfelt conscience and feeling guilt perhaps. Because, I feel guilty about things I've done but I can kind of get over that. But I know in there really the difference between right and wrong. I know when I'm doing things wrong. So what I have today through (with) God in my life or perhaps God talking to me through my conscience or perhaps my conscience is God. I think that's probably what it is. I think really God is my conscience. Or that's how I can really; for me really access God in my conscience. And I know when I am doing things that I shouldn't be doing. Today what I have through my programme is a choice. I can do that if I want but then I'd regret it and then I have to go through the process of . . . . Or I can choose to do something differently. So that's how my conscience has grown, is developed over time, or my awareness of how to work with my conscience not against it. So really what I am doing is working with God not against God. I'm choosing to try to live in accordance with God, God's principles today.

I: Thank you Adam. And the next question is: How did you develop alcohol addiction? You told the story. What is alcohol addiction? When did you realise that you have been addicted to alcohol? How did you try to manage your alcohol addiction? You pretty much explained all these things. Do you think you want to add anything?

A: I just think that alcoholism is a progressive disease. I will always be an alcoholic. I'm still an alcoholic. I am an addict but I just don't drink or use drugs anymore, you know. One day at the time through the programme of recovery and having God in my life, that's simply that. When did I realise? I think I've probably realised for a long time. And I used to remember I always say to myself: "I am a cocaine addict." But the thing is, the difference is that I didn't know what an addict was. I didn't know what an alcoholic was. That's the difference, you know. To my understanding an alcoholic and an addict is "powerless over those substances," "powerless over their addiction." Other places, other techniques, you know that's 12-step recovery understanding. Other places would say: "That's not true. You're not powerless over it. You need to change. You need to . . . ." I don't know. Somebody would say: "Look, if drink is a problem, is getting you in trouble, just stop doing it." If it was that easy—great. But for me it wasn't. I couldn't stop doing it. There was a long time I didn't want to stop doing it. I had to get to that point where I was broken. I was on the complete rock bottom. And the rock bottom for me wasn't losing my flat, being out on the streets, picking up a blood-borne virus disease, you know, AIDS, HAV, or something, it wasn't using heroin. My rock bottom was the total internal mental torture and anguish, you know, and ultimately suicidal feelings. And when I talked about sitting on the edge of my bed, you know, I felt broken up, I swore I would never to use again and a day later I was. And the feeling—I wanted to kill myself. That for me, that was when I realise this is more than just trying for years to stop using. And things got obvious when you realise it but it was a moment of clarity which I believe God gave me because he knew I was ready at that point. Or he knew that I was ready to go into the next part of the journey and start learning a bit about recovery which was: "Adam, you're not gonna stop using by yourself. You haven't got the willpower. What you need is, you need my power." Now coming to these meetings I learned about this programme of recovery which gave me the power. That's what I have today.

I: Thank you Adam. The next one is; you pretty much covered everything but I will just read them and if you want to add anything: What were your moral views before your moral, spiritual, and/or religious transformation? What is morality? How did you deal with moral dilemmas? How much did morality matter for you? You talked about this but do you think that you should add something about morality?

A: Much of it I think I spoke about before.

I: You spoke about right and wrong.

A: Yeah. I mean again I think that has to do with my conscience really. I knew the difference between right and wrong. You know it's like, another thing my mum is said to me is that: "You're very wilful child. You are full of self will." Well that for me is really what makes an addict an addict and alcoholic an alcoholic. So full of self will, I was self will run riot. And I would do anything to get what I wanted at the end. So if there was any difference between right and wrong to be honest I didn't really care. As long as I got what I wanted it didn't really matter about anybody else. You know, so, really at the end I knew the difference between right and wrong. And I understood, I did have, I had some morals, you know, like . . . . But then you know, my morals got, you know, the boundaries. They've got further and further, you know. It's like, I never thought that I would have taken cocaine, lots of cocaine. I've never, ever thought that I would, you know, I've never thought I would manipulate my mother for money. I've never thought that: one day I went around to visit my grandfather who was bedridden with emphysema, a lung disease. And my mum is taken my grandmother away on holiday. And I went around to chat to him and to make him a bit of dinner. And I've picked up some cocaine and I had one line. And I went in and spend 15 minutes with my grandfather cause I was so, I couldn't wait to get away. And I was chopping up cocaine on my grandparents' kitchen site. Now if somebody has told me years ago that I would do that I would have said: "There is no way that I would ever be that disrespectful." My grandparents' house! The things they've done to help me over the years after my dad left, and the love and care and the presents they bought me for my birthday and Christmas, and just to get the love that they gave. My morals at that point obviously were fallen back from what they would have been. You know that's kind of an example really the lengths that I would have gone to.

But one day, you know, the last year of my heavy using before I kicked my girlfriend out, a few weeks before, I asked to borrow £20 off my girlfriend. I was so desperate to get some cocaine. She said: "What is it for?" I said: "I wanna go and get some shopping." And she said: "Well, I don't believe you. I know what it is for." And in a fit of rage I smashed my flat up, totally. I threw a glass against the wall. I kicked things over. I got a table and threw it. I pulled the wardrobe over. I just went ballistic. Now again if somebody would have said to me that's what you would do like an animal, like an absolute animal, like an animal which has been caged and somehow it got out and running; in fact worse than animal; in fact that's disrespectful to animals. I was like a savage. That's where my addictions led me.

You know, again, you know, that happened. I can't change that. But what I choose to do today is to live differently. I tried to do; my morals are more . . . ; I believe I've regained my sense of good values and trying to do the right thing. You know, I'm not perfect; I'm not trying to be perfect. I spoke about St Francis's prayer. I like the idea which is in the values and morals there. I am not trying to be a saint, you know. I'm just trying to do the best that I can today because I think I owe it to myself, for first and foremost. I owe it to my family. You know, my family don't know half of the things that I did. But my mum says that she's proud of me today. She doesn't know about the cocaine and that. But she knows about the alcohol, you know. She knows I don't drink any more. And she knows what I do for my recovery. She knows that I do a lot of meetings; that I help other people; the changes in this career. She is very proud of me. And that's, you know, again I continue to do this stuff. For me, it has to be for me ultimately but for my family as well. But also today I've got a duty towards God. Because, if God is done this for me . . . . God has come and transformed my life, you know. You know, I see a lot of people out there. People coming here that are smashed and I might try to tell them a little bit about the true recovery I do and they don't want to know because they are not ready. Some of these people, they may find it eventually. Some of them will die. That's the reality. But what I do, what I have today is: I have an obligation, I have a contract, a deal with God, you know. God helps me to stay clean and sober on daily basis and I will go and bring this message out to others. If I am doing that I need to be practising the stuff. You know, I need to be . . . . You know, I can sit here and talk the talk but I need to then go and walk the talk. I need to go and practice. There is not a lot of preaching but is all about putting it in action. I can't change through reading words in a book, I need to read the words and then go and practice those things. So I'm going to the gym. If I go to the gym I don't get fit and toned by sitting and reading a book. I read the book of what to do and then I have to pick up the weights or get on the treadmill or the bike. It's the same stuff really. I'm trying today sincerely to be a better person, you know. Sometimes I already mess up with it and that's what makes me human. That's the humility part of spiritual principles. I've got faith today. I have faith and trust in God today that he's put me on his path for whatever reason; perhaps to help other people; perhaps he just seen that I had enough. In some sense where I was, when I finished, you know, I see some people in much worse positions, places. I'm just grateful. And I didn't say a lot about gratitude. I'm really grateful for what I've got today. You know what I mean. I am alive. I am clean. I've got everything that I need. I'm grateful for that. I'm really grateful for it. There is a thing that people say: "A grateful addict and alcoholic doesn't need to use again." And that's true. I have gratitude in my life today. Gratitude ultimately goes to God because that is what has turned my life around.

I: Thank you Adam. You pretty much covered a lot of what we're saying in these questions but if you feel like you need to add something feel free. The next one is: Did you practice spirituality before your moral, spiritual, and/or religious transformation? What is spirituality? How did you practice spirituality? How much did spirituality matter for you at that time?

A: The answer is, "No." Perhaps at times I thought I was when I was smoking a good quality skunk, when I went travelling to Australia, in my early 20s in New Zealand. Sometimes taking hallucinating analgesic drugs like LST or magic mushrooms I thought perhaps they were creating some kind of spiritual . . . . The answer is, "No." I didn't practice anything spiritual. I thought maybe at times I was. Sometimes again I might read a book. I might read a book on meditation. Not practice it but think that I was doing something spiritual. But that isn't to me.

I: The next one is: Did you practice religion before your moral, spiritual, and/or religious transformation? What is religiousness? How did you practice religion? Did you have religious affiliation? How much did religion matter for you?

A: Again I didn't practice religion. No. I was not forced to but I was told to go to Sunday school. I was taken to Sunday school by my parents. Like I've said I believe; I always believed in God, you know. And really my belief in God hasn't really changed that much. I've just still believe really. Spelt ultimately what I do, like I've said before I have a belief that God is one God and everyone has his own conception. I was christened so I suppose ultimately if anybody said to me: "What religion are you?" I would say: "I was, Church of England." I'm not practising but I quite happily today am going to sit in a church and pray. I in fact, a little while ago, I was going to church on Sundays. I stopped going simply because circumstances changed and something else came up. But I will definitely go to church again as much as I would come to sit in a Buddhist temple. Before—"No." Like I said the only times really that I ever prayed was to say: "God get me out of this. Get me out." You know, which didn't work because I was making demands. I wasn't sincere in saying: "God, actually what I really need, I really need you to help me." I was saying: "God if you get me out of this I would never use again." And that didn't work. Although, thinking about it, both spiritual stuff and religious stuff, if I think about it; I would like the thoughts of perhaps doing something spiritual or religious. It was always there in my mind but I just never did anything about it. As I said, the drugs and alcohol were the solutions for years. When I stopped working . . . . Really ultimately I guess in a sense I have become religious. I just prefer to say that I'm spiritual. If somebody said to me: "Oh, you're religious." I think, I would be a bit probably, I would be painting an untrue picture of somebody that, you know, they don't go to church or anything like that. I think I would be sort of not being truthful. I think spiritual to me means that I can sort of have more of a . . . . It doesn't have to be one set religion. I can use my spirituality and I can draw on different, you know really picking, the best way to say it is, pick and mix. I can have a little bit of what I like.

I: Thank you. Okay, next one is: Did you experience moral, spiritual, and/or religious transformation? You talked about this. How did you experience this transformation? When did you experience this transformation? May you identify anyone who played any influential role in the process? How much has this transformation changed your life?

A: I think I probably covered all that just a part from the last part which would just highlight that recovering addicts and alcoholics are been through what I've been through. And they knew what I've been through because of the similar stories and that they recovered in the same way as I have, which is now what I do. I passed on the message. When I leave here now, half-past seven, I go to a church to set up a meeting. People will come to the meeting. We sit and I share, and we share about what worked. The people that do trust the recovery; that's how I learned about this, you know.

I: The next one is: What was the impact of your transformation on your life? You pretty much covered it. Basically compare your morality, spirituality, and religiousness before and after the transformation. How did the transformation impact your understanding of morality, spirituality, and religion, and their role in your life? How much did morality, spirituality, and religion matter for you after your transformation? Yeah, you pretty much cover all of these.

A: Yeah, I think so. May you just say the last bit again?

I: How much did morality, spirituality, and religion matter for you after your transformation?

A: It matters very much. Do you know what I mean? It's my life today. It's how I have to live my life. I live my life on a spiritual basis. I have to, you know. I have to practice the stuff that I'm doing to be spiritually fit. If I'm not spiritually fit that's when I'm in trouble. You know, there is no doubt in my mind about that. I practice this stuff. I work the steps which gives me access to God. I am growing in my understanding, you know. Sometimes I don't really know what. I keep continue to do this stuff simply because I don't want to go back to what my life was like before. Why would I? When my life is without doubt; I cannot put any kind of measurement of how much better my life is today. But what I've really got is just real, normal life. That's all I've got. It's nothing, you know . . . . What I've got is, I don't use a day at the time but what I've got is a normal life. I don't get, you know, a medal or a certificate or anything like that or like a room of people clapping me. It's simply what I have today, is just a normal life. But it's more than that really. There is a sense to me of a different dimension. It's like for me I'm in a different dimension than I was before. And on this earth I believe there are different dimensions. I believe in a spiritual dimension. I believe I'm in a different spiritual dimension than I was before, you know.

I: Thank you Adam. Next one is: What was the impact of your moral, spiritual, and/or religious transformation on your conscience? Compare your conscience before and after the transformation. How did the transformation impact your conscientious behaviour? How much did the voice of your conscience matter for you after your transformation? You pretty much talked about all these. Do you think that anything else should be added here?

A: No, I think that's covered.

I: Next one is: What was the impact of your transformed conscience on your recovery from alcohol addiction? Compare your recovery before and after the transformation. How did your transformed conscience impact your recovery from alcohol addiction? What is the role of your transformed conscience in the maintenance of your abstinence? May you identify anyone who played any influential role in the process? I think you covered it.

A: Covered. Yeah.

I: Next one is: May you share your future plans related to your recovery? What is the role of morality, spirituality, and/or religion in them? What is the role of your transformed conscience in them? Do you plan to share your experience with others who need help in recovery from alcohol addiction? That's all covered, I think.

A: Yeah. To continue to pass on the message; keep on growing spiritually; to keep on developing my relationship with God, which really, really, I am just on the start of my journey. I am new in it. I'm not gonna sit here and pretend I am some kind of spiritual giant or religious. I'm not whatsoever. I'm really in a kind of a spiritual kindergarten really. And perhaps I am about to sort of step out and maybe going to spiritual primary school, perhaps. But I am on a start of a journey, but it is one that I want to stay in. That's my intention but to do that I know that I have to pass it onto other people. It has filled me with excitement, and wonderment, and hope, faith, courage. I never had that. I never had that. Today, I have that. My life is transformed without doubt, without a question. No doubt about that. My life is transformed today. Because ultimately I have God in my life, my conception of God.

I: Thank you Adam. And the last question is: May you formulate the main theme of your life story? And the sub-questions are: What is the place of alcohol addiction in your story? What is the place of conscience in your story? What is the place of morality, spirituality, and/or religiousness in your story? What is the place of your moral, spiritual, and/or religious transformation in your story? Basically the main theme of your story and the parts which make it.

A: The main theme was: I was wrecked. My life was an absolute . . . ; my life became a mess. I don't blame myself. I don't look at myself. And I don't hate myself today. I don't look at myself and go: "I am a bad person." I just, whatever, whatever happened, you know . . . ; I still don't really know exactly why it happened but, you know, . . . (age omitted due to confidentiality) years old I wanted to end my own life because of my addiction. And you know I hurt myself and a lot of people along the way. I was like a wild wind of chaos. You know, I wasn't brought up like that. I was brought up to be a good person, you know. I don't think I was a bad person. The thing is this: I'm not a bad person that is trying to be good. I believe today I am a sick person that is trying to be well, you know. I have a spiritual maladjustment. You know, I am; I have a threefold illness.

Appendices

In a moment of clarity I discovered God. First of all I discovered, I understood I was powerless. In that moment I prayed to God sincerely: "Help me." And God stepped on and helped me. That was the start of that new part of the journey till what brought me to what I'm now four years later. Okay, coming up three years clean; year of not really doing what was suggested to get this stuff. Then I started to practice it properly. And you know, I believe in a moment of real surrender, you know, I believe that I surrendered to God. I sincerely said to God: "All right, you are the boss. Here I am. You can have me. You can do what you want with me." And, you know, from that point really I've learned through the 12-step programme to live differently. Because of that I've had, what I would call a "spiritual awakening," "a psychic change." You know my whole psyche is changed; my whole thinking; my behaviour. I am in touch with my conscience today. I am in touch with other people, you know. You know in my core I am still a real selfish person but I am learning to be less selfish. I'm learning to be more considerate. I have hope in my life today. And I do wanna keep on walking this path; I would like to get closer to God. I don't fear what happens to me when I die anymore.

I believe God, you know, I mean ultimately I guess God has saved me not to make life hard for me and to make things difficult. That's not to say I won't experience life which could be very difficult and hard. But, what I know today is that I've got God there to help me through it. You know, what comes to mind is that story of the footprints on the sands. You know, there can be difficult times but when you know onshore where there are one set of footprints is when God is caring me because I'm finding it too hard. That's what I've got today. I'm walking hand in hand with my creator. You know, I have the spirit, God's spirit within me today. Yeah, that's, you know, I was on the brink of destruction and today I'm living, breathing as a normal human being. When sometimes I . . . . You see I think working in the industry where I'm working not particularly with 12 steps for recovery or the God based recovery, I am working in a harm minimisation type of recovery, that perhaps some of my colleagues don't know about the 12-step recovery and the God thing. My thing is that I was not as bad as some of the other addicts that come here. I'm not saying I am as bad or my stories are worse than theirs are. But what I think, probably not a lot of people realise, is that I was on the brink of destruction. I was distracting, you know. What God is done for me is taking me from destruction. And today I'm just living normally, you know. I can't express enough gratitude for that, you know. And that's it really, you know. I just continue to try to do the best I can and to keep on walking forward no matter what comes up, no matter how hard it gets, no matter how . . . . It's not easy, I think, walking on the spiritual path, I think, you know. I don't have today; I don't have drink, drugs. I can't, you know, go out and just meet women and go and do . . . . You know, I had to change, you know. So, therefore, I am not constantly changing the way I feel. Everything I'm experiencing today is real, real emotion. I feel deep profound emotion. I have my past, my conscience history resurfacing. And it can be very, very painful. I don't have the luxury today; not a luxury, maybe that's one of the better way describing it. I don't have the luxury of substances today to take away that pain. But what I do have is fellowship of people that I can talk to—support. But ultimately what I have; if they have to take everything away, everything away; if I took everything of my life away I would be left with just me and God. That's what it comes down to; comes down to God at the end of the day. Everything that I do, everything that I think; everything I do, think, do, and feel, and breath, my conscience, my every single muscle fibre, every single part of me today is about my relationship with God. And that's it, that's it. And I will continue with that.

I: Thank you very much, Adam. Today the 4th of 11th at 6:57 we're finishing the interview and I'm very thankful for the story you told me.

A: Thanks, Yordan.

*__Note of clarification:__ Daily Spiritual Experience Scale (DSES; Underwood, 2006) and Perceptions of Conscience Questionnaire (PCQ; Dahlqvist et al., 2007) were filled in by all interviewees during the interview. The completion of DSES and PCQ was moved from pre- to post-interview schedule, after the first two interviews, in order to avoid any possible interference with the genuine character of the story. The use of DSES and PCQ was discontinued due to their very marginal importance in the development and major findings of the research.

Appendices

Alex (2011). Personal interview (Conscience in recovery from alcohol addiction), 09 November.

Interviewer (I): Okay this is an interview which basically is open. You will tell me your story and the guidelines are the following: Structure your life story in chapters. Think about their names, summaries, and progressive links. Without interfering with the genuine character of the story can you identify the role of the following topics in your life narrative: conscience; alcohol addiction; morality; spirituality; religiousness; moral reformation; spiritual transformation; religious conversion and/or affiliation; the relationship between morality, spirituality, religiousness, and conscience, and recovery from alcohol addiction. How will you summarise each of these chapters? What progressive links will you make between these chapters? So, I will have these here just to remind you if you want. What I read now is listed here. You can keep it next to you as a reminder if you want. But basically tell me your story.

Alex (A): All right.

I: Tell me your name first and . . . yeah.

A: My name is Alex. I was born in . . . (year omitted due to confidentiality) to mother and father. My mother, she felt ill with postnatal depression and I was put into care as a baby. I've got put back with my mother three years old, roughly. And there we didn't really; they were not churchgoing people. So sort of like, my life, it didn't have God in it at all from a young age.

Conscience: My mum taught me; my mum, my father taught me right from wrong, which I don't think they've done a very good job.

Morality: I knew right from wrong. It was sort of like what I made up as right from wrong. You know, sort of like you don't hurt people. You don't do things wrong. You don't steal. I've got sort of like done stealing from my mum and dad.

Spirituality: I met spirituality since I've been around the homeless charity (HC, name substituted throughout the transcript due to confidentiality). It's always been around the HC when I first went to the local church (LC, name substituted throughout the transcript due to confidentiality). I've got more out of spirituality since I've been going to the . . . (name omitted due to confidentiality) church.

Alcohol: I've used that as a dealing mechanism for the way that I was brought up. I was bullied as a young child. I've got really hurt when I was young child. I was bullied from the age of 13 till 20. And then alcohol and drugs; they were a big part of my life as a way of acceptance, acceptance in life.

Drugs: Big time; I smoked a lot of cannabis, hash. I would say when; I mean; I lived with a woman for 14 years. I helped raise her children or raised her children. And sort of like I put more of my morality; I taught them right from wrong.

But sort of like religion has never come into my life at that part of my age; I mean sort of like till I was about 35. That's when religion took over in my life when I've come into the HC; when I started going to the community centre for homeless (CCH, name substituted due to confidentiality); when I started going to the short term hostel for homeless (STHH, name substituted throughout the transcript due to confidentiality); in and out, in and out of the STHH. But sort of like it was always I used to go to, what's the name of it, down the . . . (name omitted due to confidentiality) road and not the . . . (name omitted due to confidentiality). There is one church down . . . (name omitted due to confidentiality) road that I used to go to for Sunday dinner. And it was sort of like it was always there but sort of like it was always meeting people that were on alcohol. Everyone sort of like used to go in there drunk. I used to sort of like coming there drunk.

And alcohol has been sort of like; I've been weaned off of alcohol through the HC. Because sort of like the HC has said that alcohol is not a way of dealing with your life. So sort of like if you ask for God to be in your life then he will help you out with your substance misuse. And now I don't drink or smoke marijuana. I have little bleeps every now and then but sort of like . . . . But I don't go to church as often as I should do. I pray to God every day pretty much before I go to bed or when I wake up in the morning. This might be one of the shortest interviews you have ever had because sort of like I still sometimes I don't feel that God is working in my life. And I wish he was but he cannot change my life. It's only what I feel inside that would change my life. And the way that I deal with the way my life is going. And alcohol has killed my legs. Now, sort of like my legs are not working too well. And, certain other parts of my body that are sort of like . . . made an impact on my life. It's really hard one for me to do Yordan because sort of like God is worked in my life but mainly through the people that have been around me. It has not really had an impact on my life. I've got my own guidelines; it's right from wrong. It's sort of like treat people the way you wanna be treated yourself. So treat people right and they will treat you right. Treat them wrong and they will treat you wrong.

All the way through my life or from the latter part of my life, from 35 to 45, God is been chasing me. And he's been hounding me, not being hounding me but sort of like he's been there to sort of like help me to try and change my life; to try and change the way that I look at things; the way that I look at myself. And it's slowly working. And it's just coming; I mean until I'm dead I wouldn't know whether it's worked in my life. So sort of like it would only be on my deathbed that I would actually be able to say whether it's worked. This is as much as I can say. Because, sort of like I don't know until I'm dead if it has worked in my life. What more can I say to that?

I: Tell me more about your alcohol addiction. How did it start? How did it develop?

A: That was through being bullied. So sort of like when I was younger I was bullied and sort of like it was verbally bullied rather than physical bullied; physically, I could have taken it but sort of like I had one fight in my life. And I was 11 years old. And I beat the lad. I won the fight. I went back home and I've got beaten up by my dad. And he beat me up worse than I've come out of the fight. And he beat me up because sort of like I've come back with a ruined uniform. I mean it was properly mashed. So my dad, he beat me up because sort of like I ruined my uniform. And he put more value to money, then he had to buy me sort of like a new uniform, rather than the fact that I won the fight.

Now sort of like in my early years as a teenager, religion, it wasn't as it should be now, as it is now. Religion is better. It is much livelier. And it is more welcoming. You get more sense of belonging. The church is more inviting. And it's more; it is hard for me to put in words, but is a good place to go. When I was younger it wouldn't have been such a good place to go. You know sort of like people would have gone by and walk past it and all that sort of things. People would have thought more negatively about it. But nowadays it's more culturally acceptable. And I wish that church was more like it is now when I was younger. Then I would have had people to talk to. They would have helped me through my problems. The way my life was being . . . ; the way I was being treated; the way I was being bullied. And I would have had more strength; sort of like it wasn't there. And now people should find out more about religion at younger age. And I believe there are a lot more younger people that go to church. I mean sort of like when I go to church and sort of like they do the worship. Then, sort of like they go off to their children groups. And sort of like the church half empties. It is very few people in the church; sort of like, say 50 percent; 50 percent of the chairs are empty when they go off to their groups. So sort of like when I was younger it may have sort of like 10 percent of the chairs empty because sort of like there wasn't so much for the children to do. And you've got more young people, teenagers, and sort of like going into the 16–17 year olds. They are going up to their groups to learn about God and to learn about religion. And they . . . ; it carries on. So sort of like the more people go to church now the bigger the churches are got to be. The more people are inclined to go to church because sort of like church is a good place. It's where you learn morality. It's where you learn how to be sort of like conscientious, conscious in the way that you live your life.

And so for me firstly church is a good thing to go to. And I wish that more people went there. The only problem is; I mean sort of like, the church I go to; they couldn't build it as big as they wanted to. But that was for a reason. So that they do more services. They get more people. They pack their church out every Sunday. So they do three services in a day. They do two in the morning and one in the evening. The LC—it is always packed. And there have sort of like; they have two services in a day or three services in a day, early morning, late morning, and then they do one in the evening for teenagers where they just sit down on the floor. So sort of like a lot of younger people are going to church nowadays. So they get to sort of like respect each other. It is all about respect, respecting people and having God in your life to lead you in a good way. And sort of like not have an outside influence. The outside influence is governed by the people or the church or the church leaders. Whatever the church leader decides to use in his sermon reflects on the attitude of the people that are going to church. So I think the church should be bigger. And more people should go. And I wished that it happened more in my life. So that in my life I would have had more guidelines; I would have learned; I would have been able to express the way that I've been bullied. I would have had more support than I did from my mum and dad; through church rather than my mum and dad. Because, my mum and dad had their own problems. And my mum and dad might have had their ways of dealing with their life; with postnatal depression, sort of like in the 60s it wasn't really dealt with properly. So sort of like church would have been a better thing for them. And would have helped my mum out. But now you know my mum and my dad; they didn't really interact with people. They didn't have a lot of friends. They didn't teach me how to interact with people which it all had an on-going reflection of the way my life turned out. That's it, pretty much.

I: What about the drink? When did you start drinking? And how did it develop? And what impact did it have on your life?

A: Drinking: I started drinking when I was about 15. I started smoking cannabis or hash, as it was called then, at the age of 15. But I used

Appendices

that as, sort of like, a way of being accepted into a certain group. And it just built and built and built. And I was sort of like going to work. I was smoking hash. And sort of like, that was accepted as long as I've done my work. And then that job ended and then I started doing . . . . I met a woman in a small town (ST, name substituted throughout the transcript due to confidentiality). I was sort of like, I was hanging at the door next door. We were just chatting and that would be it. And sort of like, next thing we went out for a drink. And then we had: two nights we went out having a drink. So drink and drugs coming to my life at the age of 15, and they continued through my life all the way until 43–44. I've been away to a rehab. But sort of like, come a sunny day—it's a sunny day. So sort of like, I messed up the rehab.

This is the longest period since I've been in the other hostel for homeless (OHH, name substituted throughout the transcript due to confidentiality). That's sort of like, I've been abstinent. I've had little blips, little lapses. I've had one lapse on smoking which I'm still sort of like; I've got a pee test on the 25th of this month. I mean I had a pee test yesterday and sort of like there was a glimmer of a line. I should have two solid lines by the 25th which will keep me in here into, sort of like, Christmas period. So alcohol has always brought me; it has been a way of escaping reality because sort of like I didn't like reality. I hated reality. I hated my life. I hated everything that has gone on in my life. Because sort of like, the bullying had an effect on my life; it had effects on the certain part of my body. And sort of like—I don't feel whole.

And now I am going to Christian counselling. I haven't been to church for a few weeks, quite a few weeks. But sort of like they talk about me being an active member of Christianity. But sort of like because the alcohol has killed my legs I'm not an active person. So sort of like all I've got is me or my head; walking around on a pair of legs that don't work very well. So the alcohol has killed them. And I still get prayed for. I get my legs prayed for to sort of like make them better. But sort of like, the doctor says, my legs aren't gonna get any better. So sort of like, this is the way I am. And alcohol makes them worse. So sort of like that's why I stay away from alcohol and drugs. I can't do it. I can't smoke weed because of the house that I live in.

Even though that's the best antidepressant I can come up with, I can find. And God made marijuana. And he put it there for a reason. But I can't go down that route because it's for the government to say what's right and what's wrong. And if the government says it is wrong then that's it. But if the government turns around and says it is legal to sell alcohol which ruins so many people's lives. It takes them away from God. Because they got hangover on Sunday morning and sort of like they can't be bothered to get up and go to church.

So really if I had God in my life, earlier on in my life, then it would have made my life better. So sort of like it was my parents' fault for not being religious. It was my own fault for not being religious. But I didn't know what I would get out of church when I used to go to church when I was younger. It was all done, you know, sort of like hymns; and they were sung; it was, sort of like, done by organ. It didn't have a band. It didn't have so much cheerfulness, rejoicing. It wasn't as lively as it is now. So sort of like, church is taken a long time to come around to the way that it leads its worship. And sort of like, the sermons; they are put more in an easier language or terminology, whatever. It's easier to understand, what the preacher is preaching about. So sort of like, nowadays church is much more accessible to turn on with more people. Because sort of like, the ministers; they have a more relaxed way of teaching and people's problems are different now. So they look at different ways of teaching. And I don't think it should be preaching. I think it should be sharing. That's the way I see church. It's more of a sharing; a sharing of wisdom rather than a preaching, or telling someone they should live their life in this way. It's more of a sharing how life should be lived; how they should progress in life. I don't know whether that's done you any good.

I: I have some questions after that. But if you may tell me more about how bad was your alcohol addiction.

A: Pretty bad; pretty bad. I was drinking. In the end I was drinking, say 12 cans of K (cider), a bottle of vodka a day. I stopped smoking weed when I lived in a hostel for homeless (HH, name substituted throughout the transcript due to confidentiality). I used to smoke weed and I just used to get on with life. And sort of like, I've done many things within the HC. Everybody knew, not everybody, but sort of like, quite a lot of people knew that I smoked weed. And alcohol made me aggressive, nasty towards other people. Alcohol is the worst addiction that anyone can take on board. It's the worst substance. It's worse than heroin. It's worse than crack. I mean even though people who take heroin and crack; they end up going to prison. Then they get off the heroine, and then they come back out, and they do the same over, the same over. I've never been to prison through the alcohol. I've lost my license three times through the alcohol. I've lost countless numbers of jobs through the alcohol. Alcohol is being the worst thing that's ever been in my life.

Weed is one of the best things that's ever been in my life. But sort of like . . . . See, but I'm talking more about substance misuse and I glorify, I glorify weed. But sort of like, God was the one that created weed. He didn't create it to the strength that is grown nowadays. Because it's sort of like, technology gets better. And then with technology, people use the technology to make it stronger. It's like alcohol; once upon a time they can only make alcohol so strong. Now they can make it really, really strong. And so like people don't understand how much, how much they are drinking; how it affects your body; it's just a life-killing drug. And it's legally free. It's legally sold in the streets. I mean you can go to Tesco's 24 hours a day and buy alcohol. You can go in there and steal it. I've never stole alcohol. I begged for alcohol. I begged on the streets to get alcohol, to get drugs. Alcohol and drugs are not good. And sort of like, if more people go to church then they would understand more about drugs and alcohol. And they will learn more about God's grace to help you to get through your life. That's pretty much it, man.

I: Okay. Let's go to the questions, which if something hasn't been covered the questions will reveal it and then you can add to it. So the first question is: How do you perceive your conscience? What is conscience? How did it develop? How does it function? About conscience.

A: All right. My conscience: my conscience; it tells me what's right and what's wrong. I knew that when I was drinking and driving my conscience would tell me that it was wrong. But sort of like, my addiction to alcohol; it outweigh my conscience. It's sort of like, my conscience didn't kick in. It should have said: "No." But my brain said: "Yes." So sort of like, that's why I was drinking and driving. And every time I would go to court for drink driving then my conscience kicks in even more. And then I've never broke the law while I was under a ban. So my conscience comes through. But sort of like, if my conscience has worked properly in the first place I would have never drunk and drove. So sort of like, I would have kept my license. I haven't had my license for 10 years now. And I can't trust myself to get my license back because I would go drink driving again. So there is no point of me having a licence because my conscience wouldn't stop me from drink driving. That's that one.

I: Okay. Next one is: How did you develop alcohol addiction? You spoke already about this but if you want to add anything about it. What is alcohol addiction? When did you realise that you have been addicted to alcohol? How did you try to manage your alcohol addiction?

A: For many years I didn't; I didn't try to control it. I used to wake up in the morning. I drive to an off-licence—I drink. I'd buy some cans of beer. I'd drink them on the way to work. When I've got to work I do my work; tea-time comes; I used to go to the off-licence to buy a couple of cans; go back, had my sandwiches, smoke a joint, drink a couple of cans and go back to work. And then I'd do the same at dinnertime. I'd do the same at tea-time. Then I'd buy more alcohol on my way home from work because I was carpenter, I earned good money. So I could afford to drink. And sort of like, my reasons for drinking were to escape the away I felt about my life.

And now I can't do that because of the house that I live in; the rules; and sort of like I keep the rules. So sort of like, alcohol has been taken out of my life through the place where I'm living, pretty much. If I could drink which I have done since I've been in this house; which they found out about and sort of like I am on the last, my last warnings of being in this house. If I drink again then I am gonna lose my bed. I've been caught once for smoking marijuana. And they understand why I smoked marijuana but sort of like it's not tolerated. So sort of like, that's not in my life anymore. I would not do it because I would not lose my accommodation, the people that are around me, the people that care for me.

And they all are religious. Everyone believes in God. And they are trying to help me to find God. So sort of like, I try not to do anything wrong because I believe; I believe in what they believe in. I believe in God, but sort of like, I just don't feel it as much as they know it. And that's why I persevere and persevere. And sort of like, I'm trying to get him in my life. I'm trying to let him in. But sort of like, it's my old ways of dealing with life; I think God might have the hump with me because I'm still letting them; influences influence the way that I feel. So sort of like, it's just letting go of them; it's letting go of those old influences that will help me towards having faith in God.

I: Okay. The third question is: What were your moral views before your moral, spiritual, and/or religious transformation? What is morality? How did you deal with moral dilemmas? How much did morality matter for you? You already mentioned it but if you want to add anything about it. So we're talking before your moral, spiritual, and/or religious transformation.

A: The spiritual transformation is still happening.

I: In terms of morality. What were your views of morality before that?

A: I've always believed in sort of like: treat others the way you want to be treated; respect other's points of view. But when alcohol was in my life then I didn't have very good morals. But now I've got good morals. I've got good moral understanding. I respect other people's views. And I'm quite good at morals. So sort of like; but that's only because of the people that I've lived with. But I've always had good morals. I've always treated people the way they treated me. So it's sort of like, it's mutual respect. So sort of like, I've always been a moral. I've always had respect for people. I've always treated people the way they should be treated. And I expect to be treated the same way. So sort of like, that's all I can say on morals. It's pretty much: treat people the way you want to be treated yourself.

I: Do you see any difference then; as you said when you were drinking you didn't have good morals. Do you see any difference between your moral understanding when you were drinking and now when you're not drinking? Is there any difference?

A: Morals go out of the window when you're drinking because the alcohol overtakes the way that you feel; the way that you act towards people. Alcohol impairs the way you think. And sort of like, it affects you in such a way; at first you start drinking and sort of like, you're all right. And then you drink a little bit more and it gets a little bit worse; then sort of like, you drink more; and it depends on what sort of drink you're drinking as well. But sort of like, the more you drink the worse you get. And sort of like, you don't care about what people think. You don't care about what they believe. Your inhibitions are gone. It's sort of like, you treat people terribly. So sort of like, drink is the worst drug because, sort of like, you don't have respect. You lose your respect for people. You lose respect for yourself. That's all I can say on that one.

I: Okay Alex. The fourth one: Did you practice spirituality before your moral, spiritual, and/or religious transformation? What is spirituality? How did you practice spirituality? How much did spirituality matter for you? You already mentioned a few things about this.

A: Yeah.

I: Do you want to add anything?

A: No. All right.

I: Okay. The next one is: Did you practice religion before your moral, spiritual, and/or religious transformation? What is religiousness? How did you practice religion? Did you have religious affiliation? How much did religion matter for you? You already mentioned about this in relation to your past; anything to add about this?

A: When I've got kicked out of the ST or the relationship that I was in, there was no spirituality in there whatsoever. But since I've been around the HC spirituality has come into my life, and I've tried, and I've tried but unfortunately alcohol keeps on coming into my life as well. When I was living in the STHH; I lived in there, and sort of like I had 28 days in, and I had 28 days out, 28 days in, 28 days out. And sort of like when I was in there I was going to church, I was going to the LC even when I was living on the streets. So sort of like, I was living under a bridge down Tesco's. I still went to church on the Sunday to sort of like trying to grasp some sort of spirituality that would take me away from the drinking. But because where I was living it was always sort of like: it would be cold, it would be damp, it would be . . . ; it is sort of like . . . : How do I get to sleep at night? The easiest way to get to sleep at night is to drink. So sort of like, alcohol has always played a big part in my life; to sort of like, be able to survive those nights. And in sort of like, when I've got into the HH then sort of like, it got a little bit better because, sort of like, I wasn't drinking but I was smoking. So sort of like, it was always an outside influence that was taking me away from God. So sort of like, now not drinking, not smoking it takes me a little bit closer to God. Because sort of like, God can see that there is no outside influences.

And when I go to church, when I praise God, it is just me and God. And sort of like, things are getting better. The more he sees me as a person with no outside influences, he sees the person I am. And he understands what I've gone through but sort of like, there is no quick fix with God. It's sort of like, you can't just walk into the church and sort of like bang you're fixed. You have to keep doing it, keep practising, keep going, keep going, keep going. And sort of like, you build up friendships within church, which saying it to you now it makes me feel that I should go to church more, then build up these friendships within church. So sort of like, this Sunday I will be going to church, which is good. So sort of like, you coming down and asking me these questions are actually persuading me towards church. So "the proof is in the pudding." The more you talk about it the more it brings it to want that you got to put more in. The more you put in the more you get back. But it's sort of like, it's just building that relationship. And sort of like, I think it can get better.

I: Thank you. Next question: Did you experience moral, spiritual, and/or religious transformation? How did you experience this transformation? When did you experience this transformation? May you identify anyone who played any influential role in the process? How much has this transformation changed your life?

A: I would say living in the OHH has brought it to me more than when I lived in the HH. Even though, sort of like, I had lovely people around me. I had Roger; I had Rebecca; I had you around me but sort of like, not as much because Rebecca was my key worker. But sort of like, I feel that; I went to the LC which I think was too big a church for me. Where is now I go to the . . . (name omitted due to confidentiality) church which is a smaller church. But sort of like, after I got kicked out of the HH I went to live in my own place. And sort of like, my drinking got worse because, sort of like, the place I was living was horrible. And sort of like, it affected my legs; which through alcohol has killed my legs. So sort of like, then coming into the OHH, and sort of like I've been stronger off the drink and the weed. And now is the time to put more into church but sort of like, is feeling bad about myself, about my legs, not being out to be as active as I can; alcohol has killed me. But I've got a little bit of life left in me and sort of like, I've got to put more of that into going to church. So sort of like, the OHH has done me a favour.

I: Next one is seven: What was the impact of your transformation on your life? Compare your morality, spirituality, and religiousness before and after the transformation. How did the transformation impact your understanding of morality, spirituality, and religion, and their role in your life? How much did morality, spirituality, and religion matter for you after your transformation?

A: The transformation hasn't quite happened yet. It is still on-going. So sort of like, I know God is good but it's still in progress, work in progress. So sort of like, that's why I say that I should go to church more. And I should get more involved with the people in church which will give more of a transformation. So I got to put more into it.

I: Okay, number eight: What was the impact of your moral, spiritual, and/or religious transformation on your conscience? Compare your conscience before and after the transformation. How did the transformation impact your conscientious behaviour? How much did the voice of your conscience matter for you after your transformation?

A: So having this interview is giving a little bit more; is giving a little bit more substance to the transformation. It's telling me to go to church. It's telling me to build on; it's because the transformation hasn't happened yet. So sort of like, me doing this interview is sort of like, at first I looked at the questions and sort of like, "I can't see it," "I can see it." But sort of like, the more we go through the questions the more I feel that I should go to church to find that transformation; to actually say that God makes a difference in my life. Even though all the people that work within the house are religious, and they go to church, and they believe in God one hundred percent. I would say: "I would be 70–75 percent." So sort of like, I've got a little bit so down. So the more I go to church the more my belief would get greater and the transformation will work.

I: Okay. Thank you Alex. Number nine: What was the impact of your transformed conscience . . . . You said it's in progress. So we can interpret it as in progress, can't we, the transformation? What was the impact of your transformed conscience on your recovery from alcohol addiction? Compare your recovery before and after the transformation. How did your transformed conscience impact your recovery from alcohol addiction? What is the role of your transformed conscience in the maintenance of your abstinence? May you identify anyone who played any influential role in the process?

A: Deborah, Allan, Susan, Henry, you, everyone plays a part in my transformation. Living in the house; living under the rules of the house; they all are playing part in that. Because it stops me, sort of like, going back to drink; my legs, everything—drinking just doesn't do it for me. Smoking doesn't do it for me. So sort of like, my transformation would only work through God. So that backs up the reason why I should go to church; why I should pray to God; and why I should pray to have a personal relationship with God outside of church when I'm going to bed; the things that I read; the people I talk to; the people I associate with. Not going back to the people that, sort of like, take me the wrong way; mixing with people that take me the right way.

I: Okay. Thank you Alex. Okay, number ten: May you share your future plans related to your recovery? You already mentioned a few things but if you want to add anything. What is the role of morality, spirituality, and/or religion in them? What is the role of your transformed conscience in them? Do you plan to share your experience with others who need help in recovery from alcohol addiction?

A: Without a doubt! But I would say to him; I mean there was a young lad here, Ian. So sort of like, he didn't believe in God. And I said to him: "Go to church." There are a lot of people I have said to: "Go to church. Go to the . . . (name omitted due to confidentiality) church. It's really a nice church. So sort of like, it would have an impact on your life. You will find a way out away from the alcohol. Because sort of like, it's mixing with people that have got good morals that will take you away from your alcohol addiction or drug addiction." And I've spoken to other people that don't live within the HC. That sort of like, find that they have got nothing to do in a daytime, or they've got nothing to do in the weekends. If they go to church then they will find people that will help them to stay away from the alcohol and drugs. So, yeah, it is working in my life. But sort of like, God is working in my life. I'm just passing on the Word of God and how it works in your life. So that's the answer to that question.

I: Thank you. The last one: May you formulate the main theme of your life story? What is the place of alcohol addiction in your life story? What is the place of conscience in your story? What is the place of morality, spirituality, and/or religiousness in your story? What is the place of your moral, spiritual, and/or religious transformation in your story? The main theme.

A: The main; the main thing is substance misuse doesn't do you "no favours." It's living in reality but sort of like, giving God the place that he deserves to be within your life. Make sure that you keep him close at hand and think of him every time that you feel that you're gonna slip, have a lapse, relapse, go back to, sort of like, your old ways of dealing with life. Keep strong and keep pursuing God because sooner or later God is gonna come in your life. Pretty much that would be it.

I: Okay. Thank you Alex. This is the end of the interview with Alex at 11:08.

Ben (2011). Personal interview (Conscience in recovery from alcohol addiction), 15 November.

Interviewer (I): I'm recording and this is an interview with Ben taking place on 15th of 11th—1:20. And the guidelines for your story are the following: Structure your life story in chapters. Think about their names, summaries, and progressive links. Without interfering with the genuine character of the story can you identify the role of the following topics in your life narrative: conscience; alcohol addiction; morality; spirituality; religiousness; moral reformation; spiritual transformation; religious conversion and/or affiliation; the relationship between morality, spirituality, religiousness, and conscience, and recovery from alcohol addiction. How will you summarise each of these chapters? What progressive links will you make between these chapters? These same, what I read here, guidelines are here. So I will put them here, just if you would like to have a reference there. And basically feel free to develop your story.

Ben (B): All right. As far as I see it, my alcohol addiction started in the mid-90s. Would you like me to go back earlier than that with my life history?

I: If you feel that it is important for the story please, yeah.

B: For my career after school I went to a hotel college. I went through a hotel management, "...". (name omitted due to confidentiality). And I really enjoyed these works, working very hard. And it's something that I was having a social drink, a glass of wine with a meal. Or, maybe go out on a day off—a pint of beer during the day and that was my extent of my drinking. In the early 90s my father took ill at home in . . . (name omitted due to confidentiality) which was about 4 hours' drive from here. So actually I came into a situation where I was in the manager's position in a private company and nowhere to move. Either I would stay in the manager's position for years to come very comfortably, or I would make a change, and I would move home to be near my mother and look after my father's heart conditions. So I actually gained employment in . . . (name omitted due to confidentiality) with "Quick Save" food stores as a relief store manager. And so I moved back up, back to home. Initially this was good. I was there covering holiday relief, sickness, and opening new stores just where my area manager wanted me around . . . (name omitted due to confidentiality). And then it changed. Managers were getting suspended and sacked for pilfering, stealing. And I would get a call: "Meet me at midday in such a car park. Don't go in." And my area manager would go in with his team. Walk out the manager who they suspended pending an enquiry. And I

Appendices

would be handed the keys and the security code in the car park. And just to say that, you know: "Run these stores till I get in touch with you and I will find a replacement." So this was happening month after month of the similar occasions like this. So you're walking called into store. The staff would have just seen their manager suspended even fired. They knew he might have been stealing. So staff have probably been stealing themselves. They've been turning a blind eye. And for their intense purposes you are from head office and you're their worst enemy. And I wasn't married at the time. So I was living at home. I was getting at home after 14 hour days and covering a takeaway on the way home, living alone. And that's what turned me to go to the bottle in the evening for support just to blot out the pressures and harassments of the day. It just became an on-going habit.

I was always a home drinker not a pub drinker. But I would always have a drink at home. And it got into my mindset that no matter how hard the day is I would leave all these thoughts behind, or that wasn't necessarily true, and go home and just have a drink and forget about it all. And then restart a new morning again back at work, which I did. I always did keep working. But I was drinking through the evening, not through the night but through the evening, but regularly. And this is where my dependence on alcohol really took hold. But surprise me until recently when I realised that although I was in hotels, and I was doing stock controls for food and beverages, and I had access, I had entertainment allowances, I could have all the food and all the drink I could have had if I wanted, I didn't abuse that. I put that down for two reasons. One, I didn't need to. I wasn't under the pressures. And I enjoyed my work. And, also the other fact was that I kept myself extremely busy. Maybe working, I would be working six days a week, maybe plus coming in only one day off. So you didn't actually have a lot of time to actually think about yourself. But I think that in its own way has identified itself that I've grown or haven't grown used to a leisure time with myself which is to my detriment. And so that's why being alone or having too much free time is not healthy for me.

So this time for doing the "Quick Save" it did cause me problems with drink. It only cost me, well not to say only, it cost me my job when I lost my driving licence. So that really was quite a shock on that. I did actually drink . . . . Sorry! I did drive one day while I was banned because I had a store which was very hard to get to through public transport. And that day my car was recognised speeding and then they realised. And I was disqualified from driving. And I did receive two months prison sentence for that. That was okay. That was correct.

Appendices

Coming back from that I just did part-time jobs; and then got working with ". . ." (name omitted due to confidentiality). And I was able to work five days a week in that. And I was having a drink but not so heavily. So, I mean, I was still dependent on the bottle at that time. And, you know, I still was maintaining work but I don't know to what degree I could have really choose so much more. I was only really just studying myself and just going through emotions. And it wasn't a hard position. It was enough for comforting at that time.

But then I met Clare in a walking group. So in that time I was happy and happy spending time with Clare. And we got married. My drink, it did decline to a great degree. And, I would still, may be have a drink when I got back in. But then not drink through the evening so much. But this after we have been married for 10 years pressures started to build with my sister who was diagnosed with cancer. And she lived in this south coast English town (TSCET, name substituted throughout the transcript due to confidentiality) and not married and lived alone. And we were travelling down on weekends, down to TSCET to see her in between her chemotherapy trials. I found this very stressful. And I just tried to blot this out. I did go back to drinking heavily then in this time. And that also affected my health, physically and mentally. I was physically gone in a cycle of about six weeks of 18 hours of vomiting not feeling nauseous but just the vomiting.

I was also distancing my wife which I didn't realise at the time from that. She was coming and making some tea, and I would lose my appetite. And I didn't realise how much of a slap on the face for her that really was that I wouldn't eat. She would be working as well and she would cook something that she wouldn't cook for herself, a gentile amount, and then that food might have been snacked at latter on but this really was starting to annoy her. But she felt not comfortable in speaking to me about this. And so being an alcoholic I've never assumed that. I was bringing money into the house. We were running along fairly, I mean. I wasn't going out at night because I would have had a drink. So I didn't want people to, you know, being in a close proximity of people may be in our church home group. We still attended the church. And that was something that really Clare then didn't want to go out on her own for two reasons. One was, she didn't want to leave me alone for my own safety. And just so she could make sure that I was okay. But also she wanted not to go out on her own and people see. She didn't want to be labelled as an alcoholic's wife. And, to be out on her own. So she wanted to do kind of . . . . She didn't condone my drinking but she wanted to not support it either but just to cover it. So she did protect me in that and did become my carer.

But my physical health, I mean, I stopped cycling for over a year before coming to this residential rehabilitation centre (RRC, name substituted throughout the transcript due to confidentiality). And that really was just due to fatigue and muscle wastage. And just initially I had a mini stroke in February which the doctor said is just a warning. It's not necessarily to do with the alcohol: "Is just your lifestyle—not eating properly, not drinking properly, cholesterol levels, and just all that put into the whole equation and how that works out." If I hadn't decided to come to the RRC for that purpose—or I came for the purpose of my health really. Because I knew I had this repeated vomiting times which means I had no warning. So I had to actually have a bucket next to me in bed or the side of the chair or sometimes when I was working from home at the desk. You just feel a cough coming and it will just follow as a vomit. So I had no preparation for anything, not to run for a toilet or a sink or whatever. But in coming to the RRC I came for myself, for my physical self and it took nearly two months with counselling to work out why I really came to the RRC. I didn't appreciate, I mean, I was in denial about this and how much I hurt Clare. And, if I hadn't actually decided to come to the RRC she would have not divorced me but she would have found another house locally and she would have carried on working. And she would have stayed away till I've got myself right again, in using a bit of tough love. But I had no concept of that.

But through this programme now at the RRC I've been able to draw out my root issues of half blacked bonding with my father. He's been very busy. He was a doctor. He also worked in the main medical politics in this south east English city (TSEEC, name substituted throughout the transcript due to confidentiality) of . . . (name omitted due to confidentiality). And if the government had a medical situation there were asking for an official statement. And so, that was extra upon his operating lists in hospitals. So he was in TSEEC two days a week. So his home life was very minimal. But he was a very strong Christian man. And he held a job of treasurer at the church. So at the church, morning and evening, I had a Bible class in the afternoon called "Crusaders." So Sunday for me was a very busy day. Never really sitting down I'd had a quick lunch then I would be out in the afternoon; back for a quick tea then out for church in the evening and then back to school. I used to entertaining myself really and playing with other school friends who lived locally. And I didn't realise what sort of effect that would have on me, of insecurity and all these underlying issues, you know feeling not worthy. A big turning point for me, not that it turned me to alcohol initially, but my father changed my O level positions. I had a choice between geology and biology. And I chose geology because I enjoyed the walking and the outside life. I wasn't going to go into medicine like he was. I was gonna follow my grandmother actually into catering. And that was always agreed; the backing was there and that's why I went into a hotel school. But my father said: "Look, it would baffle me." My father said it would baffle him if I didn't do biology because he's a doctor and you know people would wonder. And so he actually changed that without my knowledge with my headmaster. I vowed secretly then that I wouldn't do well in biology. I passed my other exams in general science but biology—I gave no effort. And I actually got no support from my father. He actually wasn't there when I did my biological home works. But that's, I think, I was suppressing all that because I really enjoyed the hotel life in the hotel management and the structure and the busyness and late nights and early mornings, and I tried on it. I think it's only after that stopped, I changed my work cycle, and also pressures that all the suppressed issues were really just coming up. My weaknesses were coming through. And I was looking or didn't know how to control or how to seek support. So it's all, I think, I probably was, I mean, if I had a different career not hotels I could well have been an alcoholic earlier. So I think it was just waiting to, or I don't think is a gene that you get in the family. I just think it's something you absorb in your formative years and that is just waiting to see then how you react with everything. Basically I was weak to react and I chose the weaker option. That's why I chose alcohol as a strength from that. I'm rambling a bit, sorry. What else can I give you? That's put it in a nutshell really, on that.

What I remember about my childhood was, I didn't use to get punished even when I damaged my mother's car as a young teenager. A situation where my neighbour had MOT failure and I was just started junior course about 11. And this car couldn't be—is passed fixing. So he said: "Do you want this car to tinker on." I did enjoy tinkering. That's one way I used to amuse myself. And I was driving it up and down our drive soon enough to go forward and reverse. And that one time I was reversing it with using the wing mirror on the front of the car but not door mirrors. We didn't have door mirrors in those days. And I didn't see my mum's car. And I forgot that it was parked there and just bashed straight into it. And this sort of old, solid car crumpled at the front by the headlamp beam. It didn't break the headlamp but it pushed it down. And my mother came out. She heard the bang. And she just said: "Oh, you know, you just wait until your father gets home. You just wait inside." My sister got back from school. And she was full of glee cause we always were in competition together. And she thought that I was gonna be "murdered" for it. My dad came back from work and he said: "Well," he looked at it and said to me: "I am not paying for that." And he went inside and we had tea together. And, you know, I still couldn't understand that. I realised that: "Well why should he pay for it?" But I thought there would be a consequence for that. But there wasn't a consequence. So it's all very strange.

Other situations like that: We would go away on a holiday. We went to a beach mission in North Wales. It would be for two weeks. So far he actually drives us down during the first weekend. And we'd settle into hotel. And then he'd go back to work during the week. And then he'd come back in the weekend to spend the weekend with us. And then he'd go back for the second week. And then he'd come back to take us home. We thought that, you know, he got a bit of free time at home working and playing golf. So he just left my mother and my sister and myself for the two weeks, half of our main holydays. We didn't appreciate that at the time. But this has had an effect. And something that my father still doesn't accept. I thought he would do as a medical man but no, he doesn't. So I don't go down that line anymore. But I'm going through forgiveness to cleanse myself of that. So we just helped him, obviously. I'm gonna go and see him and have a meal with them this weekend when I go back home. So that was a big stumbling block.

I have hurt him as well because they are teetotal. But I'm not sure whether it's that because I shielded them from my drinking. And when I saw them I've made sure that I haven't been drinking the night before. So there is no alcohol around, or you weren't under the influence of alcohol. You know, it became as a shock when I announced that I was going to this rehab. And I think that was also a general shock for them in the family, really that, you know, their son has failed. He has become an alcoholic. That you know it's . . . . If I hadn't decided to come to this rehab I don't know where my life would have gone. I did go to a church and was involved in certain parts in issuing weekly notices. So it's very strange that I can't actually call a church or church family as accountable because I actually fooled them, really, or fooled 95 percent of them. So they know now but at the time a lot of them didn't know. So it was really quite strange that, you know, you can be very devious, manipulative all these different trades.

Sometimes I do strange with words with having this mini stroke. I always get a bit jumbled.

So, how to go through the conscience, alcohol, and addiction? My conscience really was about: I knew what's wrong and I hid it from people but it didn't stop me drinking. It was my form of support in that. And my home, and to some get in the cupboard there, having a bottle in the cupboard there was a form of support. And that was, I knew it would be there, and so when I arrived home after work—that was great as a security. Although I knew it wasn't the way to handle it was great for the moment, temporarily.

Morality: I didn't have any sexual morality or that. And I didn't need to steal to fund my drinking. So as morally I did, well, lie to my church and hide the fact from it. And I just had to work with that, lying, and that week after week. So yes, I mean, I do put my hand up to that. And hiding it from my parents. And my wife allowed me to drink; sounds awful to say a little bit, maybe one or two drinks a night, thinking that that wasn't a problem. Which I suppose initially probably wouldn't be a problem but with my history, and when extra pressures came on, that's what caused me to drink more again and to relapse again. And that's really what put the pressure on Clare. I had to almost try and hide the extra drinks I was having from Clare. So it did make you a liar, you know, this devious on that. But I think in her heart she knew but she didn't want to upset anything—or how to approach it, or I wouldn't be in a fit state for her to discuss anything, to talk about it. So she has a lot of guilt at the moment.

Spirituality: I was a Christian. And I'm a Christian now. I don't think I ever stopped being a Christian. But when I turned to alcohol for my support to blot out my days when I was working with "Quick Save" I made alcohol my idol, my number one idol. And so that replaced God as my idol. And so I thought more of alcohol that I did of God at that time. So I walked away from God at that time. And I felt that alcohol to me was more important, in having this physical sensation on that. Thankfully now which I've been able to come back and being forgiven by God and with the power of Holy Spirit, and I'm really enjoying my life now. And it's strange to build a confidence of speaking to people and not with a quiet voice which used to speak with shallow breaths in case there was any alcohol lingering on your breath. You wouldn't have made conversation with people. And I've just noticed now, just this last week since I've moved to the second stage and to the . . . (name omitted due to confidentiality) here that certain members of staff have said: "Oh well we would like to interview you for an update in

Appendices

counselling." I said: "That's fine." You know: "Can you do tomorrow morning." I said: "No. I'm working tomorrow morning." "Oh yeah that's right." "Can you do this morning?" And I said: "Oh, I've got to see my counsellor until so and so and be free after 11 o'clock." And he said: "Well, perhaps that would be convenient for me but can we meet at teatime." And initially I should have turned my back because normally if I was going back to my old self I wouldn't arrange an afternoon meeting cause I knew that I would have had a drink by then. Something that cut me out of the social life in the evenings, and having no meetings, and keep myself working alone on the afternoon. Although I didn't drink at work I would make sure I would be able to finish work early or work from home which I was able to do. It was just quite strange to have that feeling of: "Why am I worried about having an afternoon meeting. I've got this time now free."

I've got it just now—rethink who I am, and what I do with my thoughts, and how I act on my thoughts. I kind of say to my wife: "I mean drinking is like a temptation and no one can swap temptation. But that's what you do with temptation. That is a sin if you act on that temptation. If you reject the temptation, and hit it back, you know, then there is no sin there." And the thought of drinking, yes, I would always gonna think of drinking. The craving, that's become less and less. And my triggers are really into the worry side of things and how my feelings are more than passing a pub. Or I do have to control myself in a supermarket where you see the beer or the bottles on sale and just not putting one in the basket. And I just bypass of that. But that's controllable, I know that. I would not buy anymore beer or alcohol. But just trying to have like a firewall for all these thoughts that come in. So like an email coming in and you get these junk mails. So here's the firewall. Yes, you had it. It is received, it is recognised as junk, as not a good thought and gets rejected. And that's the way I'm working at the moment. I try to move on from the fact that I'm leaving the RRC and not having that big stick over your head with having that you can be tested any time. I don't think that's a true way to say: "Oh. I haven't done a drink for eight months." Because, you know, I can be tested any time. But because once I move out of here I won't have anybody testing you, you know, with the breathalyser. As I didn't touch drugs but only drink is my problem. So I've got to really get my own mindthought about my own attitudes of coping with stress and worry. And free time is something, something that at the moment since I moved into the second stage of the residential rehabilitation programme (SSRRP, name substituted due to confidentiality) I'm working three days a week. I would be able to come back home in the afternoon. And I like to have some free time there. You always twirling your thumbs and thinking: "What could I be doing, or what should I be doing, or shouldn't I just be relaxing?" And you feel guilty in that because you know that: "I don't want to have a drink which means I am thinking about drinking in a reverse way." So it's not me fighting a craving for a drink but is just trying to find something to occupy my mind and my time in that.

Religiousness: I have got into a local church here now. And I have given my life. I did give my life to the Lord as a Christian. And I have come back walking in that way now although I did stray and turn my back on the Lord. I don't think it cuts you off from being a Christian but he will if you knock on the door and say: "Look, please forgive me." He has opened that door for me. And he says: "Come back in. Come back into the family." I find a real warmth in that. I find it easier moving back into the church because I am married, in my early 50s and my wife also wants to join in with the church. When she comes down, she comes down once a month, and people have been keen primarily to talk about issues about alcohol not necessary directly with me but just how I've treated Clare. But they want to relate this to a personal level with them which they haven't discussed with anybody not even the church leaders. That they would have someone in their family, and they are wondering how to react and what's best to do in that. And also just to find someone to talk to, talk to quietly, who can understand what they're going through because very few people really understand. My wife has had counselling provided by work through the NHS. And that was really a total turn off for my wife. It left her more upset than . . . ; or more negative than positive. And even church members who don't understand addiction, don't really understand the root causes of addiction, that is not just going for a bottle. Addiction is not just leaving the bottle alone and just not drinking. You have to deal with the root issues. And that is very hard to find people who actually understand that. And Clare is struggling with that at the moment even in her own church. And it's surprising the church I'm going to at the moment, which I am actually doing my volunteer work at, six different people have actually come up to me about family issues they have and just not asking me for guidance but just to come alongside with a bit of empathy. And so, they know they can come and speak confidentially, quietly to me about that. It is actually tremendous. I'm not putting myself there as a counsellor in no way but they actually pulled me out cause they know, I am coming from the RRC,

I've had a problem. It does give me a bit of encouragement that they can see a difference that, you know.

I can explain my past actions and that. Now I realise about how my past actions have affected my life, affected Clare's life, and how detrimental that has been. We're now rebuilding our marriage. And so it's getting quite exciting really. We're going through almost like a courting stage again. Because I must admit that although I was drinking carefully I was drinking throughout our marriage. So Clare hasn't really known a 100 percent of Ben. She might have known a good deal of Ben. But now she's going back a 100 percent of Ben, alcohol free plus someone who more understands his own inner self which I never did before. Before I was able to keep busy and bounce around and go from job to job in my progression of employment. So it's quite strange really that sometimes when we go home quietly she would ask me about something to explain it to her. And she is a senior physiotherapist. So she has a medical knowledge. But she just needs understanding of the inner person. She wants to come alongside. Because, with our groups here, in our time here, in our thought processes we had the training to go in a straight line. And she doesn't want to be drawing away and just want to becoming in staying in tandem, staying in contact with that. But that is working for me at the moment. And that's a real blessing.

Moral Reformation: Well I suppose my main moral issues were lying to people, hiding, deceit on that of my drinking, and hiding. That must be the effects and the signs of alcohol: that be a smell, slurred, speech. Do we forming this? I really just had to draw a line under my past life. I can't change my past life but is to bury it and to move ahead, and look for guidance of how I am going to rebuild my life. But now not actually hide or have any hidden cupboards. So that I'm not actually trying to hide any secrets which I think will in turn bring me all into a more confident person. While I was in the hotels I used to be quite confident. I used to be in massive ceremonies, at functions. I used to be able to, you know, keep teams of people going, be the banqueting or be the house-keepings or whatever site in the hotel laundries or be the leisure. But with me drawing into myself I found I've really been digging a hole and just getting deeper and deeper. And the only way out is just to get a ladder which I've used as Jesus, the Holy Spirit to climb out of this hole and to fill the hole and to walk away. And you never forget that hole. You don't forget that if you are digging a hole you would get dirty under the fingernails. So that's still would be there. But it wouldn't be there to attack you. You say: "Oh yes but

I've passed that. And now I've stepped on from that," so really just having a new life. That's coming through.

That leads into the spiritual transformation really or having a new life in Jesus. And that has really; it has blessed me, and the warmth I've got at this church. People have been genuinely . . . ; they have been cautious; they haven't had known what to expect. They have had some not so good experiences with some residents or ex-residents from here. But each resident is totally individual. And I just thank them for their honesty of taking me at my face value. And the more I am with them the more they can see who I am. I taught myself into volunteer's job there because . . . . I suppose it is a bit manipulative because it is something I knew I can do. But it wasn't something that I used to be doing. But it means I could, I was doing practical work there in facilities, maintenance. I was doing a bit of admin. And they have a coffee shop there as well just to, partially to help. But basically if someone needs a hand doing anything they are there to do it really. I'm very pleased that the minister or one of the ministers there took a trust in me to offer me this volunteer position for 18 weeks not knowing what he was going to get. He knew me from the RRC coming here once a month and from Sundays. But that's not really knowing the real Ben. But now he's saying, you know he said: "You kind of undersold yourself." But I wanted to really use the volunteer's time to prove that I can actually get myself up, breakfast, wash, shave, out to work 3:30 in the morning, cycle seven miles down to this church. Then do a day's work and cycled back and get tea, and then go out to different groups in the evening, evenings and weekends are free. And that's one aspect I am still working on towards, you can actually prove that I can get myself back or to get back into full-time employment. So I am really glad that people don't bear, what's that word, like a memory of my past life. That they're happy to start with clean slate as I am starting with a clean slate. And we're moving ahead afresh. So spiritually I see it as an opening, and it's really just trying to let the front waters in, and not make myself defensive. I do feel myself growing in that way bit by bit. I've probably covered religious conversation, affiliation.

Religious conversation and affiliation: well I do like to go to the church. And I do like to go to the studies. And I do want to hear more about what I've lost in hiding myself from God in that. So, yes, I am really putting myself open for this now. Just to make myself available to take on board, you know, Jesus and what he's saying to me and guide me and lead me. Because I can make so many decisions but I got to make sure they are the right decisions. And with God's righteousness, so I need to put those decisions before God and find, you know, which ways are opening, which are good ways, which, you know, are maybe not so good ways. And I just pray daily that, you know, God's gonna be a light to my path. But this light would be a torch in my hand, so I can actually see only a little bit ahead of me every day. So you don't know you got reached the junction but you can just see where these bends are, and just follow the path bit by bit, and just find your way through. It tickles me about that. As in Proverbs three, verse five or something it says: "he will make your path straight." And going back, that's you think: "Oh, path straight." You know we are on a straight line on a motorway. But if you look at different or the original translation coming through it's: "he will direct your paths." So he will actually show you which pathway to go on that. There is a better translation I find that that's what it is showing: "We don't know the best way, and we don't just keep heading straight forward and just ignoring all the side routes; that's all the side roads on that." But it is having an effect on me at the moment.

"The relationship between morality, spirituality, religiousness, conscience, and recovery." These are all really blending in together for me. We might have touched on a few of these. But I think it is giving me a freedom to be my natural self which I'm not sure what my natural self is now. I had so long, nearly 20 years of drinking, handled drinking heavily that's nearly half of my lifetime. And although I have been working throughout that period of time I've also been planning of how I can drink around my work and plan, plan, plan, and also shield, hide, hide behind masks. And people haven't got to know the real me. They only got to know the Ben that Ben wants to let them have a look at. So now it's sort of if I am not open for to be attacked, as in saying attacked that means I am going to be attacked by the devil. I know he is still out there constantly trying to get me back. But I'm not going to be attacked by people through my insecurity at the moment. They're trying to comfort me and strengthen me and build-up muscle on my bones. And so they are keen to accept the open Ben. And just that I've really come with all left behind, my all trades, and come with very little just what I want to rebuild, and give what I can at the moment. And then built on what I can and my knowledge, my skills, my DLY. You know I find that really encouraging. And I do feel my confidence coming back a bit. But it's a bit a slow process. It's always something you felt second-class and always hiding under a shadow. And it's now you are walking in a bright light, and it's so bright, and the shadow is so small; it's under your feet and you cannot hide there. And, you know, that is so confirming. It's so giving you so much confidence and that. Here I am. This is what I do. Yes, I will do my best. And, you know, I do see it working.

How I summarise these chapters. I can see my life going through of having a bit of a lonely childhood, not having a strong bond to the father. But my father never did any ill to me and always wanted the best for me. And within reason would always . . . , yes, he would buy things for me as during special times when that time was right for a present. Yes he would, I mean. There's never been any negative approach from my father at all on that. But then growing through I didn't realise how much I have suppressed my feelings, my core issues. And that even took me nearly eight weeks in the RRC to draw them out from inside me. And something that has been stacked in my subconscious and I haven't really thought of that, I haven't even tried to think about it. And it's even that; it is something that I haven't emotionally searched out. I never thought, I never presumed that I had a problem, had a weakness with that. So it has been very enlightening. Then you can now actually work out why you do things. And so it's really just to reconstruct, remould my lifestyle on that.

Progressive links between: I think from going from chapter to chapter, from stage to stage I've thought I had a bit of lonely childhood, but growing through, but that gave me more a desire to perform, to work, and to achieve in employment. And I was able to achieve all this myself. Well, with the blessing of my parents. But it was a natural way to go through, go ahead. So I was very kind of, very pleased with myself. The way I was actually able to achieve employment and working around the country and able to work in private hotels. So in each stage I wanted to get to move on the ladder to a new stage. I had to really move to a new job, to a new position. For that really all was quite sustaining but in the false sense of security really that I was striving to do better and better at work and put all my eggs in one basket. So I wasn't actually spending much time with myself. Now what this goes down to: now I'm going to have to spend more time to get to know myself and with Clare and with being comfortable and finding new leisures and pursuits; be it reading, I mean. There is nothing wrong in a bit of television, but being selective and not being just totally television all night just watching having everything just thrown at you and just watching over. But it is the highlight of the fact that once I changed then my weaknesses really came out and my insecurity and my worries and my low self-worth, and that I wasn't strong enough to either go to my parents, birth parents, and talk things out. I didn't feel confidence in that, which I think has come around through from the childhood. And I also then turn my back on God whom I did know. And I just used this alcohol, just to have my idol, my suppressant. And I don't condone it now but it did have an effect which, you know, suppressing everything but in that way I still had to pay the consequences now for that. And for I do believe that now at this stage I have the choice now to live a clean life. Thankfully I haven't damaged my body internally. And so now I've got a clean sheet to go ahead. Use my history of my life skills and work out which are the good skills and which are the negative skills which is very important really cause I think I have been very naughty, very devious, and lying to a lot of people, deceiving a lot of people. So I think to understand this, and just to make myself aware of what I am doing, and just analyse my life. And I am really quite excited now of what is ahead. I don't know where I'm going to live, where I'm going to relocate after here. I'm not doing that just to people please as in Clare. But the household holds so many not bad memories but so many memories of "Ben carries away" and "how I walked through the door." She sees such a change. She thinks it should be a time for change. I know we should move forward together. So I'm just stepping into a new area now just wanting to bring with me my positive skills and now my more understanding of myself and of my issues. And how I can just adapt these and get back into society and full-time employment and back into my marriage.

I: Thank you for the story. Please try to cover the questions as much as they have been left uncovered. You don't need to add anything if you feel like you have covered it. So I will go through all the questions and then you think whether you need to add something. The first one is: How do you perceive your conscience? What is conscience? How did it develop? How does it function? Do you want to add anything in regards to conscience?

B: I think I've covered conscience really, you know. I've realised I've deceived a lot of people. And also deceived myself on that of hiding the drink and thinking: "I could drink and not be dependent on drink."

I: Second: How did you develop alcohol addiction? What is alcohol addiction? When did you realise that you have been addicted to alcohol? How did you try to manage your alcohol addiction? I think you pretty much covered all of these. Do you want to add anything?

B: No, yeah.

I: All right. The third one is: What were your moral views before your moral, spiritual, and/or religious transformation? What is morality? How did you deal with moral dilemmas? How much did morality matter for you? You spoke about morality. Do you want to add anything about morality?

Appendices

B: No, cause that's, I didn't go down to sexual immorality on that. So, no.

I: Okay. The fourth question is: Did you practice spirituality before your moral, spiritual, and/or religious transformation? What is spirituality? How did you practice spirituality? How much did spirituality matter for you? You mentioned it already that you were a Christian.

B: Yes I was a Christian before that. And yes I was quite an active Christian. I suppose one thing I didn't mention was that, it probably goes without saying, but in hotels you do have to work weekends occasionally. So I didn't have a regular Sunday out. And evenings sometimes were—you didn't have always time to go to different groups. So if I wasn't there I wasn't missed cause they would say: "Oh, Ben was working." But yes it upsets me that I did choose alcohol instead of God to be a support. And I do recognise before coming back that I did turn my back on God on that. But I have gone back to him through this door. He has opened a door for me.

I: All right, thank you Ben. Next question is: Did you practice religion before your moral, spiritual, and/or religious transformation? What is religiousness? How did you practice religion? Did you have religious affiliation? How much did religion matter for you? This has been covered more or less. Anything else to add to this?

B: No.

I: Okay. Did you experience moral, spiritual, and/or religious transformation? How did you experience this transformation? When did you experience this transformation? May you identify anyone who played any influential role in the process? How much has this transformation changed your life?

B: I suppose my transformation I put down to my counsellor here actually because I didn't realise where I was at. I didn't come here; although, I was an alcoholic I didn't come here thinking that I was an alcoholic. I came here for my ill health. I knew that alcohol wasn't helping me. But I didn't put the two together. So there is a term called "denial" which covers a lot of things. So it was actually: I put my counsellor high on that list for that. It was my pastor who had lived previously in this area who gave me a prayer letter, a newsletter from the RRC which he still gets. He said: "Have a look at this and see if this can help you. It may not help you." So he was the first opening. But the major opening was my counsellor just drawing out from my subconscious, my inner self so I can actually understand myself and then work or still in work, preparing myself. So yeah, that's my counsellor.

Appendices

I: The next question is: What was the impact of your transformation on your life? Compare your morality, spirituality, and religiousness before and after the transformation. How did the transformation impact your understanding of morality, spirituality, and religion, and their role in your life? How much did morality, spirituality, and religion matter for you after your transformation?

B: All right. My morality and my spirituality have been totally transformed since my recognition of my alcoholism. And it just really opened my eyes again after how far I've strayed and got away from God. And so coming back into God's presence for guidance and to cleanse my body of my past which I am not happy with but I cannot change my past. But we can change our future, or we can shape our future. So spirituality now is paramount for me. And into that comes morality—not lying to people or not deceiving people, not hiding from people which will give me a confidence to be available to speak with people. Thank you.

I: All right. Thank you. What was the impact of your moral, spiritual, and/or religious transformation on your conscience? Compare your conscience before and after the transformation. How did the transformation impact your conscientious behaviour? How much did the voice of your conscience matter for you after your transformation?

B: All right. My conscience. Before I didn't realise but I was walking around with a huge burden, like a huge sack on my back. And I was carrying that around everywhere I went. And it was like having a dark cloud over my head. And now after this transformation, now the sun is shining and the burden, the load has been lifted from me. So now actually I am able to concentrate just on the future way ahead. I'm free to look up instead of struggling, looking down, trudging along. So now I'm looking to start the sprint, start to jog, and start to sprint. Enjoy the fresh air and freedom.

I: Thank you Ben. Next one: What was the impact of your transformed conscience on your recovery from alcohol addiction? Compare your recovery before and after the transformation. How did your transformed conscience impact your recovery from alcohol addiction? What is the role of your transformed conscience in the maintenance of your abstinence? May you identify anyone who played any influential role in the process?

B: All right that's quite a question.

I: Some elements were covered but anything else which you would like . . . .

B: I think that does cover, I mean, what happened in my transformation. I mean, I must put my praise to my counsellor who through . . . ; as my counsellor is a Christian also, but he's there to try and help and guide but not push. But he doesn't tell you to do things. He will sometimes advise but he always draws out and works on whatever you tell him. And I am amazed what I actually would come out and tell him for my counselling session which I have no idea I was going to come up with. And how he can draw on certain emotions like when we talk about my father, that you know, these subconscious emotions arise which are not brought on consciously. So I'll put my counsellor there.

I: Two more questions. May you share your future plans related to your recovery? What is the role of morality, spirituality, and/or religion in them? What is the role of your transformed conscience in them? Do you plan to share your experience with others who need help in recovery from alcohol addiction?

B: All right. My aim is starting with a religion—yes. I would be continuing that. I'm glad that my new church knows that I've come through the RRC. And they know I have gone through the first stage and I am on the second stage. So they know where I'm at. But they know I'm not out of the woods yet. I'm still in recovery. And so that is good. But I will let them support me in that. And you know I will; I'm keen to join in all groups that I can there, just with learning. In my job at the moment I work with two ministers there. And just to see how human they are during the week. And just having little chats. And we get so much words of wisdom just over a cup of coffee. Obviously I mentioned about my conscience. I think we covered most of my conscience but yes my freedom. And that's really lifted my burden.

I: Okay. The last question Ben is: May you formulate the main theme of your life story? What is the place of alcohol addiction in your story? What is the place of conscience in your story? What is the place of morality, spirituality, and/or religiousness in your story? What is the place of your moral, spiritual, and/or religious transformation in your story? The main theme.

B: I think just as a synopsis: Growing up I unknowingly absorbed in my formative years the lack of bonding with my father. So I was really feeling . . . . I didn't know what I felt then I just knew how to occupy myself. "Was I not special enough?" "Was I not good enough?" Low self-worth and all these coming through. I think once I—alcohol started once, well, became an issue; once I changed my career and moved into working in a new environment, living on my own, under pressure, and returning home on my own to an empty house, and just letting pressures overwhelm me. And I weakened and took alcohol obviously as the answer, not the correct answer but as the answer at that time. I now see how my past growing up and my issues have been inside of my subconscious, and how they come out and emotions, and emotions lead to feelings, and feelings need to be dealt with. And it is now for me to judge how I deal with my feelings. Not to supress them with alcohol but to take them to discuss with somebody. Or if they are minor feelings to take action, to do action force, to go and do something active, to break that thought pattern. You know, and also to speak to God and Jesus and with the power of the Holy Spirit to help me. I do appreciate I still have to take day by day, you know, and that would be hard, honest. But I'm confident. It's awful. I'm saying I'm confident that, you know, I will be strong but I just wonder if I got to stumble. But that's there, that's probably the devil there, always there prodding you, trying to see if there is a weakness. If there is a weakness he will try and prod it. I got my eyes on Jesus.

I: Thank you Ben. Now we will finish the interview at 2:33.

Jack (2011). Personal interview (Conscience in recovery from alcohol addiction), 20 November.

Interviewer (I): Okay, I am recording now. This starts the interview with Jack on the 20th of the 11th—3:48. And the instructions I want to give you in regards to your story are: Structure your life story in chapters. Think about their names, summaries, and progressive links. Without interfering with the genuine character of the story can you identify the role of the following topics in your life narrative: conscience; alcohol addiction; morality; spirituality; religiousness; moral reformation; spiritual transformation; religious conversion and/or affiliation; the relationship between morality, spirituality, religiousness, and conscience, and recovery from alcohol addiction. How will you summarise each of these chapters? What progressive links will you make between these chapters? All these guidelines are here just for you as a reference. But feel free to develop your story.

Jack (J): Okay. Okay. Basically I'll just give testimony really.

I: Exactly, exactly.

J: My name is Jack. I come from my home country (MHC, name substituted throughout the transcript due to confidentiality). I come from a small village. It's one of these places where everybody knows everybody. And it was a nice place, you know, the area in which I lived in. I was very lucky, it was very nice. But for me it was all to do with life at home. You know the place in which I lived played no part. Home life for me as a kid, as a child was very, it was horrible, to be honest. My mother, she suffered from depression. Actually it was the result of my grandmother who died. And as a result of that, which was her mother, seems to be a part of my own mother died with her. And there what seemed to be a normal family that everybody else would have . . . . I had two brothers and we always enjoyed life with our family. But from that, and I think I must have been an around and about eight or nine years old. When my grandmother died a part of my mother died. So, therefore, any love that she had for us seemed to have just died with her. My mother suffered from depression. And as a result of this she would deal with her depression by—she would be quite violent. She would be quite, you know, just towards us. As kids we seemed to be the object that she would take her anger right on. You know, she would always tell us that she loved us. But when she is in this place when she's not doing so good, it was just mayhem really. As a nine-year-old boy you don't understand what depression is. As far as I was concerned this lady, this woman, my mother just didn't like us. She had a hatred for us. We were just a hindrance. We were just there as some form of like a punch bag really. And it was quite disturbing at times, to be honest. There were times things would be so violent when you couldn't go to school. You would be beaten so badly really that your . . . ; it was something that you couldn't even wear clothing. It would be too soar to touch your skin, you know. And she would do these things and then she would break down in tears. But for us as kids you know, it was very, very disturbing we wouldn't like quite. You could not go to the house and play because as far as she was concerned: "If you are in the house I can see what you're doing you can't get the blame for anything," therefore, she had peace of mind. But for us it was like prison. You know, we would watch our friends play at the window. You know, people would call to the door to see we would come out and stuff. And we would be sent to the door to say: "No." You know it was very embarrassing. It was a time of my life to be honest that it was just horrible. And I can remember at the age of about 11 I took a lot of pills. You know, even at that young age I didn't want to live anymore. You know my father, he had a bad heart. And he always had a lot of tablets and stuff around the house. And I remember just getting them all together putting them inside and just taking them. And whatever happens—happens. You know, and praise God, you know, nothing happened.

I grew up as being of one religious group (ORG, name substituted throughout the transcript due to confidentiality). We would have to go to Mass probably four–five days a week. My grandfather was a caretaker of the chapel. So, therefore, on the Sunday after the service we would clean the chapel. On the Saturday we would clean the chapel. We used to go over and ring the bells and stuff. You know we would always be involved around the chapel. More to do with the fact that my grandfather was a caretaker, which was good for me because I loved my grandfather. I loved being around with him rather than being at home. So looking after the church was like a means of getting out of the house. I can remember this continued through for me even throughout my school days.

You know it was very embarrassing, you now. We would always have the cheapest of . . . . You know, we would always have things. But you had the lower brand of everything. You know, you would get mocked a lot at school and stuff. And my defence in all of that would be to . . . ; I just became like a fighter, you know. Anybody that would say anything I'd too then would became quite violent because the way I was being treated, inside me there was a lot of anger and stuff. And I would have no interest in school. I would sit all day just looking at the window. But teachers would ask me a question and I would just give them the answer. And it was always that part of me that they said that I could do well. But I showed no interest. You know, I was very fearful and didn't know how to mix with people. And the only people that I tended to get along with were other angry people. And that seemed to be the people that I associated with. In school I was probably very lucky in a way. I would hang around in a group. And the group that I would hang around with nobody really gave us any bother. Because it was one of these things that, you know, if you know one person in the group then you know six or eight. And this continued all the way through my schooldays. Quite often we became like bullies, you know, within the school and stuff. I was getting attention. I was getting recognised. Not for anything good but you know I was getting recognised, you know. And I was liking it. I knew it was wrong but I liked all these things.

I remember probably at the age of 13 or 14; from the age of about 12 to 14 I used to run away from home a lot because there was no stability, there was no love in the house. I had two brothers and we all had split up really. Many went into care homes. And my younger brother, he went to ". . ." (name omitted due to confidentiality), like a prison sort of thing, because of his behaviours and stuff. But, for me for some reason I couldn't even get into a boy's home. I used to tell lies about some of the . . . . Even though the appearance I was getting was a lot, I used to try and make it sound worse. And still I could never for some reason get into a care home. So I was always the one that had to stay at home and be around that, you know, that atmosphere.

I think about the age of 16 or 17 I went to live with my grandfather. Things were just too much. And at that stage you know I left school. And that was experience for life—it was quiet at night. I was allowed to go down the town and be with the guys. And none of these things I didn't know how to control. So very, very quickly I would find myself getting into a lot of bother. It didn't matter what trouble could be brought to the door because I didn't live there no more. And for me because of the way I was treated through all these times and my father . . . . My father was a great man. Very quiet man he would never raise his voice. He would never lift his hand. He would just tell you he's upset, or he's annoyed with you. And just by talking to you in a nice way you would know he was upset. And you know you would feel it just as much. But the fact that he was so quiet he allowed things to continue. You know, it's almost as if he was afraid of my mum sort of thing. He would never let you disrespect her or raise your voice to her because he knew of her illness. "That's your mum and you don't disrespect your mum. No matter what she's still your mother." And that was his . . . . He would just stand by all night and day. But to me I just saw hatred.

Probably at age of about 17 or so I've begun working and things. And soon after I left my grandfather's house. And I went to live in a group, well in a house with three other people. It was a shared house. And these people were all involved in drugs. Like for me I wasn't really involved in drinking and haven't been involved in drugs because there was so much fear, you know. If you would to take a drink or even take a smoke and get caught you would get killed. You know, and we were even afraid to do something wrong. But I began drinking. The drinking at first was very, it was just drinking. But for some reason it allowed me to forget about stuff. You know I was able to relax. I was able to chill out a bit. I found myself then I would hold on to this drink. It wasn't everyday but just when I got too much, when I allowed things in my head to take control, I would take a drink and I would chill. And that's the way I was for a while. Some of the other people in the house were on other drugs. You know, some were taking heroin. Some were just smoking weed, you know, and taking LSD and all that sort of stuff. And I would be the sort of person, somebody said to me: "Try this." And I would try it. Cause, you know, with the way I was feeling, with the way my life was, you know, every day for me was so hard. You know, I just, every day I just relived all those horrible days. And you still have to go down the street and smile at people. And you still have to go to work. And you still have to do . . . . But inside I was, I was a mess. I was very false because I was always smiling at folks. But for me inside was just empty.

Soon after I was working. And I enjoyed working because in my head I would be resting a lot. And work always helps. You know, the more I worked the less thinking I had to do. And soon I became like a workaholic. You know, go to work in the morning and . . . . But I wouldn't go home at night. I worked really, really late, hard at night. Until it got to the point where I was so tired and, you know, I would be really angry then because the bad moods would come in and stuff. And then I would start to think of the past. And then I would get really rebellious. And then I wanna carryout evil stuff. You know the man became really worked and stuff. Then I became very angry with my family and stuff. And for a long time I'd just, I wished them dead to be honest. Because I had no love for them. Soon after the drink problem begun to become more of a problem and so was my attitude. Any people that I had around me were starting to drift away from me. Because I was becoming somebody that they didn't like. You know, I was like, I was just like a time bomb. And people would have stayed clear of me. This continued for a couple of years. I was very, just angry at the world, you know, with the place and different stuff. And there being from MHC is very easy to get mixed up and things. Things that don't concern you can soon become of interest. And there I would start, you know, being of ORG and I've found myself living in areas where we would dislike people of another religious group (ARG, name substituted throughout the transcript due to confidentiality). I would play a lot of rebel songs. Songs that would get me windup. And then I would go down the streets myself on my own or with a couple of people. Then the people of ARG go and I'd just beat them up. Simply out of, you know, just hatred. Not known the person, the guy doesn't even do anything wrong on you but, you know, when you're in with people, and you've been noticed. You know and I wanted this. And I thought to myself: "If I'm not getting noticed for doing good things I'm gonna get noticed for doing the wrong things." And then this continued for a while. I became quite bitter towards the community of ARG. And soon I got myself in a bit of trouble.

In year 2001 I was in a relationship. It wasn't a good relationship at all. But the girl fell pregnant. And something at that point was telling me that: "If I can give to this child all of the stuff that I missed out on." You know, this was a great opportunity. So things changed. My thinking began to change. I stopped drinking. So I did. I stayed away from people that I associated with. It was pretty much just myself and the girl involved. And we were looking forward to this time when the child would be born. And in the October 2001, my son is called Scott, he was born. And there was a very exciting time. You know, everybody wanted to come and see the baby. But when my family turned up to the house I flipped. And I kicked my family out. I wanted to stab one of my brothers. I've just seen a lifetime of anger on my doorstep. I didn't want it there. But I didn't know how to react. And I didn't know how to control it and I just flipped. My family run away and we had no more contact.

After about four or five months I started drinking again. I would take my child out. We would go down the town together. People would see us together. And then I'd turn into the bar and have a couple of drinks and stuff. At first did become quite sociable just having a few beers. I wanted a drink but I wanted to be seen, you know, with my kid. So I was very deceitful in many ways. After nine months or after seven months the drink became really heavy again. And at nine months the mother of the child asked me to leave. I had a licence and stuff at the time and I began drink driving and stuff. Just out of anger I would drive around and I would get caught. And I lost my licence. And then the period of the year leading up to losing the licence I was quiet again. Then I had a fine and I didn't pay the fine so I just went to prison. And then when I was in prison I met different people. But they had contacts and things for when I got out where I could go, you know, meet with them and be part of their groups and stuff. And I lived in a very particular political party (PPP, name substituted throughout the transcript due to confidentiality) end of MHC really. For me was just fun some of the stuff that the guys were getting involved in. And I didn't really want to be involved in. I just wanted to be seen with these people. So then I became very angry and bought knife and ended up back in prison. This wasn't for a long period of time.

When I came out of prison again I was just on self-destruct. You know, I would become very angry, very emotional, very unstable. Every day for me was just—I wanted to die. And that's the way I was. I would keep going in and out of psychiatric units and stuff. Believing that I was— just my head was gone. You know, I would constantly be a threat to myself, a threat to others. At this time I wasn't allowed any near my child or anything because I was very unstable. Which looking back on it was a good thing. In . . . (year omitted due to confidentiality) I got into a lot of trouble of which I had death threats issued to me: one to me and one was officially handed into the police from the local paramilitary unit. There were two death threats placed on my life. And I went to visit a priest who lived quite near. They had many connections within paramilitaries and stuff. When people had committed things, crimes and they would talk to these priests and stuff. But I went to see and this priest became like gold for me. And more they were keeping talks with the paramilitaries the longer I would be kept alive really. In . . . (year omitted due to confidentiality) it was the early, probably January—February talks came to an end and I was basically told that I have 48 hours to leave MHC or I would be shot dead. I left there and I got a flight. But it was quite strange because I met a guy who was a part of a group called ". . ." (name omitted due to confidentiality) which was a Christian group. And they came over to be a part of this, where the priests were just as a retreat or conference. The guy told me about a residential rehabilitation centre (RRC, name substituted throughout the transcript due to confidentiality). He didn't know, you know, anything about it but he just knew that it was a place to go. I wouldn't have any money or anything but it would be a place where I could work. They help people with drink. They help people with drugs. And I needed to leave the country. So the very next day I left got a flight and came in to here.

And that's when I arrived into the RRC which would have been May or June . . . (year omitted due to confidentiality). When I came here I was very rebellious. I was lost. I needed help. I wasn't willing to ask for help. My head was so focused on going back to MHC. And you know just having revenge on these people who put threats on my life. I knew where the people were. I knew where they lived. And at that time I wouldn't take a lot to pay a visit really to any of these doors. I was very wound up. And I was in a place where if I were to do anything stupid that would have been the time. In my time here, just to say, I didn't like it. People were constantly being nice to me, which I didn't know how to accept. People were getting help with their alcohol addiction, their drug addiction. Everybody was happy, clappy, you know, just being Christian. And everything was God, God, God. And to be honest with you it had done my headache. You know, I started to believe that maybe these people were worse off than I was, you know. But I stuck around for one simple reason—I didn't have anywhere else to go. I was in fear. I didn't know who knew where I was or what I was doing. So I could really close the doors. And I was pretty much, I was afraid. After about four or five months I've been here I hadn't changed. I was forming little groups in the house that were very negative trying to bring other people into my way of thinking. Creating my own squad, you know. And I was asked to leave because it was affecting other people's opportunity of rehabilitation. And I knew at that point when I was asked to leave that: "You know, this is it." I have to go and these people were right here and I'm gonna have to face these people. And the pastor when he opened the door to put me out all of the sudden it just rained. And the rain came down so heavy I never seen rain like it. And he said to me: "I don't think I could put you out." He said: "I think this is a sign for you to stay." But me not believing it and me not really; I was caring but I wasn't gonna show I was. You know and I was very: "Well, if I have to go I'll go." You know and he says: "No." He says: "Wait there." And he went away and he came back. And he says: "They are going to give you another chance." Because he felt the Lord has said to him to give me an opportunity. And that I would change. So I thought: "Okay."

My first initial plan was to do all the things they asked me to do and proved that they don't work. And so I carried out all these things they were asking me to do. And I began to feel that things were different. You know, I felt I wasn't feeling angry anymore. And I wasn't struggling to go. I wasn't going against everything. For some reason I seemed to have slept into a place where I was feeling comfortable. And I was beginning to become more aware that maybe, maybe what this guy has told me is true. So I thought to myself: "Lord, you know, if you're real I need you to do something in my life because I can't continue." Because I forgot to mention but just before I came into the RRC when the talks stopped I tried to take my own life. I went down to the local B&Q centre and I bought 500 mils of roundup weedkiller. And I just opened it and I drank it, the bottle of the weedkiller. And I was very ill. I fell to the ground instantly. I was in a lot of pain. And you know I was rushed then into hospital and stuff. But it wasn't till I came out of the hospital and that was before I came here. For me it was like things were beginning to change. And I couldn't let these people see that I was beginning to change. Because that goes against all the negative stuff that I have planted into the other guys. You know these little groups that I have formed. You know that we have been doing a negative group. I was beginning to see how wrong that was. And many of these guys left because I convinced them that this was never gonna work. And they left. They left their opportunity of rehabilitation. I don't know where they are today. I don't even know whether they're still on drugs; if they are on drink; if they are alive; if they are dead. That was my fault. You know I planted those seeds in these people.

After a while things were changing and I started to move up into a position of responsibility here. And for the first time in my life, you know, I felt a part of something. The love that these people had for me wasn't because they wanted anything from me. They just wanted what was best for me. So I started to grab a hold of that. Things were changing for me. I still had no contact with family. It was very much just me here doing what we do. After a while I decided to, you know, thinking a lot, I'm gonna hand my life over to the Lord, which I did. Soon after that I got into contact with my mother. And it was very difficult because when I left MHC as of ORG their next contact with me was as far as they were concerned I was of ARG. So not only had I left with death threats from the paramilitary groups, the . . . (name omitted due to confidentiality) and stuff; it was basically thrown back into their faces that I have become part of the other site. So that was very difficult, you know. My family, they liked the changes that were in my life but they don't acknowledge as far as they are concerned: "You are of ORG and you will always be of that ORG and that's the way it is." My mum still suffers from depression. I know God is very much in my life today. Quite often she would ring me, maybe twice a week. And she would ring me and say: "Look son I'm not doing very well today. I've just cut my throat. I've just cut my wrists. I took a lot of tablets. And by the time the ambulance gets to me I would be dead." And this could be at two o'clock in the morning. And then she would hang up. And she leaves you with these thoughts that she's gonna die. Before I knew the Lord, you know, to me that's something I could never have coped with. You know, as much as you're full of anger, and as much as I prayed for that. For a long time I prayed that these things would happen to her. When I became to know the Lord things changed. But I know she would be okay. Each time she tells us I know that she's just seeking attention. And I know that she's gonna be okay.

My conversion wasn't anything spectacular. I just found myself one day in a place where everything was different. All the anger had gone. I was no longer thinking about alcohol. I was no longer thinking about drugs. I was no longer alone. I was no longer seeking revenge. The people who had threats on my life I actually thank them for today. Because that put restrictions on my life. That put me in the place where I had to change. And there like most people like us if you think you've got another life you use it, don't you? You play all your cards. I didn't have any. Many guys, we have to come into the community. They come and they go. Because they constantly try to use the last of their resources. But for me I didn't have that. For me it was life and death. And you know it's good today. Things are good.

I am the house leader now for the centre. I now speak at prisons. I go to . . . (name omitted due to confidentiality) prison. I go to other prisons all throughout UK. I am very much involved with the homeless on the streets. I have contact with my son again which is very, very slow. But we've been away for so long apart we don't really know each other. We have a love. We have a bond between us, just a father and son thing. But we don't really know each other. My mum even though she's very messed up she rings me for advice. And we still don't talk about what I do. You know, it's just she knows that I pray a lot. And she just settles for that. She can't tell people where I leave, what I do. Because then afterwards they are at risk that their son is over here working for the community of ARG. You know the born again thing, you know, it's not a way of life over there, either for ORG or ARG. And that depend on what stage you are on, depends on the area which you can live in, you know. I do have family who are, who still live in a very PPP areas. And they still don't . . . . I have no contact with some of my family now for probably seven years. But the Lord showed me

Appendices

a new way of life. And it's me, it's not important the people that I've left behind. It's what's now. It's where we go from here. Recently I've just got involved in a relationship. And it's amazing because it's the first relationship in my life that I can say honestly that, you know, I love the person. And all of what's happened in my past leading up to this—I've just been build-up of teaching. Because from someone who wanted to die every day. From someone who wished so much hatred upon their family. My son was of no interest. You know, my drink came first. Drugs came first. Women came first. Women—they were just objects. I had no love for them. I had no respect for them. Because, as far as I was concerned, the feeling was mutual. People have mistreated me, and therefore I was gonna mistreat them. But today, today life is a genuine life. And, you know, a very grateful day really to be honest, to be a part of the ministry I am involved in. It is so big and it's growing so well. And, you know, the past is the past. You know, my thinking today is totally different. From being so disturbed, so wicked, so violent to just, I just want to love people today, you know, and just to encourage people in that. Because to be honest with you, is the love of these people that won me over. You know, feeding up on my attitude. Feeding up on my negativity. Talking to me, you know, in a way that you . . . . They would say: "Look! You can't do this. But this is the reason why." Before everything in my life was: no, no, no, no—no explanations. You don't ask for an explanation. Not that it mattered, it was just—no. You know life is different as a Christian. You know the world we live in, we live in a wicked place. But you know I just, I just fully, I give everything to the Lord today.

I have everything to live for. I have so many opportunities coming up. In fact this morning, you know, I was on the way to another church simply just to tell the people about who we are and what we do. To talk about God and to have no shame; to talk about him as your father and as your friend and as your saviour. And if I was to do that before at home where I come from you've be laughed at, mocked. And these are people who have a religion but they don't have a relationship. They just pray. They don't know who he is. And they don't know who they are in him. But to me he is everything. He's a lifeline for me. And he has proved that many, many times. You know I've put the Lord to the test many times. Even though Scripture tells us not to do that I have done that. I went out of my way to test him and to test his love for me. And each time, you know, he has come true and faithful for me. Not always getting what I want but the outcome would always be much greater. So yeah, life for me is just: from a boy who grew up very fearful, very angry, very lost, no hope, no future just a path of destruction till somebody who today—I couldn't wait to help you, you know. If God added nothing else into my life from this day onwards I would be still so happy because I've got everything, you know. And that's good. You know, I never thought that this day would come. You know, everything I said about these people at the beginning was just out of not understanding. But when you open yourself up and you allow God to do work in your heart the things change. No doubt about it. Yeah, life is just great today. That's my testimony.

I: Thank you so much for your story. And I will go over the questions and if you don't feel like adding something to the question don't worry we will go further. But if you feel like you can add anything in regards to the elements of your story according to the questions please elaborate as much as you want. The first question is: How do you perceive your conscience? What is conscience? How did it develop? How does it function?

J: Conscience. Before I knew the Lord I don't think I really had a conscience. You know I . . . ; it was normal or what seemed to be normal: to think and act and behave the way I did. And because of the way I was mistreated, you know, I thought I could justify my behaviour. Now that I know the Lord I am very much aware that everything what I've done in the past and regardless of the way I was treated I had no right whatsoever to treat people the way I treated them. You know I have done wicked things to people to get self-recognition, just to be noticed, just to be part of groups that were wrong from the beginning. Those things, I don't dwell on those things today, you know. I've asked the Lord for forgiveness in those areas. For long time I was quite . . . . When I first got saved, I was very ashamed of who I was. Even when I read Scriptures. As a matter of fact because I do preaching things now, I did a preach a while back. And I don't normally have a title for a preach but on this one I had and it was called: "Exposure." And that I felt as I read the Scriptures that I was being exposed. And I've never felt exposed before. And I could see myself exactly for the person who I was, and who I am today. And I didn't like who I was. I can't change those things in the past. But today and tomorrow I can do things differently. When I do things wrong I know I'm wrong. And I put things right now as and when things happen. Because to me my conscience is very alive at the moment, you know. And, yeah, I am aware on a daily basis of the things that I do that are right or wrong. And unless I put them right I've no peace in my life.

Appendices

I: Next question: How did you develop alcohol addiction? What is alcohol addiction? When did you realise that you have been addicted to alcohol? How did you try to manage your alcohol addiction?

J: How did I know I had an addiction? I didn't know at first. It was just something I took to escape. Because my thoughts were so bad and stuff I just drank a lot. I've drunk to the equivalent of what my thoughts would be. So if I wasn't feeling so bad I wouldn't drink as much. And when it was really bad I would drink more. People quite often told me that I had a problem. I didn't believe them. I believed that I had everything under control. I believed that the drink that I was taking was simply just for my own purpose. But I didn't believe I was on any form of . . . , you know, I didn't think I had a problem. Soon after I realised that I did have a problem, but I've done nothing to control it. By the time I realised myself that I had a problem I didn't really care and I just, I just kept going. My need to change didn't really become known to me until I came here. You know, because up to that I had no reason to leave. So if drink was gonna be the very thing that was gonna kill me so be it. I'd just keep drinking. But since I've come here in . . . (year omitted due to confidentiality) I haven't had a drink whatsoever. When you come in here you actually come off all addiction. So I had to stop smoking. I had to stop drinking. Any form of medication I may have been on—everything stops. It's called: "cold turkey." But I knew then, after the threats and stuff, and I knew when I got here, you know, that I had a problem. I just I wasn't prepared to ask for it. But I was pretty much aware that I had a problem and that I need it to deal with it, of which over a period of time that began. But it was just to find myself in that place where it was very good; the way, you know, God is so good. I didn't have to struggle with him. It just seemed to have went. It's hard to explain really but I asked for something to be taken away and it was. Whether at first I put a dying to it because is not available, is not around me, I don't see it, I don't smell it, nobody really talks about it, or may have just been an answer of prayer. You know, I believe that it was prayer. And I believe that very much so. I do. I believe that the things that I asked for he granted. So all those years I've been in that place. Firstly, not knowing I had and then not really caring till now, you know. He has been very gentle with me, the Lord, you know. My biggest problem here wasn't coming off the alcohol, my biggest problem here was getting to know who I was. You know that's right—struggle.

I: Thank you. Next question: What were your moral views before your moral, spiritual, and/or religious transformation? What is morality?

Appendices

How did you deal with moral dilemmas? How much did morality matter for you?

J: I didn't have any moral views, you know. Every man for themselves, isn't it? Take what you can get, as and how you can get it. That's the way I thought. Today things are different. You know I'm very much aware of each person underneath, you know. It's just different: a lot more respect for people and their possessions and property. You know, a lot more grateful. I don't have a lot but I'm very grateful for everything I do have. I had no respect for anything, for other people's life, but I had none for even of my own life. I had no respect for anyone at all. I just was somebody who had been mistreated. And I was gonna do the same thing—very selfish, very, very selfish. But not today—things are much different, yeah.

I: Thank you. Next question: Did you practice spirituality before your moral, spiritual, and/or religious transformation? What is spirituality? How did you practice spirituality? How much did spirituality matter for you?

J: No, I've never practised any of that. You know, anything I've ever messed around with would be wiki boards and stuff. You know, we would just blame everything that has gone wrong really and definitely nothing godly. I had no love for God. I had no respect for God. I didn't know who he is. We just prayed to him as being of ORG because it's what we had to do. He didn't mean anything to me. And today he's everything. You know—no. I'm sorry. No. No desire even to practice it or even to get to know him. After my conversion and after I've seen what he has done to my life and other people's lives I made it my business to get to know him. And I spent as much time as I can seeking the Word and getting to know who he is.

I: Next question: Did you experience moral, spiritual, and/or religious transformation? How did you experience this transformation? When did you experience this transformation? May you identify anyone who played any influential role in the process? How much has this transformation changed your life?

J: For me the transformation was just very; things just became different and that was it, you know. I just found myself one day in that place where it was like—I have respect for things. I have respect for people. I began to love people. I wasn't angry at people. Yeah, there was nothing—it just happened. It was very much just like—he just made it easy for me. So, yeah, when I knew things were different I just . . . . At first I was just a bit frightened about it. Because when I realised that things were different

Appendices

and things were changing it was almost as if I had no more excuses. It was almost as if he's brought me in that place, he's answered all my prayers. He set me up and he says: "Right. I know you recognise me in your life. What are you gonna do about it?" I could very easily go back to the way I used to be. But the desire to do that wasn't there anymore. The desire to move forward and to continue with this was all I could think of really.

I: I had another question before this. One question I missed which I am going back to now is: Did you practice religion before your moral, spiritual, and/or religious transformation? What is religiousness? How did you practice religion? Did you have religious affiliation? How much did religion matter for you?

J: No, I never practised any. I used to go to Mass and stuff but simply I was supposed to go. You know, I had to go. But no, I had no love for it. And the things that I've done as being of ORG .... ORG was just the title; was just a name for a group of people who didn't like another group of people called ARG. And that's all it was. Yeah, that's all it was.

I: You mentioned, to move to the other question you answered before about the transformation, you mentioned conversion. Can you explain it more to me?

J: Oh, the conversion for me was just, as I said; it was very—things just changed.

I: Was that in a moment of time somehow, or it was over a period of time?

J: It was over a period of time. There was no sudden change. For some people I know that at their conversion they couldn't sleep at night. But for me it wasn't like that. I think, I had changed for two months before I realised I had changed. You know it was like almost as if he just let me slide into it rather than a sudden thing. Probably cause a sudden thing may have just frightened me and which I would have rebel against it. No, for me it was just—I just—I had more of a joy. Because the joy that I had up to that point I only seen it in another people. So this joy that I've seen in these people I was beginning to experience. You know, I wasn't fearful anymore. I was having a laugh. Every day was genuine. You know, we used to have this corner that we called "the seat of mockers," where I would just spend all my time. And I just find myself no longer being at that place where that's all I would be orchestrating my own selfish motive things. Things were just different. I had a lot of peace, you know. And the hatred that I had for my family—that was gone. At first I didn't have a desire to know them. I didn't have a desire to may be make things right. But I didn't hate them—no more. It was almost as if that that door is closed. That's not important. It's now, you know, the journey had begun sort of thing. That was the path I head along with. You know, I love my mother to bits today. I understand today. When you're older you realise that she wasn't well. She has an illness. She's full of depression. It wasn't hatred. It wasn't that she didn't love me or she didn't love my brothers or my father or anything. It wasn't that she had no time for us. It was just—she wasn't well. But I allowed that to eat me for years, robbing me of the peace of my life. So I just found myself at that place where I had peace. That chapter of my life was over.

I: Thank you. This is part of the same question—the transformation. May you identify anyone who played any influential role in the process?

J: Yeah. You know because of who I am there are many people who played a part in, in who we are. Other guys who were maybe just on the same programme as I was. I've seen other people changing. My pastor and his wife played a big part in my life. The ministry that I am involved in. And even though it is a rehab in the world sense we are a church. So that family of us here was always present. And no matter which of the other centres we would go and visit you are treated as a part of the family. I remember sitting at the anniversary. It was the . . . (number omitted due to confidentiality) anniversary of this place. I remember sitting in a tent and I was looking around. And I thought to myself: "I have a sense of peace." And I just knew I was at the right place. I didn't understand everything. People around me, some looked worse off than I did but others were filled with joy and stuff but I just knew that I was where I was supposed to be. And the fact that people, especially now, a lot of what people said to me at the beginning I am now experiencing, now at that six years, you know, down the line. You know, all the things that they say would be restored. I've been restored. I know that everything has been, but it is. So the thing is because of that, because God has honoured his Word I can see the truth in what my pastor and my leaders and different people had said to me. So I know they've never lied to me. And that's something; that is just the honesty in the house that has always captured me. Because I didn't always like what they told me. Quite often they would be very direct with me. But they were always open and there were always honest. And I admire that. And maybe in the way I was, I needed to be spoken to directly. Because if I thought I could get won over somebody I would have done so. And these people recognised that in me, so therefore they treated each person according to each person. And some people are fragile, others are a bit—you can speak to them a bit differently. For me it was very—you had to speak hard and you had to speak direct. But in every situation they did it in love. And even after they had rebuked you or cracked you for anything you still felt loved. So it wasn't that you've been rebuked and you can't do this. There is a love and a peace that came with it. And that won me over.

I: Thank you. Next question: What was the impact of your transformation on your life? Compare your morality, spirituality, and religiousness before and after the transformation. How did the transformation impact your understanding of morality, spirituality, and religion, and their role in your life? How much did morality, spirituality, and religion matter for you after your transformation?

J: I think we've pretty much answered a lot of that. So what was the question, go again?

I: What was the impact of your transformation on your life? As you said we covered it pretty much. But in terms of morality, spirituality, religiousness—how did you understand them: back before the transformation and now after transformation? And how much do they play a role in your life?

J: It's everything for me today. You know, the Word of God is food, isn't it? I don't leave the house each day unless I've spent time in the Word. As far as other people notice it, you know, the impact that it's had in other people—people see it. People are not afraid of me today. You know they don't want to avoid me today. They like to be with me. They like my company. You know, when I go to churches, other churches, you know, I am at home no matter where I go. And I am very honoured really to tell people on a regular basis really of the things that God has done in my life. You know, I would have been embarrassed to talk about God. You know, you don't talk about Jesus and things, that's for weirdoes, isn't it? But for me today it's everything. You know, my total understanding of life itself is different today. People, you know . . . ; it's a different direction; it's a different world really. I don't any longer have thoughts of what the world has to offer. It doesn't appeal to me. It doesn't offer me anything that can sustain what I need on a daily basis. For me my life now is within the ministry. It has been for quite some time now. And it always will be. So yeah, once I didn't care but now I make it my business to tell people about God and try and change other people's views. You know, because they are many people who don't have any morals. I tried to identify with them, people. But then I tried to say to them: "Look, you need to change, you know."

Appendices

I: Thank you. Next question: What was the impact of your moral, spiritual, and/or religious transformation on your conscience? Compare your conscience before and after the transformation. How did the transformation impact your conscientious behaviour? How much did the voice of your conscience matter for you after your transformation?

J: Like I said before, you know, before I never cared. And then after my transformation, the conversion, I began to get convicted a lot. You know, I was very ashamed of a lot of stuff that I've done. Some of those things I've been able to put right. But there are other things I can't. You know, the anger that I had towards my family. My father died while I was here and I wasn't saved at that point. The bitterness that I held against him for not may be being there, for me was still there. When my father died I never even went to his funeral. You know, to this day I've never seen my father's grave. But that's not because of anything, that's because of—I can't go home. I live in a place where I can't return to. And that's difficult. You know, as I've said my views have changed. You know before I would have no morals and all I wanted was revenge. But today even in not being able to see my father's grave and not being able to see my family, all of those things, I've still got peace. Things are just different.

I: Okay. Next one: What was the impact of your transformed conscience on your recovery from alcohol addiction? Compare your recovery before and after the transformation. How did your transformed conscience impact your recovery from alcohol addiction? What is the role of your transformed conscience in the maintenance of your abstinence? May you identify anyone who played any influential role in the process?

J: When my morals changed everything changed. You know, my need for a drink, my desire to drink, everything, you know, had left. It definitely prevents me from going back to that way of life. Because I see, life today is much more valuable, today. Life for me before was with no purpose. I didn't want to be a part of it. And definitely I didn't appreciate it. But today, you know, life is different. Other people, yeah, I've seen how other people have changed. And that encourages me. I always get encouraged when I see people change. Because you know, it's almost as if, how would you put it, you know I'm not alone in that. They are many people who struggle with that. And my whole thing is different today. You know, is gone from one of hatred to one of love. And the desires that I have are so different than anything, you know, from a negative to a positive. It doesn't mean that I see the positive in everything. It just means my understanding is different. And in that understanding with perseverance you get the positive. It would come really. It just makes me appreciate life today more and people and the importance of people. I spent many years alone. I always described it as: "You can put me in a room with 100 people and I would always feel alone." But today, you know, I am real. I don't feel alone ever. I feel really blessed today, just excited about life. Life is exciting, isn't it?

I: Thank you. Next question: May you share your future plans related to your recovery? What is the role of morality, spirituality, and/or religion in them? What is the role of your transformed conscience in them? Do you plan to share your experience with others who need help in recovery from alcohol addiction?

J: Life for me is in the ministry. I believe it is my purpose given from God himself to continue within what he is revealed to me. I don't believe that he changed my life and changed my thinking just so that I could have a better life. I believe he is much more involved, it's much deeper than that. And I believe just as other people have encouraged me, you know, I believe he wants me to continue in that to encourage other people. For me at the moment I just see the ministry that I'm in; the people that I work with, I am feeling very much at home with; I can identify with these people, you know. I can sympathise with them. And I can empathise with them. I believe that because my own thinking has changed. And I see the value in people. And I believe that my conscience has been changed. You know, I believe that helps me a lot to understand other people. And to spend more time with people. And to be a bit more sensitive with people and stuff. Because you know, I wasn't the perfect person. You know, and I've been forgiven much. If I was to take the time to think about my past, all the things that I did, I still did them. But we get guys coming in who are doing the same things. And we can only be a testimony to them. The words: "I can't do this" are no longer an option really because I have done it and so can they. And I'm just encouraging people. As far as religion is concerned I don't use the word religion really. Religion itself, I feel, just traps people. You know, I see it in my own family. You know, they are just trapped in something that they get no self-worth in. They definitely have no freedom. When they leave the place of worship they just go straight back to how they lived their life. As for me when I hear the Word it convicts me and I know I have to change. I can't just go back, you know. I can't play two people. You know, I just can't do it. But as far as my belief is concerned I will do my best to encourage other people in that and to bring them to a place where they too will accept Jesus as their Lord and saviour. Because he's the only thing that can sustain us really.

Appendices

I: Thank you. The last question: May you formulate the main theme of your life story? What is the place of alcohol addiction in your story? What is the place of conscience in your story? What is the place of morality, spirituality, and/or religiousness in your story? What is the place of your moral, spiritual, and/or religious transformation in your story? The main theme.

J: I don't know. I think it all now is to glorify God, I think. I believe I wouldn't appreciate today . . . . You know, I don't have any regrets now of my past. But, I think in order to have experienced all that I've done and all that I've been through I would not have appreciated what I have today. You know, this would have been just something else today that I would have taken for granted or abused. But today I see the value in life from my experiences of the past. You know, it's changed my whole way of thinking. You know, it's taught me that the values of true morals, Christian teachings, self-discipline, and all the very things that we should apply in our lives from the beginning anyway, all the things that we should be taught. I think my family tried to do a lot of that but it has never gonna work—they are just religious people. You know, there is no relationship. So then everything just became routine rather than principles. And to say, yeah, I'm glad of my past today. It's the value I would have today. It just taught me how to value people, to treat people. And it's just respect really for people. Yeah, we're living in a world where it's hurting, isn't it? It needs change, you know. And I think if God had not come into my life when he did I'd be dead today. Cause my life was over. As for now my life has just begun. You know, I've got everything ahead of me to look forward to.

I: Thank you. Thank you. This finishes the interview with Jack at 5:15.

Appendices

James (2011). Personal interview (Conscience in recovery from alcohol addiction), 15 November.

Interviewer (I): Okay, this is an interview with James starting at 11:05. And the guidelines for the story are the following: Structure your life story in chapters. Think about their names, summaries, and progressive links. Without interfering with the genuine character of the story can you identify the role of the following topics in your life narrative: conscience; alcohol addiction; morality; spirituality; religiousness; moral reformation; spiritual transformation; religious conversion and/or affiliation; the relationship between morality, spirituality, religiousness, and conscience, and recovery from alcohol addiction. How will you summarise each of these chapters? What progressive links will you make between these chapters? Now this is for you. What I read is here just to remind you. Otherwise feel free to tell me your story.

James (J): Yes. Are you ready?

I: Yes.

J: Hello. My name is James. I am an alcoholic.

Chapter 1: Yes! I started alcoholism at a very young age. By the age of five or six I was drinking alcohol to block out domestic violence really that my mother suffered from my father. In the week my father would be a normal everyday father. I used to fear the weekends because when it came to Friday I knew what would happen. Friday, Friday night they would go out. They will get intoxicated. They will come back. We were really fighting, my father with my mother. My mother would be bruised or battered basically. Sometimes he used to come off from work on Fridays. And I used to pray to God above that he would go for a couple of bottles, bring them back to the house, fall asleep so that I could pinch a drink. So basically go to sleep. Yeah. Block out what would happen. This went on for a number of years. That is basically. That is all I can say for chapter 1. That is the start of my life story. And that is the summary of chapter 1.

Chapter 2: This went on for basically a number of years—hitting. Yeah. So I mean, I felt, I felt helpless, I felt. I felt basically a loser really. There was nothing I could do. I was frightened. I was upset. I was worried. I was angry. I was fearless of. I was in fear, sorry, for my mother's safety. Then, then basically he's carried on. Then by the age of about 10 or 11 I was drinking, I was drinking when I could. Still hating the weekends because I knew what was going to happen. It carried on happening for like a while longer. And then one day my mother had enough. My mother decided basically to—basically decided to leave. She had enough. That's it for chapter 2. It's just a bit of the background of my life story. As time goes on it will become a lot more interesting and a lot more, you'll be able to see how I turned my life around.

Chapter 3: The progressive links basically with alcohol and my childhood memories were just, basically; I used to be able to have a drink so that I can't hear screaming, basically. I can't hear the screaming of my mother getting, getting hurt. Getting hurt in the way that; basically people say: "Love works in mysterious ways." That was something that I could never ever quite, quite grasp was the word I am looking for. To grasp why the lady would put over there for so long because . . . . By this time I basically hated my father. It was just, just my mother was a punch bag and I was helpless, hopeless, fear, fear was the word I am looking for really. Fear that, fear that they wouldn't go out. Fear that he wouldn't have too much to drink, basically. Fear of also, fear of him not bringing the drink back for myself so that I can block the pain out. This is, this is a very, very short chapter. But that's it for chapter 3 because I was starting to get into things that I found very, very, very important to the way I have changed my life around. So the summary of chapter 3 is just the links of chapter 1 and 2 depending on the violence, the drink. That's it.

Chapter 4: Chapter 4 is—once I started going to school then. I started going to school. I started going to secondary school. But by this time I was drinking, yes. Drinking. I wasn't going to school. Wading school, drinking, hanging around the street corners, hanging around where . . . , hanging around the street corners that, to be part of the crowd. To have love of friends that I never, never used to have of my father. I was very close to my mother. But I never used to have it of my mother, of my father sorry. So I started drinking. And then one night at the age of 14 . . . ; this is where, this is where it starts getting interesting now. By the age of 14 I was strong. I had a fight with somebody. I put him in the hospital. I had six weeks in detention centre. I did the six weeks. It was meant to learn me a lesson. But I thought it wouldn't. It would have but it didn't. Then I came out of prison thinking that I would strike the lad. Yeah. Then I behaved and everything. I started drinking heavily then, heavily, heavily every day, every week where I could bother. Every week when I could get a drink I would get one, yes. I spend in lifetime in prison, in and out, two years here, three years there, 18 months here, nine months there, 12 months here. I was spending a very, very, very long time in prison. Same old story: go in prison; do the sentence; come out; get drunk; go back into prison; get arrested. But the violence was escalating. I started stabbing somebody.

Appendices

Hitting someone with armours, bats. Then I met a lady. I met a lady and my life really turned around. My life really turned around for the better. Well so I thought. And that is the end of chapter 4. The summary of chapter 4 is now was starting to get to know the old James.

Chapter 5: As I was saying, I had a relationship with a lady on and off for a long period of time. I had a little daughter with her. My daughter is now 17 years old. I'm trying to get in touch with her but because of my alcohol addiction I was really a loser and a waste of time. Nobody wanted to know anything about me. So my daughter is 17 years old now. I don't think my daughter has ever, ever seen her father without a drink. Yes. My partner and my daughter left me very shortly after two more prison sentences. I did one for 18 months for violence on a police officer. I bit the police officer's ear. And then I just got six months for drunk and disorderly when I didn't get into police car when I should have. The police arrested me and I was fighting. So by this time Erica, my partner, had enough of me and said: "James you got a choice to either make your mind for me or the drink." By this time it's easier said than done. Yeah. I am absolutely raging drunk. So I, I carried on drinking. I carried on going around into her house when I was intoxicated, ballooning, arguing; police coming; getting arrested. This, that, the other. So she had enough. She had enough. And that was it. The last summer I saw her was, I would say about 1999. The last summer I saw my daughter was when she was 10 years old. She is now 17 as I've said. So basically, then, then I was violent, arrogant, street-cornered alcoholic that . . . . I had a reputation in the town that I lived: "James is drunk because he's violent." Basically that is it for chapter 5. Now it's starting. Now I go to chapter 6.

Then I left my home town (MHT, name substituted due to confidentiality) because, basically I've done everything I wanted to do. I was a pain in the backside and basically I had no friends, no partner, nothing at all. I then moved to this north west English town (TNWET, name substituted throughout the transcript due to confidentiality). I moved to TNWET. When was it? About 2001 I think it was. No, not 2001, I'm sorry. About 1999 I moved to TNWET. And then I met a girl. I met a girl who was basically a drinker like myself. She used to like a bit of amphetamines like myself at that time. Basically, to stay out longer and drink longer. I met a girl called Sally. Me and Sally had a child. Yeah. She already had one child that was living with the grandparents. Living with Sally's mum and dad. And that was taken off her because she couldn't basically handle it with the drink. We got the news that she was pregnant. And we went up to Tristan and Nancy, the child's grandparents, to tell them the good news. I'm sure you can imagine the look on their face when they . . . . She got one child that was with them. They weren't very pleased. But they give us the benefit of the doubt, themselves and the social services. They give us the benefit of the doubt. It was like . . . . They said: "We'll keep an eye on you but you can keep your child." So we kept the child. They kept an eye on us. Then one Thursday night we had an argument. We had an argument while the child was with us. Yeah. And because we were arguing on the street the police came. The police came. They rang Tristan and Nancy. And they took the child. Tristan and Nancy took the child with them away. Now as that was going on . . . . As that was going on Tristan said. Sorry. As that was going on Tristan said, that's the child's grandparents: "Over my dead body you would ever see Wesley again." So they took him away. Me and Sally split up. Sally went away. And I haven't seen Sally since, since 2004, 2004.

But by this time I was on, the word I'm looking for is; I was on, I was on, the word I'm looking for is; I was on a slide, very, very different, very, very fast slide to alcohol dependency. Yes. I was already an alcoholic but it was really getting, spiralling out of control. Basically I was unmanageable. I could not manage. And then I had, that's the word I'm using, is: I got nothing; nobody loves me; a bit of self-pity and everything else. So I moved from TNWET. And I moved to a place called "another north west English town" (ANWET, name substituted throughout the transcript due to confidentiality). Yeah. We're now in, we're now in 2005. I moved to ANWET. No, sorry. Christmas Eve, 2004 I moved to ANWET. Yeah, it was 2004. I moved to ANWET. No, sorry. It was June 2005, sorry, summertime. I moved to ANWET. I had nowhere to go but I; I am an alcoholic, I'm an alcoholic anyway but I was raging, raging drink about this time. Anything I could get my hands on I would drink. Yeah. So they said: "Alcoholics, find alcoholics." And you can imagine, it wasn't long before I was on the pub bench drinking with the crowd. This went on through summer. I had a few times when I got arrested.

I had a few scripts with, with a . . . . I had a few scripts with a very, very serious, serious, not accident, serious, serious mistake. I was once on the bank of this north west English river (TNWER, name substituted throughout the transcript due to confidentiality). There was a breach and TNWER, and I was that intoxicated that I fell off, I fell to sleep. And it was lucky that TNWER were not coming in. Otherwise I would have been washed away. But back to the story. So I carried on drinking. Yeah. I carried on drinking to this state of . . . . I was sleeping rough; I was on the

Appendices

streets; I was living for pillars' support; sleeping in wheelie bins; sleeping wherever I could get my head down; drinking. Yeah. And then, then—August 2005 I met a lady, a girl called Charlotte. It was just a drinking colleague more than anything. But we bumped into a guy in 2005. We bumped into a guy. And the guy I thought was okay. So we were going to this town on the English coast (TTEC, name substituted due to confidentiality) for the weekend. We got off the train on this north west English city (TNWEC, name substituted due to confidentiality). And every time I went to the toilet the guy was coming onto the girl. So we ended up arguing and fighting. So we ended up fighting. I took him outside. And I was fighting with him very, very badly. Yeah. I was jumping on him, on his head, and things like that which I shouldn't have been doing. So the police came. I had arrested. I got bailed. This was June 2005. I got bailed. I went back to court in September. I got bailed again. Yeah. I got bailed again until after Christmas, January. Now here comes. In December, in December 2005 on Christmas Eve I was drinking, basically, on the streets—I was living. I was drinking, I was intoxicated. And this gentleman, two gentlemen actually who said to me: "Hi." So I said to them: "Have you got the time;" or, "Have you got a pound;" or something on that weight of length. Yeah. The gentleman started laughing. But he was laughing with his friend, or I thought he was. But at the time I thought he was laughing at me because I was on the streets, homeless—nothing. So we ended up fighting. We ended up fighting. Basically we were rolling around the floor. With me living on the streets I had a knife on me. I took the knife out and penetrated his body three times: once in the ear, behind the ear, once in near the artery, and once in the chin. Yeah. The man was on the life-support machine. I got charged with attempted murderer first. And then got it dropped to section 18 with intent. And then got three years imprisonment for public protection. That is the end of chapter 6.

Chapter 7: For the offence that I was fighting with, I got 12 months to run concurrent. So I'm looking at four-year sentence now in prison. And imprisonment for public protection, where you can't come out until the public think that it is safe. Whilst in custody I still drank, I still drank. I drank hoodge; what is own brew; what is made in prison. Yeah. So I still drank for the first six months because when I first got the sentence, a life sentence means: you are not getting out unless you really, really behave. So I drank for the first six months. Then started to, to realise that nothing, nothing is gonna . . . . It is not gonna change anything. Started getting your head around the prison. I was in prison. I was still violent. Because

Appendices

in prison you got to wear a mask. You've got to not let people think that they can take advantage of you. And then I had a few fights and that. Then that's the end for chapter 6.

I: Chapter 7.

J: Chapter 7. Yeah. That's it for chapter 7.

J: Chapter 8: I am . . . . I was, I was doing anything I could in prison just to basically get out of my prison cell. I was gaining a few qualifications. Just things like that. Just to get out of my cell because it was locked up all the time. Yeah. Then it was one Sunday, one Sunday a friend came up to me and said: "James I'm going to church are you coming?" "Church, No!" So then he said: "Come on James you—no lose!" So I decided to go. So I went to church. I liked it. I liked it. Yeah. So I started to go. I used to go every Sunday for two years. Two years. No, sorry—for a year. Then I should have been out off for my parole in 2008. But by this time is July 2009, now. And in July 2009 I am waiting for the parole board. And the parole board said to me: "Now, do this, do this, do this, and we'll have looked at you in 12 months' time."

Now in July 2006. Yeah. Eventually when I've gone into jail I got told of a top judge, yeah, and top psychologist that: "You are a waste." The judge said to me: "You are malice to society. You are danger to the public. And it is highly unlikely if you would ever be released from prison." Now I got a judge saying there to me in 2009: "Do this, do this, do this, and it might happen. So, go away." So I went back to my room. And I decided, I decided to pray basically. Yeah. I decided to pray that I may be getting out of prison in a year. So I started to pray. I started going to church. And things started to happen that would have never, never happened before. Just simple things like, like: you start getting . . . . Things started going on your way that would have never gone on your way in the past. So that happened. That carried on happening until, until June 2010. Yeah. June 2010. I went before the parole board again. And the parole board said to me: "Have you done everything that needs to be done." I said: "Yes I have." It said: "Right. We would have a look at you again in 12 months' time." So I said: "No problem." So I carried on behaving as I behaved. And it got to, it got to the case where I started to go to church on a Wednesday then as well as the Sunday. So that was, skipping forward to, basically, to where, to Christmas 2010. That is the end of chapter 8.

Chapter 9: We got Christmas over the way. I got off that call. But I was a lot more focused. I was focused on that maybe a chance here. So Christmas comes out of the way. On Tuesday night a lad comes through my door: "We got a parole day for you. It is 2011 . . . (date and month omitted due to confidentiality)." Skipping on to 2011 . . . (date and month omitted due to confidentiality), I go in front of the parole board and all my probation officers, and all these are saying to me: "James, you could be getting out!" Whatever! So then I saw the parole board. I was there for an hour. And that parole board said to me: "We'll let you know." Two days later I got a letter through my door. Yeah. Yeah. "You're going home, to a residential rehabilitation centre (RRC, name substituted throughout the transcript due to confidentiality)." "To RRC!" I was over the moon, I was, and decided that enough was enough. By this time, by this time I was well into, I was well into being a Christian. Yeah. Now this Christian thing in prison is not the same as out here because it locks up. But, when I did get a release from prison, yeah, when I got to the gates and the gates opened, before I got through the gates, yeah, I was handed £1,000 in my pocket, which was my money. Yeah. Now the gentleman, the Holy Spirit says: "Well." Right—was with me. Because I come from this south Yorkshire town (TSYT, name substituted due to confidentiality) on my own, hundred and seventy miles away with £1,000 in my pocket, an alcoholic. Yeah. And I knew myself that I had a . . . . I hit, I hit rock bottom and the time for change had come. Yeah. The time for change had come for myself that I was very, very, very focused. Well, very focused to the case of: "I need to change." Yeah. That is the end of chapter . . . .

I: Nine.

J: Chapter 9. Going to chapter 10 now.

Chapter 10: By this time I am in the RRC. And within the space of three weeks I felt a spiritual transformation because I went to a church with the RRC called ". . ." (name omitted due to confidentiality). And whilst there they said: "Anybody who is on the fence come down to be, to be—hand your life over to Jesus." And all of a sudden all the residents of the RRC went. And all of a sudden I started to sweat. I felt dizzy. I went downstairs to get blessed and everything. Whilst there I was swaying with, and the Holy Spirit was swaying with me. It was a very, very nice experience. Since then, since then I cannot get enough of church. I cannot get enough of praying, meetings etc. Do you know what I mean? I mean the transformation in myself; I mean even my peers and even people here, counsellors, staff have even noticed the transformation in me. I mean every time I go to church now and I pray I know the Holy Spirit is in me. He's overwhelming the spirit that I have in me. I'm singing. I'm praying. I am at the front. I am there for everything. That to me is one transformation that at times I cannot believe myself. The transformation that I've changed in myself. I mean I have. I mean. I don't know what it was. Yeah. I mean. It's like, it's like I've been blessed. It's like, he has searched me in the reason that I do not know what it is but I walked on now because I've got the man right at the side of me and I have no worries. And that is end of chapter 10.

Chapter 11: Religious conversations. I mean. There is at least once, sometimes more, twice, three times where I take myself away because I need to watch for his guidance more than anything. Guidance, where it's like: "Father is it right to do this?" Because he's, this man, the guidance that this man has given me is quite unbelievable. I mean. He, he guided me to the RRC. He guided me to the RRC. He has got a purpose for me. Yes. And, and like a lot of people now, right, we're for ever in his debt. He is the saviour. He is the one that, he's the one that I owe my life to. He saved my life. He saved my life because if he hasn't taken me as I was I would be dead now. I would be dead. I would be dead cause I would have either drunk myself to death, or I would have killed somebody with the alcohol in me. And he's . . . ; he guided me. He guided me for a reason. He's got a purpose for me. And I am forever grateful for that. I am forever grateful, I am. I mean the relationship between spirituality and religiousness is kind of overwhelming, I mean. You can see the gentleman here. If you can see the gentleman on the Sunday night in church he is a completely different man. He is up, he is worshipping. Right! Because he thinks it is his right to go to there. Because you always got to remember he took me as, as basically down and out. That's all. These are the only words I can use—down and out. Yeah. And I was frightened to go into church. I was frightened of people seeing me at church. What! No! No! He's no good. I mean. Now, now I've been, I've been in the RRC five and a half months. I mean. I've just spoken to my counsellor today. And my counsellor said: "The transformation in you James is quite unbelievable." Yeah.

Recovery from addiction: Yeah. There is only one word that I can use. The Father and the Holy Spirit have set me free from addiction. The Father, the Holy Spirit, my willpower, and people basically that believed in me. That's the only one I can say—believed in me. But the major one is God. He is the major one—God and the man who died for us—Jesus Christ. They are the main ones that believed in me and, yes, and I believe in them now—me. I do. And basically he saved my life. And now the conclusion of what I was, of the life story that I have told. Now the grandparents of my son have been in touch with the RRC. Yeah. I'm trying to find my daughter. I'm expecting letters by an agency. So the only words I

Appendices

can say are believe in the Holy Spirit, believe in the Father, believe in Jesus Christ and you'll go right. Thank you very much Sir.

I: Thank you James. Now 11 questions.

J: No problem Sir.

I: You may have covered them already. If you want to add anything please do, if not tell me and we will go on.

J: Okay. No problem.

I: The first question is: How do you perceive your conscience? What is conscience? How did it develop? How does it function?

J: What do you mean?

I: Conscience.

J: Yeah. My conscience, I mean while I was drinking I didn't use to have any conscience. Yeah. I didn't use to have any conscience, guilty conscience, shame, anything. Now. Now the conscience I have got, yeah, is all right. You cannot change the past. The past is gone. The past is gone. The conscience is on the future. And the conscience that I have got now is: I will live alcohol free; I will live with friends, proper, proper friends; I will live with friends who believe in me. I have people that will believe that I will succeed. And I have got people who do believe that I am a gentleman. So my conscience is clear. And my conscience is good now.

I: Next question is: How did you develop alcohol addiction? What is alcohol addiction? When did you realise that you have been addicted to alcohol? How did you try to manage your alcohol addiction? You covered this pretty much.

J: Yeah.

I: Do you want to add anything?

J: Yeah. Yeah. Like I've said in the story I covered it. I was a typical alcoholic. I haven't got a problem. It's other people that have got the problem. It's other people that are picking things. It's other people. But now I can take responsibility. And I can take responsibility for my own actions and say: "It was me that had the problem. Everybody else was right. And I was wrong." But now, now I am on their wagon and I am right as well. That's me Sir.

I: The third question: What were your moral views before your moral, spiritual, and/or religious transformation? What is morality? How did you deal with moral dilemmas? How much did morality matter for you?

J: All right. My morals, my morals when I was young, I haven't had any. Yeah. All right! My worries were at the end of a bottle. And at the end of the bottle was where was the next one. Are you with me? Now my moral

Appendices

responsibilities are my life, my life, my future. I cannot change the past but I can change the future. Learn by your mistakes. And my morals now are, hopefully, get in touch with my children, finally. Seeing them for the next time. But, if that doesn't happen is not the time yet. Jesus Christ knows when the time will be. And that will do me.

I: Next one: Did you practice spirituality before your moral, spiritual, and/or religious transformation? What is spirituality? How did you practice spirituality? How much did spirituality matter for you?

J: I didn't. Like I said, I didn't believe, I didn't believe, I mean. I used to just say a prayer when I was on the streets at night to get up in the morning. "Jesus please guide me." It was whilst in prison, like I've said in the life story, that I started to. But now I am really, really, really established Christian now, really. Yeah that's it.

I: Next one: Did you practice religion before your moral, spiritual, and/or religious transformation? What is religiousness? How did you practice religion? Did you have religious affiliation? How much did religion matter for you?

J: At the beginning region didn't really matter. I mean, because like I said all my morals and everything were upside down. Now, now like I've said I'm a really established Christian, now. I prayed three times a day, sometimes more. I go to church as many times as possible. I am nearly into home groups. I go to Alpha courses. I go to Alpha course. I went to Alpha day last Saturday. I am really into Christianity now.

I: Next one: Did you experience moral, spiritual, and/or religious transformation? How did you experience this transformation? When did you experience this transformation? May you identify anyone who played any influential role in the process? How much has this transformation changed your life? You covered it pretty much. Anything else to add?

J: No, No, No. Because, like I said to you, I got touched by the Holy Spirit at church. So that's it.

I: If you are to identify any influential role in the processes whose role will that be?

J: It was the role of the . . . . It was the role of the Holy Spirit. And it was the role of God and the role of Jesus Christ and myself. It was also the role of the pastor who was in front of me. And the pastor that was on the back of me. Yes Sir.

I: Okay James, thank you. Next one: What was the impact of your transformation on your life? Compare your morality, spirituality, and religiousness before and after the transformation. How did the transformation impact your understanding of morality, spirituality, and religion, and their role in your life? How much did morality, spirituality, and religion matter for you after your transformation?

J: Like I said, when I came to the RRC I was going to different churches every single week. Every week we go to a different church here at the RRC. When I got touched, it was kind of, it was kind of for me, because now I live forward to the next meeting of the church. Like I can't wait for Wednesday when is the Alpha course here. And then I can't wait for Sunday to go to church. Then next week when I move over to the second stage of the residential rehabilitation programme (SSRRP, name substituted due to confidentiality) I can't wait for Wednesday. There will be a home group on Thursday. I can't wait for Sunday to go to church twice. So it's really changed me, it has. Really, really changed me.

I: Okay next one: What was the impact of your moral, spiritual, and/or religious transformation on your conscience? Compare your conscience before and after the transformation. How did the transformation impact your conscientious behaviour? How much did the voice of your conscience matter for you after your transformation?

J: I mean, I mean like . . . ; I used to worry about everything. I used to worry about what's this gonna happen, what's this gonna happen, what's this gonna happen. Since I got touched I don't worry about anything. Even people are saying here, now: "James you are so laid-back." I'm so laid-back because I have no worries. I have no fears. I've got the man at the side of me. Are you with me? If there is anything that I was gonna do wrong he kind of says: "Hold on a minute." Yeah. That's it. That's good.

I: What was the impact of your transformed conscience on your recovery from alcohol addiction? Compare your recovery before and after the transformation. How did your transformed conscience impact your recovery from alcohol addiction? What is the role of your transformed conscience in the maintenance of your abstinence? May you identify anyone who played any influential role in the process?

J: I mean, like I said when I was in prison things started to happen that I never thought would happen. Yeah. I mean, the only person, the only person that played a major role is Jesus and God. Because they are the people that I prayed to. Because you've got to remember that this gentleman that is speaking here is a gentleman that has got told of two, of one, sorry, of one top judge: "This man is a danger to the public and a danger to society. This man will never be released." Yeah. Now right, for somebody, somebody like Jesus and God to say to me, say to me: "I'm not bothered what you've done in the past. I've got a purpose for you. Come on. Come with me." Yeah. And they're the only people that play major roles in my life. Yeah.

I: Next one: May you share your future plans related to your recovery? What is the role of morality, spirituality, and/or religion in them? What is the role of your transformed conscience in them? Do you plan to share your experience with others who need help in recovery from alcohol addiction?

J: Yes. Yes. There's only one thing I can say about my story. I've got God on my side and God is the man who keeps me on the straight and narrow every day. I pray, I pray to God. I pray to God: "God please send me through this day." Right! "Alcohol free and another day clean and sober." And God has planted the seed. And the Holy Spirit says: "Well no more, no more, no more alcohol." And I would just like to share this opportunity to say that: "Anybody who hears this story and you have got a drink problem turn your life over to somebody who can manage your life." Because we admit to God that we cannot manage our lives on our own. Yes. So we turn our life and the will over to a higher power that can manage. And up to now he's not done so bad on my life and I am quite happy. Yes.

I: Yes James, thank you. The last question: May you formulate the main theme of your life story? What is the place of alcohol addiction in your story? What is the place of conscience in your story? What is the place of morality, spirituality, and/or religiousness in your story? What is the place of your moral, spiritual, and/or religious transformation in your story?

J: Like the story says. I started drinking because to take away, to take away emotions, and take away pressures, and take away rejection, yeah, emotional and everything else. Then I thought it was normal to have a drink. I thought it was normal to have a drink. I thought it was normal to see domestic violence. But it isn't. But then alcohol started to get hold of me. And before I knew who I was, before I knew who I was, I was having a life of crime, domestic violence, crime, prison, in and out of prison. Just the only word that I can use is dog's life, is the word I am using—dog's life and a waste of time. But then it cost me a life sentence in prison. Not to wake up. Yeah. To be patted on the back really by Jesus Christ and say: "Listen. I died for you. I got a purpose for you. Come with me." So I started to turn my life around with the help of God and with the help of Jesus Christ. Yes. Then things started to happen, as I said earlier on in the story. And then things started happening. There was, there was, there was an odd journey,

Appendices

don't get me wrong. There are times when I was saying: "Come on, God! Why are you not answering my prayer?" But I think everybody knows that God does not answer all the time straightaway. But as time goes on he does answer the prayer, he does. He does answer the prayer. And he answers the prayer where, where it was like—a typical example today. I actually have seen probation today. Yeah. I've been praying. I've known that I've got to see him for a week. I've been praying for a week because I have to speak to Yordan, this gentleman in front of me. It would coincide. I saw Bruce. And Bruce said: "James, it is not a problem." So he does answer, just little things. But he answers big things as well. But don't forget there is a lot of people that he has to answer to, so. Keep praying and he will answer your prayers. He will. That's all.

I: Thank you James. Thank you very much. This will be the end of our interview on 15th of 11th—11:56.

Luke (2011). Personal interview (Conscience in recovery from alcohol addiction), 11 November.

Interviewer (I): Okay, we're recording. This is an interview with Luke taken on 11th of 11th starting at 2:08. So the following guidelines are in reference to the story: Structure your life story in chapters. Think about their names, summaries, and progressive links. Without interfering with the genuine character of the story can you identify the role of the following topics in your life narrative: conscience; alcohol addiction; morality; spirituality; religiousness; moral reformation; spiritual transformation; religious conversion and/or affiliation; the relationship between morality, spirituality, religiousness, and conscience, and recovery from alcohol addiction. How will you summarise each of these chapters? What progressive links will you make between these chapters? And these same guidelines are here for you to remind yourself. So take your time and develop your story.

Luke (L): Well my name is, as you said, Luke. I'm ... (age omitted due to confidentiality) years old, born in West Africa (WA, name substituted due to confidentiality). I arrived in this country in ... (year omitted due to confidentiality); and now leading the church. And so I was born again in 1991 in this country. And since then I believe God has taken my life through reefs and buns. I've been pastoring this church for seven years. And before I started pastoring the church I've been an assistant pastor for about two or three churches. My story is not spectacular to me but I've always used it to tell people about the greatness of God's deliverance and the power of God to transform people.

I started drinking at an early age when I was 14 through friends and through family. I believe the first I remember so vividly was related to the first night I believe in ... (year omitted due to confidentiality) when we were in primary school. I was referred to a good secondary school. I went to my father's first wife. All served the local gin, the high quality 100 percent alcoholic gin. She was the districts' distributor. She had the shop. But then my father was no longer with her because this was the first wife he married and separated, my father was no longer with her. From design her grandson came to live in the same house where he was living for another month. So we reunited the relationship through the grandson of my father's first wife. So as soon as I've gone there all of them knew me but I didn't know them, because obviously his mother and brothers knew me, his uncles knew me. So I just entered in the family. We were leaving about 5 miles apart in the same town.

Appendices

My first touch of drink was I believe the 31st of December . . . (year omitted due to confidentiality) because I remember the year before I went to secondary school in . . . (year omitted due to confidentiality). We finished eating and the woman preserved a special drink for people in her bedroom, the bedroom that was attached to the shop. "So my son come and take a bit." So I took a bit in the same pan where we used to eat. It wasn't a glass it was something that we sell now, is just like taking water. Apparently in the same ball we used to take water, from it we also drank. And from there if you believe we went to church. And in the church I didn't see anything. We were just laughing and then we came home. And that was the start of it I believe because when I was drinking it, it was a bit short but not regular.

But when I went to a secondary school apparently it was a Catholic school. It was supposed to be a very good school and it was. The secondary school in . . . (name omitted due to confidentiality), in my home country, (MHC, name substituted throughout the transcript due to confidentiality) is one of the top schools even now. I can recollect the whole thing. It was run by SVD, funded from America. My first experience of drinking on campus happened when I was in form one. Because the white fathers, those in America; they thought it was fun to drink the local pub wine. This was of lesser alcohol content than the one that I drank first. The one that I drank first was 100 percent alcohol. And people say that if you pour it on the ground, on the cement, and if you light a match it would be a blue flame—pure, pure alcohol. But this one; they took us one day to the next village walking, one holiday. And we tested the palm wine. They call it "Pama." It is very low-level alcohol. But if you're not a drinker or if you're not somebody who drinks you get boost. You definitely get drunk. And then you go. And some people drink it and get drunk anyway. In the morning it's okay but then in the afternoon it continues to brew and by the evening is so tough that people who drink in the evening only one "calabite" full, like two of these cups, and then another cup will knock you down. So I remembered very well; so we went and we drank it. They took us together in a convoy like taking children to the park exploring the woodland. Then we enter it as we never lived there and then we took it on from there.

Then things started rolling and I started going with friends. Against school there was a village, not where we went with the fathers but another village, where every Saturday, almost every Saturday, me and my friends from form one, every Saturday, we go there, drink the local gin, the stronger alcohol mixed with the palm wine. The locals called it "..." (name omitted due to confidentiality). That's a mix of palm wine. So we come at times and in order to show that we are macho: I can go out there, drink, go and vomit, and come and sit down again. And do vomiting that I would take as fun. So every Saturday we sneaked out after breakfast, and come there just before lunch, and we would get back before supper. And we were so popular in the school, me in particular. When I went to secondary school, form three, we were still going regularly from form one, from ... (year omitted due to confidentiality). When it became ... (year omitted due to confidentiality) when I was in form three my seniors in the sixth form would come and ask me to go with them. I was so popular with them. So the drinking became consistent. So during the holidays we were drinking a lot; we were drinking a lot. So that's how it started. So it started in the secondary school and I went to sixth form, that's the secular sixth form. But it was in the town where the booze was really available. You go to school but you'll get it. So the drinking continued. And we were going to nightclubs and that thing. So the drink became part of me. All my family knew that I was drinking.

So it continued till I went to the university. And the drinking continued and it became every day; holidays—we were drinking. And whatever it goes. I wasn't drinking beer or palm wine I was always going to the big stuff, the refined alcohol. So it was a bit, as I reflect now it is much, too much. You don't see it when you're going into a different.... But the thing is that you want to go and drink. And somebody to know that you are addicted—the outside is that when somebody who buys drink for you or you drink with as soon as you part: "So I'll see you tomorrow," you think it's an appointment to go and drink. So the following day you are looking forward to go and to meet them and drink. So it was all that. So it's a bit like when you are becoming addicted you don't know until you are. And nobody would admit: "I am an addict" until he goes to a point. So I was drinking and thank God .... When I had some friends in the politics and so making the politics; and I had many friends who were lawyers and when I go to their home they don't buy me, how do you call it, the whiskey and other things but they go for the local gin. And I was drinking everywhere. I go, drink, I had to sleep three nights before I was coming home. And so it was. I was a very heavy drinker and also smoking.

So after secondary school, after university I went to teach in this West African country (TWAC, name substituted throughout the transcript due to confidentiality) and the drinking continued. And because

Appendices

I was drinking, the landlady had a shop and even sent beer because she knew I was drinking. So when friends come we would buy beer. And when friends would invite us in TWAC; they are popular; they all know us; and they all have been there; and they come, and we go, and we drink, and we come back late. Whether we're going to school, gymnasium or not, a teacher, it doesn't matter we were drinking. I mean in TWAC it became more acceptable because as immigrants, and I learned that about the immigrant population, the only thing that is as an entertainment, for example. And people were coming traveling from other areas to come and meet us. One thing that we do in TWAC is that we go get money and buy beer for them when they come. There is ceremony in our culture: you take to somebody water first and then probably a drink, and so it becomes part of it. And because we were drinking, and because it was that drinking culture in TWAC as well of very heavily drinking . . . ; because in every spot there is a place where they open a shop where they sell beer and they get more money than even selling food. So we went to that culture and there were a lot of my own nationals (MON, name substituted throughout the transcript due to confidentiality). And we knew ourselves. So drinking was that there was no value judgement attached to it. There was nothing that we would get, go and drink. And at times we would go for loosing up in town because that is what follows it. If you're drunk and you don't take care of it and involve yourself and it happens. If you're married men it was important that there were girls around there. So when you drink the next thing is that you fall into that trap; which we have done; married men who would go to visit in their homes or to faraway towns they all have girlfriends in; they also have girlfriends in, what do you call it, like in the brothels. Every big hotel turned into a brothel because that was the money that attracted the attraction that they had.

So in TWAC the drinking continued so much throughout. I was in TWAC to . . . (year omitted due to confidentiality). It continued throughout even affecting my girlfriend—you'll lose certain things in life because of that. Because the girl that I wanted to marry from TWAC—I went and prepare. One of the uncles said: "No. I will not give you to this man to marry." Because the man of teaching was no good. You see! And the girl's mother and the girl became sad. So I came back to TWAC and I went back in the following year. I went to see the girl and to say hello because it was a short trip. And I left money with her uncle. The following week the girl was there. She was going to go to Germany but she said: "Let's go and try if the relationship would work." In TWAC the conditions that we were in were not that much. However, I think when she went I didn't hear about her. I think it was because of the drink. Because I think she was coming to watch closely. She didn't care about lack of facilities or nothing. I believe that she didn't come back and I didn't hear from her because it was drinking that if I didn't stop drinking then it can continue.

And it continued and I left where I was in TWAC. I was in the South and I went to the North; the same drinking continued. And in the North it was worse; not where the Muslims are in the middle of it, but it is where we call "culture of drink"; even a young boy would drink the local brew beer. Whiles in MHC like the 14-year-olds probably 16-year-olds would not drink; they are not allowed to drink, not yet; "Why should they drink?" But there they don't mind; they can give it to them. But the alcohol is not that much; it looked like food, the local millet that is brewed. But it passes from bare food to alcohol. It's just related to the content but after drinking more you get drunk. So where I went it was a village/town and the only big shop was a beer bar. And what you call it "a chemist," the one that opens the provision shop. So we were friends with the guy who served there. That's how you waste away your time. And another teacher who joined me also liked his drink so we would team up. And friends that we go to visit as I told you earlier on, when MON meet in TWAC, I think is something related to the immigrants' sort of culture, they drink. Wherever we go, we go and drink most of the time. When you go and visit somebody they say: "Let's go and drink." Then we go and drink and come back. That's how typical it is. That is a form of entertainment. But the entertainment gradually . . . ; because alcohol is very addictive in my case I believe that I was addicted. So anywhere, I expect; it's the mind. You expect the person to buy you a drink. You thought yourself you're going there, part of the plan: "I am going to visit but I know that he is going to buy me a drink." It might not be the reason to go but it might be an incentive to go. So when you go—you go because you know. So it became part of it.

Well alcohol and spirituality—wipes. I mean if you're addicted and you're in spirituality. Yes you can; you didn't know how spiritual you want to be; or you are determined because spirituality, as I now understand it, is probably: you have a theology but you're not a committed Christian. You have been baptised into a church; you have been confirmed as we do; and you have really gone to church once or twice in your youth and in another time and you know that there is a God. You don't deny the existence of God. So people can say: "I have some kind of spirituality because I relate to things that are not of this world, things that are spiritual. God is spiritual.

So if I believe in it, that's a bit of spirituality." So I believe I did. I did have. And I think it was very strong.

Because I remember when I went with my dad to church to be confirmed. So every time; there was once in TWAC; this was with my friend and I drank. And I need to emphasise it. After travelling I went to visit my friend. Our job was gone and we were waiting for money. So I was in the capital of TWAC. Then one day a friend comes and we started to go to one of MON who was preparing a local drink and I started drinking. And one thing, it was unplanned. The thing is that you don't plan when you are going to drink, just unplanned. After six o'clock I didn't see anything. I don't remember anything until the following morning. It hit me a bit. Because what did I do? What did I say to my friends? What conversations did they have? And to make it worse at that moment, that is conscience which moved, that I could have behaved badly to drink. What has happened? So I just was the guy who was drinking near. Why? Why was somebody knocking on my door to sell me drink? But one thing is to be assuming—you should not behave like that, you see. So that in away a bit I saw; I became more like: "What's happened really?" And my friend never told me. Then one day the friend was in there; I was in the same university with him. And he knew that in the university I was drinking a lot. Then I came down with the drinking; it subsided. So we were lucky as to go to church. That's what he said. He has invited me to go to church. He takes his beer one or two but he goes to church. And we started to go to church. And then I started thinking of me seriously stopping drinking. So I for a while used willpower instead of God's power. So I used my own power: "I want to stop. I want to stop." Then it turned unsuccessful. Once in a while I will drink.

Then we left TWAC. I left TWAC in . . . (year omitted due to confidentiality) to come over. Before I came over I went to my dad, my dad's home. I was going to see his relatives somewhere, not from where we live but in another region in MHC. He didn't tell me anything, he knew I smoked. He told his nephew whether there is anything that he can help me to stop smoking. He said: "Later we would talk about it." But later it turned out it wasn't a good idea. They were going to go to ". . ." (name omitted due to confidentiality) to a human to draw something on your tongue and that would cut it off. So you need a supernatural thing to do. And that guy is, I would tell you, the chief sorcerer but he knows it because he's there and I believe that he's done something with the sorcery concerning those sorts of fetish and all that African traditional religion; and it would have gone

Appendices

in. But I believe that it was God who saved me from that. Knowing of what he was going to use on me later because that could have brought in something else. It was not a medicine and it was not a prayer. Anything that is not medicine, medical or prayer can have some spiritual implications in the future. So I also tried: "Okay, I would stop." So I did for a long while.

So when I came in the country I was not drinking. Not at all. Then I went with friends and we were working. And there was a time when we were going to a party but through immigration we were caught. So I was in that cell for three days. So when I came out my friends said: "Let's celebrate." So when I was drinking I was drinking the heavy stuff and so: "Let me take a small bottle of Guinness." And that started the trail again. So I've stopped—started again; stopped—started again.

Then the drinking continued. It became serious again. So even my friends who brought me to drinking again were good friends from MHC where I used to know them. So we knew ourselves before I met them here. And when we met before in MHC before I met them here we were also drinking. And I happened to have; to go out with their sister. It was drink that broke up the relationship. One day I went and drank and I spoke anyhow so then it became a bit of a bad thing for the family, so we just "got in there where the parents were." It's a bit of drinking that can take you, alcohol. When you start drinking and losing your mind and track of what to say then anything that doesn't make you to stop and you go for it again that is an indication of addiction.

Addiction is that something that you take you can't go away with. You have to get it into your system. Addiction also affects your outlook; because it affects your demeanour; affects your external disposition because you could be sad in the following day and as soon as you get any drop of alcohol it triggers your whole system again. And it could be physiological. Addiction is physiological as well because it goes and also attacks; not attacks but affects your physiology, your system. Because part of it goes in the blood; and when alcohol goes in your blood and sort of you are elated, when you take the alcohol. But really alcohol can affect your system and your physical body as well. Because that's when addiction becomes out of hands. When you're weak and you get a bit of alcohol you become strong. You feel that. It means like; it becomes like, what do they call it, something that strengthens you; but it's all in the mind.

Okay, so after this incident and working with them the police came and I went back into drinking again. Where friends were drinking their friends expanded. I know; you know somebody and you will go to parties.

Appendices

And every weekend we were going to parties. We were looking forward to it. And I had been drinking Sunday still about 5 p.m., 6 p.m. because the next day I was going to work. And when the time goes to nine because I've been drinking heavily Friday evening, Saturday, and Sunday at times you know that things are going rough. It is going to affect your work as well.

Well, it will be that my friend advised me to go to church. The friend that I was with; he wrote to me; the guy who said that he would like to go to church. He went to Germany and chill for a while and he wrote me: "Go to church it might help." I did not hate church. No, I didn't. I loved it but I never got good because if you are addicted you want to feed your addiction and nothing else. When you have money you won't get your food but you feed your addiction.

So in the morning we were so drinking, so much in the morning that before 12 they don't sell alcohol but we went to the shop that we knew that they would sell it to us. And I remember that we were living opposite the police station. They would sell alcohol to us outside the hours. And I changed, and I went, and we met. And we met them on the road and we went to a party that was that close to them, it was dangerous. And I was drunk. After that day I couldn't spot where we went. They took us into a grotty nightclub, and we came out, and we came home as well. Then I used to go to the pub once in a while. When the pub that I run to was closing the drinking was then at home or at parties. That's where the drinking was but you are always looking forward to, you are looking forward to go and drink. So that is a little that pushes you. But the level and the reason that we had; that we were there because the way we've been teamed that we had to work. So during the working time; or during the working time we would drink as well. But after work is when we would drink a lot or probably, not probably, mostly during the weekends, during Friday evenings— a time to sort of let your head down.

So after I went back into drinking then I went to stay in the same place. And one day I saw; I had a relationship with another woman; after I was with their sister I had a relationship with another woman and I quickly moved in with the woman. Then is when I started saying: "Boy you have to cut the drink." Because my drinking became worse and I decided I'm not going to drink. So that's really helped a bit. But I went back into drinking again. So I believe that about six or seven times I stopped it and came in, stopped it and came in. Because I wanted to stop. Because when it gets very bad I think: "Did I do the right thing? Is that the proper way to behave? I should stop." Later I went to work for . . . (name omitted due to confidentiality) council as a community coordinator. And I was drinking.

I was living the most serious parts of my life around this time between . . . July and . . . (years omitted due to confidentiality). The reason is that some of the things that I did were indications that really, really you are addicted. Because you would find the tiniest excuse to drink; there is no inconvenient place to drink. Even if you wouldn't get any place to drink you would skim and get innovating ways that you can drink because you're so looking for it. I was working for . . . (name omitted due to confidentiality) council and I was drinking. I started there in . . . (year omitted due to confidentiality) as a community coordinator in the town hall. I was going for interviews, meetings for the council, taking notes and agendas like a community secretary. I left there and became an employee in the housing industry (EIHI, name substituted throughout the transcript due to confidentiality). And I was still drinking as an EIHI. There was a culture that we were going to parties in the afternoons and in the evenings. Then it went on in that way.

In one occasion we had a party, I drank and didn't see anything. Somebody dropped you home. I went and took the car without insurance, without licence, and I drove the car to another party in the town hall. And I drank a lot and I drove home. And the next day I said: "This is really, really bad." Because when you're addicted you don't know you're drunk. There were no drugs involved. I didn't do drugs. But the addiction to alcohol can be so serious. Addiction to alcohol, because this is what I did; I think I was: "What happened! It was that!" If you had the license is dangerous, and insurance; but you do have none of it. And the car is not registered on your name. But why do you go and take it to go to another place to drink more? That's what addiction can drive you into. But all I believe that as soon as you start thinking your conscience will pull up on you. I believe that the conscience is something you know that is right but you are not able to do. Your conscience will prick you. The conscience would know, this is good and this is bad.

Because I believe that God has given us basic conscience by breathing into us. So through this man became a living soul. Part of it is our conscience. God's nature is in us. So man failed but the conscience is with us. So it became like: so you know wrong from right. So you know that this is right and this is wrong. And conscience is also determined or mould out, either way by the laws and the norms of the justice society. Then when you are betrayed, and this is bad, and the law says this is bad. So when you do something that the law has said that this is bad your conscience will prick you that you have done mean thing. But in terms of when you are under alcohol you throw everything overboard. You don't consider anything until after the event. You probably become moral, you become sorry but because of the addiction you would do it next time again when you have a drink. Because what you did for your conscience to prick on you was fuelled by alcohol. And you're controlled by the need to drink. It's become a need instead of entertainment. Addiction has translated, how do you call it, pleasure into a need. So you need to have alcohol once a day or twice a day. And if you drink once then it calls for more. I don't remember who said: "Deep calls for the deep."

With alcohol and religion I believe that some people say that: "You can drink and go to church." But as I was brought up, I knew that you don't drink to go to church. That is my standard, yes. But then I was drinking and I wasn't going to church either. After that incident of driving without licence I went safely home.

I also remember an incident where . . . ; that incident, it was for a period of time; I was a cleaner for a time to supplement. The people there said: "Oh, Luke, take care." It lasted so far . . . ; beer you can take it, yeah . . . ; because of addiction I went beyond. And I remember—serious. I remember I came to that company; it was the managing director's cabinet I went to and pour some drinks, and I was drinking, and it became too much, and I added water to it. You see how addiction can take you. This really can be a criminal offence because you have been drinking and gone beyond the refrigerator to the drink cabinet. And it can even poison because you have added water to alcohol, whiskey bottle, so that the amount you poured was so descended that you would be caught. You see the point. So it is between the criminality and trying to order yourself. So when you are addicted; when I had two pounds and I want to buy beer for myself you actually have mind and would say: "No." So lies and deceit also accompany because you need to feed your addiction. And you do some unusual things as well.

So during the same period between . . . ; talking about between . . . and . . . ; I am talking about when I became an EIHI, between . . . and . . . (years omitted due to confidentiality) it became very serious. So whenever I was working with alcohol I would go and drink. I could buy but: "Why did you take it?" And it turns to; I was also not doing the cleaning during the weekend, I could get time to buy my drink while I still needed drinking. And the girlfriend I was with said: "Let me go and help you." I said:

"No." Because what happened, I would go and drink. So pushing people away in order to get and attend to yourself. And as an EIHI I would finish work, and I would go to the shop and buy quarter size whiskey and four cans of the highly alcoholic lager, a special brew or "Super Tennents" with a very, very strong alcohol. So every night after work—quarter size whiskey and these four cans, and it's a deadly cocktail. And I want to drink it before I go to do other job. Do you know what I did? I would go to the telephone kiosk as if I'm ringing and I would start drinking. Because if there was a place nobody knew me I would be like those sitting on the bench. I would get a bench and drank. Because people know me as a highly built . . . and no bench, I resorted to little phone kiosk. And nobody is coming to see that you're drinking. Because you're addicted you were able to do so many things.

Fortunately during that period, at the end of it, we were going to churches here and there; . . . (name omitted due to confidentiality) church, Church of England. I was going to Church of England. Yes, Sunday was a sober time but Saturday becomes a bit, it's all about you. Especially when I stopped drinking I was going to church. When I started drinking I didn't go to church. There was a day in . . . (year omitted due to confidentiality) December somebody said: "Let's go to a church." I think that my girlfriend knew this guy. And I think that the drinking was becoming too much. And she said: "On the 31st normal people go there and we need to." Somebody gave me a whiskey bottle that would be that size. So I remember I had it by my site and I was drinking. So I said: "When are we going to church?" "7:00." "Okay, 16:30, my last shot." No, because I know that you can't drink and go. I've forgotten that when you drink the effect can take longer time than while you literally taking the glass to your mouth. I forgot about that. Why, because I needed to drink. I would get any excuse to drink. So we went. And then there were a lot of calls, and then I properly became a committed Christian.

Then, I started going to church. It was far away from where we lived. So I wasn't drinking. Then, what happened was that I started doing my project diploma in . . . (name omitted due to confidentiality) studies. Then, I started drinking again. And that was worse than any of my life. And at that time I wanted to stop. I was drinking and smoking heavily. I wanted to stop. So for one year I didn't feel all right, but I was still doing it, and I believe that because I've been born again the spirit of God was fighting against drinking in my conscience. This is coming under conscience. The spirit of God came; God's conscience came; put into your life and working.

So in another way previously where you don't feel that guilty when the spirit of God comes in your life, as it says, the spirit of God convicts us. So there is a serious conviction not by my own assessment or what is written or societies have said but the consciousness. The conviction comes with the Holy Spirit in my life. So I was even calling when I was alone: "Oh, Lord come and help me." Because I was so much frustrated drinking and smoking—that I was doing it.

Gradually the girlfriend I was with; her two children were there; the girlfriend I was with has junior sister who has married a pastor that was going in the Bible college in TWAC. And the man was coming to visit. I've got into chasing women as an EIHI. Because of the drink, I would buy drink and would have an affair in the afternoon and come and continue my work which is highly unethical. But it continued. And I knew it would be for ever because of the drink. So when that man came; that pastor came; that's when we went and just prayed. I received the baptism of the Holy Spirit and that was it. And I went out and went to meet another girlfriend, you know. I wished to smoke. And I went to McDonald's. I don't remember why we met. I needed a cigarette. "Give it to me." I took two puffs and I couldn't do it again. So I had to stop because of the prayer that we had. It didn't take much time. It didn't take long on the deliverance from addiction. We were just praying. We started speaking in tongues. The man prayed breaking the addiction with that prayer and that was it.

So since then if I have a sip I might but I don't remember. I was having a sip probably in a cough mixture. Some people say probably there is an alcoholic in the cough mixture. There was a time my friends, despite my drink I think, they did a little. I didn't know. I didn't taste it. I didn't know what they have done. I was okay. They were laughing when I was doing the drinking. "Oh, they were laughing, so they did." But I was laughing. I didn't take it seriously, about it, because I think they did only a small thing. So I just said: "Don't do that again." They were testing whether I'm still of. They didn't do it maliciously because they were good guys and they were expecting that I was not drinking again.

And when I became born again I had a strong desire to go and talk to alcoholics; to speak Christ to them. But I was a bit "big" Christian. And I think this is something I regret not doing. I didn't know how to approach them. I didn't know whether they would receive me or so. Because I had that strong, strong thing to go and speak to them.

Well morality and addiction; the whole morality, spirituality, religiousness, conscience, and recovery from alcohol addiction. Recovery from alcohol addiction is that now you're not moved, you are not, you don't act because of alcohol addiction. Now you can think clearly. And therefore, you can consider things that you're going to do whether good or bad; whether your religion accepts whether this goes; the way to do things.

Normally, I'm not saying that people are perfect. But when you're recovering from addiction then you cannot blame anything for your decision that you make because the decision you've made maybe fuelled by alcohol. Of course alcohol; you went to drink alcohol, therefore, I believe there is no excuse for it. So I believe that morality; when people are addicted morals are thrown through the window. Because their primary purpose, everybody alike, is to feed their addiction. They have a sense of morality but the addiction, to feed their addiction takes precedence over morality. Then some might even forgo the spiritual outlook that they've obtained because if you don't deal with it, it continues.

And now let me subtract a bit. I don't argue about whether we should drink as Christians or not—all alcohol is Adam's. All I see is that all the drinking that I needed to drink I drank it already. So I guess I'm sacrificing that pleasure that I had for the God who saved me. Because in the Bible probably is fair that it is implicit in it. So many people take so many verses so it is good to state that the Bible didn't legislate. I'm not going in depth now but to me I believe whether smoking, eating, the Bible is saying, it's implying for us to keep our bodies; for us to maintain our bodies. Because I believe a good body can house—would be a house of God if the body is a temple of the Holy Spirit. And God worked through the apostolic council by Paul saying that when you take God's temple to love a prostitute; if you lied in bed with a prostitute you have taken the body and damaged it. You have damaged it. Yes, I think that God know that they would do all those things. The sins of alcohol; to me I was alcohol addicted; the scenes and the places that they do go are not places where the Holy Spirit wants to be. So as a Christian I would not? Yes I would not go.

It makes me more conscious in order that now these days I don't blame people for being addicted I rather sympathise with them. I rather empathise; not sympathy; not that I'm pitying them. It makes you more understanding of people. Even if they are not addicted you find it very difficult to deal with certain situations. You know that you've been there before because is very difficult to get out. And I don't subscribe to willpower. That's a Christian: I surrender it all to God; because I came to God. And since he has put the spirit of the Son in me why should I use my own strength since God's power is within me to help me. So I believe as it comes

Appendices

to addiction I know it is just prayer nothing else. Because through prayer that I was delivered. That's why I know my experience. It wasn't anything as: get the patch; do not smoke anything. I was smoking and realise that they are all gone purely through the prayer and through the spirit of God. Because one year I was like going through the valley of shadow of death. All the time you are watching yourself and you're saying that you should stop; you don't feel happy after you smoke, or you've been drinking, you feel bad. Because you know, something in you tells you that this is not what it should be. So that's where the conscience would come in. And the conscience is the level of God's consciousness in us. The conscience that all human beings possess—because to know from good and bad. Yes that's it.

Summarise each chapters: Well, from my infant age I drank and it's gradual. And starting school time I also drank a lot. And it was voluntarily. The money that we had we use it for alcohol. And for some people it doesn't matter the roof or where they are. So they put you in Catholic school. They put you in school where there is discipline. And canonically; yeah canonically I wasn't bad, years I was on top. But still I was drinking. Most of your youth when you go and drink I think you lose so many things that you don't realise. Because the addiction becomes entrenched. Because for every addicted person wherever you have a chance you drink. Whenever you have that chance you go and drink. So deeply; that deeply to set up the root to be deeply addicted to alcohol. And also when I grew up since I was in the university it became like not a fashion but like a badge of honour. And you don't care who thinks of you or not. Even the women in the university's big campus when you go and mention me by name they would know me because I'm a regular visitor, you see. So that much and what comes with it is a reputation going down; people looking down upon you. And I remember when we were visiting my friend; the father gave me a name because in the afternoon I would drink and passed off there. So you think you're walking straight but you're not. You see all these things are; there are things that come into play.

But the most important thing is that some of the moral issues that are attached to it. Some of the things that you do; some of the things that you do—deceive. I don't remember stealing; because it was not stealing going to get the money, because my father had a shop. When the shop is there and when people come, we have quality price and single price. So when people see single prices about things they think this take single prices money. And on the record I've sold it in a quality price. So there is a bit of money on it. That is not a profit. That's for my dad not for me.

But I needed it to go and drink. So all this got into it. And if you want to drink you develop undercurrent trends which show that you are being addicted. Addicted person depending on the level of addiction would deceive people to buy them; would coerce people to buy them; or beg people to buy them; but it might go beyond stealing to feed your addiction; and commit criminal offence because then you develop other character which is because of the addiction. I think; Are we here?

I: Okay, yeah.

L: Thank you.

I: I have few questions now. I will read them and the sub questions. If you want to add anything please do. If not we will continue until we exhaust all of them.

L: Okay.

I: So the first one is: How do you perceive your conscience? What is conscience? How did it develop? How does it function? You already covered a lot about these.

L: Yes.

I: Do you want to add anything about conscience?

L: No.

I: Okay. The second one is: How did you develop alcohol addiction? You talked a lot about this. What is alcohol addiction? When did you realise that you have been addicted to alcohol? How did you try to manage your alcohol addiction? Do you want to add anything?

L: Yes. What you never, never knew. I've never come to a conclusion at any time that I was addicted. All you know is that you like the drink. You see, probably other people but me, I've never thought I liked the drink. And I thought that it's because of my family that I should stop. But they said that I was drinking and I thought that I probably am drinking too much. But coming to a realisation that you are addicted, in my case I came to realisation that the drink caused so many problems. And the woman that you want to go with says: "You don't have to drink." And her mother said: "That is an incentive to stop." But being addicted—"No"; I'm checking myself in, or I'm expected to seek help for addiction is something that has never occurred to me.

I: Okay. The third question is: What were your moral views before your moral, spiritual, and/or religious transformation? What is morality? How did you deal with moral dilemmas? How much did morality matter for you? You spoke about this. Anything else to add?

L: I was basically; because I was afraid of my dad I was basically on a place of good or bad and I always wanted to do the right thing. You see. I wanted to do the right thing but going back in the period that passed, I would hurt people unnecessary and all that. But the moral view I said before is; know so many women and going there; because of addiction I was going to so many women and people that you don't know for one last chance and other things. The old days are something that was fuelled by the addiction because if I was not drinking I would not be at the spot where I would chat to people and go in bed with. And for some people some of their belief is that if I've not drunk I'd have not done anything there. So that is how you get this. But like that time I was intrigued by the Christians and what they had. Because one thing that I did was that after I drank I went in the bus. First, the double-decker you can smoke apparently which I think was not necessary. I was reading and smoking at the same time. Before they did that change you could even smoke in that time. But then I would be reading and I felt some kind of peace there. So something was in me but it's not coming out. And I believe that, as I said for the recording, the spirit of God, God's part is in us before I became born again at least. You see, God breathed into us and we became living souls. That conscience God put in me was still there.

I: Okay. Next one: Did you practice spirituality before your moral, spiritual, and/or religious transformation? What is spirituality? How did you practice spirituality? How much did spirituality matter for you? You spoke about this. Do you want to add anything?

L: No. No.

I: Okay. The next one is: Did you practice religion before your moral, spiritual, and/or religious transformation? What is religiousness? How did you practice religion? Did you have religious affiliation? How much did religion matter for you? You already mentioned it.

L: Yes. Religion as well as spirituality; I think that religion: as a Christian denomination I am Presbyterian. I think that's my religion; that's spirituality, yes.

I: That's before your conversion.

L: Yes, because I believe; I said I knew there was something bubbling up in me. Because at the end I dreamed sages from early, early age about 10, 11, 12. And I started, I remember getting out of my bed and praying. And somebody when I was sleeping was laughing at me. You see, I was young but I knew that there is something in me but I couldn't lay hand on it.

I: Okay. Next question: Did you experience moral, spiritual, and/or religious transformation? How did you experience this transformation? When did you experience this transformation? May you identify anyone who played any influential role in the process? How much has this transformation changed your life? You already mentioned all these.

L: Well, there is one more. There was one man—my friend in TWAC. He was going to church and he was gentle but he drank. But his drinking was not elated, just one bottle of beer and that's it for organisation at that end. Also when I came here my extra common-law wife also played a part. Why, because when I went to her and her mum was there, she said that I should stop drinking. I said: "Oh, yes." I went there, I think and this was a time when I drank and I misbehaved a bit. So since then I started to be a gentleman who never used to drink. But when I've got the job as an EIHI, you know, we would crack opened the champagne. And that started it. And they were drinking champagne, champagne. Then I started it again. That's what I'm saying between . . . March and December . . . (years omitted due to confidentiality), that period. And I started at . . . (name omitted due to confidentiality) and delighted up to July . . . (year omitted due to confidentiality), that's where I had the preacher praying and I just became born again. One person who did was the Reverent from MHC; he is a bishop now; who prayed and then the drinking and smoking got stopped.

I: Next question: What was the impact of your transformation on your life? Compare your morality, spirituality, and religiousness before and after the transformation. How did the transformation impact your understanding of morality, spirituality, and religion, and their role in your life? How much did morality, spirituality, and religion matter for you after your transformation? You spoke about all these.

L: Yes.

I: Do you want to add anything?

L: No. That's right.

I: Okay. What was the impact of your moral, spiritual, and/or religious transformation on your conscience? Compare your conscience before and after the transformation. How did the transformation impact your conscientious behaviour? How much did the voice of your conscience matter for you after your transformation?

L: Before the transformation as I said, before that I believe I was person of morals, meaning morals in general. I would not do anything bad, I would not swear off. I was honest with friends and very loyal to friends and people around; telling the truth and didn't hide anything from anybody.

Appendices

So morality; I was always doing the right thing as generally acceptable. And when I was challenged it became a bit more because I felt that I had been cheated. However, when the transformation came in I became conscious. Because my transformation started with me receiving the baptism of the Holy Spirit and being a committed Christian. So that changed the particulars, the Word of God and the other things. So when I compare that now because of the path and as a ratio my Christian growth after; after the prayer incidents and deliverance; and when I look back there are so many things that I shouldn't have done. Because especially with sexual immorality that is—that shouldn't have happened. Yes, sexual immorality shouldn't have happened. And I started to become . . . . Oh, God. There is a period that I started blaming people for socially immoral behaviour. But one day it crossed my mind: "Look! Look at you before you became a Christian. Look at the life you were living especially with the youth." You see; "Now you are married. You have children. And you have responsibility; so what about them? What sort of things that they should do?" So I would rather pray for them, counsel them rather than condemning and judging. So that is what has now happened.

And even it has continued until recently. Of course to my leaders in church I say that I don't want any judgemental pronouncement, any condemnation pronouncement from the pulpit in the church. Because it is for people; it is a hospital. People should be looked after. There is no doctor who goes and blames you. He looks after you. Even the arm robber is looked after before they go in the police. Even the arm robber who has been shot; they treat him or her (to make sure we are politically correct: you treating him or her) before when you know that her life has come back to her and she can speak; and she's then ready to speak. Because of the preservation of life it is very, very important to them before considering what the person has done. So it has changed my outlook. And I think it has continued to change my outlook. And it is given me my ministry as based on Isaiah 61. "The anointing of the Lord is upon me to preach to the poor and bind the broken-hearted and pronounce liberty to the captives." I believe people who are alcohol addicted or do immoral things, they are captivated. And Jesus himself looked for the same scripture from Isaiah; that's it the Ministry of Isaiah. So as a Christian I know how to bring people from brokenness into holiness. And part of it is that part of the brokenness can be through addiction, through rejection, through so many things. And it goes deeply into the head. Why people become addicted? Why people become addicted to cocaine; therefore, there are prostitutes. And where they come from there are so many things happening; from rejection to everything; deep, deep things. I'm not going into the root causes of things other than looking at the branches and the fruits. Because if you are concentrated on the branches and the fruits you would be deceived and you could never get it done.

I: Okay. Next one is: What was the impact of your transformed conscience on your recovery from alcohol addiction? Compare your recovery before and after the transformation. How did your transformed conscience impact your recovery from alcohol addiction? What is the role of your transformed conscience in the maintenance of your abstinence? May you identify anyone who played any influential role in the process? Anything to add to this one?

L: No.

I: Okay. May you share your future plans related to your recovery? What is the role of morality, spirituality, and/or religion in them? What is the role of your transformed conscience in them? Do you plan to share your experience with others who need help in recovery from alcohol addiction?

L: Well, I mean the last part I have been doing it over the years. Even at work not in the Christendom; even at work. And, as I said, also transformation is to look at first not alcohol addiction-wise but all in my Christian life as well. Because I think basically I don't like people who judge and accuse people without reason. Because I think as it is said: "people notice for reason." So I said: "Do you know about it? What do you know about it?" If you bring something to me I will question you about that. I don't like people who are always putting people down and judging them. I think that's what affected me without me thinking about it. Because this is so . . . . Even my wife when she comes to tell me she has to be very careful when she tells me something because I will question. And I will not accept anything just on the surface. And if you knew somebody who comes to me and does say something to me, and then they go back; some of them I know that there is a basic issue with them. So I need as a pastor and a person with whom God is working . . . . And God basically wants to transform people. It is a restoration process that is going through. And I always tell my wife that she cannot be intercessor and be an accuser. Because Jesus interceded, he didn't accuse us, he forgave us. So, no matter what the person has done, it is to help this person to come through and identify certain causes which the spirit of God would identify to you or knowledge that you know.

Some, he puts them to people who are trained to go deep down into them. There was a case of a woman; this woman, thanks God I spoke with her on the phone. I met her in 2006 when we were working between . . . (name omitted due to confidentiality) and I was giving her a lift. I interviewed her. But later she was behind and we were going to share a car, later. She was so sad; serious eye bags because the daughter; the married life; it was all wrong. The daughter would give her problems. So gradually we were talking and praying, and I referred her to a counsellor, a Christian counsellor. And thank God today the mother and daughter, they get on. The woman is now in the uni. From where she was she went to university. And guess what course she is doing? "Psychology and criminology;" because she is taking that experience. So, therefore, when I'm dealing with people now I have to know that people can change. And God's Word for people refers well that we change. The person has to cooperate; but we can; from the experiences we can get. Because I cooperated but people helped me on that road to cooperation, to cooperating. Why? Because they spoke into my life. They explained the situations and knew where I was going. Because somebody said: "If you don't stop drinking I am not with you." The person is helping you to identify the problem. They're helping you to take a decision to stop what you are doing. And it becomes positively getting on. In all things the people get the person to sit down and think: "Oh, this is wrong and I need to . . . all being that I cannot help myself." Then I believe that 50 percent of the problem is sorted because "their help desk" offers all the help that we can get. But it is we taking the first step to see the help. And God will help us to get the right people to help us.

I: Thank you. May you share your future plans related to your recovery?

L: Oh, future plans! Future plans of recovery: I'm not directly into the alcohol or any addiction recovery. But my future plans that I have and now coming to me. I don't know whether it's related to it but I think it should be. The other way is that getting people from brokenness into holiness. It's exactly what I need to do to establish them. And also one thing that the basic causes of addiction, I believe, one of the big things is rejection. But if people know their stand in the Lord then their identity in Christ and that they've received Christ's love they won't depend on substances or drink in order to suit their pain that would land them into alcoholism. And that is what I'm doing. I'm going to start freedom in Christ in the church. And I'm going to talk about Christ and the centrality and the uniqueness of Christ; about all Christian life. So when you say freedom in Christ they will know the person who has given them the freedom. And after that we will be doing discipleship about what Christ did. Not what Christ will do. We're not going to speculate. We're going to the Bible to see what Christ did. So that we are disciples and we will follow the master. We have to know the master and what he did. Not what commentators are saying what he would do in the circumstances. Because now you see all over: "If Christ was there he would go to the pub. If Christ was there he would have been homosexual. If Christ was there . . . ." You see! But what Christ did actually do? So that is this. All this I believe is to go to the root cause. To get the love of God into the people's life so it prevents any form of addiction.

Because with my children I'm taking the high standards. I've now confiscated my son's laptop because he was really addicted to films. So I say: "Come and do your homework downstairs." Every morning we would meet. I meet them between 20 and 30 minutes to share a prayer before they go to school. So that is that and I'm using that to give examples and in that time that is all right. Because you are addicted to Internet. And other addictions are so clever that if you're not careful the picture just come on and hardly is the picture that you see. But then when they log on things come up. What you accept multiplies in your life. What you are exposed to influences you. So in our children; in my own children if they are less exposed, not exposed to as if we want them to be exposed; we can expose to them by controlled exposure so that we give them the right Christian meaning, the Christian stand on the things in life. Then it will help them. Because by just exposure coaches drawing out the pleasure and let them to focus on, how do you call it, the pleasure of it, not the dangers. It would become difficult. They can go in and as soon as they go in they'd become addicted. That's why we need to in order to prevent for my own children and then they are going to return to the church.

I: Thank you. And the last question is: May you formulate the main theme of your life story? What is the place of alcohol addiction in your story? What is the place of conscience in your story? What is the place of morality, spirituality, and/or religiousness in your story? What is the place of your moral, spiritual, and/or religious transformation in your story? The main theme.

L: Work in progress. Because I was work progress. I believe that God has called me but I went through there. I thank God, he doesn't push me into it. But he let you remain in there until things happen. And it was there alcohol, I mean addiction, and then came friends and other things. I used to cling to friends. I was so much attached to friends because I didn't stay with my mum. And my dad also went to work. So we were alone in the house. So when I was there I had no supervision. But I think that that developed kind of rejection spirit in us. So you get closer attached to people. So you get something that would make you happy and you hold on to it. Because of my father working out that they divorced. My father was working in the farming. And they anyway divorced and I had to stay with my uncle. So I believe that the background started, you see, or can have serious implications in the case of addiction. How you develop it. Because psychologically you know that you need satisfaction, you need human touch, and you need certain things that they can sort of give you what you have lost. Alcohol and addiction I believe are substitute for the lack of love for something, principal that you haven't got. But it takes . . . . I'm saying this because of afterthought, the hindsight.

Because I was one time in my break time and I came to . . . (name omitted due to confidentiality) conference. We came to a church and talk about edifying, rejection in the spirit, having people doing things. And I believe God opened my eyes that there were some differences in the church. Most of them—what they had; a certain attention, and their names and their pictures came. "This man, the father died when he was young. This woman was alone like me, and the mother and father travelled, and then she was alone. The boyfriend took the money and then they negated her. So her behaviour is all that and if you say 'no' to her then there is a problem." So the message is that the rejection is in the past. All including myself, my wife, and our first daughter did not say anything. For I realised that all this have got a deep, deep source. So when the deep source is investigated and dealt with the alcohol and the addiction will go. But thank God for his Word and the Holy Spirit, and the power that he has given us. Then prayer also can let things go. Prayer can resolve the addiction before they are thinking through. Because the person should know to think it through with the Word of God. Oh yes, the teaching of the Word, I am also convinced that it can help thinking through. That to me is how the person recovers from addiction. That's how I believe that the Holy Spirit would open his mind to the past not to condemn again but to know that these are the things that they did. Because I believe that no experience is wasted. So my experience, I believe God wants to use it to help others not only with addiction but when people are finding problems with behaviour, behaviour problems, yes.

I: Okay. Thank you Luke. We will stop recording now.

Mary (2011). Personal interview (Conscience in recovery from alcohol addiction), 10 November.

Interviewer (I): Okay. So, this is an interview on the 10th of 11th with Mary and the instructions are simple: Structure your life story in chapters. Think about their names, summaries, and progressive links. Without interfering with the genuine character of the story can you identify the role of the following topics in your life narrative: conscience; alcohol addiction; morality; spirituality; religiousness; moral reformation; spiritual transformation; religious conversion and/or affiliation; the relationship between morality, spirituality, religiousness, and conscience, and recovery from alcohol addiction. How will you summarise each of these chapters? What progressive links will you make between these chapters? So this is all here if you want to remind yourself. And then take your time to tell me your story.

Mary (M): So should I just tell you my story, yeah.

I: Exactly, yeah.

M: Basically one of four children I was born in a European country (EC, name substituted due to confidentiality). My father was in the army. My family—Christian. Not actually practising Christians. But I did go to convent when I was very young girl. Purely because that was the nearest school. And my father developed alcoholism when he left the army. We moved back to this country. My mother lost three children after my youngest sister was born. And during my early years I was a bit of a sounding board for her basically. Because of my father's alcoholism she was often depressed. And because she lost her children. And I seemed to bear the burden of her sorrow. I don't know really. My father's condition deteriorated. He was hit by a car. Prior to which his condition deteriorated and his alcoholism worsen. He went to work in a bank and embezzled a lot of money. And he did the bank basically. He left us all. But then I suppose his conscience brought him back. He came back. My mother made me; I was not very old at all, possibly seven or eight; and she made me so plead with the bank officials. They came around to our house. Plead with them not to jail him, which I found extremely difficult. And all the more so because my father was sat in the chair and I knew. Because he was a very proud man. He was a major in the army. He was very successful as job. And he descended into this alcoholic who just embezzled money. Yeah. Physical, mental, psychological rack basically. And I know that when I was speaking to his bank officials the shame for him must have been huge. And I found this really dramatic. Then I was never really close to my mother. She was more close to my brother and my young sister, I would say. She was a little bit frightened from my old sister.

And then eventually I started sniffing "pasturent" stuff when I was young about nine. And I don't know why. We always queued up randomly on the street. We always queued up and sniffed my father's petrol camp. And it was always me that really enjoyed it the most. I don't know why if that was anything to do with the addictive nature or what. I was really enjoying doing that. I also loved sniffing rapid markers. Things like that. And anyway I started drinking in my early teens. I think the first time I got completely legless I was about 13. I went into a youth club. And my friends and I decided to take some booze and I took a bottle of sherry. And I just drank the whole thing. And all I can remember is sitting on the swing on the way to the youth club and seeing the ground coming up towards me. And next thing I knew I was back in my bed at home. And the youth club leader actually brought me home. I had no memory of what happened after the swing. And basically alcohol has always been very accepted in my family. And I would say that most of my family are alcoholics. And I've lost several members of my extended family through alcoholism as well.

And, yeah, I started drinking on a regular basis. Going out to clubs when I was 14; usually weekends. I flunked school. I couldn't concentrate on school at all. As I said, during this time my father was hit by a car and comatosed. And he was transferred to a hospital in this south east English city (TSEEC, name substituted due to confidentiality) for ex-army officers, I think. And he subsequently died from pneumonia there. And then as I got older I just did a shop job. And then I went to work in a hospital. And when I was working in the hospital admissions officer said if I wanted to do nursing. So, because I flunked my O levels and I've got couple I did a couple more. And then I applied for nursing posts in this English county (TEC, name substituted throughout the transcript due to confidentiality). I moved to TEC. I was really sad, really homesick, and not so much, not for my family, only for my younger sister and for my boyfriend. I had a boyfriend I left behind who used to take heroine, which I didn't realise until I walked in on him one day. But he destroyed his mind really. And I knew that there was not future of that relationship because drugs changed him massively.

And I did nursing. And then I moved back from TEC back to . . . (name omitted due to confidentiality) and started working on neurology ward. I found it very depressing because neurological diseases are really cruel. So I moved to intensive care ward place, which was a bit crazy for somebody like me. And I really enjoyed looking after patients who went through cardiac surgery and had none event for recovery. And that was great. I really enjoyed that aspect of it. Occasionally, we had trauma patients in. And there was one particular case. I think I was oversensitive then. A lot of the other nurses could deal with things a lot better than I could. From an emotional point of view. And this one little boy came and he was 10. He fell out of the back of a van on the motorway. And he came in. And because some of the nurses on the unit were laughing on something really unrelated, the sister said: "Do you mind looking after him." He was already presumed brainstem dead. But he was kept alive on life-support machine. And she said: "Would you mind looking after him for next three shifts that you work." So I think, you know, for the family sake, so I can build a rapport with them. And I did look after him. And it was awful because he was lying there. He was pink. He was breathing because of the machine. His heart was functioning normally. He was pink, he was warm. His family were sitting there, praying, praying for him to be, to start to be alive, for signs of life. And I had to frequently obviously check neurological observations, check signs of life. And there were not any. And then that in retrospect, I didn't realise at the time, but that's really had a huge psychological effect on me, I would say. Because, yeah, after three days he was deemed to be brainstem dead, after they did the brainstem dead test. And I felt really guilty actually because his mother consoled me. And I've really felt that I failed in my role. And I will cry about right now.

And then, anyway, I think shortly afterwards, anyway I've got, I met my ex-husband, now my ex. And we had children. And I left nursing. And everything was fine, I was really happy. I think until children started to getting into an age when they no longer needed me. I lived life, taking them to playgroups, going to school book club, and I did a lot of things with them I suppose—proactive. But then I grew old and they needed me less. And I . . . . My ex-husband, I don't know; he is very good in belittling people. And he presents it as humour but it is not. It is really hurtful. It is quite demeaning, quite derogatory. But he says it in a joking way. He says: "I was only joking, what's the matter." But it is not. I think after years of that it actually chipped away of me, you know, my self-esteem. And at the end I was drinking more and more and more. And it got worse. And I wish in retrospect, we should have got divorce a long time before we did. And I did. I would get drunk and I'd say: "I want to divorce blah, blah, blah." But he'd always try and patch things up and it's sort of saying: "I love you blah, blah, blah." And, you know, we carried on. We just muddled through really. Which was a mistake, huge mistake.

And anyway my drinking got worse and worse. And I ended up going to this detox facility (TDF, name substituted throughout the transcript due to confidentiality). I went to CDAT. And I was referred to TDF. And I was put into detox. And I spent two weeks there. And I came out, and I was under the false impression—I could control alcohol, which was a mistake. And I started drinking again. And it wasn't long before I was back to what I was drinking before every night. I had no work to get up to or anything like that. I had tried to return to practice course, which I did. I completed it in three months but I chose not to go back to nursing. I did not want to do that. I didn't know what else to do. And my husband, my ex-husband earned a good salary. There was no need for me to go to work. There was no need for me to do, there was . . . . I had no purpose basically. And so I stayed at home. Yeah, I started picking up earlier and earlier each day and every day. And as the days go on each day earlier and earlier.

And then we moved. And during that time, I sort of felt in love with a man who worked next door. But nothing came of that. And I told my sister-in-law who told my ex. And I couldn't stop thinking about this man I did fall in love with. And that made my marriage worse because the more I loved this man the less I wanted to stay with my husband, being with my husband. But neither of us actually took steps for divorce, which was huge mistake. And things continued to get, to become much worse. And I went into . . . . I went into few rehabs. I went into . . . . Do you want me to name them or there is no point?

I: As you feel.

M: All right. I went into . . . . I went into . . . . I've been into ". . . ." I've been into ". . . ." I've been into, how is it called, they changed the names, now is called ". . ." but it was ". . ."—I've been there twice. I went into ". . ." (five names omitted due to confidentiality) for a secondary care one time. But that was after I've done the rehab. I went into the secondary care. They voted that I was safe to go out on my own. I went out on my own. I thought, this is my only opportunity so I bought some vodka, drank it, went back to the house. They breathalysed me and they put me out. That was that. Then I went . . . , I've been to more but I can't remember the names. I've been to about six in total. I've also been after that as well. I went to hospital few times. I went . . . . I am getting . . . . My years are all mixed up. But I went into hospital in between some rehabs and then after the last rehab I went in more so. And I ended up . . . . And during this time my husband actually asked me, my ex-husband asked me for divorce. And I know that he met this woman that he worked with, who is now living with. And during the time of my worst alcoholism my children lived with him. And I lived in this house. I moved into this house in this large English village (TLEV, name substituted due to confidentiality), not far from the family home.

And I got in such state; I developed muscle wastage; I was double incontinent. Out of hours nurses have come in. They have come in few times a week for a short time. I stopped eating. I had to live downstairs. I had bed downstairs. I had to commode downstairs. I had to walk in frame. I used to phone a local taxi company to go and get me booze and they would. Sometimes my friend went to get me booze. She didn't want to but she knew that if I didn't have the booze I would fit. I forgot to mention that over a few years I started developing fits. And they became grand mal seizures. And they became more and more frequent. If I didn't have booze I did. And the worst thing was, it was as a vicious circle. If I didn't have booze I would fit. And if I did have booze at least I wouldn't know I was having a fit. But it would mean that I was going to have more fits. So it was awful. I would have booze in order to be oblivious to the fits. But, obviously the more booze I was having the more I was likely to have the fits. So I was terrified. Obviously, terrified of the fits because I used to feel them coming on. And then my head would always turn to one side. And I could not move it, and I knew the fit was coming on, and I was going to grand mal seizure. That absolutely terrified me. Yeah, I was in this terrible state. And sometimes I've managed to . . . . I got up first thing in the morning. I would have . . . . I would start drinking. I used to have squash first and then I vomit that. Then I started drinking wine. I always had to have booze there in the morning because I couldn't function without it. I started having wine. I would be sick. I would be keeping sick. But I would keep going until some of it was going into my system. And then eventually started shaking and eventually I would be able to kind of crawl out of the house. And the shop was only 50 yards from the road. And I would get to the shop and then I would get back. By this time my ascites was awful. Do you know what ascites is?

I: No.

M: It is fluid. Basically my kidneys were packing up and because of the liver—liver disease. You got fluid in the peritoneal cavity. And so I couldn't even do, I couldn't even do my trousers up. And one day I walked up to the shop. And I was walking backwards with booze. I would fall over in the shop frequently. The shopkeepers were really kind. There wasn't a lot they could do. They weren't ignoring the fact that I was drinking and just sit and trying to make money out of me. They knew that I had to have that drink, you know. And one day I was walking back from the shop. And my trousers just fell down. And I couldn't. I knew because of what would often happen. If I bend forward or anything I just go straight over. I completely lose my balance. My muscle wastage was so bad I couldn't get up again. And that happened to me couple of times. And I knew that I couldn't put the shopping bags down because I wouldn't be able to pick them up. And I couldn't put my trousers up. If I put my bags down I have to lean down to pick them up and I would be over. So I actually walked on the street with my trousers down my legs. Shocking state to be in. And all I could do was just . . . . I just couldn't wait to get through that front door basically. And I felt on the stairs numerous times. That's why I lived downstairs at the end. And in and out I had detox for few times in this general hospital (TGH, name substituted due to confidentiality). And then finally culminated in me ending up in the intense unit. And my ex-husband came around into my house and found me hallucinating. I could have sworn I saw a child outside the window screaming. So he called an ambulance.

And I went into hospital and spent there about a week. I developed arboreus or acute respiratory distress syndrome. And I had an alcoholic hepatitis. And I had an organ failure basically. Everything packed up. And then after I've tried to stick around as I could I was coming to the wards for two and a half weeks, something like that. And then I was physically well enough to go home. And the consultant who happens to be a friend of my ex-husband knew my history; well he would anyway. And he knew exactly what I was like. And he said: "You're going to go home and drink, aren't you." And I said: "No, no, no." But I would have. That was my intention. And he knew. And he said: "Will you go to a mental health hospital unit (MHHU, name substituted throughout the transcript due to confidentiality) for a few days, which is . . . ." I don't know whether you know the MHHU.

I: Yes I do.

M: And I said: "No." So got the psychiatrist involved. And they sectioned me. I went in there for a few days. And I'm so glad that they did section me. Because it made me put everything into perspective. I finally realised I hadn't. . . . I saw people who had lost their sanity. I finally realised, you know. I hadn't yet lost my sanity. I hadn't yet developed cirrhosis. And I suddenly realised. I suddenly put everything into perspective. And I felt a huge appreciation for my life for the first time. That's it basically. Because the doctor had, the consultant had told me: "If you go home and drink basically you will develop cirrhosis. You will need liver transplant. And you won't get one." And that time in the MHHU just made me realise how fortunate I was. And they even, I mean, when I've seen my gastroenterologist since, he said: "You know that you really shouldn't be sitting here, you should be dead." I shouldn't; if you go by the books, theoretically I shouldn't have lived. And I am so grateful that I did. I was looking at life in a whole different way. All things we take for granted.

And, oh yeah. And in the interim this vicar came around into my house when I was really poorly. I mean everybody else, my whole family sort of dropped me as an old cake. And everybody and people, sometimes I would be on the ground, on the pavement, and people would walk passed. Those completely, you know, ignored and dismissed of the human being, I think. And this is the vicar called Evelyn—the local vicar. And I hadn't been to their church. I had not been to church in years. And she tried to help me. And she came in. And she gave me her phone number, and she said, you know, ... And she would arrange to come back but I didn't answer the door to her. And she did come back but I've never answered the door. And I really appreciated that. Out of everybody, she was the only person who would have any time for me.

Yeah, after the MHHU I started going to her church. And I think I see. I think I understand. I think the problem nowadays seems to be a lot of people do not understand what it means. I mean I haven't read the Bible. But I don't think . . . ; I think a lot of people from what I can gather from groups and stuff; I mean from AA for example; a lot of people are put off because the word "God" is mentioned. And I think, I think there is a lot of misunderstanding about what is said in the Bible. But I think of . . . . I've just had a different problem with my . . . . I'm doing a counselling course, counselling skills course, every Friday. And I've said about; and we've been talking about empathy. And I was saying to her that sometimes empathy can be—you can be too empathetic. This can be a bad thing for an individual, sometimes. She said: "No. You can never be too empathetic." She made me do my homework all over again. So I've been looking at that. And I think that because of my experience I don't think you can ever be too empathetic. But I think compassion can be, can be harmful to the individual. I feel that's what I got now. Because I've not only got empathy, I've got understanding. That's what I feel. And I've got compassion. And sometimes that can be a bit unsafe for me. Does this make sense?

Appendices

I: Yeah. Do you feel that this will be like the story itself, or you want to continue up to today? I have some questions to cover after but I want to be sure that you feel that this is the story.

M: Yeah. To date, I've decided that, I've decided what's important in life. And what I really want to do is I want to help other people who are going through misery basically as best as I can. And use my horrible experience to help others. That's how I feel. But I've just got to be careful it's not of my own expense. Because I do get a little bit too involved. And that's it.

I: Okay. Thank you. Eleven questions; some of them you may have covered already in the story. But anyhow, I'll read them and then if you should consider that you don't have to add anything you don't need to. If you feel like you need to add something in regards to the questions feel free to develop it as much as you want.

M: All right.

I: The first question is: How do you perceive your conscience? What is conscience? How did it develop? How does it function?

M: Yeah. I've got another problem of mine. I think my conscience is too much, I would say. What I feel now is I don't feel, I don't feel I'm answerable to anybody except to myself. And I don't believe that anybody can give me as hard a time as I give myself. I've always been one of these people, I sat down, and I ponder about stuff, and I think about stuff. Sometimes too much. People have told me that. And I do and I worry about everything. I worry about how other people have . . . ; if they have misinterpreted things I've said. All sorts of things. And I think that has contributed to my alcohol problem.

I: Is that all you think about conscience when you think about your conscience, and what it is, and how it functions.

M: I think I'm too hard on myself. And I think I have good conscience. I think, or what I would say myself. I do believe I'm morally good person. And I mean I've done bad things. I mean, look how I left my children down. You know, but through my alcoholism I've said some horrible thinks to some people on the way. But I've never, I've never done anything really bad. I've done lots of bad things. I can't say that. I have. But I think on the whole I have got a good set of morals. And my conscience is fairly clear.

I: The second question is: How did you develop alcohol addiction? That's—you elaborated a lot. What is alcohol addiction? When did you realise that you have been addicted to alcohol? How did you try to manage your alcohol addiction? You said all about this. Do you want to add anything?

M: No. The only other way I tried to manage it, I did do a few home detoxes with my ex which was not good. Because in the rehabs, they never worked for me because as soon as . . . . I was fine when I was there, I was happy but as soon as I came out of these doors, I was back to the same situation. And my sobriety was gone.

I: The third question is: What were your moral views before your moral, spiritual, and/or religious transformation? So basically what I'm implying here is that there has been some moral, spiritual, and/or religious transformation which has taken place either simultaneously or through a period of time. This is what I'm implying in this question. What were your moral views before this transformation? What is morality? How did you deal with moral dilemmas? How much did morality matter for you?

M: Yeah it did. It always has done actually. But, not as much as now. No. Yeah. Probably more so now, I think. I'm more aware of my responsibilities, definitely. I do feel I've gained quite a lot of understanding, more understanding of others. So—more tolerance and perspective.

I: The fourth question is: Did you practice spirituality before your moral, spiritual, and/or religious transformation? What is spirituality? How did you practice spirituality? How much did spirituality matter for you?

M: No, I used . . . . I've always believed in God but I didn't bother going to church or anything like that. And when I was praying I was half-hearted. I was praying for selfish things. But now if I pray I really mean it, and I really believe I'm heard.

I: Thank you. The fifth question is: Did you practice religion before your moral, spiritual, and/or religious transformation?

M: No.

I: What is religiousness? How did you practice religion? Did you have religious affiliation? How much did religion matter for you?

M: No, I didn't. Religion was definite sort of on the backseat. I didn't go to church or anything like that. I didn't really think about it.

I: Okay. The sixth question is: Did you experience moral, spiritual, and/or religious transformation? How did you experience this transformation? When did you experience this transformation? May you identify anyone who played any influential role in the process? How much has this transformation changed your life?

M: Oh, the vicar Evelyn. She played a big part and she had a big influence on me. And, I don't know. I just feel after what the doctors have told me, and the depths to which I plummeted, I do actually believe that I've been given a second chance because I know that I shouldn't be here. I've always felt, I've always felt like when we went to "Lords." And if I went to church before I've always felt like shedding a tear and I get quite moved. So there has always been that. I have always been very aware that to me that I believe in God and Jesus and . . . . And I guess it's only recently that I've actually looked to God and Jesus and I feel that they're looking back.

I: Is there something which prompted you to do this, to influence this change. Like you mentioned the vicar Evelyn. And you said that when you were in the MHHU you kind of felt that life is . . . .

M: I felt blessed, I felt blessed. And you've gonna think that I am crazy now. You'd probably think that I should be back in the MHHU. But really, really unusual things have happened to me during my recovery. They might just be totally coincidental but some bizarre things have happened. I can't even pin by them but they have been . . . . I'm not nuts honestly. Maybe, maybe is just wishful thinking. I don't know.

I: If you remember to mention any of them. If you feel comfortable to mention any of these. What are these things?

M: Yeah. I don't know what. For example, I help this young lad who is only 25. He called me cause I was on the structured day programme then. And he was desperately, desperately in need of detox. And he came from horrible home environment where he basically wasn't going to get sober there. And he called me and asked me to meet him after CDAT. So I did. Oh I lost my chain of thoughts. Oh yeah. I helped him to detox anyway. And he went to monastery. I didn't. That was nothing to do with me. He was Catholic and his family arranged that. And then he went to monastery, and he went back to his family, and the same thing happened again. And he called me again. And I managed to get him detoxed in hospital that time. And yeah, when he was in hospital my friend and I were thinking about setting up this sort of crisis home. And we went to visit this rehab in . . . (name omitted due to confidentiality). Just to know what sort of support services were around. And they said to us: "Why do you want to visit this place?" You know. And I said: "Oh." We used him as an example. And I told him that we used him. And he didn't mind. I said: "We got this friend Anthony, he needs a rehab, so you know. We just want to find out about the rehab." It was all fictitious. It was made up because we just wanted to know more about what they were offering there. And then, blow me down, his auntie phoned me for some reason that very day. And said: "We're thinking putting him in a rehab." And I said: "We've just seen a rehab. And it is ideal, it's perfect." And, no, she didn't even mention, they weren't going to send him, to put him into a rehab. They didn't know what to do with him, I don't think. And it was so bizarre. And then she ended up basically taking him into a long-term rehab. And he's there, he's still there now and is doing extremely well. Just lots of little things like that have been happening.

And it was like when I phoned Betty here for my friend Ella, she was having, oh, she started self-harming. And she was having a bit of a crazy time. And I was really concerned about her. She hasn't been put on structured day or anything like that. And I phoned Betty. And I said: "Ella really needs help." Betty said: "You know, there is nothing we can do at this very moment." And then she said she put the phone down. And as soon as she put the phone down a caller came through and said that they wanted to cancel their counselling sessions. And so Betty said: "Counselling session is free for the following day." So she phoned me back. It was all very coincidental. This is probably wishful thinking but I almost feel as if divine intervention. There have been a few things like that.

I: The next question is: What was the impact of your transformation on your life? Compare your morality, spirituality, and religiousness before and after the transformation. How did the transformation impact your understanding of morality, spirituality, and religion, and their role in your life? How much did morality, spirituality, and religion matter for you after your transformation?

M: It means a lot to me now. I don't, I don't, I'm not. I go to church every few weeks. I'm not a big church goer about it. I do enjoy when I go. To be honest with you the first time I went to church I thought, I was thinking to myself: "I don't, I don't want to mingle with the people that go to church." I know a lot of people go to church because for the social site of it. But that's not why I go. And they often say: "But why didn't you stay for coffee, we have coffee and all afterwards or whatever." And I don't want any of that. I just; what I said to myself the first day I went. Cause I know that everybody in TLEV is probably seen me staggering around, down the road, and all the rest of it. And it could be hugely embarrassing for me to go in and all these people seen me: "Oh, here's the local drunk," type of thing. I'm not going for anybody else, just going for God and for Evelyn. And that's all. Only Evelyn and God himself that I was going to church for. And they do still keep coming up to me and asking me for coffee and stuff like that. And I don't want any of that. I know a lot of people go for the social aspect but that's not me. I just want to go there and I probably would go more often if people left me alone when I was there. But I do find when I'm there, a lot of the sermons, I do feel that since my alcoholism that I have a greater understanding of what has been said. Whereas before I think a lot, about myself, a lot of the language used in the Bible and in sermons it doesn't seem to make a lot of sense. But now I feel it does—a lot of things.

I: Thank you. Next question is: What was the impact of your moral, spiritual, and/or religious transformation on your conscience? Compare your conscience before and after the transformation. How did the transformation impact your conscientious behaviour? How much did the voice of your conscience matter for you after your transformation?

M: Well. I mean now I'm far more . . . . I don't think is, I've got to stage, I don't actually, I don't feel a great deal of guilt from alcoholism because I perceive it as an illness. I can't believe that I was in any sane frame of mind to continue pouring alcohol down my throat knowing what it was doing to me, knowing what it was doing to my children, knowing what was going to happen to me. So I don't believe I was thinking sanely at all. So I don't actually. I don't think I had a bad conscience during my alcoholism. And I don't think I got bad conscience now. Did I explain myself?

I: Do you think that there has been any impact from the spiritual or religious or moral experience which you have undergone to your conscience. Like, when you were, during the period of alcoholism, how did you feel in respect to your conscience, and what happened after the transformation? How do you feel now? So if you kind of try to compare these two.

M: Well I think, when I was drinking alcohol, yeah, you become very selfish and disregard the other people but mostly you're disregarding yourself. But now I have more conscience not only towards other people but towards how I deal, treat myself as well as other people.

I: So do you think that this change which has happened has anything to do with the spirituality, with what you experienced.

M: Yeah. Because suddenly I love myself. While before I didn't love myself. So I think if you don't love yourself you can't really love others. I don't know. I think with alcoholism you don't have love for anybody, do you? You don't, you don't have, you don't think about anybody, you just think about that bottle. But now, yeah. I mean: How other people are feeling? How much more I am aware of other people's feelings and my own. And I just want to treat everybody and myself as they should be treated.

I: Okay. Next question: What was the impact of your transformed conscience on your recovery from alcohol addiction? Compare your recovery before and after the transformation. How did your transformed conscience impact your recovery from alcohol addiction? What is the role of your transformed conscience in the maintenance of your abstinence? May you identify anyone who played any influential role in the process? So basically now you're thinking about your transformed conscience. What was the impact of the transformed conscience on your recovery?

M: Oh big, I suppose. Because, since my sobriety, as I was saying, I have a lot more appreciation for people, for myself, for life. And value people and life so much more than I did before. I can't explain that. It is difficult, isn't it? I knew I'd treat them accordingly and myself. For before I didn't put value on anything other than the bottle. And that is because now I am, I mean, I enjoy somebody's company so much more than I enjoy a bottle. I enjoy people, you know. I love people. I love myself. And I hate that stuff. It is difficult for me to explain. So I treat people a lot better. I'm kind of a lot more thoughtful. And I do have compassion for people. I understand. I like to think that I understand people's misery. I have an insight into certain, certain things that cause people misery. And I do feel for them. And I can show them empathy because I know the misery of it.

I: So you relate this change to your transformed conscience now. What has happened with your conscience is influencing what you're telling me.

M: I can show a lot more empathy because I know what other people are going through. I know the misery and why they are doing it. Because to me it is escapism. You just want to escape. You just want to block everything out, all emotion, everything. So I understand why people are doing it. So I'm a lot more tolerant, a lot more tolerant.

I: Next one: May you share your future plans related to your recovery? What is the role of morality, spirituality, and/or religion in them? What is the role of your transformed conscience in them? Do you plan to share your experience with others who need help in recovery from alcohol addiction?

M: That's exactly what I want to do. I'm doing, I'm doing the peer mentoring course at . . . (name omitted due to confidentiality). That's the hospital, NHS. And I am. Nina is going to let me know when they start the peer mentoring group here. And also I'm going to do mental health first aid. And I'm also; I'm doing a counselling skills course. And I'm also going

Appendices

on this petals course which is by . . . (name omitted due to confidentiality). They are paying for me to go on it. Have you heard about petals course?

I: No

M: It's all about teaching and again mental health and addiction. So I'm trying to learn as much as I possibly can of how to help people. Because, ultimately that's what I want to do. That's what I think. Even though I did years of nursing, I mean I've been alcoholic for much more, far longer. Not drinking to massive excess, obviously I wasn't when I was working, but my main experience is in alcoholism. So I would like to share that and hopefully help other people who are going through it now.

I: And what is the role of spirituality and conscience in this desire to help others.

M: It has been a problem because people, people don't want to hear about your spirituality. People don't, people try to get away from the word "God." So I don't even bringing out. I don't mention it because as soon as you do they would think is raving matter. You know, they do, don't they?

I: The spirituality and your transformed conscience—do they help you in regards to this desire to help others?

M: Yes, definitely. I feel that, I feel that I have purpose now. And I feel that I have a legitimate reason to be on earth. And I feel, I hope that what I do, what I'm doing is not drawn upon but . . . . I just hope I am doing the right thing. When I pray, I pray for guidance. I want to know if I'm going wrong, if I'm doing things wrong. It is important to me. I want to know.

I: And the last question: May you formulate the main theme of your life story? What is the place of alcohol addiction in your story? What is the place of conscience in your story? What is the place of morality, spirituality, and/or religiousness in your story? What is the place of your moral, spiritual, and/or religious transformation in your story? The main theme and the place of these themes, segments we mentioned.

M: I almost feel reborn. I'm no longer fearful of death. I'm no longer, how to say, I don't feel accountable to any other person except myself and God. And I finally feel content and loved.

I: Thank you. This ends the interview with Mary on the 10th of 11th at 4:13.

Max (2011). Personal interview (Conscience in recovery from alcohol addiction), 15 November.

Interviewer (I): And now I am recording. And this is an interview with Max—4:23 of the 15th of 11th. And I will read the guidelines for the story. Structure your life story in chapters. Think about their names, summaries, and progressive links. Without interfering with the genuine character of the story can you identify the role of the following topics in your life narrative: conscience; alcohol addiction; morality; spirituality; religiousness; moral reformation; spiritual transformation; religious conversion and/or affiliation; the relationship between morality, spirituality, religiousness, and conscience, and recovery from alcohol addiction. How will you summarise each of these chapters? What progressive links will you make between these chapters? All this information is here. I'll leave it in front of you. And please feel free to tell me your story.

Max (M): Is this from an early age or just my addiction?

I: Whatever you consider relevant for the addiction please include it, and for the recovery.

M: Okay. Up until 2008 I hadn't drunk alcohol for 18 years. And I've been totally abstinent. I was, what you call, fairly successful. I managed a drug rehab. I was managing a drug team; active within the church community, leadership there. I taught in a local college. So for a period of 18 years relatively I had been happily married—two children; seen as probably middle-class and successful. But I was very driven to succeed. I was very driven to, you know, almost being on the right place at the right time, seen as successful. That comes from childhood because I lived in quite a rural community. We were quite poor; never went on holiday; dad worked away. Eldest brother was very violent when he drank. So I didn't spend a lot of time at home but always kind of vowed that actually if I had an opportunity I would change that. So from probably about 16 after I left high school with no qualifications I went back to college; worked in horticulture quite successfully for 14 years. Before my career changed in . . . (year omitted due to confidentiality) when I went into the care industry; working in a drug rehab where I myself opt to manage that. I stayed there for eight years. That was a Christian rehab. After eight years they decided to take the Christian message out so I transferred jobs. I went to work for social services. And soon, well within 12 months I was managing my own team. Church-wise—very active within the local church; very driven in a sense in that to be in that place. So a lot of my self-worth, a lot of my feel good came from how well I was perceived.

Appendices

And then probably . . . (years omitted due to confidentiality), I lost my younger sister Zoe. And Zoe and I were 12 months, 15 months apart. We grew up together very, very close because of my brother who, as I said before, used to get violent when he was drunk. He used to beat us up. He used to drag us out of bed and give us a good kicking all that kind of stuff. So we grew very close and she died suddenly in about . . . (years omitted due to confidentiality). And, you know, I heard about it when I was at work. I've got the phone call from my father, went home, and I was back at work for the next day, kind of just put it on one side. And then 18 months after that; no six months after that my eldest sister had a heart attack. And she brought me up as a child. My mum was always very busy out at work and it was my eldest sister who brought me up. So I related to my eldest sister more as my mum than my natural mum. And she had a heart attack where she worked, at the hospital. And if she hadn't worked in a hospital she would have died. So she is very, very fortunate. Then 12 months after that my eldest brother, the one that was violent, he died in his sleep. So, within a period of about three years I lost my younger sister, my eldest brother, nearly lost my elder sister. And I've never dealt with grief. I just worked hard. I just threw myself into work; threw myself into church; threw myself into home. And then my wife was ill for 12 months. And so, I was working, church, coming home, nursing my wife, doing all the housework. And I got very, very tired. And she got well again after about 12 months. And within two or three months of that my mum was diagnosed with cancer and died very, very quickly. So in a period of the last six years I've lost my sister, my brother, and my mother with my eldest sister; so a lot of grief. And I started to drink again in . . . (year omitted due to confidentiality) because of that.

I didn't feel, because I was driven, success orientated, I didn't feel I could talk to people at work about what I was feeling. I felt my position at church . . . ; I didn't want to expose that vulnerability that I am struggling. My wife at the time was just recovering from illness and I didn't want to burden her, you know. And in a sense we were growing apart for that 12 months she was ill because there was no emotional or physical contact because of the chronic fatigue. So I started to drink again after 18 years abstinence. And that really, you know, of course broke my wife's heart. And I started to drink from a bottle of Guinness. Within two, three weeks I was drinking half a bottle of Scotch; walking in the dark after work. And it just escalated. Up until October . . . (year omitted due to confidentiality) when my wife walked out, left me—another loss; but she was having a relationship with somebody else in the church that we both led. So I just drank and drank and drank.

I knew I was doing wrong but I just didn't like what I was feeling; really spiritually I died. So any kind of involvement with church had died. Conscience-wise I resigned from work because I knew I couldn't work with people with drug and alcohol problems and actually be drinking or manage simply outside of that. So I took time off sick and then resigned. So I was left with nothing just all the house and all the bills. I lost everything in the divorce after been married 25 years. And I ended up really from October . . . (year omitted due to confidentiality) just bumping along, just drinking myself into oblivion. Towards the end of November I started a relationship again. And in November . . . (year omitted due to confidentiality) I started another relationship with an ex-work colleague. I knew it was wrong but I just wanted the comfort of a female. So we got into a very difficult relationship because I was drinking. And I was all over the place. I spoiled her life really. But that was because I was so unhappy with myself. I'd failed. I didn't feel I can go anywhere. So I just drank and drank.

And then, in March . . . (year omitted due to confidentiality) I came to a residential rehabilitation centre (RRC, name substituted throughout the transcript due to confidentiality) for six months. During that time of abstinence I kept in contact with this new partner. And we agreed that after six months I can move in with her and the children and you know be happy family as it were. But during that six months of being here I kind of rewoke that spiritual side of me, my faith side that has been so important for the previous 18 years, 19 years when I was abstinent. So when I did leave after six months in August–September . . . (year omitted due to confidentiality) I knew, I was very uncomfortable with what I was doing but I was committed to it. So I went and moved in. After six months they wanted me to stay and do the second stage of the residential rehabilitation programme (SSRRP, name substituted due to confidentiality). I said: "No, I will, I will go and give it a go." Because I liked the attention and I felt good. It was a family again. There was a lady in my life, a woman in my life. And all those kind of external things made me feel good but internally I was all over the place. And spiritually I knew that actually the more sexual that relationship got, the more intimate . . . ; I've just come through a divorce; I have not finished grieving for my wife. But also from a spiritual point of view I knew I was doing wrong. You know, after living abstinent and being in the church for 18 years you kind of . . . ; there are, you know, obvious links of what's right and what's wrong, that kind of moral perspective. But within a month of going back in . . . (year omitted due to confidentiality), you know, September—October my new partner didn't like me going to church; didn't like me keeping in contact with here; didn't like me keeping in contact with Christian friends I had. So I became very socially isolated. I found it difficult to get work. I still remained abstinent, you know; didn't drink at all. And then it got to the Christmas of . . . (year omitted due to confidentiality) and I kind of woke up just before Christmas and just realised this is just not what I wanted but didn't feel I can get out of it. I felt trapped. And I started to drink again. And drank probably heavier than I've done in my life. From December, January, February when my partner kicked me out I just drank, stole. Morally I became; well I didn't have any morals as long as I drank. Spiritually I was totally divorced. All I needed, all I wanted was to drink myself into oblivion really because of this situation I've got myself into; nobody else's responsibility but mine. So when I got kicked out in the February I lived rough for a period of time in shades, garages, sofa surfing till people have had enough. Even my father put me up for a bit and, you know, I stole from him. And he asked me to leave. So I ended up living rough again. And in March I contacted the RRC again. I couldn't get any funding to come back. I was lost. I was broken really. And, you know, whether people agree with it or not I was able to come up for an interview. I spoke to them here. They offered me the bursary fund but it would have to go through the panel because I couldn't get any kind of local authority funding. And in their wisdom they said I could have the bursary fund. But I was so desperate to get here I actually lived for four days in the woods, rough. Just so I could be here. And that was probably the worst four days of my life. And actually, the last night, Monday the . . . (date, month, and year omitted due to confidentiality), I was having detox in the woods. I prayed to the God as I understand it and said: "Either open the door or actually take my life." I was that kind of morally, spiritually broken, physically broken. I knew that I would probably die if I carried on drinking.

So on . . . (month and date omitted due to confidentiality) I came in. And I was ill for about three or four days on the back end of my detox. But I was very, very fortunate. I'm now in the second stage of the programme here, the . . . (name omitted due to confidentiality) programme, which is kind of going back out into the community, which is formed with difficulties. You know I am . . . (age omitted due to confidentiality). You know I had everything as according to the world, you know, a house, a new car, position, everything on the surface—good. But I've lost all that.

And I came in, as I said, to the RRC on . . . (month and date omitted due to confidentiality) with four bags. And as I look back I can't separate the fact that actually morally if I look back at my life, you know, I lived a good life I think for 18 years. I was what you call successful. Then when my wife was ill there was no physical contact. I started to slip into Internet porn and stuff like that. I was looking for some form of escape. And then the drinking came after that. Even now if you look at of the link between how well I was spiritually to some of these decisions I made morally, there is a distinctive link for me. Spiritually I became less careful of, less interested in. I started missing church even though I was leader, one of the leaders. All those kind of things; the lies and the deceits that came. Then morally I became more, you know, destructive really in decisions that I made in my life. So the more I drank the more I stole. Spiritually, my awareness or my willingness to be accountable spiritually diminished. And therefore, the moral side and alcoholism were for me hand in hand. Because morally I couldn't live with myself. I knew what I've done. I knew I've broken my wife's heart. I knew I've done things wrong. I couldn't cope with what I was feeling. I couldn't cope with the sense of failure. I couldn't cope with the sense that I could no longer cope while I've always been a coper and you know very success driven. And that kind of realisation emotionally, you know, influenced my decision to drink. Because the drink actually stopped all that process; or by drinking morally I became . . . . If I would looked at it I made some real bad decisions and knew that they were wrong but the desire to still those emotional disturbances through alcohol was greater. So the link between all three for me is, you know, spiritually if I'm not well then for me morally I'm making impaired decisions; the more impaired decisions that I make the more likely I am to drink, you know. So over the last three years spiritually I started to, because I was tired, I was exhausted, spiritually I became very inactive, very inert. Morally I started making some bad decisions. Once I started that road then it was a matter of time before I drunk.

And as I look back now, you know, it breaks my heart, when you talk about conscience, it breaks my heart; the people that I've hurt and damaged. And I would love to be able to put those in a package and send them off, and they wouldn't bother me anymore. But during the seventh—eight months I've been here now, seven months, part of the recovery process for me is not just walking away from those people, an element of conscious, conscience really of who I've hurt, who I've damaged, who I've stole from; it would be very easy to say: "Well that's in the past. I know I can't help that. You know I was drinking, tha, tha, tha." But an important part of my recovery is been trying and then endeavouring to make contact with those people. And to try and what AA call—"make amends." To write to them and say: "Look I can't excuse it. I've been out of order, tha, tha, tha. Please, you know, if you can, you know, I'm really sorry." That's been a hard journey because some of the responses I've got though I expected them, to see it in black-and-white, you know, kind of rocked my world a bit. But I've been through all those people. I wish I could financially give back what I stole but I can't. But that would be a way of covering in a sense the harm that caused. And I know, I look at my partner when she kicked me out in February. I had contact with her, you know. And she wrote a very open and honest letter two weeks ago. And some of the things that she wrote were really quite hurtful. But that was because in my conscience as it were, you know, that right and wrong, the morality side of things, I realised she was right. There is no hiding from it. I wish I could have said: "Yeah that was because I was an alcoholic." No! I chose to drink. And because I chose to drink that behaviour came with it. And you know I hurt a good woman. I damaged that relationship. I damaged the children's life. I don't know whether I would ever be able to repay or repair that. You know, I wish I could go back in time and do things differently but I can't.

So in my recovery from alcohol addiction keeping short accounts where there is offence, where there is difficult relationship is having the wisdom to understand that some relationships' amends can be made, you know, even today even living in the community like the RRC. But there are some relationships where you can try and make amends, you are not gonna get anywhere, and is having the wisdom to say, you know: "I would be polite. I'm not gonna get anywhere. But I've just had to put that down to experience." But also realising that actually for me is important of keeping short accounts. You know, if I've offended somebody, or I think actually I could have done that better then I would go back. Because for me that link of uncomfortable feeling that I've offended or hurt somebody, you know, if I don't deal with that then it just builds and escalates. And morally then I start making impaired decisions whether that's to shut down, to isolate, not go to groups, not go to church, not go and be socially active. Then I start to put myself in a place of vulnerability to relapse. So keeping short accounts, keeping well spiritually are really keys to my alcohol recovery really, my alcohol addiction. And you know for me, as I said before, repeating myself, they cannot be separated, you know. If I'm not doing well spiritually, as I said before, then morally, conscience-wise I make bad decisions, bad choices. I don't like what that feels so I look for something to kill the pain. And obviously over the last three years that has been alcohol. So for me my on-going recovery is depended first on my spiritual side, you know, my relationship with God, relationship with church, and keeping good relationships. And making sure that I don't do anything that would destabilise social relationships really. So, if I look at choices, for example if I use . . . , you know: I still long for female company. You know, I still as a man of a certain age, you know to be quite blunt, I haven't had sex for a long time, you know. So those are natural desires within me, natural wants, natural needs if you want. But I know at the minute: a) that would be wrong spiritually, but b) I'm still not well. I'm still learning to live alcohol free. And that would be a distraction to what I'm doing here. So that would be; the reason I said that is because morally that would be a wrong choice at the minute. It would be wrong for me but it would be wrong for the female, you know, the female that I would be involved with. Because it would be about me meeting a need rather than relationship. So morally and conscience-wise that's a poor decision. And therefore, I would be susceptible to that because in a sense it would be a need-based decision. It's no more, it would be no different than picking up a bottle of vodka again. I need something so I drink. I need to silence the voices—so I drink. You know, I need sex so I put myself in a position where I can get that. It's all need based. And for me they are connected. So in a sense you've got down here: "the relationship between morality, spirituality, religiousness, and conscience, and recovery from alcohol addiction." Without repeating myself they are all critical building blocks. And it depends of how well I build them that will influence my on-going recovery.

One of the big transformations that's taken place has probably been my willingness to attend church, to be open to spiritual things. Because, as I said before, my wife left me and she was having a relationship within church. I was very antagonistic towards the church and spiritual things. That hasn't happened these last six–seven months. I've really become quite vulnerable in that area and really begun to be open. Though it's not been easy the benefits are there for me. So that spiritual transformation has taken place. Morally, the fact I'm physically well and spiritually I'm vulnerable is really improved my moral decisions, you know. I'm clearheaded; spiritually I have a good understanding of what's right and what's wrong, what's right for me at the minute. Therefore, my moral decisions are moral, you know, they are sounder. And therefore, my conscience is clear. I sleep better. I'm able to act and respond better in relationships rather than being in that active addiction which is all need based. I found that early on in my addiction that actually I related to people not because of the person but because of what I can get from them; and what are they for me—to drink. If that makes any sense. And therefore, having a clear conscience is enabled and morally being refreshed, spiritually being, you know, transformed as you got here and alcohol free, I'm able to relate back to people as people. And that's critical I think for my on-going wellbeing really. So that's what I can say.

I: Thank you Max. We move on to the questions. And the questions may repeat things which were already shared. So if you feel the need not to add anything please just say it. If you feel the need to add something, please elaborate as much as you want. The first one is: How do you perceive your conscience? What is conscience? How did it develop? How does it function?

M: "How did it develop?" "How did it function?" I think is . . . ; there is a . . . ; for me my conscience developed; and why is that. It's a break. It's my mind letting me know that I'm going into an area that might not be too good for me or is good for me. So I don't want to say it but I will say it, it's kind of a right and wrong mechanism. It's my body actually naturally telling me: "Hey, old Max, you know, warning." So it actions a warning, a break and I can choose to override that if I want to. It developed I guess through . . . ; I don't think anybody ever told me what was right and wrong, I naturally knew that. But it got shaped very much by my early influences from my mum, my dad. The fact—mum wasn't present, dad wasn't present—my sister brought me up. So those were the real influences on my conscience, you know, about what was right, what was acceptable. And because, my sister was only a teenager at the time, she was going through her own adolescence, her own kind of forming her character, she was bringing up this baby, you know. I guess some of that development was flawed. So I put that, as I said before that is a warning, my conscience is there to say: "Hey, you know, if you do this the outcome may not be too good."

I: Second question: How did you develop alcohol addiction? What is alcohol addiction? When did you realise that you have been addicted to alcohol? How did you try to manage your alcohol addiction? You covered pretty much all of these. What I heard and didn't hear the explanation of it was, you said: "18 years of abstinence." So what happened before these 18 years? Something wasn't mentioned. If it is important for the story . . . .

M: When I grew old because my brother was violent with alcohol I've always said I was never gonna drink. And at the age of 14 I was abused by a neighbour. And I drank a bottle of cider the day after. And I liked the way it felt. So even though I said I was never gonna do it, I did it. I went through school okay; 16–17 I got myself on an apprenticeship. And I started to drink quite heavily when I was about 18–19 with a group of lads I was on apprenticeship with. And not that it got out of hand but it got a regular thing. And then, I've got my wife. We got married. We've got two kids. I was working in horticulture on a ruler estate in the middle of nowhere. So my wife was bringing up two children. I was out for work all day. She was socially isolated. But I would go and play cricket and sport because I was quite active sport-wise at weekends. So I've always had Saturday and Sunday, Wednesdays and Fridays. And I would drink regularly, quite heavily on those occasions. And eventually she said: "Look, stop or I'm off." And I didn't. She went back to her parents for a bit. And then we got back together. But when we got back together I stopped. And then, I was 18–19 years without. But then again I guess, as I said previously, you know, I picked up again because I didn't feel it; I had a head full of emotional baggage that I didn't feel. I've trapped myself in a sense of this performance mentality that I didn't feel that I could actually expose this vulnerability. And I remember doing the weekly shop one day in 2008, early 2008, I sat in Morrison's car park in . . . (name omitted due to confidentiality) in the car and drank a bottle of Guinness. And there I just liked the way it felt. I knew it was wrong but I thought I could, you know after so long, I could handle it. And I liked the way it felt and it built from there really to live in homeless, you know.

I: Thank you. Third question: What were your moral views before your moral, spiritual, and/or religious transformation? What is morality? How did you deal with moral dilemmas? How much did morality matter for you?

M: Is this before I drank or after?

I: Before.

M: Before I was probably very legalistic, moralistic. So having things done in the right way at the right time was very important to me. Even down to stuff like punctuality. I hate being late or hated other people being late. So doing the right thing at the right time was that kind of aspect of moral living; conscious, you know, conscience was critical for me, you know. In a sense it was a structure to my life, you know. Making sure that; is part of that drivenness, that performance, you know, that sense of being in the right place, being dressed right, saying the right thing, behaving in the right way. And in a sense it probably; it was a mask that I wore and deep down I guess I've always feared that morally I was, you know, vulnerable or, you know, corrupted in some ways. And I guess when I started drinking again morally I just became inert. I just became; it became a passive part of my life. You know, drink was the most important thing. And, as I said before, the spiritual transformation woke me up to the fact that actually I damaged so many people over the last three years. You know, I've lost a wife; struggling in relationships with my son, youngest son, you know, my partner and her children, my father, my sister, you know. So that transformation has rewoken actually. Morally I was corrupt kind of confirm that belief I had. And instead of running away or hiding behind the structure I've kind of taken those barriers down and said: "Okay, yeah, I am responsible for this. I am responsible for this pain." I can't go back and financially recompense people. But what I can do is actually recognise that actually I wasn't a nice piece of work; I wasn't a nice person to know. Not because the alcohol made me that way but the alcohol released all that negative feeling within me. So the spiritual transformation; that's probably morally made me look at the damage and the responsibility aspects of my life.

I: Thank you. The next one: Did you practice spirituality before your moral, spiritual, and/or religious transformation? What is spirituality? How did you practice spirituality? How much did spirituality matter for you?

M: Yeah, no. The spiritual aspect of my life is really quite important now. It is very important. If I'm well spiritually what it means for me is actually a relationship with God. It means praying, meditating, going to church, being accountable in relationships, reading. Did I say reading?—reading the Bible. Oh, I can't think . . . . That's what spirituality means. It's a daily walk, a daily discipline. Not that is easy, because it needs maintaining. And I guess that has been part of the transformation. But now meditation, daily reflection it's all part of that spiritual transformation. And I need to do that for my emotional well-being, you know. So I'd spent a lot of time getting build-up from nature. You know, I love water; I like bike riding; I like being in the open; being in the garden; all those kind of things. Those are really important factors to me. That's part of my spiritual well-being, you know. It's time when I reflect, time when I make sense of my life really. And a part from those three years I guess I've always been quite spiritually alert.

I: Thank you. Did you practice religion before your moral, spiritual, and/or religious transformation? What is religiousness? How did you practice religion? Did you have religious affiliation? How much did religion matter for you?

M: Religion and spirituality, I don't know what's the difference. In those 18 years when I was abstinent I wouldn't say I was religious but I was properly more legalistic. And for me religion is about, you know, right and wrong. It's very parallel to a moral code of life, you know. "You do this. You don't do that, tha, tha, tha." Where spirituality I think for me is less informal, it is more informal sorry, more informal, less rigid. So I wouldn't say I was religious. I was probably quite zealous over certain things. But when I was drinking I did become religious. I did become very legalistic to justify what I was doing, you know. So I would use the religious law as a way to protect myself from other people. You know: "Why you haven't been to church." "Well, because x, y, z is happened in church I don't feel like I can be part of that." And that would just define me staying at home and drinking. But nobody knew I was drinking. They just thought I had an issue of religious issue, you know. So I used it when I was drinking.

Now I wouldn't say I'm religious. I think probably I'm more spiritually pliable, more laid-back, probably know myself, it sounds silly. I am . . . (age omitted due to confidentiality) and I've gone through all that, you know. As I said before on the tape about what I've been able to achieve. But it's almost as . . . (age omitted due to confidentiality) now I actually know myself better than I did when I was 16. So spiritually I'm probably, you know, more in tune with who I am, what I am. And therefore, probably less structured as religion or you know if that makes sense. Anyway it makes sense to me.

I: The next one: Did you experience moral, spiritual, and/or religious transformation? How did you experience this transformation? When did you experience this transformation? May you identify anyone who played any influential role in the process? How much has this transformation changed your life?

M: The transformation took place, as I said earlier, on . . . (month and date omitted due to confidentiality) when I prayed in the woods: "God if you are there open the door or take my life." And the fact that I was there the next morning and I was able to come in because it was never certain I guess was God saying: "Yeah, I am there. And I've opened the door." So something set me back. I didn't expect God to answer in that way. So that was a critical element of my spiritual transformation. And I think the fact that actually though I was physically alive something did die in me that night when I prayed that desperate prayer. Something, whether it is, that I'd come to the end of myself, humanly, you know, and I needed some influence from elsewhere. I don't know. But something did die. And I think that's been a critical part of my spiritual transformation. That reliance of what I can do, my performance, how I am perceived as I talked about before, you know, it led me in a sense directly to living rough in the woods, you know, all in my own strength. And I think that night I realised that actually, you know, I can't do this anymore, you know. I am broken, vulnerable person. And God opened the door. So that transformation took place from there and there have been several people that played influential parts in that, you know—some of the staff here. But particularly a lady called Dana who works in admissions. And when I got offered an interview, and I missed an interview, and I messed them about, I was drinking and tha, tha, tha. And she was the lady that went to the panel. And she fought for me to come on the bursary fund. And put a neck out, you know, put a neck on the block as it were for me. And that's always stayed with me. That actually when I was in the pit and I couldn't see anything good in me actually somebody saw something in me and was prepared to stand in the gap, you know. And she did that on the basis of her faith. And those things stayed with me. Those things are precious to me. So that was when, as I said, the transformation took place in the woods. But the influential part was probably more from that lady called Dana who works in admissions. Very powerful, you know, why would somebody do that for me like.

I: Thank you. Next question: What was the impact of your transformation on your life? Compare your morality, spirituality, and religiousness before and after the transformation. How did the transformation impact your understanding of morality, spirituality, and religion, and their role in your life? How much did morality, spirituality, and religion matter for you after your transformation?

M: As I said, afterwards it's critical; they're all, you know, foundations of my recovery. So if I'm spiritually well, morally, conscience well then I was well. But the warning signs are if I make impaired decisions morally or conscience-wise, so any kind of deceit or anything, if I start to wobble on it and if there aren't conscience and morality it affects me spiritually. I am vulnerable so that's critical to my on-going transformation and future. How did they influence my wife? Well, I was divorced from my wife.

I: Your life, sorry.

M: Life. Oh, life yeah. They've been critical since I've come here, since . . . (month omitted due to confidentiality) really. Looking at and taking responsibility for my actions. That's not just a spiritual element, there are some morals, kind of responsibility to what I've done, you know. Even going back to paying back fines, not fines, loans that I had with DSS and stuff like that. There is, you know; it's actually not doing the right thing for the right time for the sake of doing it, doing it because I want

Appendices

to, because it influences how I feel about myself. So the conscience, the spirituality, and the morality are critical to my on-going transformation.

I: You mentioned about your spirituality in terms of before your transformation, like you have been always spiritual.

M: Yeah.

I: And in this regard how can you compare the spirituality then and there and here and now in terms of recovery.

M: I think I've touched on it previously when I said that actually when I was in church for those 18 years I was very performance orientated; so, it came from, not from a genuine source. In a sense of actually I was more interested in how people perceived me than who I really was. Where is now my spirituality is actually being comfortable in who I am before God rather than through the eyes of another.

I: Okay, thank you. Next question: What was the impact of your moral, spiritual, and/or religious transformation on your conscience? Compare your conscience before and after the transformation. How did the transformation impact your conscientious behaviour? How much did the voice of your conscience matter for you after your transformation?

M: Okay. As I said before, my conscience was totally revoked when I was drinking; I didn't give monkeys. Afterwards it was a painful process of choosing to listen to my conscience in respect to what I did and how I treated people. And that's still an on-going process. And, as I said to the previous question, actually my conscience is a warning sign that things are not well. And if I override that I reap the consequences of that. My conscience really; if I can go to bed at night and realise that actually today I had a good day I sleep better. If I go to bed at night and I realise that there is a conflict between me and somebody else or in something that I've done then I make amends the next day. So it's a way of keeping me well.

I: Okay. Thank you. Next question: What was the impact of your transformed conscience on your recovery from alcohol addiction? Compare your recovery before and after the transformation. How did your transformed conscience impact your recovery from alcohol addiction? What is the role of your transformed conscience in the maintenance of your abstinence? May you identify anyone who played any influential role in the process?

M: All right. I think I probably touched on that one already in a sense that actually my conscience is key to it. Before I didn't give monkeys. In a sense I drank to silence it. But then when I came here I couldn't silence it, and I had the choice whether I listen to it and do something about it, or I

Appendices

don't. And if I don't I'm vulnerable to drink. So I chose to do something about it. So listening to it and keeping it healthy just like a pot plant, you know. If you keep it nice and fed and watered and well then it will grow. If I decide to not give it sunlight or not give it water then that will impair my function as a human being.

I: Okay. Thank you. Next question: May you share your future plans related to your recovery? What is the role of morality, spirituality, and/or religion in them? What is the role of your transformed conscience in them? Do you plan to share your experience with others who need help in recovery from alcohol addiction?

M: Yes to the last one. I indent to share it. My future plans are to probably resettle around here, right in the south around the . . . (name omitted due to confidentiality) area. To find some work where I can be happy rather than driven, you know, or performance led. So at the minute I am doing voluntary work and I'm loving every minute of it, you know. So it's giving without receiving. Because I've taken a lot from people with or without their permission; so giving back. And then, probably I'll end up, hopefully going to Bible college from October next year. I can only do that, as I said before, as long as I haven't anything lurking in my conscience or in the moral decisions that I've made. So they play a critical role again in my future plans.

I: Thank you. The last question: May you formulate the main theme of your life story? What is the place of alcohol addiction in your story? What is the place of conscience in your story? What is the place of morality, spirituality, and/or religiousness in your story? What is the place of your moral, spiritual, and/or religious transformation in your story?

M: All right. Alcohol in a sense has always been something related to either fun or escape, nothing else, no kind of social aspect to it. Although, well I guess fun is good but mostly it has been around escape. So my alcoholism has always been about shutting something down or escaping from a situation. And therefore, I kind of learned from that that actually I do struggle when emotionally I am in pain, or I'm in conflict or afraid of something, and I'm looking for an escape path. And I guess alcohol is always done it for me; so, that kind of element of . . . , you know. And also now that I'm in that kind of a recovery process I can see that actually if I drink, morally, conscience-wise, spiritually I don't exist. You know, I become defined by the bottle that a drink. Where is actually if I keep myself in the recovery process, keep the conscience and morality side of my person well by dealing and taking responsibility even for things that

Appendices

I don't want to, even that are uncomfortable then actually I become less vulnerable to alcohol. Is that making any sense at all? And the spiritual side of things is for me, you know; without that spiritual I am . . . ; for me that is key. Because if I'm not alive spiritually then my conscience is dulled, my moral choices in life are dulled. And I get a lot of joy and a lot of peace from studying not just the Bible but Celtic Christianity which is around. You know, treating people well; respect; you know, nature; all that kind of stuff. And for me I get a lot of peace and emotional wellbeing from that. Where is if I drink or escape I lose all that. And I don't want to lose what I have at the minute, you know. If you look materially I had a wonderful house, I had a brand-new car in the drive. My wife and I, you know, used to get nearly a hundred grand in a year joint salaries, so we could afford holidays. To come here with four bags through that transformation, through that taking responsibility for my actions, to actually being in a place where I don't feel that I have to prove or drive myself or be performance led and have that kind of contentment in my life— is a good place to be. I don't know if I answered the question but that's my answer.

I: Thank you Max. All right, and then with this we will complete this part of the interview and I will stop recording; that's 5:14.

Appendices

Paul (2011). Personal interview (Conscience in recovery from alcohol addiction), 15 November.

Interviewer (I): This is the beginning of the recording with Paul on the 15th of 11th at 2:51. In regards to your story these are the guidelines: Structure your life story in chapters. Think about their names, summaries, and progressive links. Without interfering with the genuine character of the story can you identify the role of the following topics in your life narrative: conscience; alcohol addiction; morality; spirituality; religiousness; moral reformation; spiritual transformation; religious conversion and/or affiliation; the relationship between morality, spirituality, religiousness, and conscience, and recovery from alcohol addiction. How will you summarise each of these chapters? What progressive links will you make between these chapters? All this information is here, just for you to use it as a reminder if you want. And then please develop your story now.

Paul (P): Okay. My name is Paul. Obviously that you know already. I was born on the . . . (date and year omitted due to confidentiality) to a Christian family. And I have two brothers and two sisters. I'm in the middle. And growing up was quite good. I had all the benefits the normal child was born to have. I am fortunate, I'm blessed that I come from a very loving family who are very supportive and everything. And they have been like that all through my life. We were three at one stage when I was born and I was the only boy. And even behind my middle name . . . (name omitted due to confidentiality). If it's translated culturally it means, "my thinking, all my worries are over." Because my dad desperately wanted a boy and he got me. And due to my cultural background the first son like assumes responsibility, you know, when the father grows old, you know, and everything. So there was a lot of joy and everything surrounding my birth. And I grew up well. Then my other brother came from my mum. And I had a stepbrother cause my dad had another wife.

So I got sent to boarding school. And the certain attention I was getting wasn't the same anymore. And I did feel it a bit. I was a bit nervous of being in boarding school. But I went along with it. And they were quite innocent days in boarding school at the beginning. I was quite athletic. And I despised those that smoked, drank, or anything like that. And there was a senior that was in school. It's now that I'm grown and mature that I realised that he was actually using drugs. Then I walked into his room and he was injecting himself. And oblivious of what was going on I asked him of what he was doing. He said that he was sick and things like that. Then he later told me that: "They are not pharmaceutical injections but that's much better than normal injections." And he asked me whether I wanted to try. And I said: "No. I wasn't interested." I've always hated needles till today, you know.

And I went on in school, and curiosity grew more as I grew older and took of alcohol and smoking that came up. And most of my friends didn't try anything like that because we were all from fairly responsible mums. And bear in mind, anyway, nobody drank in my family. And they told me about. That was this friend I had who told me a lot about alcohol. And it arose my curiosity. One holiday changed the whole pace of my life. I went home for Christmas. And my dad does keep alcohol in the house for his guests and everything. But he personally or anybody else in my house doesn't take. So this Christmas they all went out, and I came back home and opened the cabinet and found the alcohol there. It was a bottle of brandy. It was a fine bottle and I was attracted to that particular bottle. Not actually the content. I opened it and sipped it, and it's really burned me. That was my first taste of alcohol. It took two, three more sips and I felt it, you know. I was practically drunk because I was . . . ; the whole place was spinning around and I ended up throwing up, all that kind of thing. And my dad found out and he wasn't happy with me. And there were consequences for that.

I went back to school and told my friends about my experience over the holiday and they laughed at me. And they told me that I should have started with beer instead of spirits or rum. Beer is much lighter and . . . . One thing led to the other and we started sneaking out of school and drinking and stuff. So, but there they sold it more in bottles not pints, and everything. And one bottle was okay for me. And all that kind of stuff. It did happen, we continued and everything. And in terms of my sexual nature, you know, I was still a virgin and things like that. And this friend of mine who told me about the alcohol was the same person that talked to me a lot about sex and things like that. And the next thing, I sneaked out of school with some friends, and we went into a brothel, and I lost my virginity there. And we did drink there too. And gradually my eyes were beginning to open more and more and everything.

And when I came home on holidays we did meet up with friends. There were girlfriends and things like that and I was more aware of how to be open with women and how to handle alcohol a bit and things like that. But bear in mind growing up I had kind of a low self-esteem. Which now that I've grown, I've realised that there was no reason to have a low self-esteem but it was inbuilt in my mind. And I always wanted to be more than what I was. And I was extremely shy. And this was where alcohol formed an incredible partnership with me. Because it brought me out of my shell and I really blended into the crowd and everything. The parties, the ladies, the guys they all loved the high me not the normal me cause the normal me was more reserved and quiet. So this carried on for years.

And I started drinking at the age of 14. I think, yeah, at the age of 14. And it went on for years into my late teens and early 20s. It didn't reach a stage where I depended on it for anything yet. But the more I grew older the more I started drinking. It didn't affect my school at all or anything like that. I was still athletic and everything. But when I started smoking a lot it affected my athletics. I was very good at basketball. And it really affected my game and everything. I couldn't play full for quarters and things like that. But little or nothing it didn't mean anything to me then. But gradually I dropped the sport's part of me. I got into partying and things like that.

And I went off to school, school of preliminary studies, is like an access course back at home before you go to uni, year two. And that was my first experience of living alone. I had an apartment. My dad bought an apartment for me and I lived there. And during this stage of growing up I did have good friends who didn't do anything and were normal. But I looked at them as boring. And they always invited me to join them for fellowship and things like that but I always neglected them. And I totally ignored the moral values of Christianity and everything I grew up learning. So there in the school of preliminary studies I—that's where I took a nosedive into the life, you know, in terms of sex, partying, and alcohol. I got introduced to marijuana. I did smoke it on one or two occasions but I didn't like how it felt. I just put it away. And I don't really have a problem with marijuana. I can see it and totally decline to smoke it. Yeah, things got nasty a bit. And my dad did come to see me in my apartment one day, and it was completely clouded with smoke, and people were drinking and smoking in my room, and that's when my dad knew that there was an issue on ground.

I came home on holidays, my attitude, my behaviour were becoming weird. And they started picking up that something was wrong. And they asked me and I always denied it. I told them I was tired and things. With the time they realised that I was drinking. But I was to an extent still well-behaved, you know. I got into uni. I got into uni and mixed with the wrong crowd again. For me the problem always rose from the company I kept myself with. Because I was easily influenced by friends. Even days when I didn't really feel like drinking just because they drank I would follow them and drink. And I was like chaff being blown by wind, you know, anywhere the direction would face like I'd face there too.

My course in the uni was five years. I did well for the first three years but I really got deep into alcoholism. And I was drinking before I'd go for lectures. And during exams I would be high. I would go to write a paper with a hangover. And that was where my girlfriend did complain and everything. She didn't drink or smoke. But she tried her best to like stop me but I didn't listen. And it affected our relationship. For one she was the loveliest person I've ever met but for no reason I just broke the relationship because my friends told me that she was boring and I should get somebody that is more like me. And I did find that person. And it was just the match made in hell, let me just put in that way, because we're not building each other constructively in anyway.

So yeah, I joined the ". . ." (name omitted due to confidentiality) back at uni and which turn out to be dangerous at the end of the day. I got attacked in my apartment and I was threatened and asked to leave. The school nerds threatened to kill me and things like that. I had to come home and everything. I told to my dad that I couldn't go back to that school. He found the way. He sorted things out. He got a transcript for me and changed my university. But the problem wasn't really about the alcohol. Because there were people that were actually there to help me out of it. But the problem was I just run into with these boys, I had to go for my safety. I'm getting to this different university. I just totally stopped going for lectures. And I was just drinking. And it was just about women and alcohol every single day. I've lost weight and everything.

That's where the issue of rehab came up. I needed help. My sister who is a doctor, our first born, had a colleague who told me that he knows of a place. And he took me there. And I just spent a week there because we were still smuggling in alcohol and cigarettes and things like that. And I was even drinking more there than the outside. And I went out one day on a Sunday and I just called that they should pick me up. Because it's actually my dead body they might come and carry from that place cause I'm actually drinking more in there. I came back home and continued drinking. Another option came in a different state in my country. I went there and spent eight months. And when I was living they were making recording. They do it for everybody when you're living. And the staff and all the other clients there come and advise you of what you should do when you leave. And one thing stood out for me; it was "stay away from old friends."

And I did stay for 10 months clean after that. But I went against the rule. I was seriously warned about, "staying away from old friends." I went back to them and they drank, they smoked but they knew where to draw the line. That was the difference between me and them. And we would go out, and I would have a soda, and they would drink and smoke and tease me and everything. I really felt bad and asked for a bottle. And that's how I relapsed. And these same friends who pulled me back into it moved on with their lives. I got into another rehab. And I was into this rehab for three years in an out anyway. I relapsed—they took me back. I relapsed—they took me back for three good years. And I didn't really get help there. So my counsellor thus met me and told me about this place. And my parents were planning on bringing me to England for treatment. And I was interviewed on the phone and finally got here.

What stood up for me during all this period of time till I got here was that I was deeply emotional and it wasn't only about alcohol. And I always thought alcohol was the main problem. But there were other emotional links to my problem; things like sense of inadequacy, you know, not leaving up to the expectation of my dad or my mum or my family. Because things really went bad, and my dad was a politician and had sensitive positions in government, and my behaviour was a total disgrace to that image. And all my life I wanted to live like this particular person.

I use this analogy all the time. I have a pair of size 10 Reeboks, classics, very nice, just size 10. But every time I wear them there are kind of tight. And they hurt my feet a lot every time I wear them. And that's how I picture the life I was living. It was glamorous, it was good on the outside but every time I lived it, it really hurt on the inside, you know. And there is this other pair of shoes I have. They don't really have a name. They are torn and really ugly looking but they are very comfortable and everything. That's how I see life right now. It's not really comfortable, is not a joy ride or a honeymoon, and it could get ugly at times but I'm comfortable living that life, you know. I have inner peace now and everything.

And since coming here I've reinvented myself. I found my voice. I talk to people. I relate to people without that shyness there. And I don't have to feel adequate to express myself in anyway. And I've really grown spiritually knowing God. I know here that people are a bit sceptical about God. And only handful of people mostly believe in God. So I mostly keep my spiritual views to myself and if confronted I do give my input, what I think about spirituality. It has been quite a remarkable journey.

And I've been here, I stayed here for five months and I was in the last week before I moved to the second stage when I had a lapse. I went to see my brother in this south west English city (TSWEC, name substituted due to confidentiality) and we had an argument. And I just went for a drink, which showed me clearly that the problem is not just alcohol. I still have emotional issues which I haven't been talking about with my counsellor. And now we talk about self-worth and my belief system. And not assuming what people think about me but actually confronting them and finding out what they think of me because I really felt belittled by my brother. And that's what drove me into drinking. My brother who happens to be 10 years my junior but he's in uni and he's doing quite well for himself. And, yeah, I had that lapse and damaged the relationship with my parents, you know, with the people I love the most. Since then, I was able to build myself back up but I was pulled back 12 weeks on the programme for relapsing and using alcohol while in the programme. I did the 12 weeks. The lapse was the best thing ever happened to me. Because I really realised then what my problem was. And I have to deal with the man himself not the alcohol. And having dealt with those issues I've been okay. Challenges have come my way and I haven't drunk or anything like that. It has been quite a remarkable journey.

I: Thank you Paul. Let's go to the questions. Now I'll read the questions and the sub-questions and then if you consider that you want to add something feel free to elaborate as much as you wish. If you consider that you don't need to, you don't have to. Then you just need to let me know and we will go further. So the first question is: How do you perceive your conscience? What is conscience? How did it develop? How does it function?

P: I'm a very conscious person and I sometimes go with what goes on in my conscience. And I believe in it a lot. And I understand it to be the inner thought of myself, being, you know, what goes in my mind. And how I react towards issues that come across my way in life and everything. Yeah I deal a lot with my conscience in life.

I: Okay. How did you develop alcohol addiction? What is alcohol addiction? When did you realise that you have been addicted to alcohol? How did you try to manage your alcohol addiction? You've covered several of these things but if you have to add something please do.

P: Yeah. I just started it out of curiosity. It became an addiction because an addiction is everything we love doing. And I loved, I loved drinking because of the pleasure I derived out of it. That's why it became an addiction for me, a harmful addiction. And it is there where it became a problem when I started depending on it for daily living.

I: Okay. Next one is: What were your moral views before your moral, spiritual, and/or religious transformation? What is morality? How did you deal with moral dilemmas? How much did morality matter for you?

P: In terms of morality I look at it as a human being as a whole, the things you're supposed to do. And to link it with the conscience we are having a clear conscience knowing we've done the right thing. And morality, I grew up knowing the proper morals of spirituality. I believed in God, no sex before marriage, you know, the 10 Commandments. Everything about spirituality I was taught growing up. But I decided, I took a conscious step; to link it with my conscience again; I took a conscious step to drift from what I've grown up learning.

I: Next questions may be similar but if you consider to add something please do. Did you practice spirituality before your moral, spiritual, and/or religious transformation? What is spirituality? How did you practice spirituality? How much did spirituality matter for you?

P: Yes I practiced spirituality. I went to Sunday school, church every Sunday, and Bible study. I did everything that normal Christian would do. But doing and believing are two different things. My spiritual state of mind was that I would do all the basic things everybody would see on the outside but I was not in peace in the inside. So I had a very turbulent internal spiritual sense, sense of well-being. So spirituality level is growing now, is growing back up. I talked the talk but I did not act the act if I was to put it that way.

I: Thank you. Did you practice religion before your moral, spiritual, and/or religious transformation? What is religiousness? How did you practice religion? Did you have religious affiliation? How much did religion matter for you?

P: Yeah, religion. I would say I was a Christian but not a practising one. Because the life I was living was the complete opposite of what I believed in. And I believe religion is something you believe in and you stick to and follow all the morals. But I've never followed the morals of Christianity.

I: Next question is: Did you experience moral, spiritual, and/or religious transformation? How did you experience this transformation? When did you experience this transformation? May you identify anyone who played any influential role in the process? How much has this transformation changed your life?

P: In terms of transformation, it's happening here today. I've realised that God really loves me and has given me one chance after the other. Because if it was death I would have been gone a long time ago. But the spiritual awakening came for me when there was a time I drank so much, and I was withdrawing, and I was really vomiting blood. I passed out. And there was a dark path I saw. And it was later revealed to me that that path was hell because of the life I was living. So yeah, I do believe in the afterlife, and God has given me this opportunity to come here and build my identity, build myself, build my spirituality, you know to be a better man.

I: And next question: What was the impact of your transformation on your life? Compare your morality, spirituality, and religiousness before and after the transformation. How did the transformation impact your understanding of morality, spirituality, and religion, and their role in your life? How much did morality, spirituality, and religion matter for you after your transformation?

P: After the transformation—it has made me who I am today: a confident, happy, to an extent peaceful man. And there is a lot of joy each day I derive from communication with God and telling him about my problems. My view about it, about the transformation, is that as a Christian I always expected all the answers to be there immediately but doesn't work like that with God. Therefore, meaning that you have to be patient and you have to persevere in terms of relationship with God. And having understood that it does really help me a lot.

I: Thank you. What was the impact of your moral, spiritual, and/or religious transformation on your conscience? Compare your conscience before and after the transformation. How did the transformation impact your conscientious behaviour? How much did the voice of your conscience matter for you after your transformation?

P: The voice of my conscience told me what I was doing wasn't right. And the people that were around me, I was hurting them. And they don't deserve it. So I had to use my conscience to come here and make up my mind to do the programme and get the best out of it. Because the programme is workable if you only put an effort in on your own. And that is what I've done here. I picked up responsibility in taking control of myself. I'm making sure I do it. And I always pray to God and he helps me and shows me a path that I can follow. You can't attain spiritual or Christian perfection but you can at least make an effort and that's just the way it works with God. You make mistakes and he picks you back up. And you go on track and keep on fighting that fight.

Appendices

I: Okay. What was the impact of your transformed conscience on your recovery from alcohol addiction? Compare your recovery before and after the transformation. How did your transformed conscience impact your recovery from alcohol addiction? What is the role of your transformed conscience in the maintenance of your abstinence? May you identify anyone who played any influential role in the process?

P: I would say that people here in the residential rehabilitation centre (RRC, name substituted due to confidentiality) have contributed a lot. Because they've opened me up to spirituality more and they believed that God actually loves me. So it has cleared my conscience in terms of impact; it has cleared my conscience a lot. And I have a clean slate in my heart. And whatever I'm doing wrong my conscience always tells me: "You know where this will end up if you follow this path." So I'm more self-aware of my conscience, the power of my conscience. I am more self-aware about it. And you can either use your conscience to build you or destroy you. But mine has actually been building me. That's my view.

I: Thank you. Next question: May you share your future plans related to your recovery? What is the role of morality, spirituality, and/or religion in them? What is the role of your transformed conscience in them? Do you plan to share your experience with others who need help in recovery from alcohol addiction?

P: Yeah, definitely. I plan on being along with them. We are all brothers of the same struggle. And we need to be there for each other. But there are some links that cannot just be tied at all because they are meant to be broken. So it does bring a challenge to you. Of course your conscience—you always feel. I feel paranoid at times: "What have I done wrong?" Or even when somebody hasn't done wrong you have an idea that somebody has done something wrong. It has been very helpful. And honestly since this cleansing of my kidneys, kidneys—sorry, of my conscience—that's helped me a lot to just understand my addiction better. You understand! And as I get along with the programme I receive credible and assertive advice.

I: Thank you. The last question: May you formulate the main theme of your life story? What is the place of alcohol addiction in your story? What is the place of conscience in your story? What is the place of morality, spirituality, and/or religiousness in your story? What is the place of your moral, spiritual, and/or religious transformation in your story?

P: My life today in terms of spiritual transformation. My life today: it should be a witness to others that God does answer prayers. That even in the midst of a storm he has to help you use your patience and you persevere to walk with him. So in all those categories you mentioned I see myself fitting into all of them because it has been a complete change. And even my family have noticed it. And a relationship that we hardly even spoke but now I'm talking with them and everything is going so great. Life has never been better. And it thus has made a complete transformation for me; and me having a clear conscience. Even when I'm going through confrontations and I knew it is not my fault I don't get the hump about it because my conscience is clear. So I'm more in tune with my conscience now on this stage of the programme.

I: Thank you Paul. This will end the interview at 3:19 with Paul.

Sam (2011). Personal interview (Conscience in recovery from alcohol addiction), 16 November.

Interviewer (I): And now I am recording, and this is an interview with Sam taken on 16th of 11th starting at 10:48. And now I will read the guidelines for the story. Structure your life story in chapters. Think about their names, summaries, and progressive links. Without interfering with the genuine character of the story can you identify the role of the following topics in your life narrative: conscience; alcohol addiction; morality; spirituality; religiousness; moral reformation; spiritual transformation; religious conversion and/or affiliation; the relationship between morality, spirituality, religiousness, and conscience, and recovery from alcohol addiction. How will you summarise each of these chapters? What progressive links will you make between these chapters? Now all these guidelines are here listed for you just as a reminder if you want to consult them. But please feel free to tell me your story now; starting with your name.

Sam (S): Yeah. All right. My name is Sam, you know. I obviously suffered through alcohol addiction and genuine addiction. I have a compulsive personality, so everything I do, whatever but . . . . My life story starts off in my mind from my childhood. It started after alcoholism wasn't necessarily a part of the family but it seemed normality for everybody to do drink. And so I didn't drink at all, you know, until I was about 16. But through my school years is where my trauma first started. I was really, really, severely bullied. You know, things like: when I was younger I had big ears and people used to pick me up by my ears and call me FA cup; call me this and that. And then I had ginger hair so they called me "ginger nut." And then this progressed onto just other minimal things but they all to me were adding up to diminishing my character and making me what you call withdrawn from society even at the age of eight.

So then when I got to the age of about 13, you know, this is a bit that I don't mind telling to anybody now but it's a big part of my story. I didn't have puberty till I was about 17–18. So when I was going in the showers and whatever people would take the piss, if you don't mind me swearing, and say: "Here comes needle dick for he had a pubic hair to wee out of it." And you know just generally, you know, I felt absolutely destroyed. And then it made it worse for my best friends, so I thought at school, talk to me about the same thing. So I thought I was abnormal. So I didn't want to go near girls in case they thought, you know, there is something wrong with me. But, as I know now, people develop at a different age. But during school people see something wrong with you and they like to use it to have a laugh.

So at 16 years of age, you know, I used to always watch my dad who used to hide this stuff, which I know now is alcohol, behind the bag of sugar. And I used to wonder why he did that. So one day I thought to myself: "I would have a taste for whatever is up there." So I went behind looking about and then I picked up this drink. And I took a little sip. And at first it was sort of: "Oh, it is a funny, funny flavour in my mouth." But straight away, you know, it made me feel like Popeye, you know my arms were bulging. And I felt superhuman because of this one taste of alcohol. So then I thought, you know, (I'll try not to swear too much because obviously . . .) but you know I thought this stuff can help save my life. Because if I take a sip of that everything everybody says about me would go away. So you know my dad also brought me up very disciplinarian. He was regimental because he was a soldier. So: "Don't do this. Don't do that. Don't touch anything!" So my life was full of fear. So this stuff that I've found now, which was alcohol, took away fear. So yeah, from day one for me now looking back I drank alcoholically because I used alcohol to change the way I felt. I didn't use it to go out with the boys and have a drink. I used it to make me feel someone different. So that's where alcohol started in my life. And I was also a bit of a compulsive gambler at the time. Because, when I gambled with all the flashing lights and all the horses around me my mind wasn't focused on the real life, it was taken away, and I was in a dream sort of world. So you know, that's also took me away from reality. Which are the two addictions that brought me to where I am and where I've been?

So then I started work and you know I would like a drink now and again. And then I met my lovely wife who was Jessica and she was working in the same bakers. Well, first of all she was working in the fish and chips shop. And I used to go down there every night because my mum used to like fish and chips. And I used to say to this girl: "Can I have fish and chips." And she would laugh. And I used to come back thinking: "I really fancy her." But I was so shy and I couldn't talk to her. And I laughed back now because I joked to myself when she said to me: "Do you want salt and vinegar on your chips." I came away thinking: "She fancies me because she's asked me do I want salt and vinegar." So after six months she started working in the bakery I worked in. And once after I had three or four pints of lager I thought: "I'm going to ask her out." So I went in and I asked her out. And she said: "Yes." And my expressions at the time were; I would use a swear word; I thought: "What do I do now?" because I was expecting a "no." So then Jessica became a big part of my life. Obviously she was younger than me. And you know I've fallen in love. But to make me feel good when I went out with Jessica I would sometimes drink a bit more to make myself funnier. So if we were with her friends who were younger I would be funny. A little note: the progression of alcohol, you know, was taking its toll.

So we got married in . . . (year omitted due to confidentiality). And we stayed together all in all about 12 years but six years of marriage. And then I had a lovely son called Leslie who was born in . . . (year omitted due to confidentiality). And that was the best thing that ever happened in my life. In one way it was better than marrying Jessica. It sounds strange because it's something I created. No one could take away the fact that Leslie is my flesh and blood.

So in . . . (year omitted due to confidentiality) my wife Jessica started taking ill. And she became very irresponsive to what was going on around her. And she left me in . . . (year omitted due to confidentiality). And three months later she came back to me, you know, because she said: "Don't you want your wife?" And she came back. And she was filling Leslie's milk bottles with mustard and things because now knowing she didn't know what she was doing. And I would take her to places and she would say: "We've already been there yesterday." So I started to panic and think: "Something is wrong with Jessica." So I took her to the Mental Health Team. And they said: "She's suffering from some form of nervous breakdown." So they took Jessica out for the afternoon, her brother and sister. And then she never came back to me again. So I would receive phone calls: "Stewart is doing Jessica's head in. You know she's getting worse. Can you please tell your mental home?"

And at the same time my mother was dying of cancer. So I had to try and pretend to my mother that Jessica was at home washing her hair or doing this. But really all I wanted to do was to hug my mum and say: "I'm in trouble. My wife left me." But I let my mum die in peace. Because she said, the happiest thing she knows is that she's dying knowing that I'm happy. So by now I started picking up vodka instead of lager. Because I remember back from childhood: "Ah, alcohol helps with pain." So I started drinking to help me get stronger. So the stronger the pain the stronger the drinking need. But by now it took its toll on me and I was at work and never noticing that I had drink problems. And my boss who was very kind at the time said: "You know, you need help." So I went into rehab in . . .

which is . . . (names omitted due to confidentiality). And I stayed there all in all for nine months. But after about three months, you know, in there I have become life and soul of the party. Because I learned that I didn't need alcohol for people to like me. And I thought: "I am gonna speak to my wife and say: 'I want to see my child.'" And I said: "I don't wanna speak with her parents because it's me and my wife who had the child."

So then my counsellor, one day, was very strange, strange of me. Normally if I would play badminton he was cheering me on but that day he was like something was wrong. And he took me into a room on my own and he said: "Sam, I've got something to tell you." And I thought at the time that she was asking for a divorce. Because I've been told she was getting on with her life and, you know, to leave her be. And I thought: "Fair enough I would go on with my life." But then my counsellor said to me: "She's been in a coma for six months. And she's got '. . .' which is . . . (details omitted due to confidentiality)." I didn't understand what that meant. So I went to the hospital to see her in this south east English city (TSEEC, name substituted due to confidentiality). And she was five stone and shaking, you know, just like . . . (details omitted due to confidentiality). So you know, from then I was devastated.

I stayed in the rehab, got through the nine months and got a flat. But when I came out I came out to nothing. You know, my wife was dying, my son was gone so I returned straight again to alcohol to ease the pain. So after this Jessica died, after about a year and a half of being in a coma. And I wasn't allowed to see her at the funeral. I wasn't allowed closure. You know to say goodbye. But I thought: "Bollocks, I would carry on drinking because if I drink nothing matters, you know, nothing at all matters in life." If somebody hurts you, you just drink a bit more, and you can just forget about them. So then this led me back to being on the streets again. And I would wait for doorways and flats to open so I can sleep on the floor in the doorways and things like that. So this went on for quite some time until I found the accommodation for homeless (AH, name substituted throughout the transcript due to confidentiality) which is actually in this south east English town (TSEET, name substituted throughout the transcript due to confidentiality). And obviously they put me up in the AH but I couldn't recover at the time. But they did find me a flat. But I sort of laugh now because as I sound recovered—but the flat was right above the off-licence. And I thought: "That's not the place to put an alcoholic, above the off-licence." So within two or three weeks I was drinking again. Because in my life now all I wanted to do is drink myself to death, you know. Drink was never about enjoyment. It was just about killing, you know, numbing the day. So I carried on drinking. And the only time I would ever give up was when I ended up in hospital. And I would be on the drip. They drove me out for two weeks. And then I would come out and return to drinking again.

So after that I then moved to another town (AT, name substituted throughout the transcript due to confidentiality) where I found the short term hostel for homeless (STHH, name substituted throughout the transcript due to confidentiality). No, I came straight to a hostel for homeless (HH, name substituted throughout the transcript due to confidentiality). You know, and I thought: "Oh, this could be the chance to reignite my life and start it again." But in the back of my mind there was still nothing to live for. I still hate myself from being a child. I miss my wife obviously. You know, as I said, she was only . . . (age omitted due to confidentiality). But I tried my hardest in the HH. And, you know, what I was doing in the HH I wasn't drinking but I was gambling which was an addiction still. So I wasn't recovering there. All I was doing was staying sober and doing the right things. I was still taking myself out of reality.

I wanted to believe in God because the HH was about God obviously. You know, God is at the centre of recovery for me now. But at the time I was angry with God. Because he has taken away my wife in my mind and my mother at the same time. So I thought: "Why the two most important people in my life would God take away at once." So I couldn't forgive him. You know but what I saw in other people in the HH, you know, with the staff and people I can still see that there was something in it. But I didn't want to believe it still because I thought it's not gonna happen to me, it never will. So I would go to the local church (LC, name substituted due to confidentiality), watch people's faces and: "Not at all. It is not happening to me." But I realise now it wasn't happening because you have to work with God. He can't just do it all for you. You know, you can pray and whatever but if you don't follow the instructions or: I get taught; little sort of voices in my head that would say: "This is the right thing to do and that's the wrong thing to do." And I didn't know that was God telling me or whoever but I will always do the opposite. I would go with the bad. Because the devil played the biggest part in my life is that: "If you go gambling you don't have to worry." But then during the HH I returned to drinking. For a while I thought I would start with one, start with two, and then before I knew it I had three or four warnings. And then I was asked to leave.

But some of the parts I missed out during my story are when my wife was dying I realised that she was in a psychiatric unit and the only way I could get to see her was by getting myself into the psychiatric unit. So what I would do I would, you know, snatch my wrists. But I started just by snatching my wrists to getting into the psychiatric unit to be with my wife. And it didn't work because they put me in a different psychiatric unit. So I hadn't really gone in there because I tried to kill myself, it was a way of desperation. But during some of my stays in the HH I returned to self-harming. And the manager at the time said: "You know, you've become too much of a liability." He said that it's very unfair what I'm doing to other people's minds and whatever because it was; I can't think of the correct words; but that was just frightening for the other people knowing that I was cutting myself to bits. So I was asked to leave because of that sort of behaviour. Not that it wasn't tolerable but it was hard for people to deal with.

So then about a year after that whenever I was on and off the streets, in and out the STHH then I would really try to kill myself. You know, I sat in the graveyard by the . . . (name omitted due to confidentiality) pub and I waited till three o'clock because in my head that's when Jesus died on the cross—three o'clock. And I have gone into the pound shop. I didn't have any money left so I stole a standing knife and I had some cider with me because I needed to numb the pain. So I waited until three o'clock and then I slashed right down the middle of my arm. And I thought that was it because I've gone deep through the arm. And I thought: "That's it I'm going to die now." But obviously I woke up and the police found me. And I got stitched up and that was that. But then I found self-harming which became another addiction. Because if I was in pain because I've been chucked out of, say the HH for example, or if I was in pain because I thought of Jessica dying once I cut myself and found the blood running down my arms it was a form of self-satisfaction in the sense of: "That's why I was in pain and not because of what had happened." I would look at my arm and think: "Oh, that's what's wrong." I don't know whether that makes sense but to me it deflected the pain. So I used it as another addiction to stop feeling pain. I would put pain on another pain.

So then I was sent down to . . . . From the HH and the STHH they said: "I was very difficult to deal with." You know, my patterns of behaviour were not aggressive, not upsetting but they needed some more serious help. So I was sent down to a rehab in . . . (name omitted due to confidentiality). And I went down to . . . (name omitted due to confidentiality). And I was obviously very nervous. It was a Christian rehabilitation. But it was more of a working environment rather than a rehab, which I used to get very frustrated about because I had problems I needed to deal with.

And the moral they used down there was, "if you do a bit more hard work you would forget about the pain." So even then I knew that that's not how you deal with issues. You need to talk them through. But instead they say: "Clean out the milk tank. Clean out this." And I used to swear quite a lot and say: "I'm here for counselling not to clean out the milk tank."

So I got quite fond of my boss down there. You know, he was, I don't know, he took me under his wing, as they say. And he had been there three years so instead of now being a student he had become a staff member. So you know, I started to open up for the first time because I've been nine months without alcohol, nine months without gambling. So I didn't self-harm there. So I was just raw. So I opened up to him. And I told him everything I never told anyone before. Bit by bit, I wouldn't do it all in one go. And I trusted him. Then I looked up to him not necessary like a god but because he was . . . ; he could quote every scripture in the Bible, this and that. I saw him as someone who knows everything but within reason, within reason. So he would give me treats and take me out. Unlike the other people who couldn't go out of the rehab I would go out. So I felt, you know, special. And some of the things, you know, like I said about being in the showers and stuff like that I talked about that for the first time to this man. And the things that I told him he would use them to make me feel good about myself. He would turn it around and make me feel good. So we started training in the gym.

And this is the bit I do hate because another man's life is still in turmoil. We started training in the gym. And then he said, you know; he took pictures of me with his phone when I was doing the weights and he was telling me he wanted to show me how my muscles were developing and stuff like that. And me like a fool I thought: "Yeah, that's what he's doing. What a kind man, you know, was me to feel so good about myself." And then I lifted up the weights one day and then I was putting the blinds. I know that this is not about swearing because I don't believe in swearing that much but in situations I have to. He grabbed me by the bollocks. And he said to me: "You're all right down there." And he said: "What were you worried about at school?" And then I thought something wasn't right. I really thought something wasn't right to do that. So I sort of dismissed it. And I thought it was a laugh, sort of in my head. But then I thought there was something wrong. So then he kept wanting to go into the gym. And I didn't want to go there anymore because I didn't feel comfortable. But we shared the same caravan. So we went out. And then he took me into a pub. And we went into the pub. And he said: "You know, you would be

Appendices

all right if you can have a drink because you are with me. You would be all right." So I had a couple of pints because I thought: "If Noel says I can have a couple of pints, why not? He's my boss. He's my manager of the . . . (word omitted due to confidentiality)." So then after that we went back again because after I had a drink he started talking about other deeper things and then . . . . And then the next time we went out he started making sexual advances towards me. And he kissed me. And you know, I hate to admit I kissed him back because I was so fooled by the way he treated me like everything I ever wanted to be treated about. And I've had a couple of drinks. And I was very, very confused. I know I wasn't homosexual or whatever but I've been groomed and I didn't realise.

So I came back to AT for the weekend because I couldn't get out of what had happened. I was devastated. I thought: "For once in my life somebody treated me for who I am and didn't want something out of me." And instead I realised he wanted, whatever he wanted, sex. So I talked to the people of the homeless charity (HC, name substituted throughout the transcript due to confidentiality) that I knew. And they said: "It is best to go back to face the truth." So I went back and faced the truth. And we sat in front of the head pastor down there. And there were two other witnesses. And all that the head pastor said was: "I could see this coming." And I said: "What the hell do you mean?" And he said: "Noel has problems with homosexuality." He said: "And now God has brought that out. Noel can deal with it." And I said: "What, so I had to go through what I had been through so God can bring out this." I said: "If you knew this six months ago why didn't you tell me." And you know he said: "You haven't got a problem." He said: "You're not gay, are you?" And I said: "No, I'm not. But I am very, very confused." I said: "I started to believe that I could be. And I didn't know." And I just swore again. And I said: "My life is a mess now." I said: "I've been here for a year." And I said: "I feel worse than I did before I came." I said: "Putting my trust in somebody and it had been broken." And I said: "You've being the head pastor knowing that this is what this man or . . . ." I still see him as a friend. Because then they said what has happened in his life. And I thought: "Well, why didn't they work and deal with him and help him instead of putting me in a vulnerable position as a new student."

So I left there and kindly the HH put me back up again. And from then on I started drinking from day one. And the manager at the time said: "This is too much." And he tried to detox me. I was allowed to drink a couple of cans per day to cut down, to get down to a serious level or to a level. And then I get it a bit confused from there. I started to think of what has happened. Because everything now is happened so quick. But I finally put down the drink. I think it was . . . (year omitted due to confidentiality). I put down the drink, or . . . (year omitted due to confidentiality), whichever it is. I put down the drink but at the time in the house, it wasn't very, how shall I say, constructive. There was a lot of drinking going on at the time. A lot of drug use which was known to the management at the time. And I found it very hard to stay sober but I did. And I stayed sober for eight months. And I went over to an independent accommodation with support (IAWS, name substituted throughout the transcript due to confidentiality). Finally, after getting sober for eight months, and at that time I met a lovely girl called Carol who now happens to be my wife.

And after about three months of seeing her my birthday came along and she hadn't done what I expected. My dream is: I never met a girl like this, so spiritual and I was expecting something special for my birthday. And the way my addict works, you know, if I get upset I'd turn to the drink. And so I got upset, so I turned to drinking in the IAWS. And I was asked to leave. And I tried to commit suicide again because I couldn't handle it. And when I came back out they moved me from the IAWS back into the HH where I tried to get sober again. And then I left moving to . . . (name omitted due to confidentiality) with Carol. And what I can see in Carol really sort of made me start to believe in God again. Because after my experience in . . . (name omitted due to confidentiality) my whole trusting God had gone. Totally, I just couldn't see because this pastor, as I say see him now, laughing and just saying: "Good. God can do his work." And in my head was sounding: "If God can only do his work through something like this happening then there is no God." That was my . . . ; I have to be honest, there is no point in painting everything black and white because . . . . But I can see something in Carol. This aura around her—that was peace. And I thought I want some of that. And lucky enough without me doing any other work as such it was rubbing off. You know, I was getting this peace, this and the calmness, not knowing that God was working through Carol making me a lot calmer person.

But then . . . (number omitted due to confidentiality) years ago; no; . . . (number omitted due to confidentiality) and a half years ago I decided I wanted to end my life again for the final time. And this time it was final. And I've got a blunt knife. I planned it. I haven't drunk too much. And I thought if I get a large blunt blade it makes the cuts so they won't bleed. So I managed to push the large blunt blade through my stomach and it didn't bleed much but it made a big hole. And then because I had planned what

Appendices

I wanted to do I was able to stuck a small knife insight and cut away my stomach because I didn't want to wake up and for real, you know, I didn't want to wake up. So I tied my dressing gown and obviously I collapsed. And three hours later or whenever Carol found me on the floor. And they stitched me up. And I was starting to getting . . . ; I wasn't happy at the time because I had enough. I've just lost the last chance with my son after this incident.

So after that I drank again . . . (number omitted due to confidentiality) years ago. I relapsed after about eight months clean. And it was the worst drinking in my life. I didn't feel suicidal but I just wanted to drink, drink, and drink. And Carol left me, you know. And being an addict and alcoholic it was all her fault. I thought: "How selfish of her to leave me, you know, in pain." Because I didn't realise that when you have an addiction you just destroy other people's lives. They sit back and watch you die or . . . these were her words: "You are killing yourself." And she came back two weeks later in . . . (month and year omitted due to confidentiality), and I was saturated with urine. The bed was saturated with urine. I didn't understand this, didn't realise this was going on. I don't know where I was getting my alcohol from but I was getting my alcohol from somewhere. And two friends from AA came around. And they decided that I needed hospitalisation. So at the time I didn't want to go. I still had drink in the house. But they all undressed me. And the urine burns down my legs were so severe like a baby when it hasn't had his nappies changed for weeks. And, you know, to this day now I used that as my story in AA. I joke because I tried to use my sense of humour. When I'm sober now I do have a sense of humour. And people say: "Why did you finally give up drink?" And I said: "For the first time in my life." I said: "I had three beautiful women undressing me." And I said: "And I didn't even know anything about it." And I said: "That comes only once in a lifetime." I just joked in AA. And they all laughed.

So when I was in a hospital two people from AA came around. I didn't want to see anybody but for some reason I let them come and see me. And they were very spiritual. Not just from AA, you know, their belief was, God would cure everything and anything but also you need AA. While before I never knew that. I thought, you know, it's one or the other. And these men said to me: "Do you know you are in hospital because of alcohol?" And for the first time in 20 years of drinking it struck on that: "Yes, that's why I'm in hospital." Before I've thought it was because of whatever. I was ill. I couldn't, didn't want to blame alcohol because it was that,

that was the saviour. So since then I'd go to church. I'd go to AA. Every day of the week I would go to AA for the first 90 days of my recovery, once a day. And then I would still go.

So after that I went back to a community rehabilitation centre (CRC, name substituted throughout the transcript due to confidentiality) as well. You know, they gave me a great help. You know, they said: "You can't come back for 11 weeks." Because I've drunk and been thrown out of the course. And I waited those 11 weeks. And I thought: "Now I still need help." So I went to the group for . . . (number omitted due to confidentiality) week course. Then they asked me if I would take over the group. And facilitating group myself which I did and I thought: "You know, the respect that I've got from all the other clients; since someone has been through addiction; was getting through the other end, you know, it proved to them that it can be done." Where sometimes it might have an adverse reaction and people would say: "Who do you think you are? Are you better than us?" But instead they looked at me positively. So I worked for the CRC for about eight months. And in between there I applied at the AH. And I went back to the manager there and I said: "You know, is there any chance for any voluntary work?" And he shook my hand and gave me a big hug and said: "Sam I thought you are dead." And he said: "Some of the people thought that you are dead through your alcohol addiction." And they took me on. And within four months I was getting paid work . . . (details omitted due to confidentiality). And what was it?

About . . . (period omitted due to confidentiality) ago I started doing a lot more work because someone was off, and they were gonna be sacked, and I thought that I was going to get the job. And I didn't get the job. And for the first time in my life I didn't look towards alcohol to save me. I prayed for this man to keep his job, I said: "Because I don't want to benefit through someone else's misfortune. But if the job is meant to be mine is mine." And obviously with Carol's prayer and going to church that really helped. And not to want alcohol was a blessing in itself—just amazing. So that's my life up to date now.

Now I'm still doing my voluntary work. And just waiting patiently for a full-time job or whatever comes along. Just to give back what I have been given. And all along my recovery I've taken something from what people have said. It might have not worked at the time but I stored it in my memory and thought: "That's how you do this and that." So when I killed alcohol or put it to bed it was because of all the things I've been told by staff, ex-addicts, and things like that. So it all does work. So, you know,

Appendices

now I have my driving licence back. I have things like; the first thing which got back was my mobile phone. And to normal people it doesn't sound a lot but to an addict a mobile phone is: "Oh, God I've got a mobile phone." Because it is the first thing you would sell to get money for alcohol. I've got a passport. I've been on holiday. I can drive again. I'm married to my wonderful wife, Carol. Who, you know, seen what alcohol does, and she's still there and wants to support and help and goes to AA when she can. So, you know, this sounds not detrimental but: I'm glad I was an alcoholic because I've learned so much about myself through being an alcoholic that I would never have learned if I wasn't. So I can thank alcohol in one way that I wouldn't be the person I am, or I think I am now. So that's basically my life story up till now. And I just hope that it gets better day by day.

I: Thank you Sam. Thank you. Now I will pass through the questions. And if you feel like you can add something to the story in the directions of the questions please feel free. If you feel like that you don't need to, you have covered it already, no problem we would go to the next one. The first question is: How do you perceive your conscience? What is conscience? How did it develop? How does it function?

S: How do I perceive my conscience when I'm drinking or when I'm sober?

I: In general, how do you perceive conscience? And then yeah, what is conscience? How did it develop? How does it function? Yeah, you can compare both ways when you were drinking and now when you're not drinking.

S: Conscience to me when I'm sober is something that now can eat me alive but I'm a person who likes to . . . ; like if I say if I'm gonna meet yourself like today, you know, I would be there and if I am not there my conscience would eat me and say: "You know, that's wrong to do because, you know, if you promise something or you say you would do something it would play on my conscience for long." So conscience in my life is very important, you know. And I have like if I've done the little thing wrong my conscience again will eat me and say: "You should have just phoned or you should have . . . ." Because my conscience is one of my biggest beliefs, you know. If you promise or if you do—is on my conscience. And then I find it hard to get out of my life and phoned up, all done. But if I'm drinking there is no conscience because alcohol takes away all that consciousness. Because you do not understand when you're drinking that if I said to meet yourself today and I was drinking I wouldn't realise that you are sitting here waiting for me. Because I've just been getting wasted and I would think: "Oh, I'm not worried. So why is the other person worried?" So your conscience when you're drinking—there is none in my life. But you can't understand that's what happens. If somebody died for example and you all drank you can't understand why the other person is upset about that. So that's a bit like conscience: "Oh, what's the matter with them?" Because you don't have any feelings; so—no conscience when I'm drinking, not at all. And if you do you just drink a bit more and it goes away.

I: Next question: How did you develop alcohol addiction? What is alcohol addiction? When did you realise that you have been addicted to alcohol? How did you try to manage your alcohol addiction? You covered pretty much this question but if you want to add something.

S: So with alcohol addiction I don't think anybody will ever find the answer to, you know, how do you become an alcoholic or how do you get an addiction. Because when people cross over that fine line where they can't stop, you know.... I always look at that if you are an alcoholic, and you stop drinking, and you see another alcoholic drinking, and when they have been sick and throwing out blood, you know, weeing themselves or whatever if you still could choose between that and being sober then you certainly wouldn't choose to have an addiction to be throwing out blood near death. So I define alcohol addiction as a mystery to me. But I do know, an alcohol addiction is when you have one you're thinking of the next one before you even had the first one. So that's my way of knowing that I was an addict. Before I got one I want the next. And then after that is where I'm gonna get the next four or five. You're not enjoying just controlling. What are the other parts?

I: When did you realise that you have been addicted to alcohol? How did you try to manage your alcohol addiction?

S: Well I realise now. As I said in my story, I wasn't addicted to alcohol at 16. But that's when it began, as I said in my story. Because it did what a lot of alcoholics like myself use it for to change the way you feel. But you don't realise that is an addiction. But what I did to try and recover was use AA, pray; you know, try and see whether life is better without alcohol. But then it takes a long time to realise that it is better without alcohol. But when you've got alcohol inside you it's hard to control that. It's hard to control.

I: Okay Sam, thank you. The third question: What were your moral views before your moral, spiritual, and/or religious transformation? What is morality? How did you deal with moral dilemmas? How much did morality matter for you? That's before the change happened.

S: Before the change. My moral views were; I've always got them through my mum. You know, if you say you are gonna do something, you know, to be moral is that you do, do that thing that you are gonna say. And if you believe that going to church is the right and that would be my moral to go to church and not come away and then slander the church because I've been told to be there. If I believe in something, you know, my morals are to stick by what I believe in hanging out. If something is wrong like racism, such and such, to me that is immorality, you know. So my morals are, you know, if I'm saying okay I'm not a racist but then I'm talking to somebody else saying I don't like that person because he is foreigner, you know, that's not morals at all. So, you know, my morals are what I believe in is right on the personal level, you know. Do not steal. Do not slander. Do not have affairs. They are the morals I believe in. So that sums it up.

I: How did you experience this belief of morals when you were drinking?

S: When I was drinking. When I was drinking, like I said, you know I can keep saying the same answer, with drinking it would take away all morality, all of it, you know. You might start of good intentions but then when you are on that drink you don't care who you hurt in a sense, or what you may have to do to get the drink. You know, you may just steal it. You may have to lie, you know. I remember once breaking my morals, "do not lie to get money." But I went to the Salvation Army saying I needed bus fare to get back from TSEET to AT and all I wanted was the four pounds to get a bottle of cider. So you know, that's how my morals were taken away. That's one of the biggest things I learned. It is something that I hate to tell people that I've never wanted to hide my addiction because I think the more you can tell people that I had been there honestly the more people can realise that they are not the only ones and it can be easier to recover. So the worse moral that I ever did break through alcohol addiction was when my mother died and obviously Jessica was dying at the same time, which was tragic. And I just wanted to get so drunk. So I went to the bank and pleaded and lied that I needed money for my mum's funeral when really I wanted the money for drinking. And that's . . . ; I look back at that and I think: "I don't really want to say God but you know—How could you stoop that low?" But now I've realised that's the power of alcoholism. You know you would tell a lie as big as that one to get money for gambling and drink. And that doesn't hold me now because I understand that that's not an excuse but that's the power of addiction.

Appendices

I: Thank you Sam. The next one: Did you practice spirituality before your moral, spiritual, and/or religious transformation? What is spirituality? How did you practice spirituality? How much did spirituality matter for you?

S: As a child, you know . . . ; spirituality, you know, is obviously in the belief of your God of your understanding. You may be Catholic, you may be Protestant, you may be Buddhist whatever, spirituality is believing and practising. But as a child that was taken away a little bit because my mum used to suffer from epileptic fits. She would always lie in bed with the rosary beads. I wanted to get out and walk. She wanted to go to church. And my dad wouldn't let her go to church through shame of her having an epileptic fit in the church. And I was only eight at the time. And my dad would send me with my sister to church and he would go to the pub. And I couldn't understand if spirituality, and believing in God, was so good why my dad would go to the pub; my mum who wanted to go to church wasn't allowed to go to church because my dad was ashamed. And I thought: "Surely my mum would be in the best place in the house of God if she was to have a fit for people to help." So I was very misconceived at early age about God. But you know I was christened, Holy Communion and confirmation. So I did have a belief but it was always very fuzzy.

I: Okay. Thank you. The next one: . . . .

S: I'm sorry. Now my spirituality is: every day I try and hand over my will over to God, which is still hard to do because I still think I needed to do it myself. But I do pray and hand over. You know every decision I make is the one that God wants me to make. So that's how spiritual I believe I am at the moment.

I: Thank you Sam. Next one: Did you practice religion before your moral, spiritual, and/or religious transformation? What is religiousness? How did you practice religion? Did you have religious affiliation? How much did religion matter for you?

S: This is almost the same as the other one in away.

I: Yeah. If you make a difference between spirituality and religiousness then you can add something else if not then it's okay.

S: I don't know the full, at this present time, spirituality and religiousness. Because religious to me—that word now just sounds so strong, religion. Religion to me, my belief is that there is one God and there is only one God and doesn't matter, you know, which religion you are, to me there is only one God out there, you know.

I: The next one: Did you experience moral, spiritual, and/or religious transformation? How did you experience this transformation? When did you experience this transformation? May you identify anyone who played any influential role in the process? How much has this transformation changed your life?

S: Well, as I said, the only question that I can answer is, you know, my mother with her rosary beads being Catholic and because she held onto them all the time I couldn't believe that God wouldn't save a person like that. Yeah, someone else going around shooting and murdering people, blah, blah, blah, they would be saved. Yes they might be punished later on in life. But because my mum was taken away with it, she died with the beads in her hand. And again it was just distorted. Yes that's what I could answer for that one.

And Carol—her Christianity, and another lady who is coming to help in the HH, I saw what they had. The way they practised, you know, is still what I want one hundred percent. It's not there but I'm open enough to it by watching other people's spirituality and Christianity. You know, because I know they've got through their beliefs what I want. And until I practice more and learn to trust more in God it is not gonna happen just yet. Because I believe you and God have to be a team. God isn't just a leader. He is adviser. That's how I look at it. And if you don't follow his advice then he can't help you in a way that you want him to help you. He wants to team-work with me.

I: In terms of your mother's role as you said in regards to this transformation, is it positive in terms of understanding God or negative.

S: Negative.

I: Negative. And the second one you gave with Carol and the other lady . . . .

S: Positive, yeah.

I: And in terms of, you mentioned AA. And these people, you mentioned that they were spiritual and they came to visit in the hospital. Is there somewhere there such an experience which can be identified as a transforming experience, in AA or in the hospital?

S: Oh, with the person in the hospital. You know because he's so spiritual and as I've just said a few minutes ago my terminology with spirituality—I'm not hundred percent sure of. I know about beliefs. But you know, the calmness that he showed as well and the spirituality he had, in other way the way he would pray about everything, the way he would have that aura of spirituality and calmness inside him. But the positive came out that he said: "God developed AA as well." He said so. I wasn't to go to church on a Sunday after I came out of hospital. And he said: "At the moment you need to go to AA because sick people get sick; when sick people are sick they go to the hospital. When alcoholics are alcoholics they go to AA. But also God in an annual prayer is as important but at the moment you need AA meetings." But with God's prayer along the way, you know, and his spiritual beliefs that he had he said: "God always said, you still need AA." That's what God told him through his spirituality. This AA was set up for a reason. And then just going to church won't just save the alcoholic.

I: In terms of your experience, as a transforming experience, did you have any single event as such, or did you have kind of lengthy and still developing experience of change in regards to spirituality?

S: I'm not sure if it's just spirituality at the moment but I do know that it was at that hospital bed. You know, the way that man came across because of his spirituality if it wasn't for him that day, and as I call it intervention if he hadn't have come, I would have come out of hospital and drunk probably. So that was my . . . ; yeah, that was my defining moment. That man coming from church; reading me scriptures from the Bible; that night was my defining moment. And I probably don't realise how much until you've just asked me now, how much it meant to send someone like him along at the right time, the right place, reading the right Scripture. So that was, yeah, the moment I can identify if I look back. And then obviously meeting Carol and seeing in her the spirituality and the calmness and the devotion into watching God's channel and this and that.

So I'm still slowly and gradually following in their footsteps. Because—and I will go on a bit; but when you've been hurt so much and your trust has been broken you still take a while and think that you need to do it yourself. Because when you cried out for God's help before, you know, with my wife, with mum dying and that bloke and other things when you've cried out and it's not happened—we all have to gain trust whether of being God or whether of being the partner you are with. And you know sometimes I think I get confused because they say: "God will not give you anything more than you can handle." And sometimes I think: "Well, some of the things I haven't got into greater detail in the interview, some of the things I had to handle at the same time—is too much for anybody to handle." So I was thinking: "God surely you are gonna give me a break." You know but . . . . Now maybe my break is coming and I realise that I'm stronger than I was. But to me at that time I thought: "If you really are there God . . . ." But then I see yourself, Carol, and I know he's there for other people. But when I start trusting more and walking in the direction and letting go then it would become easier. But yeah I'm still making the steps.

I: Thank you. Next question: What was the impact of your transformation on your life? Compare your morality, spirituality, and religiousness before and after the transformation. How did the transformation impact your understanding of morality, spirituality, and religion, and their role in your life? How much did morality, spirituality, and religion matter for you after your transformation?

S: After my transformation, you know, because, as I said, at the moment I'm still walking. I know that, as I said, that night was a miracle that they came at that time. You know, that was God's hand reaching out pulling me from the gutter and helping me. But as for changing my morality—no. Before I drank my morals were very strong. Partly because of my mother, as I say: "If I could be reincarnated as a person it would be my mother." Because she was so real. And she believed in God so, so much. But when she was ill she would still help others and not worry about herself. And she had that love. And, you know: "That this is what you should do in this situation. Don't steal. If you need to buy something you save up"—all sorts of morals like that. You know: "You don't get credit." And my mum told me all these morals and I didn't lose them through alcohol. They were as I say "squashed," "squashed." They were still there because there would be times during my drinking that I would sober up for a while and I think: "Gee, I'm doing the wrong things," you know. So they were still there. But when I got drunk then they would go away. But they still have not left me. But if I wanted another drink the morals will go away. So when my transformation came around I'm still the same person I was but a lot stronger just in my belief about myself. You know but the way I would treat other individuals is the way I always wanted to treat them. So—didn't really change I just sobered up. Apart from, I don't know. Would you say that because of my experiences now that my heart, my desire, my passion is to help others has changed my morality. I don't know. I don't know.

I: Thank you. The next question: What was the impact of your moral, spiritual, and/or religious transformation on your conscience? Compare your conscience before and after the transformation. How did the transformation impact your conscientious behaviour? How much did the voice of your conscience matter for you after your transformation?

S: For my conscience, as I said as a child from my mum; and from my dad—gave me conscience because of his army and regiment—was: "This is right. That's right. Six o'clock you got to be in blah, blah, blah." I always had a conscience; a forced upon conscience by my dad, you know. I wouldn't treat a person like my dad treated me and my sisters. He did like that and made us very fearful but it did give you a conscience that, "that's what you should do." See my conscience is the same as it always was before.

I: What if you compare the times when you were drinking and how your conscience functioned during this time, in comparison to the times now when you're not drinking, and you are out of the drinking, addictive period of your life.

S: As I said, during the addictive period of my life, you know, when I've done the bad thing, what I did with my mum's money and all. And if it was today and I was drinking, and I didn't want to come here, I wouldn't bother. I wouldn't even phone you up, you know. I wouldn't care at the time. But if I sober up for a couple of hours I would be a bit regretful but then if I knew that I was going to get another drink in about 10 minutes it would be: "What about Yordan? It doesn't matter." You know, that sort of thing. So yeah, as I've said before there was no conscience with the drink. You might get minimal periods when you get conscience. But other times if you can see a way to get a drink, and £10 you just saw drop out of your pocket I would have picked it up, took it, and spend it. Not pull it out of your pocket but if you dropped it. But if I was sober I would straightaway say: "Excuse me Sir is this yours?" But drinking—it would be: "Oh, you know, happy birthday, you know." Because all you want is alcohol. You know, it doesn't matter who you hurt. A lot of my drinking was depressive drinking. I didn't steal much. I've just spent my benefit money which is still a lot but I was drinking myself and that was it. I didn't have to steal much because what I drank I could afford that at the time because I wouldn't pub drink. But if I had to do it that way there has to be no conscience. You know, if I can't get it I would lie, lie, steal.

I: Next question. Yeah, you were saying about this question, coming back to the previous one actually, that during the time of your struggle with alcohol the conscience wasn't active for quite some time. Now after your experience, this transformation, and still experiencing this transformation; does this transformation or does the spirituality part of this transformation have any influence on your conscience?

S: Of what, as of the things I've done during the alcohol addiction?

I: Whether this transformation has impacted your conscience. Whether there is any kind of consequence.

S: So this is your phone and I stole it when I was drinking. But now I've become sober; do you mean is my conscience now aware of what I've done during alcoholism? Now I'm trying to form; do you mean my conscience goes back and thinks about all the bad things I did when I was drinking?

I: No. I'm thinking more about the present. How does your conscience function in comparison with the past? In a way that, you're saying that during that time of addiction it didn't function well. Yeah. Now you have gone out of the addiction. And the elements you described as part of this change, this transformation are: there is some spirituality part of it and AA part of it and people part of it who have brought to you the message of the Bible or various others' inputs. And now this change which has happened to you; the question is: did this change impact your conscience? And does it still? Because you are saying that you're still in this process of transformation, being part of this process of transformation, does it impact your conscience? And if it does, how does it impact it, positively, negatively? How does it impact the conscience in comparison to what was happening during the time of addiction when your conscience wasn't so functional? Is it functional now? Does it function, your conscience? How is it impacted by your transformation?

S: Oh, yeah, thinking about it now my conscience is gone like, like they say: "When God pays you back is tenfold." My conscience now is tenfold in a way. I have the same morality and the same beliefs and the same conscience but they have become stronger. Because of what I did when I was drinking now I try hundred times more consciously to make sure I don't let people down, not through drink. But just by being here today I was seven minutes late and I felt terrible, you know. And at the end of the day it's only seven minutes, you know. But my conscience is saying: "You have said 10 o'clock or half-past ten, you should be there." So yeah, it has become stronger. I understand what you mean now. I thought—did you mean did my conscience realise what I did when I was drinking? And was I worried about what I did when I was drinking? But you mean, how do I feel now about my conscience? Yeah, as I said; I still have the same beliefs but they are stronger because now I'm sober. I've realised the mistakes I made when I wasn't sober and how damaging they probably were to other people.

I: You mean when you were drinking.

Appendices

S: When I was drinking. But now because, as you say, I've transformed, now I make sure to try a hundred percent more that I do not let people down. And I will keep, you know, my conscience like it evolves and still depend there. I couldn't do that because—no way, no way. So yeah, drink has taught me, you know, the conscience and beliefs I had to enforce them even more now. Not just through what other people have told me through AA and things like that. It is because you understand now the effects you have on other people's lives sober or drunk. Even sober if you haven't got conscience you have effect on people's lives. And drunk you definitely do. So now I've realised everything I do like trying, it just . . . ; I know is not conscience but now I am not living on the streets and I'll always be clean and shaved. I'll always be . . . , you know. Everything is changed in that way in a more positive way.

I: Okay. The next question: What was the impact of your transformed conscience on your recovery from alcohol addiction? Compare your recovery before and after the transformation. How did your transformed conscience impact your recovery from alcohol addiction? What is the role of your transformed conscience in the maintenance of your abstinence? May you identify anyone who played any influential role in the process? You already spoke about this in the last few minutes. Do you want to add anything?

S: The only thing I would add in, you know, because obviously this is the help of people's recovery as well. You know, like if I say I would gonna go to an AA meeting to myself then I go to that AA meeting because of the mere fact—I'll put it in the comparison: if I wanted to drink I would walk a hundred miles to go and get a drink. You know, so if I want recovery then I should be prepared to walk that hundred miles to go and get recovery, you know. Does that answer any part of that question? But you know keeping boundaries, keeping commitments to everything with my own conscience and things will . . . . Without that transformation, you know, without people guiding me in the right way and teaching me the ways to recover I could still slip back. But because I've learned and listened to what people like yourself say or, you know, others at the CRC and realise how influential is, you know, keeping up appointments, conscience, this, that, the other. Yes, and that's all I can answer to that one.

I: Okay Sam. Thank you. Next one: May you share your future plans related to your recovery? What is the role of morality, spirituality, and/ or religion in them? What is the role of your transformed conscience in them? Do you plan to share your experience with others who need help in recovery from alcohol addiction?

S: Well, my best answer to that now is: I plan to share my whole experiences, you know. I've never had a passion for something so much as helping other people in recovery. You know, my desire is to work for either the HC or work for the AH and anyone who needs help with recovery from alcohol addiction. But not only will I use the experiences I've had to help others I will use the experiences I've had when I failed and couldn't quite get it. And I will use that to not think: "Right, if I'm telling say John, I won't tell him how to recover I'll, what is the word we always use in AA, I will suggest, these are good ways of recovery." And I will say: "They are hurdles that we do come across. And if we failed the first time like a horse we can pick ourselves up and try and jump again. And not think that everybody can recover straightaway and give up and think—oh, they are not listening, they are not listening." Because the experiences I've had, four or five times before I've got recovered, I will use all that experience to keep trying to find other avenues to guide that person without telling that person. But you know, I will do anything I can and share any experience I've had with anybody who wants to know. And I would not say: "Oh it's easy." Because it's not. I would say: "But with perseverance you will find your way there. And if you don't find it the first time you will learn something that first time." And I would say: "Just like a book we start with the first chapter. You know, the stories are not so good." I would say: "But then second chapter; it has something from the first chapter in it. And you get to the ending and the ending generally can be a success in the book or happy story or whatever." And I would say: "That is the way alcohol addiction can happen, you know—is chapters." Step one, obviously we know, is: we are admitting we're powerless to alcohol but that doesn't mean we stop. And you know, I would like to help others learn that once they know that they have a problem that, you know, if it takes you 10 days, 10 years knowing you have a problem you will work on it one day. And I would always say to people, you know: "This is the route I chose. I didn't listen some of the times. I wish I could have changed some things but I didn't." I'd say: "But where I am at now, I am at peace, and I am happy." And just to be able to give that knowledge and help someone it's all I wish for. You know, when I do my voluntary work now, when I see somebody move on that's just as rewarding as a full-time job. As it is you know. Yeah, because when people talk about salary—what salary do you want? I would say: "One of the parts of my salary or balances is to see someone move on." I said: "Rather than

£1,000 per year." I said: "Is just to help one who would help another." And I would use . . . . I will take a bit more time on this one.

I would always help others and guide others first of all. Because I know the HC and I have strong beliefs that God is a saviour. And I'm not just saying that because we are on tape. God is our saviour. But in the first and general road to recovery every, I shouldn't say every but most addicts dislike God because if God loved them or loved us, I should have said love me, people wouldn't be in this mess. So he's the first person most of us addicts blame, you know. If this is making sense but, you know so . . . . My way of, you know, helping an addict is seek God in here and there but at the start if you say you've come to church and people say: "Eh, everyone wants to be everyone; he hasn't saved me so far." But I will use my way of AA, you know. And I will lead people through the steps. Step one is: "we are admitting we're powerless to alcohol." Step two is: "finding a power greater than ourselves which will restore us to sanity." And that power could be anything, you know. And it can be a higher power. And as soon as people hear higher power that's God? And I would just say: "My higher power is . . . ." I would say: "Let's use for example Yordan." I would say: "Can you push that tree over?" And this would be the way I would instruct people. And they would say: "Oh, no." And I would say: "Well, there is someone higher than you that either put that tree there or could push that tree over. So to start with you can use that as your higher power." And then the third one which puts everybody off is: "hand your will and your life over to God as you do or do not understand him." And then you get four out of the twenty people leave the room because the word "God" is there. And I would say: "No"; I would say; I convinced people in the CRC to go to that. I would say: "Look at it; break the 'god' down. The 'g' is a 'group.' And the 'o' is 'of.' And 'd' is 'drunks.' 'A group of drunks.' And we hand our will and our lives over to 'a group of drunks.'" First of all we've had experiences. And as you go further and get that person, you know, not fearful of the word "god" then you bring it in, or I would bring it in then. And now they may say: "And then I started realising it; they weren't group of drunks really, you know, is God without us knowing." And they say: "Yeah it is." "You know, it is," I think. You know, that's the way I want to use my recovery.

I: Thank you Sam, thank you. The last question: May you formulate the main theme of your life story? What is the place of alcohol addiction in your story? What is the place of conscience in your story? What is the place of morality, spirituality, and/or religiousness in your story? What is the place of your moral, spiritual, and/or religious transformation in your story? The main theme. Basically to summarise everything you said as a main theme of your story.

S: The main theme of my life story was and I'd say—my life was destroyed as a child. And because of my dad and . . . (word omitted due to confidentiality) people in general drinking alcohol—it seemed to be older than all and is in everything. So that is the main. The main theme of my life story is that I believe that all this stuff alcohol did was make you happy—not knowing. But the place of alcohol addiction in my story is that I didn't know I'd become addicted. You know, so with that question the alcohol addiction hit me in the face without me knowing. You know, so the alcohol addiction destroyed people's lives which I didn't realise. In some ways of them watching me dying and what I did to people through my self-harm and the alcohol addiction.

The place of conscience in my story is: none of it was my fault. My mum died. Then bustards at school really, you know, I wish I would have told my story today with more emotion but you know, the way I was humiliated at school gave me no conscience of this. You know, I drank because I was destroyed. So I didn't have a conscience for drinking. I drank because I needed something to tell me: "Get over this." And now I realise by talking to people and, you know, learning why you drink and not, you know, as people may think you just drink because you drink. And my belief is: "No." "Is not that." I didn't have such a conscience of drinking. You know when Jessica died. That's sad enough as it is. But morality, spirituality, and religiousness, as I say, religiousness was distorted—all my life, you know.

Morality: my moralities were always there until I had a drink. So I don't believe I've lost them. As I said, they were just overpowered by alcohol. But morals are still there. And the religiousness in my story was: Where was this God? Why didn't he help me and stop all these people dying in my life? And why didn't my dad go to church? I mean my dad would go to the pub and send us to church. So I couldn't understand God. But now that's totally changed. And then what is the place of your moral, spiritual . . . in the story. In my transformation now my morals are becoming a lot stronger because of human beliefs and how I've been hurt; you make sure not to hurt anybody even more especially through my bullying and things like that. I am very much trying to step in when people are bullied. And I take it upon myself to save that person.

And my religious transformation and spirituality is: I'm growing every day spiritually. I know someone's guiding me along. Because to me, you know, when I've talked on this tape that it hasn't been as emotional as it would come across because I am a bit numb at the moment. But, you know, day by day I am letting go and letting God flow. That's all what I can say. Letting go and letting God flow. And you know, as I walk he walks with me. Before I walked behind and now I caught up with God. And now I have to hold his hand and let him guide me where he wants to guide me. And don't be afraid to hand that over to, you know, to God or Carol, who could be, you know, my god at the moment. And that's, you know, my transformation. And there is someone who cares and that is a power greater than myself, which is God. So that's my . . . ; that is the main thing. The main thing of my life story is: that with correct help and guidance and perseverance, as I'm going to sum it up, you can get there and have a life, you know, as I've heard in AA, beyond your wildest dreams. You know, which I've never thought would ever happen, to wake up in the morning and think: "I like myself." You know, that's powerful. And you are not looking in the mirror with the can in your hands: "Sam, you are great person," because the drink is doing the talking. You're talking to yourself and you feel—put your head up high and walk on and say: "I've got through this journey. And God put me through this journey. So I can get it back to others." And use a negative experience and turn it into a positive one. And that's the end of my story. Thank you.

I: Thank you Sam. So this would be the end of the interview at 12:25.

Victoria (2011). Personal interview (Conscience in recovery from alcohol addiction), 21 November.

Interviewer (I): I am recording now. That's an interview with Victoria recorded on the 21st of 11th starting at 11:20. And the guidelines in regards to the story are the following: Structure your life story in chapters. Think about their names, summaries, and progressive links. Without interfering with the genuine character of the story can you identify the role of the following topics in your life narrative: conscience; alcohol addiction; morality; spirituality; religiousness; moral reformation; spiritual transformation; religious conversion and/or affiliation; the relationship between morality, spirituality, religiousness, and conscience, and recovery from alcohol addiction. How will you summarise each of these chapters? What progressive links will you make between these chapters? And all this is here for you. Please feel free to develop your story.

Victoria (V): Okay. So I was born in an Orthodox family, which is kind of a traditional Christian denomination in my home country (MHC, name substituted throughout the transcript due to confidentiality). But it's quite formal. So we weren't really practising Christianity as such. My father was an alcoholic. But he died before I was five. My mum, she remarried but then she had some issues at work, so when she was having these issues she was also drinking. So I could see that kind of pattern. My sister who was . . . (age omitted due to confidentiality) years older than me, she had some issues herself. And then she started drinking while she was having these issues but she was more like having periods of drinking when she was having these issues. But then she would come back. So I wouldn't say she's an alcoholic, or she is an alcohol dependent.

The next important element in my history was when I was 11, when I met a family. They were Baptists. So they were Evangelical Christians. They were practising Christians. So I met them when I was 11. And about half a year down the line I decided I wanted to become a Christian because I've seen the way they were living their lives, the way they were loving me. They kind of loved me as their own child. So that was, let's say for me, the first moment of conversion to Christianity. I was very, very much practising my Christianity, wanting to tell all my friends about Christianity, so, yeah, very much into it.

My problems about drinking started when I was 25. So when I was 24 I was involved in this relationship which I knew I shouldn't be. So it was something that in a way I was going against my conscience. But it was something that kind of progressed for probably one year very slowly to be kind of drawn into this relationship which wasn't good. I mean, for me having a relationship with a guy was not a good thing because of my convictions, most of all. But however, I got into this relationship when I was 24.

And when I was 25 I realised there is someone else in the equation. So it was a very difficult time because they were persons that I was working with. The third person in the equation was my best friend that I was also working with. And kind of exposing things would have been quite a big scandal in the organisation I was working. So I tried to confront the persons. They both denied. So I was kind of led to believe now it's all in my head. But I kind of had, I had kind of signals or signs that there are some things there happening. But when I had the first . . . . When I realised for the first time what's happening the first thing that I did, it was in the night, I went and got drink. And then the guy left the following day for a few weeks the country, so I couldn't contact him. So just the sort of this happening drove me crazy. So I started to drink heavily very strong spirits from the very beginning. So I was drinking till I was kind of passing out. And that's how kind of started.

It was difficult because . . . . I think the difficult bit was that I didn't have the strength to kind of clarify and put an end to the thing, to the relationship which probably would have been the most sensible thing to do. But I didn't have the strength. And then the more I was kind of struggling both with the relationship and getting more into drinking it became even more difficult. So I ended up with five years of drinking. In the beginning I was drinking in the evenings and weekends. So I was ever so quiet, quiet for a long time to function in that way. That was my kind of emotional . . . . That was how I was processing the emotions in the evening drinking and being able to cry or to just—that was numbing them probably even more. Because every day working with these two persons, every day and being; I am quite an observant person so I noticed all the little details. So kind of having to live with this under my eyes got to the point of being very difficult. So yeah, I was coping through drinking.

Then I mean the timeframes are quite difficult to remember. But it got to a point. I was a manager. So I was able to do the job though it required a lot of effort to concentrate. And sometimes I would work till 10 or 12 in the night. It was also another way of . . . . Workaholism became another way of; instead of going home and kind of thinking: "What's happening." It was just, yeah, burying myself in work. It was better for me, I thought. And so, but it came to a point probably in the last year of the five where the withdrawals would have been quite severe. So in the morning I was having the shakes. So I had to drink starting from the morning. And I would take drink to work and hide it everywhere. And, yeah, kind of top up during the day because after about three hours of not drinking I would have the shakes, so yeah. I knew all the time deep down in my conscience that it's not good, what I'm doing.

I think the difficult bit with this guy was that he had a way with words, and he had a way of playing me in which he was trying, kind of suggest that because of my drinking . . . . So he was like accusing that my drinking is my main problem not the relationship. That because of my drinking my head is not thinking straight. So he was making me doubt all my reasoning. So I started to self-doubt. And I didn't; I came to a point of paralysis in a way. And my will became very, very weak in terms of changing something, putting an end to the relationship. In terms of drinking I tried different ways to stop drinking. I was able probably to stop for a month but then I was back into it. Yeah, of course I was straggling. I think in a way I felt justified to drink because I felt that's not the main problem. So I kind of didn't want to acknowledge that the drinking is the problem because I saw the relationship as the bigger problem and as something that would justify me to do the drinking. Because: "Look! How much pain I'm having in this?" So yeah, that was, that was the story with the drinking.

About how I stopped it was . . . . In their relationship there was a point when I; things became quite obvious to me. So I kind of had a point where I felt: "Well I had enough. And I had enough of this. And I had enough of this life." I felt like I'm living in duplicity because I was a manager. And I was a manager in a Christian organisation. And living this hidden, secret life about the relationship and about the drinking. So I just didn't want that to continue. So actually when that kind of last drop happened I decided that: "I want to die." So I said I'm gonna; my decision in my head was that I'm gonna drink myself to death. So I, I know I prayed actually before starting, and I said: "God I finished with this world. If you want to get me out of here fine. In what concerns me; in how I am; my head is set now I'm done." So, yeah, I drank six days continuously without eating but I didn't die.

During those days it happened the thing, which probably scientists would call hallucinations. I felt that I was a bit kind of suspended between two realities. And it was the physical reality. But that with drinking kind of faded away. So I was kind of more aware of the spiritual reality. And actually here is to mention just one other thing. I felt at one point with the drinking, I felt that things affected or went into a spiritual realm. Because I was having this kind of premonitions which were very interesting of what's happening when it's happening. And then I was kind of going and checking, and they were happening that way. So I felt like: "Okay! This is something interesting happening." But, however . . . . So when I had those six days of drinking, and I said that I felt suspended between two realities, I felt that there was a kind of struggle for me. If kind of I'm to die or if I'm to live; if I'm to be with God; if I am to be separated. So I felt trapped in between these two worlds.

And I remember that at one point I was praying but also kind of realising that only my prayers are not enough. So I was praying that there would be people praying for me. So something can happen that I'm getting out of there. And I did have a very good friend who had a dream. The second night when I started drinking she came and knocked on my door. But of course I didn't open. And she left a note under my door and she said: "Give me a sign of life if you are alive." And later on she told me that she had a dream with me in like foetus position but that I was dead. And then she knew something happened. And then she took my other colleagues at work, and they started praying for me which was actually what I was asking when I was desperate in my prayer.

And there was another moment in those days on drinking when it was like I was seeing the person of Jesus and God saying: "This is how much I loved you. And I gave you so many kinds of warnings, warning signs along these years." And I knew there were quite a few moments when I kind of thought: "This is the sign that I should end this." But, yeah, I couldn't really act on them. I was back into the relationship and in the drinking. So, yeah, it was an overwhelming sense of how much God loved me and how costly that love was for him. So, yeah, it wasn't; I don't know how to say it, not a; I didn't have a sense of being judged and sentenced when I had that moment. It was just a very deep awareness of how much he loved me and how much I was going against him through the way I was living. And I prayed at that moment, and I said: "God please give me another chance." And I felt like God was saying: "You have another chance but it's a matter of life and death. You better take it seriously."

So after . . . . Well friends were calling. Family was calling. Of course I wouldn't take my . . . . I was set to die so I couldn't be bothered. But, yeah, after six days I had this moment and I stopped. And I just managed to ring at work, and I said: "I'm alive." And they said: "Well, we were just about

Appendices

to break your door with the police because we thought of the worse." So, yeah, I stopped then.

And then I started. I didn't want to go to AA because I used to have an ex-client going to AA. So I didn't feel safe like going there. But I contacted, a few days later, a Christian psychiatrist cause I thought: "If I'm gonna include God in my recount of the story someone else may think that I am a bit, yeah, crazy or hallucinating." So, yeah, I stopped drinking; keeping a diary that she would check on weekly. So kind of saying, kind of monitoring my thoughts and what I was doing in the morning, noon, and evening. And that for me, because I have sensitive conscience despite the way I went against it, the fact that I knew I needed to be accountable to someone, and that I needed to be honest, for me it was good enough to hold me from drinking.

So, yeah, for one year I didn't have anything to drink. Then I had a very brief lapse, like two days maybe, but just a very small amount. One year later it was again to do with that guy that I was in relationship with before. And I had few other relapses. And the pattern was me getting emotionally entangled again with this guy. And not being able to say no to him. I mean he knew me, and he knew what buttons to kind of push. So, yeah, I had fewer relapses in MHC but they were like maybe a week the longest. I had another one when I broke up with another guy that I was with. So the pattern was that emotionally unbalanced or stressful situation would lead me into drinking. And then the decision of coming to UK was because I wanted to get away from this guy cause I felt like he still had a grip on me. And every time he would kind of get into my life one way or another I would start drinking. So I said: "No. I cannot. I cannot live like this." That's why I came to UK.

And after I came to UK everything was okay for three months. And then I had a long relapse for about five months. But it was a similar pattern. A guy kind of sweeping me emotionally. And he actually brought the drink for the first time when I started drinking again. Then we kind of used to drink together. And then after, after about five months I went to MHC for a visit. I told the friends what I'm struggling with, with the drinking. It was a difficult relationship. It wasn't a relationship as such. It was just someone who was giving me a hard time. Because I was living with the guy in the flat where we were working as well and we had .... So at the beginning he was so very much in love with me. And then it started the drinking. Then we came to kind of hostile relationship. So we were just living together but, I mean sharing the flat, but I found it very difficult to cope with him. So I was drinking quite heavily. So I was saying; but again just in the evening so I was able to work; so I was saying to my friends in MHC: "I don't know what to do. I cannot go on like this." They were saying: "Come back." I didn't want to go back because I knew what it's waiting for me there, back.

So I just prayed, I said: "God, make, do something. I cannot really put up with this." And by the time I got back from MHC the guy was dismissed, so clear. But I still continued to drink for probably another week. And then I; I was kind of exasperated with myself. And the next morning after I last drank I just wrote in my diary. And it was, it was a moment of what I would call a "complete surrender." When I said: "God, I tried. I've tried all the ways to keep away from drinking." And I am a person who is quite determined, quite strong-willed. So I usually follow through when I set my head to do something. But I noticed that in what concerned the drinking, my drinking, that wasn't enough. So it was that moment when I wrote in my diary. And it was that moment of complete surrender, and I said: "God, if you don't help me I cannot do it." And that happened on the 8th of the 8th of the 8th. And I have never drunk since. So that seemed to me to be a moment of probably deep reconnection with God and reconciliation with God. And kind of acknowledging that this issue is in a way bigger than me, and that I need someone bigger and an outsider to help me. But yeah, since then I haven't drunk. And that is what kind of keeps me, I think. Because I still had obviously the emotional struggles, a guy, or other personal issues but I have managed not to drink. And actually I got kind of a mental image in my head about what is drinking. So I feel that actually when I am picking up the drink is like I'm saying to God: "Well, you know, this issue that I'm going through right now is so difficult, and it's so bigger than you. And you cannot help so I will sort it my own way. I'll dilute it with a bit of drink." So I felt that me going back to the drinking is like an obvious way of saying that I don't have faith in God. So I think that kind of associating these two things in my head helped me. And I prayed, and I said: "I know they're gonna be difficult times in my life from now on when I would be, that would be the first instinct to a get drink. But now I prefer to go through the pain of it and kind of try to be as objective and rational as you can be in an emotional situation. And kind of stick with God there in that difficult time and in the pain but not go back to drink." So I think this kind of contract that I made in my mind that: "Okay when a hard time is gonna come this is how I'm going to go through it, kind of being, sticking to God instead of going to the drinking."

Which I know rationally if I'm thinking is not helping. It's, yeah, okay, making things maybe feel a bit easier on the spot but then the next day you have the same problem plus you have the hangover. So, yeah, I think that's mainly how I see my story.

I: Thank you Victoria. Let's move on to the questions and feel free to elaborate as much as you wish according to the question. And if you see that you have covered it you can move on to the other question. The first question is: How do you perceive your conscience? What is conscience? How did it develop? How does it function?

V: Well, I don't know, I mean probably some other things that we consider bad or good are something that we are socially taught to perceive in that way. But I think there is also that, I don't know how you call it, instinct that you have about when you're doing something that is good or bad. You have that inner voice. So I would call it an inner voice, kind of prompts you. It also plays on the feeling of guilt or feeling of okay when you're doing okay. I think I have quite a sensitive conscience. I do recognise that I went against it. But I was kind of aware of it, and I always thought that I will stop. I will make things clear at one point. I just didn't have, I didn't have, when caught in the addiction I didn't have the strength to follow my conscience. So the addiction kind of overruled the voice of conscience.

I: Okay. Second question: How did you develop alcohol addiction? What is alcohol addiction? When did you realise that you have been addicted to alcohol? How did you try to manage your alcohol addiction?

V: Well, I think I've covered a bit of it. I mean, I wouldn't though my father was an alcoholic, my mother kind of went into drinking, my sister went when they had problems. Probably it was a bit of role modelling. Some would say is genetic. I don't know. I think that was my, developing an alcohol addiction was my way of coping with the situation where I felt I cannot talk about what I was going through; was kind of turning it towards myself. I wasn't a social drinker at all in the sense of drinking with other people. I was always drinking on my own. So always buying the drink and never drinking in a pub. I was always, always drinking on my own. What else did you have?

I: How did you manage?

V: How did I? How did I? Well. I said I'd tried to manage. I tried for the length of time of one month not to drink, and I was able to do that. And I was, something emotionally clicked, and I was back on it. I knew there were couple of friends who were kind of concerned and were suggesting for me to kind of get some help. But I was very resistant for the same reason that I felt my drinking is justified. So I think that rationalisation of the drinking didn't really help at all. So I kind of pushed it, the thought that I cannot manage or control it, I pushed it away as much as I could. So I think I only admitted when I stopped drinking after those three days. After those six days when I was kind of trying to drink myself to death. I remember that after three days of being sick when I stopped I went to an Internet cafe cause I didn't have Internet at home. And I googled "alcoholism," and then it kind of struck me that I am an alcoholic. And it was just then when I was kind of crying. I was kind of repeating: "My name is this, and I am an alcoholic." And I was just bursting into crying because I couldn't believe, and I thought: "Well it didn't matter whoever, whatever they've done to me I shouldn't have allowed that to take me here." But that when I googled that, and I saw that, it struck me that, yeah, I am addicted. So that was the point, just the end of—there were actually five years—I accept it.

I: Thank you. Next question: What were your moral views before your moral, spiritual, and/or religious transformation? What is morality? How did you deal with moral dilemmas? How much did morality matter for you?

V: That's a difficult one. So I knew what my moral values were but I went against them. So being in a relationship with a guy without being married to him was as a start something going against my moral views. Continuing to be with a guy even when I kind of had all the indications that things were not good I think it kind of undermined my moral stand even more. Am I missing questions? "What is morality?" I think it's living according to what you believe to be true. How do I deal with moral dilemmas? Well I didn't deal very well then. I was just overruling the moral values. It does matter how much did, okay. Yeah, I was struggling, I was struggling with making peace in my mind and obviously I couldn't really. So it was diving into this relationship which I knew was wrong. And then diving back into drinking to kind of numb the sense of doing something terribly wrong. So it did matter but . . . . So it was giving me the thoughts and the struggles but it wasn't enough to make me adjust my behaviour to what my moral values were.

I: Thank you. Next one: Did you practice spirituality before your moral, spiritual, and/or religious transformation? What is spirituality? How did you practice spirituality? How much did spirituality matter for you?

V: What is the first question? If I practiced spirituality.

Appendices

I: Did you practice spirituality before your transformation?

V: I mean, well, to define spirituality is a bit, yeah, difficult I think. Well, I said when I was 11 I kind of made that decision in my mind that I wanted to become a Christian. And I did become a Christian. I was very much into the Bible reading, very much into prayer, very much into saying to everyone about God and about what I was believing. So, yeah, I was, I was reading my Bible daily. I was praying daily. I would pray for my family, for my mother and my sister. And few years down the line they became Christians. Going to church every Sunday, being very kind of passionate about studying the Bible. Yes so I had all that. Things changed when I was in this relationship. I mean I was still doing, let's say, the routine of practising spirituality: reading the Bible and praying. I don't know. I was reading the Bible but then there was this sense that when it came to this relationship and my drinking I was shutting down. So I wouldn't allow kind of God to interfere with that. That was my box. That was my Pandora box that I would keep. I didn't want him to interfere into that. I was kind of happy to adjust my other behaviour about my work and other things to what I believed but that, those aspects, they were kind of separate. Which I know it doesn't really make sense but that's how I was functioning. And then after I stopped the drinking I hit obviously that box, which I kept was totally opened and invaded in a way. And I kind of realised how wrong it was. And I came to the point of wanting to change, to change things. What happened, actually, I haven't mentioned that in the story, was that I stopped the drinking and then a month and a half after that I resigned because I was still caught in this triangle. And I just realised that I couldn't, I couldn't cope. I mean I was sober but I realised that that is such a big part of my addiction that it wouldn't be safe for me to stay there. So I had to end up leaving the organisation I worked for more than seven years. So I was kind of attached to it but that decision of stopping, kind of reconciling with God affected very kind of practical dimensions of my life. So I resigned the job, and then I decided I'm going to go to another church because they were also going to the same church where I was going. So I decided I would go to another church. So in many respects it was like starting life from the scratch. So, no job, making new friends, going to another church. So I had to kind of put my, "put my money where my mouth is," but yeah put into practice what I was believing, yeah.

I: Thank you. Next one: Did you practice religion before your moral, spiritual, and/or religious transformation? What is religiousness? How did

Appendices

you practice religion? Did you have religious affiliation? How much did religion matter for you?

V: Probably now I'm a bit confused with what you define as spirituality and religion in these questions because for me it is one and the same.

I: Sure. In terms of definitions, they are various. But not to enter into any debate or any in-depth discussion. For you in terms of religiousness or spirituality if they are the same then probably these two questions overlap.

V: Yeah, they kind of overlap so . . . .

I: If you consider that there had been some religious type of background, as far as your family is concerned, you can mention it now.

V: My convictions in terms of faith and the theology that I believe in is: it hasn't changed since I was 11. I still believe the same things. The way of practising, it varied. But now I still have the same faith. It is a crucial element of my life.

I: And this couple you mentioned were the ones who kind of . . . .

V: Yeah, I mean through them I came to believe, yeah.

I: Thank you. Next question: Did you experience moral, spiritual, and/or religious transformation? How did you experience this transformation? When did you experience this transformation? May you identify anyone who played any influential role in the process? How much has this transformation changed your life?

V: I think I mentioned most of the things. So the persons who had a role into it were this couple that I met when my father was dead, and my mum was remarried and not living with us. I met this couple. And I think the way they loved me and they related to me was the most significant attraction, and the way they were living their life. And I wanted that in a way. And that was their influence. If I experienced moral, spiritual, and religious transformation. Yes. So it was: the first point was when I was 11, and when I decided to become a Christian. That kind of things were bubbling in me and yeah, the way I was very open about it. And very open in a hostile environment because we were under Communism and the Evangelical church was persecuted. So at school there weren't very happy with me attending an Evangelical church. So, but I was very much into it and very dedicated and committed to it. And then, the second time was obviously when I stopped drinking, and I had to come to terms with the moral kind of contradictions that I lived in for some years. So, yeah, that was the second moment of transformation. And the third, which was the last one since I last drank, it was that moment of kind of complete surrender that I mentioned. When I've just realised that my strong will and my determination are not enough, and that I need something, someone that is above me to help me be abstinent. So, yeah, kind of three key moments.

I: Thank you. The next question: What was the impact of your transformation on your life? Compare your morality, spirituality, and religiousness before and after the transformation. How did the transformation impact your understanding of morality, spirituality, and religion, and their role in your life? How much did morality, spirituality, and religion matter for you after your transformation?

V: Well to compare it, as I said, I was going against it, and I knew it. And I knew it but I didn't have the strength to change anything. So it's obviously now I am, now I'm in a place where I am at peace. I am at peace with God. I am at peace with my past. So I feel like I have that freedom because I know I'm living what I believe.

I: I think you pretty much cover it. If you consider to add anything else no problem.

V: I think I've covered it so, yeah. While drinking and being in this relationship it was this duplicity that I mentioned. It was this dualism, this double life which was quite hard to live. While now I feel like I am a whole person. And I am an integer person. So I can live with integrity which is one of the things I value very much being able to be "what it says on the tin." So, yeah.

I: Thank you. Next question: What was the impact of your moral, spiritual, and/or religious transformation on your conscience? Compare your conscience before and after the transformation. How did the transformation impact your conscientious behaviour? How much did the voice of your conscience matter for you after your transformation?

V: You know I feel that it was the other way around. I feel that my conscience impacted my moral, spiritual, and . . . . The conscience was the bit that in a way forced me to address this contradiction, this moral contradiction I was living in and kind of settled, settled it, reconciled it. Before the transformation I would say the conscience, I was putting my fist in its month, to be very graphic. And now, now I'm listening to it. I'm kind of sensitive to it. I'm trying to pick up on its voice. So now it's in a way the opposite.

I: Why it did change?

V: Because now I'm living according to my values. So now my conscience is not nagging me for going against what I believe. It's congruence between what I believe and how I behave.

I: Is that because of the spiritual transformation?

Appendices

V: If I consider the spiritual transformation my moment of surrender, my decision to put things right—yes. How much the voice of the conscience matter? I said: "Very much." I'm trying to be sensitive to it. And now it's a good guiding tool.

I: Okay. Next one: What was the impact of your transformed conscience on your recovery from alcohol addiction? Compare your recovery before and after the transformation. How did your transformed conscience impact your recovery from alcohol addiction? What is the role of your transformed conscience in the maintenance of your abstinence? May you identify anyone who played any influential role in the process?

V: So the impact of my transformed conscience on my recovery. Well if I'm to start with this one: how did my transformed conscience impact my recovery? I was coming to terms that what I was doing was wrong. And then, kind of taking practical steps into changing my behaviour. So, as I said, the fact that I was going to this lady with my diary once a week and having that accountability and knowing that I needed to be honest that was good enough for me. Well to compare my recovery before and after the transformation. There wasn't really recovery before. I had first to go through the transformation bit before starting the recovery. I mean my attempts of stopping drinking weren't really a recovery. It was a way of denying it and trying to manage it but unsuccessfully. So it wasn't. It was a fail attempt to recovery.

I: Thank you. Next one: May you share your future plans related to your recovery? What is the role of morality, spirituality, and/or religion in them? What is the role of your transformed conscience in them? Do you plan to share your experience with others who need help in recovery from alcohol addiction?

V: So in terms of spirituality and how I live my faith. I perceive my relationship with God as being personal. And I perceive that I need to have deep dependence on him to stay sober but not only. I perceive that dependence on everything that I do. Before I was very ambitious and driven and things like these. Now I feel that that shouldn't be my ultimate reason for being a driven person not a person who would do things. But it's kind of be in tune with what God wants me to do. Yes it is very much, my addiction and my recovery, it is very much a driving force behind what I'm doing in terms of work, and what I am hoping to do in terms of work. I've studied in order to . . . . So I'm hoping to become an addiction therapist. That's my dream. I've done a course in addictions. And now I'm doing a counselling course. So because I knew how hard it was for me to walk in this journey of recovery, and now I'm working with homeless people, so I see how some of them are struggling in their addictions. It is very much in my heart to be able to go along with them and help them in their recovery. It is something on my heart. I also, in the last year I attended a recovery course of 16 weeks. And I'm dreaming, hoping to be able to do something similar, to lead something similar in our town, myself. So it is, it is very much on my heart. With few of the client's, very few, I did some disclosure when felt that it would be beneficial for them in their recovery. So yeah, I did try to help others in their recovery by using my story.

I: Thank you. The last question: May you formulate the main theme of your life story? What is the place of alcohol addiction in your story? What is the place of conscience in your story? What is the place of morality, spirituality, and/or religiousness in your story? What is the place of your moral, spiritual, and/or religious transformation in your story? The main theme of your story.

V: Would that be the meaning that I attach to my addiction in my life story or?

I: All these elements coming together like in one theme of your story or a summary or an abstract.

V: I'm not sure if I have the right, if there is a right interpretation of my life story but the way I understand it is that: I mean I used to be very independent and driven person, very ambitious. And addiction was one of the things that kneeled me, put me on my knees, and it defeated me apparently. Probably it kind of made me realise my condition of not being God or God over my life but the need to be humble. And I also think that if I didn't go through these . . . . If I haven't gone through the addiction I would be far less understanding with people who are struggling with addiction. Probably I would be quite drastic in my all: "Oh, they should just stop drinking." Or I would make judgements like this. So though I felt that it was a destructive bit in my life I can see it now in a way redeemed and turned around for good, however strange it may sound. So yeah, I see it . . . . I see the addiction as being something negative obviously, so I wouldn't deny that. Something negative but that kind of turned into a good thing because this failure kind of brought me back to God and brought me back on the line of living my life in accordance to what I believe. And using the defeat of the addiction and the success of the recovery in a good way. So I feel like it makes sense. If it's about these, they are all mixed in the story, and kind of I think, I covered them.

I: All right. Thank you very much. This ends the interview at 12:19 with Victoria.

Appendices

Code System for Analysis of the Interviews with Codes, Subcodes, and their Selections

alcohol addiction	context of alcohol addiction [4]	substituting addictions [1]	
		alcohol addiction and relationships [7]	
		alcohol addiction and childhood [4]	traumatic childhood [11]
		alcohol addiction and occupation [8]	
		alcohol addiction and friends [8]	
		alcohol addiction and family [13]	
		alcohol addiction and culture [4]	
	development of alcohol addiction [18]		
	impact of alcohol addiction [4]	addiction and self-harming [2]	
		addiction and suicide [6]	
		blaming others [2]	
		destroys progress [3]	
		distorts reality and destroys life [16]	
		hurting others [7]	
	managing alcohol addiction [7]	addiction deterrents [3]	
		period of sobriety [1]	
		rehabilitation and other treatments [16]	
	personal realisation of addiction [16]	rationalisation of the drinking [1]	
	defining alcohol addiction [12]	solution vs. consequences [1]	
		I felt justified to drink [1]	
		addiction and managing emotions [8]	
		before I got one I want the next [3]	
		because when you're addicted you don't know you're drunk [1]	

Appendices

con-science	conscience development [2]	negative impact on conscience [4]	parents' role [3]
			abuse from others [1]
			difficult circumstances [2]
	conscience during the addiction [9]	deadened [2]	
		becoming a burden [8]	
		exposing conflict [7]	
		suppressed—silenced [15]	
		but I will always do the opposite [1]	
		when you are under alcohol you throw everything overboard [1]	
	conscience in recovery [12]	conscience and peace [3]	
		conscience and understanding [3]	
		conscience and discipline [2]	
		principle of mutual respect (Golden Rule) [7]	
		just to give back what I have been given [1]	
		because I've been born again the spirit of God was fighting against drinking in my conscience [1]	
	conscience's nature and functioning [11]	conscience and spirituality [8]	
		relation to emotions [1]	
		inner voice [1]	
		conscience and consciousness [7]	
future plans in recovery	helping others in recovery [11]		
	conscience in future plans [3]		
	religion in future plans [2]		
	spirituality in future plans [2]		
	morality in future plans [0]		
main theme of narrative [1]	main theme and transformation [6]		
	main theme and religiousness [0]		
	main theme and spirituality [8]		
	main theme and morality [1]		
	main theme and conscience [0]		
	main theme and addiction [4]		

Appendices

morality	defining morality [2]			
	morality after transformation [6]			
	morality and conscience [1]			
	morality before the addiction [6]			
	morality during the addiction [18]	vices	anger [13]	
			envy [2]	
			gluttony [9]	
			greed [5]	
			lust [6]	
			pride [9]	
			sloth [4]	
		with drinking it would take away all morality [3]		
	morality in recovery [1]	virtues [1]	courage [1]	vitality [0]
				integrity [4]
				persistence [0]
				bravery [1]
			humanity [6]	social intelligence [0]
				kindness [0]
				love [3]
			justice [0]	leadership [2]
				fairness [0]
				citizenship [0]
			temperance [0]	self-regulation [1]
				prudence [0]
				humility and modesty [1]
				forgiveness and mercy [1]
			transcendence [4]	spirituality [1]
				humour [2]
				hope [1]
				gratitude [3]
				appreciation of beauty [0]
			wisdom and knowledge [1]	perspective [0]
				love of learning [0]
				open-mindedness [1]
				curiosity [0]
				creativity [1]

religious- ness [1]	defining religiousness [4]	
	religiousness after transformation [1]	
	religiousness before the addiction [8]	barrier—distorted belief about God [1]
	religiousness during the addiction [13]	the sins of alcohol [1]
	religiousness in recovery [3]	moral failures of religious people [2]
spiritu- ality	influential person in spirituality [3]	
	defining spirituality [2]	
	spirituality after transformation [6]	
	spirituality before the addiction [4]	
	spirituality during the addiction [11]	
	spirituality in recovery [10]	
spirituality and religiousness [6]		
the role of experience [0]		
transfor- mation	transformation and abstinence [4]	
	transformative moment [17]	
	transformative process [27]	
	influential person in transformation [15]	
	transformation and conscience [1]	
	religious transformation [5]	
	spiritual transformation [10]	
	moral transformation [0]	
transfor- mation impact [1]	transformation impact on understanding [13]	
	transformation impact on addiction [5]	
	transfor- mation impact on conscience [9]	conscience's freedom [4]
		conscience's resurrection [2]
		conscience's cleanness [3]
		conscience's empowerment [7]
	transformation impact on religiousness [8]	
	transformation impact on spirituality [12]	
	transformation impact on morality [9]	

Appendices

Analysis Identification Table of the Relationship between Interviews, Codes, and Memos

Document name	Number of coded segments	Number of memos	Bytes
Interview–Adam	64	50	84,392
Interview–Alex	50	24	33,324
Interview–Ben	39	31	47,101
Interview–Jack	49	35	50,530
Interview–James	42	32	32,404
Interview–John	50	38	43,038
Interview–Luke	74	38	58,218
Interview–Mary	38	31	36,159
Interview–Max	42	30	39,185
Interview–Paul	57	28	24,732
Interview–Sam	109	44	65,107
Interview–Victoria	63	34	34,657

Appendices

Analysis Identification Table of Codes, their Location, and Coverage in the Interviews

(Note: The numbering of paragraphs is according to MAXQDA and commences from the title of the interview)

Interviews	Code	Begin par	End par	Coverage %
Adam	main theme of narrative\main theme and spirituality	3	3	1.14
Adam	alcohol addiction\impact of alcohol addiction\distorts reality and destroys life	4	4	1.34
Adam	alcohol addiction\managing alcohol addiction\rehabilitation and other treatments	5	5	1.70
Adam	alcohol addiction\defining alcohol addiction	6	6	1.37
Adam	morality\morality during the addiction\vices\pride	6	6	0.27
Adam	alcohol addiction\personal realisation of addiction	7	7	0.86
Adam	spirituality\spirituality during the addiction	7	7	0.34
Adam	alcohol addiction\impact of alcohol addiction\blaming others	8	8	0.87
Adam	transformation\transformative moment	9	9	1.78
Adam	religiousness\religiousness before the addiction	10	10	1.33
Adam	transformation\spiritual transformation	11	11	1.67
Adam	morality\morality during the addiction\vices\anger	12	12	1.49

Appendices

Adam	alcohol addiction\context of alcohol addiction\alcohol addiction and childhood\traumatic childhood	13	13	1.59
Adam	morality\morality during the addiction\vices\anger	14	14	0.50
Adam	alcohol addiction\context of alcohol addiction\alcohol addiction and family	15	15	1.36
Adam	alcohol addiction\defining alcohol addiction\addiction and managing emotions	16	16	2.61
Adam	alcohol addiction\defining alcohol addiction\before I got one I want the next	17	17	1.43
Adam	alcohol addiction\development of alcohol addiction	18	18	1.21
Adam	transformation\transformative process	19	19	3.61
Adam	alcohol addiction\impact of alcohol addiction\distorts reality and destroys life	20	20	0.92
Adam	spirituality\defining spirituality	21	21	3.08
Adam	alcohol addiction\defining alcohol addiction\solution vs. consequences	22	22	1.58
Adam	alcohol addiction\managing alcohol addiction	23	23	1.59
Adam	transformation\spiritual transformation	24	24	2.33
Adam	alcohol addiction\impact of alcohol addiction\addiction and suicide	25	25	2.35
Adam	morality\morality during the addiction\vices\greed	26	26	0.33
Adam	transformation impact\transformation impact on understanding	26	26	1.15

Appendices

Adam	transformation impact\transformation impact on conscience\conscience's cleanness	27	27	2.30
Adam	morality\morality in recovery\virtues\courage\integrity	28	28	1.10
Adam	morality\morality in recovery\virtues\wisdom and knowledge\open-mindedness	28	28	1.38
Adam	morality\morality in recovery\virtues\temperance\humility and modesty	29	29	1.70
Adam	transformation impact\transformation impact on spirituality	30	30	3.08
Adam	transformation impact\transformation impact on addiction	31	31	2.97
Adam	spirituality and religiousness	32	32	1.16
Adam	spirituality\spirituality after transformation	32	32	4.88
Adam	spirituality\spirituality in recovery	32	32	4.88
Adam	transformation impact\transformation impact on understanding	33	33	2.73
Adam	spirituality\spirituality after transformation	34	34	2.25
Adam	conscience\conscience's nature and functioning\conscience and spirituality	35	35	3.96
Adam	conscience\conscience during the addiction\suppressed—silenced	41	41	1.76
Adam	conscience\conscience in recovery	42	42	2.82
Adam	conscience\conscience's nature and functioning\conscience and spirituality	42	42	2.82
Adam	conscience\conscience's nature and functioning\conscience and consciousness	42	42	0.72
Adam	transformation impact\transformation impact on conscience\conscience empowerment	42	42	0.47

Appendices

Adam	alcohol addiction\personal realisation of addiction	44	44	2.69
Adam	morality\morality before the addiction	48	48	2.37
Adam	morality\morality during the addiction\vices\anger	49	49	0.98
Adam	morality\morality in recovery\virtues\transcendence\gratitude	50	50	0.55
Adam	transformation impact\transformation impact on morality	50	50	3.27
Adam	spirituality\spirituality during the addiction	52	52	0.66
Adam	religiousness\religiousness during the addiction	54	54	2.58
Adam	transformation\transformative process	56	56	0.70
Adam	spirituality\spirituality after transformation	60	60	1.63
Adam	transformation\transformative process	66	66	1.08
Adam	morality\morality in recovery\virtues\transcendence\hope	66	66	0.36
Adam	morality\morality in recovery\virtues\courage	66	66	0.36
Adam	morality\morality in recovery\virtues\transcendence	66	66	1.08
Adam	main theme of narrative\main theme and addiction	68	68	0.98
Adam	main theme of narrative	68	70	5.84
Adam	main theme of narrative\main theme and spirituality	69	69	1.51
Adam	conscience\conscience in recovery	69	69	0.29
Adam	main theme of narrative\main theme and transformation	70	70	3.35
Adam	conscience\conscience in recovery	70	70	0.39
Adam	morality\morality after transformation	50	50	3.27

Alex	religiousness\religiousness before the addiction	5	5	0.23
Alex	conscience\conscience development\negative impact on conscience\parents' role	6	6	0.38
Alex	morality\morality before the addiction	7	7	0.71
Alex	spirituality and religiousness	8	8	0.65
Alex	alcohol addiction\context of alcohol addiction\alcohol addiction and childhood\traumatic childhood	9	9	0.12
Alex	alcohol addiction\defining alcohol addiction	9	9	0.32
Alex	conscience\conscience in recovery\principle of mutual respect (Golden Rule)	12	12	0.67
Alex	religiousness\religiousness before the addiction	12	12	4.24
Alex	transformation\transformative process	13	13	2.03
Alex	alcohol addiction\context of alcohol addiction\alcohol addiction and childhood\traumatic childhood	15	15	2.11
Alex	religiousness\defining religiousness	16	16	12.16
Alex	alcohol addiction\managing alcohol addiction\rehabilitation and other treatments	19	19	0.08
Alex	alcohol addiction\context of alcohol addiction\alcohol addiction and friends	19	19	0.24
Alex	alcohol addiction\context of alcohol addiction\alcohol addiction and relationships	19	19	0.71
Alex	alcohol addiction\defining alcohol addiction	20	20	0.24

Appendices

Alex	morality\morality during the addiction\vices\anger	20	20	0.25
Alex	alcohol addiction\defining alcohol addiction\addiction and managing emotions	20	20	0.24
Alex	alcohol addiction\impact of alcohol addiction\distorts reality and destroys life	21	21	2.30
Alex	alcohol addiction\managing alcohol addiction\addiction deterrents	21	21	2.30
Alex	religiousness\defining religiousness	23	23	4.15
Alex	alcohol addiction\impact of alcohol addiction\distorts reality and destroys life	25	25	2.96
Alex	morality\morality during the addiction\vices\anger	25	25	0.18
Alex	morality\morality during the addiction	25	25	0.33
Alex	morality\morality during the addiction\vices\gluttony	26	26	0.30
Alex	religiousness\religiousness in recovery	26	26	0.63
Alex	spirituality\spirituality in recovery	26	26	0.63
Alex	conscience\conscience during the addiction	28	28	2.99
Alex	conscience\conscience during the addiction\suppressed—silenced	28	28	0.16
Alex	alcohol addiction\defining alcohol addiction	30	30	0.21
Alex	alcohol addiction\context of alcohol addiction\alcohol addiction and occupation	30	30	2.00
Alex	alcohol addiction\defining alcohol addiction\addiction and managing emotions	30	30	0.21
Alex	alcohol addiction\managing alcohol addiction\addiction deterrents	31	31	2.17

Alex	spirituality\spirituality in recovery	32	32	2.12
Alex	transformation\transformative process	34	34	0.14
Alex	transformation\spiritual transformation	34	34	0.16
Alex	conscience\conscience in recovery\principle of mutual respect (Golden Rule)	36	36	0.13
Alex	morality\morality before the addiction	36	36	2.46
Alex	morality\morality during the addiction	38	38	2.61
Alex	spirituality\spirituality during the addiction	44	44	4.49
Alex	transformation\transformative process	45	45	3.26
Alex	transformation\spiritual transformation	45	45	3.26
Alex	transformation\religious transformation	45	45	3.26
Alex	transformation\transformative process	47	47	3.53
Alex	transformation\transformative process	49	49	1.04
Alex	transformation\transformative process	51	51	2.63
Alex	transformation\religious transformation	51	51	2.63
Alex	transformation\spiritual transformation	53	53	2.29
Alex	future plans in recovery\helping others in recovery	55	55	2.99
Alex	morality\morality in recovery\virtues\humanity	55	55	2.99
Alex	main theme of narrative\main theme and spirituality	57	57	1.48

Appendices

Ben	alcohol addiction\context of alcohol addiction\alcohol addiction and occupation	5	5	4.88
Ben	alcohol addiction\development of alcohol addiction	6	6	2.94
Ben	morality\morality during the addiction	7	7	1.17
Ben	alcohol addiction\impact of alcohol addiction\destroys progress	7	7	1.17
Ben	alcohol addiction\context of alcohol addiction\alcohol addiction and occupation	8	8	1.10
Ben	alcohol addiction\development of alcohol addiction	9	9	1.83
Ben	alcohol addiction\impact of alcohol addiction\hurting others	10	10	2.88
Ben	alcohol addiction\managing alcohol addiction\rehabilitation and other treatments	11	11	3.08
Ben	conscience\conscience during the addiction\suppressed—silenced	11	11	3.08
Ben	alcohol addiction\context of alcohol addiction\alcohol addiction and family	12	12	6.33
Ben	alcohol addiction\defining alcohol addiction	12	12	2.15
Ben	conscience\conscience development\negative impact on conscience\parents' role	13	13	3.20
Ben	alcohol addiction\context of alcohol addiction\alcohol addiction and family	14	14	2.19
Ben	morality\morality in recovery\virtues\temperance\forgiveness and mercy	14	14	0.13
Ben	alcohol addiction\impact of alcohol addiction\hurting others	15	15	2.37

Ben	morality\morality during the addiction\vices\pride	15	15	2.37
Ben	conscience\conscience during the addiction\suppressed—silenced	16	16	1.09
Ben	morality\morality during the addiction\vices\pride	17	17	2.17
Ben	spirituality\spirituality during the addiction	18	18	1.45
Ben	spirituality\spirituality after transformation	18	18	3.23
Ben	transformation\transformative process	19	19	4.83
Ben	transformation\religious transformation	20	20	5.02
Ben	transformation impact\transformation impact on understanding	21	21	2.76
Ben	transformation impact\transformation impact on morality	22	22	3.06
Ben	morality\morality after transformation	22	22	3.06
Ben	transformation impact\transformation impact on religiousness	23	23	4.70
Ben	religiousness\religiousness after transformation	24	24	3.46
Ben	transformation impact\transformation impact on addiction	25	25	3.88
Ben	alcohol addiction\personal realisation of addiction	26	26	2.28
Ben	transformation impact\transformation impact on morality	27	27	6.59
Ben	morality\morality after transformation	27	27	6.59
Ben	conscience\conscience during the addiction\suppressed—silenced	29	29	0.45
Ben	religiousness\religiousness during the addiction	35	35	1.39

Appendices

Ben	transformation\influential person in transformation	39	39	1.92
Ben	transformation\transformative process	41	41	1.32
Ben	conscience\conscience during the addiction\becoming a burden	43	43	1.24
Ben	transformation\influential person in transformation	47	47	1.44
Ben	future plans in recovery\religion in future plans	49	49	1.73
Ben	main theme of narrative\main theme and transformation	51	51	3.45
Jack	alcohol addiction\context of alcohol addiction\alcohol addiction and childhood\traumatic childhood	5	5	5.83
Jack	religiousness\religiousness before the addiction	6	6	1.34
Jack	alcohol addiction\context of alcohol addiction\alcohol addiction and childhood\traumatic childhood	7	7	3.01
Jack	alcohol addiction\context of alcohol addiction\alcohol addiction and childhood\traumatic childhood	8	8	1.43
Jack	alcohol addiction\context of alcohol addiction\alcohol addiction and friends	9	9	2.47
Jack	alcohol addiction\context of alcohol addiction\alcohol addiction and friends	10	10	3.22
Jack	alcohol addiction\defining alcohol addiction\addiction and managing emotions	10	10	0.48
Jack	morality\morality during the addiction\vices\anger	11	11	2.39
Jack	morality\morality during the addiction\vices\pride	11	11	1.83

Jack	alcohol addiction\managing alcohol addiction\addiction deterrents	12	12	1.97
Jack	morality\morality during the addiction\vices\anger	13	13	2.71
Jack	alcohol addiction\development of alcohol addiction	13	13	2.71
Jack	alcohol addiction\impact of alcohol addiction\addiction and suicide	14	14	1.01
Jack	religiousness\religiousness during the addiction	14	14	2.65
Jack	alcohol addiction\managing alcohol addiction\rehabilitation and other treatments	15	15	4.68
Jack	alcohol addiction\impact of alcohol addiction\addiction and suicide	16	16	1.03
Jack	conscience\conscience in recovery\conscience and understanding	16	16	1.21
Jack	conscience\conscience during the addiction	16	16	3.58
Jack	conscience\conscience's nature and functioning\conscience and consciousness	16	16	0.19
Jack	transformation\transformative moment	17	17	0.21
Jack	transformation impact\transformation impact on morality	17	17	2.98
Jack	morality\morality after transformation	17	17	2.98
Jack	transformation\transformative process	18	18	1.60
Jack	alcohol addiction\impact of alcohol addiction\distorts reality and destroys life	19	19	0.81
Jack	morality\morality during the addiction	19	19	1.24

Jack	transformation impact\transformation impact on conscience	19	20	5.84
Jack	transformation impact\transformation impact on spirituality	20	20	3.23
Jack	transformation impact\transformation impact on conscience\conscience's resurrection	22	22	2.70
Jack	conscience\conscience during the addiction\deadened	22	22	0.53
Jack	alcohol addiction\personal realisation of addiction	24	24	4.85
Jack	morality\morality during the addiction\vices\pride	24	24	0.24
Jack	morality\morality in recovery\virtues\transcendence\gratitude	26	26	0.55
Jack	morality\morality before the addiction	26	26	0.58
Jack	spirituality\spirituality after transformation	28	28	0.43
Jack	spirituality\spirituality after transformation	28	28	0.77
Jack	transformation\spiritual transformation	30	30	1.93
Jack	religiousness\religiousness during the addiction	32	32	0.73
Jack	transformation\transformative process	36	36	3.70
Jack	transformation\influential person in transformation	38	38	4.53
Jack	transformation impact\transformation impact on spirituality	42	42	2.91
Jack	transformation impact\transformation impact on conscience	44	44	2.02
Jack	transformation impact\transformation impact on conscience\conscience's freedom	44	44	0.73

Appendices

Jack	conscience\conscience in recovery\conscience and understanding	46	46	2.77
Jack	conscience\conscience's nature and functioning\conscience and consciousness	46	46	0.73
Jack	morality\morality during the addiction\vices\sloth	46	46	0.22
Jack	future plans in recovery\helping others in recovery	48	48	4.18
Jack	main theme of narrative\main theme and spirituality	50	50	2.70
Jack	main theme of narrative\main theme and morality	50	50	2.70
Jack	main theme of narrative\main theme and transformation	50	50	2.70
James	alcohol addiction\context of alcohol addiction\alcohol addiction and childhood\traumatic childhood	6	6	2.90
James	alcohol addiction\context of alcohol addiction\alcohol addiction and family	7	7	2.63
James	alcohol addiction\context of alcohol addiction\alcohol addiction and family	8	8	3.61
James	morality\morality during the addiction\vices\anger	9	9	4.65
James	alcohol addiction\managing alcohol addiction	9	9	0.73
James	morality\morality during the addiction\vices\gluttony	9	9	0.47
James	alcohol addiction\impact of alcohol addiction\hurting others	10	10	4.89
James	morality\morality during the addiction\vices\gluttony	10	10	1.34
James	alcohol addiction\context of alcohol addiction\alcohol addiction and relationships	11	11	5.68

Appendices

James	alcohol addiction\personal realisation of addiction	12	12	3.44
James	alcohol addiction\impact of alcohol addiction\hurting others	13	13	7.52
James	morality\morality during the addiction\vices\anger	13	13	7.52
James	morality\morality during the addiction\vices\greed	14	14	1.72
James	alcohol addiction\managing alcohol addiction	14	14	0.29
James	transformation\transformative process	17	17	2.59
James	transformation\transformative process	18	18	4.25
James	transformation\religious transformation	18	18	4.25
James	transformation\spiritual transformation	18	18	4.25
James	transformation impact\transformation impact on conscience\conscience empowerment	19	19	4.78
James	transformation\transformative moment	22	22	4.44
James	transformation impact\transformation impact on spirituality	23	23	5.38
James	transformation impact\transformation impact on religiousness	23	23	5.38
James	morality\morality in recovery\virtues\transcendence\gratitude	23	23	0.20
James	transformation impact\transformation impact on addiction	24	24	2.63
James	conscience\conscience during the addiction\deadened	32	32	0.52
James	transformation impact\transformation impact on conscience\conscience's resurrection	32	32	1.51

Appendices

James	conscience\conscience in recovery\conscience and understanding	36	36	1.41
James	conscience\conscience's nature and functioning\conscience and consciousness	36	36	0.74
James	transformation impact\transformation impact on morality	38	38	1.73
James	morality\morality after transformation	38	38	1.73
James	transformation impact\transformation impact on spirituality	40	40	1.07
James	transformation impact\transformation impact on religiousness	42	42	1.29
James	transformation\spiritual transformation	44	44	0.31
James	transformation\transformative moment	44	44	0.31
James	transformation\influential person in transformation	46	46	0.75
James	transformation impact\transformation impact on religiousness	48	48	1.86
James	transformation impact\transformation impact on conscience\conscience's freedom	50	50	1.54
James	transformation\transformative process	52	52	2.28
James	future plans in recovery\spirituality in future plans	54	54	2.43
James	transformation\transformative process	54	54	1.15
James	main theme of narrative\main theme and addiction	56	56	2.04
James	main theme of narrative\main theme and spirituality	56	56	3.79
John	alcohol addiction\context of alcohol addiction\alcohol addiction and childhood\traumatic childhood	7	7	2.48

Appendices

John	alcohol addiction\context of alcohol addiction\alcohol addiction and culture	8	8	1.86
John	alcohol addiction\development of alcohol addiction	8	8	1.57
John	alcohol addiction\context of alcohol addiction\alcohol addiction and family	9	9	5.51
John	morality\morality during the addiction\vices\greed	10	10	1.57
John	conscience\conscience during the addiction\suppressed—silenced	10	10	1.57
John	morality\morality during the addiction\vices\envy	10	10	1.73
John	morality\morality during the addiction\vices\gluttony	11	11	0.37
John	spirituality\spirituality during the addiction	11	11	0.49
John	alcohol addiction\defining alcohol addiction\before I got one I want the next	11	11	0.24
John	morality\morality during the addiction\vices\gluttony	12	12	0.35
John	alcohol addiction\impact of alcohol addiction\distorts reality and destroys life	12	12	5.57
John	alcohol addiction\managing alcohol addiction\rehabilitation and other treatments	13	13	0.96
John	alcohol addiction\impact of alcohol addiction\distorts reality and destroys life	13	13	1.79
John	alcohol addiction\personal realisation of addiction	13	13	1.79
John	morality\morality during the addiction\vices\sloth	13	13	0.41
John	transformation\transformative moment	14	14	6.10

John	transformation\influential person in transformation	15	15	2.34
John	morality\morality in recovery\virtues\courage\integrity	16	16	1.17
John	transformation\transformative moment	16	16	4.52
John	transformation\transformative process	16	16	4.52
John	transformation impact\transformation impact on conscience	16	16	2.46
John	spirituality and religiousness	17	17	0.79
John	religiousness\defining religiousness	17	17	0.79
John	conscience\conscience's nature and functioning\conscience and spirituality	17	17	1.78
John	transformation impact\transformation impact on understanding	18	18	3.71
John	transformation\influential person in transformation	19	19	3.02
John	transformation impact\transformation impact on addiction	20	20	1.45
John	transformation\transformation and abstinence	20	20	1.45
John	transformation\influential person in transformation	21	21	3.24
John	transformation impact\transformation impact on understanding	21	21	3.24
John	future plans in recovery\helping others in recovery	22	22	2.40
John	morality\morality in recovery\virtues\wisdom and knowledge\creativity	23	23	5.04
John	morality\morality in recovery\virtues\justice\leadership	23	23	5.04
John	morality\morality in recovery\virtues	23	23	5.04

Appendices

John	transformation\transformative process	24	24	4.59
John	conscience\conscience's nature and functioning\conscience and spirituality	30	30	0.94
John	conscience\conscience in recovery\conscience and peace	32	32	3.27
John	conscience\conscience during the addiction\suppressed—silenced	34	34	1.25
John	morality\morality during the addiction\with drinking it would take away all morality	38	38	1.51
John	spirituality\spirituality during the addiction	40	40	1.52
John	spirituality\spirituality in recovery	40	40	1.52
John	morality\morality during the addiction\vices\pride	40	40	0.52
John	religiousness\religiousness during the addiction	42	42	1.29
John	religiousness\religiousness in recovery	42	42	1.29
John	transformation\influential person in transformation	44	44	0.43
John	transformation impact\transformation impact on spirituality	46	46	0.42
John	transformation impact\transformation impact on conscience\conscience's freedom	48	48	0.63
John	future plans in recovery\helping others in recovery	54	54	3.02
John	main theme of narrative\main theme and transformation	58	58	1.62
Luke	main theme of narrative\main theme and transformation	3	3	0.27
Luke	alcohol addiction\development of alcohol addiction	4	4	2.87

Appendices

Luke	alcohol addiction\context of alcohol addiction	6	6	2.55
Luke	alcohol addiction\context of alcohol addiction\alcohol addiction and culture	7	7	2.37
Luke	alcohol addiction\context of alcohol addiction\alcohol addiction and family	7	7	0.07
Luke	alcohol addiction\context of alcohol addiction\alcohol addiction and friends	7	7	2.37
Luke	alcohol addiction\personal realisation of addiction	8	8	2.22
Luke	morality\morality during the addiction\vices\lust	9	9	0.44
Luke	alcohol addiction\context of alcohol addiction\alcohol addiction and culture	9	9	3.47
Luke	alcohol addiction\impact of alcohol addiction\hurting others	10	10	1.95
Luke	alcohol addiction\personal realisation of addiction	11	11	0.05
Luke	alcohol addiction\context of alcohol addiction\alcohol addiction and culture	11	11	3.15
Luke	spirituality\spirituality during the addiction	12	12	1.35
Luke	religiousness\religiousness during the addiction	13	13	0.27
Luke	alcohol addiction\impact of alcohol addiction	13	13	3.00
Luke	conscience\conscience during the addiction	13	13	0.19
Luke	conscience\conscience during the addiction\becoming a burden	13	13	0.70
Luke	alcohol addiction\managing alcohol addiction	15	15	0.84

Appendices

Luke	alcohol addiction\development of alcohol addiction	16	16	1.30
Luke	alcohol addiction\impact of alcohol addiction\hurting others	16	16	1.30
Luke	alcohol addiction\impact of alcohol addiction\distorts reality and destroys life	17	17	1.61
Luke	alcohol addiction\defining alcohol addiction	17	17	1.61
Luke	alcohol addiction\context of alcohol addiction\alcohol addiction and occupation	18	18	0.98
Luke	religiousness\religiousness during the addiction	19	19	0.80
Luke	alcohol addiction\development of alcohol addiction	20	20	2.05
Luke	morality\morality during the addiction\vices\gluttony	20	20	0.25
Luke	conscience\conscience during the addiction\becoming a burden	21	21	0.20
Luke	morality\morality during the addiction	21	21	1.38
Luke	alcohol addiction\personal realisation of addiction	22	22	1.55
Luke	conscience\conscience during the addiction\suppressed—silenced	23	23	0.54
Luke	alcohol addiction\defining alcohol addiction\because when you're addicted you don't know you're drunk	23	23	0.10
Luke	alcohol addiction\impact of alcohol addiction	23	23	1.80
Luke	conscience\conscience's nature and functioning	23	23	0.15
Luke	conscience\conscience during the addiction\exposing conflict	23	23	0.47
Luke	conscience\conscience's nature and functioning	24	24	1.07

Luke	conscience\conscience during the addiction	24	24	2.19
Luke	conscience\conscience during the addiction\when you are under alcohol you throw everything overboard	24	24	0.10
Luke	conscience\conscience's nature and functioning\conscience and spirituality	24	24	2.19
Luke	religiousness\religiousness during the addiction	25	25	0.55
Luke	morality\morality during the addiction	26	26	1.93
Luke	morality\morality during the addiction\vices\gluttony	26	26	1.93
Luke	alcohol addiction\context of alcohol addiction\alcohol addiction and occupation	27	27	2.39
Luke	morality\morality during the addiction\vices\pride	27	27	2.40
Luke	transformation\transformative process	28	28	1.94
Luke	conscience\conscience in recovery	29	29	1.88
Luke	transformation\religious transformation	29	29	1.88
Luke	conscience\conscience in recovery\ because I've been born again the spirit of God was fighting against drinking in my conscience	29	29	0.16
Luke	transformation\transformative moment	30	30	1.88
Luke	morality\morality during the addiction\vices\lust	30	30	0.50
Luke	transformation impact\transformation impact on addiction	31	31	1.23
Luke	future plans in recovery\helping others in recovery	32	32	0.59

Appendices

Luke	morality\morality during the addiction	33	33	0.73
Luke	morality\morality during the addiction	34	34	1.21
Luke	religiousness	35	35	2.03
Luke	religiousness\religiousness during the addiction\the sins of alcohol	35	35	0.03
Luke	transformation impact\transformation impact on understanding	36	36	2.54
Luke	conscience\conscience's nature and functioning	36	36	0.10
Luke	conscience\conscience during the addiction\becoming a burden	36	36	0.10
Luke	main theme of narrative\main theme and addiction	37	37	2.42
Luke	morality\morality during the addiction\vices\greed	38	38	1.83
Luke	morality\morality during the addiction	38	38	1.83
Luke	alcohol addiction\personal realisation of addiction	48	48	1.28
Luke	morality\morality during the addiction	50	50	2.45
Luke	spirituality\spirituality before the addiction	56	56	0.62
Luke	transformation\influential person in transformation	58	58	1.83
Luke	transformation impact\transformation impact on understanding	64	64	2.68
Luke	transformation impact\transformation impact on morality	64	64	2.68
Luke	morality\morality during the addiction	64	64	2.68
Luke	transformation impact\transformation impact on understanding	65	65	3.16
Luke	future plans in recovery\helping others in recovery	69	69	2.52

Luke	future plans in recovery\conscience in future plans	70	70	3.03
Luke	future plans in recovery\religion in future plans	72	72	2.81
Luke	main theme of narrative\main theme and addiction	75	75	2.21
Luke	main theme of narrative\main theme and spirituality	76	76	2.85
Mary	alcohol addiction\context of alcohol addiction\alcohol addiction and childhood\traumatic childhood	5	5	4.29
Mary	alcohol addiction\context of alcohol addiction\alcohol addiction and childhood	6	6	3.19
Mary	alcohol addiction\impact of alcohol addiction\destroys progress	7	7	2.86
Mary	alcohol addiction\context of alcohol addiction\alcohol addiction and occupation	8	8	5.35
Mary	alcohol addiction\context of alcohol addiction\alcohol addiction and relationships	9	9	3.39
Mary	alcohol addiction\managing alcohol addiction\rehabilitation and other treatments	10	10	2.59
Mary	morality\morality during the addiction\vices\pride	10	10	0.51
Mary	morality\morality during the addiction\vices\sloth	10	10	0.85
Mary	alcohol addiction\context of alcohol addiction\alcohol addiction and relationships	11	11	1.64
Mary	alcohol addiction\managing alcohol addiction\rehabilitation and other treatments	13	13	3.52
Mary	alcohol addiction\impact of alcohol addiction\distorts reality and destroys life	14	14	5.48

Mary	alcohol addiction\impact of alcohol addiction\distorts reality and destroys life	16	16	4.47
Mary	alcohol addiction\managing alcohol addiction\rehabilitation and other treatments	17	17	2.11
Mary	transformation\transformative moment	19	19	3.04
Mary	transformation\influential person in transformation	20	20	2.20
Mary	morality\morality in recovery\virtues\humanity	21	21	3.55
Mary	future plans in recovery\helping others in recovery	23	23	1.02
Mary	conscience\conscience during the addiction\becoming a burden	27	27	0.41
Mary	conscience\conscience's nature and functioning	29	29	0.29
Mary	alcohol addiction\managing alcohol addiction\rehabilitation and other treatments	31	31	0.89
Mary	transformation impact\transformation impact on understanding	33	33	0.76
Mary	transformation impact\transformation impact on spirituality	35	35	0.68
Mary	transformation\transformative moment	41	41	1.81
Mary	transformation\transformative moment	43	43	1.13
Mary	morality\morality in recovery\virtues\transcendence	43	43	1.13
Mary	morality\morality in recovery\virtues\transcendence	45	45	7.37
Mary	morality\morality in recovery\virtues\transcendence	46	46	0.33
Mary	transformation impact\transformation impact on religiousness	48	48	4.48

Mary	conscience\conscience during the addiction	50	50	1.63
Mary	conscience\conscience's nature and functioning	52	52	0.74
Mary	conscience\conscience during the addiction\becoming a burden	52	52	0.69
Mary	conscience\conscience in recovery\principle of mutual respect (Golden Rule)	54	54	0.20
Mary	morality\morality in recovery\virtues\humanity\love	54	54	1.40
Mary	morality\morality in recovery\virtues\humanity	56	56	2.46
Mary	alcohol addiction\defining alcohol addiction\addiction and managing emotions	58	58	0.93
Mary	conscience\conscience in recovery	66	66	1.03
Mary	future plans in recovery\helping others in recovery	60	62	2.60
Mary	main theme of narrative\main theme and spirituality	68	68	0.50
Max	alcohol addiction\context of alcohol addiction\alcohol addiction and occupation	5	5	3.47
Max	religiousness\religiousness before the addiction	5	5	0.48
Max	alcohol addiction\context of alcohol addiction\alcohol addiction and family	6	6	3.49
Max	alcohol addiction\defining alcohol addiction\addiction and managing emotions	6	6	0.45
Max	alcohol addiction\development of alcohol addiction	7	7	2.42
Max	conscience\conscience during the addiction\exposing conflict	8	8	2.63

Appendices

Max	alcohol addiction\impact of alcohol addiction\distorts reality and destroys life	9	9	0.83
Max	alcohol addiction\managing alcohol addiction\rehabilitation and other treatments	9	9	4.84
Max	conscience\conscience during the addiction\exposing conflict	9	9	1.76
Max	conscience\conscience's nature and functioning\conscience and spirituality	9	9	0.64
Max	conscience\conscience during the addiction\suppressed—silenced	9	9	0.66
Max	morality\morality during the addiction\vices\gluttony	10	10	0.32
Max	spirituality\spirituality during the addiction	10	10	6.83
Max	morality\morality during the addiction	10	10	6.83
Max	conscience\conscience in recovery	11	11	5.22
Max	morality\morality in recovery\virtues\humanity	12	12	8.43
Max	conscience\conscience in recovery\conscience and peace	13	13	1.05
Max	transformation\transformative process	13	13	3.83
Max	transformation impact\transformation impact on conscience\conscience's cleanness	13	13	1.05
Max	conscience\conscience in recovery\principle of mutual respect (Golden Rule)	13	13	0.72
Max	conscience\conscience development\negative impact on conscience\parents' role	15	15	1.03
Max	conscience\conscience's nature and functioning	15	15	3.12

Max	conscience\conscience development\negative impact on conscience	15	15	0.11
Max	alcohol addiction\development of alcohol addiction	17	17	4.76
Max	transformation impact\transformation impact on morality	21	21	2.49
Max	morality\morality and conscience	21	21	2.44
Max	conscience\conscience in recovery\principle of mutual respect (Golden Rule)	21	21	4.93
Max	morality\morality after transformation	21	21	2.49
Max	transformation impact\transformation impact on spirituality	23	23	2.73
Max	religiousness\religiousness during the addiction	25	25	2.63
Max	religiousness\religiousness before the addiction	25	25	2.63
Max	spirituality and religiousness	25	25	2.63
Max	religiousness\religiousness in recovery	26	26	1.34
Max	transformation\transformative moment	28	28	2.99
Max	transformation\influential person in transformation	28	28	2.65
Max	transformation\transformation and abstinence	32	32	1.59
Max	transformation impact\transformation impact on spirituality	36	36	1.03
Max	conscience\conscience in recovery\conscience and peace	38	38	1.88
Max	conscience\conscience's nature and functioning	40	40	1.62
Max	future plans in recovery\conscience in future plans	42	42	1.83

Appendices

Max	main theme of narrative\main theme and spirituality	44	44	5.61
Max	spirituality\spirituality in recovery	44	44	5.61
Paul	alcohol addiction\context of alcohol addiction\alcohol addiction and childhood\traumatic childhood	4	4	0.36
Paul	alcohol addiction\context of alcohol addiction	3	3	4.34
Paul	religiousness\religiousness before the addiction	3	3	0.36
Paul	alcohol addiction\context of alcohol addiction	4	4	3.64
Paul	morality\morality before the addiction	4	4	0.25
Paul	alcohol addiction\context of alcohol addiction\alcohol addiction and childhood	5	5	4.77
Paul	alcohol addiction\context of alcohol addiction\alcohol addiction and friends	6	6	3.70
Paul	morality\morality during the addiction\vices\lust	6	6	3.70
Paul	morality\morality during the addiction\vices\envy	7	7	1.29
Paul	alcohol addiction\context of alcohol addiction\alcohol addiction and friends	7	7	3.15
Paul	alcohol addiction\development of alcohol addiction	8	8	2.78
Paul	religiousness\religiousness during the addiction	9	9	0.36
Paul	alcohol addiction\development of alcohol addiction	9	9	4.75
Paul	morality\morality during the addiction	9	9	0.36

Paul	alcohol addiction\context of alcohol addiction\alcohol addiction and friends	10	10	2.84
Paul	alcohol addiction\impact of alcohol addiction	11	11	3.14
Paul	alcohol addiction\impact of alcohol addiction\destroys progress	11	11	3.14
Paul	alcohol addiction\personal realisation of addiction	11	11	0.14
Paul	morality\morality during the addiction\vices\lust	12	12	0.23
Paul	alcohol addiction\impact of alcohol addiction\distorts reality and destroys life	12	12	3.36
Paul	alcohol addiction\managing alcohol addiction\rehabilitation and other treatments	13	13	3.82
Paul	alcohol addiction\managing alcohol addiction\rehabilitation and other treatments	14	14	3.70
Paul	alcohol addiction\context of alcohol addiction\alcohol addiction and friends	14	14	3.70
Paul	morality\morality during the addiction	15	15	0.20
Paul	morality\morality during the addiction\vices\lust	15	15	2.30
Paul	transformation\transformative process	16	16	2.99
Paul	transformation\spiritual transformation	17	17	2.05
Paul	transformation\transformative process	17	17	0.19
Paul	transformation impact\transformation impact on understanding	18	18	5.39
Paul	conscience\conscience's nature and functioning	20	20	1.34

Paul	conscience\conscience's nature and functioning\conscience and consciousness	20	20	0.34
Paul	alcohol addiction\defining alcohol addiction	22	22	1.40
Paul	morality\defining morality	24	24	2.22
Paul	morality\morality before the addiction	24	24	2.22
Paul	morality\morality during the addiction	24	24	0.61
Paul	spirituality\spirituality before the addiction	26	26	1.65
Paul	spirituality\spirituality in recovery	26	26	0.23
Paul	religiousness\religiousness during the addiction	28	28	1.22
Paul	religiousness\defining religiousness	28	28	0.38
Paul	transformation\transformative process	30	30	2.64
Paul	transformation\transformative moment	30	30	1.09
Paul	morality\morality in recovery\virtues\transcendence\humour	32	32	0.43
Paul	morality\morality in recovery\virtues\transcendence\spirituality	32	32	0.43
Paul	transformation impact\transformation impact on spirituality	32	32	2.18
Paul	alcohol addiction\impact of alcohol addiction\hurting others	34	34	0.22
Paul	conscience\conscience during the addiction	34	34	0.27
Paul	conscience\conscience in recovery\conscience and discipline	34	34	1.53
Paul	conscience\conscience during the addiction\exposing conflict	34	34	1.04
Paul	conscience\conscience in recovery	36	36	2.56

Paul	transformation\influential person in transformation	36	36	0.65
Paul	spirituality\influential person in spirituality	36	36	0.66
Paul	transformation impact\transformation impact on conscience\conscience empowerment	36	36	0.27
Paul	future plans in recovery\helping others in recovery	38	38	2.92
Paul	future plans in recovery\conscience in future plans	38	38	2.92
Paul	transformation impact\transformation impact on conscience	40	40	3.37
Paul	transformation impact\transformation impact on conscience\conscience's cleanness	40	40	0.68
Paul	conscience\conscience's nature and functioning\conscience and spirituality	40	40	3.37
Sam	alcohol addiction\context of alcohol addiction\alcohol addiction and childhood	3	3	2.68
Sam	alcohol addiction\context of alcohol addiction\alcohol addiction and childhood\traumatic childhood	3	3	0.16
Sam	alcohol addiction\context of alcohol addiction\alcohol addiction and family	5	5	2.60
Sam	conscience\conscience development	5	5	0.40
Sam	alcohol addiction\defining alcohol addiction	5	5	0.40
Sam	alcohol addiction\development of alcohol addiction	5	5	0.63
Sam	conscience\conscience development\negative impact on conscience	5	5	0.09

Appendices

Sam	alcohol addiction\context of alcohol addiction\alcohol addiction and childhood	5	6	2.60
Sam	alcohol addiction\context of alcohol addiction\alcohol addiction and relationships	6	6	2.13
Sam	alcohol addiction\context of alcohol addiction\alcohol addiction and family	7	7	0.60
Sam	alcohol addiction\context of alcohol addiction\alcohol addiction and family	8	8	1.36
Sam	alcohol addiction\development of alcohol addiction	9	9	1.85
Sam	alcohol addiction\personal realisation of addiction	9	9	0.15
Sam	alcohol addiction\managing alcohol addiction\rehabilitation and other treatments	9	10	1.93
Sam	alcohol addiction\development of alcohol addiction	11	11	2.46
Sam	alcohol addiction\context of alcohol addiction	11	11	0.53
Sam	alcohol addiction\impact of alcohol addiction\distorts reality and destroys life	11	11	0.29
Sam	alcohol addiction\managing alcohol addiction\rehabilitation and other treatments	11	11	0.33
Sam	alcohol addiction\context of alcohol addiction\substituting addictions	12	12	0.23
Sam	spirituality\spirituality in recovery	13	13	0.08
Sam	spirituality\spirituality during the addiction	13	13	0.35
Sam	conscience\conscience during the addiction	13	13	0.33

Sam	conscience\conscience during the addiction\but I will always do the opposite	13	13	0.05
Sam	alcohol addiction\context of alcohol addiction\alcohol addiction and family	13	13	2.22
Sam	morality\morality during the addiction\vices\anger	13	13	0.06
Sam	alcohol addiction\impact of alcohol addiction\addiction and self-harming	14	14	1.61
Sam	alcohol addiction\impact of alcohol addiction\addiction and self-harming	15	15	2.07
Sam	alcohol addiction\managing alcohol addiction\rehabilitation and other treatments	16	16	1.46
Sam	alcohol addiction\managing alcohol addiction\rehabilitation and other treatments	17	19	7.36
Sam	religiousness\religiousness in recovery\moral failures of religious people	19	19	2.49
Sam	alcohol addiction\managing alcohol addiction\period of sobriety	20	20	1.53
Sam	alcohol addiction\defining alcohol addiction	21	21	0.12
Sam	alcohol addiction\impact of alcohol addiction\addiction and suicide	21	21	0.10
Sam	religiousness\religiousness in recovery\moral failures of religious people	21	21	0.69
Sam	spirituality\influential person in spirituality	21	21	0.13
Sam	morality\morality during the addiction\vices\anger	21	21	0.14

Appendices

Sam	alcohol addiction\defining alcohol addiction\addiction and managing emotions	21	21	0.06
Sam	alcohol addiction\impact of alcohol addiction\addiction and suicide	22	22	1.37
Sam	alcohol addiction\impact of alcohol addiction\blaming others	23	23	0.13
Sam	alcohol addiction\impact of alcohol addiction	23	23	2.38
Sam	morality\morality in recovery\virtues\transcendence\humour	23	23	0.07
Sam	alcohol addiction\impact of alcohol addiction\distorts reality and destroys life	24	24	1.28
Sam	transformation impact\transformation impact on understanding	24	24	0.53
Sam	transformation\influential person in transformation	24	24	0.53
Sam	spirituality\spirituality in recovery	24	24	0.01
Sam	transformation impact\transformation impact on religiousness	24	24	0.25
Sam	transformation\transformative process	24	24	0.25
Sam	morality\morality in recovery\virtues\humanity	25	25	1.99
Sam	spirituality\spirituality in recovery	26	26	0.58
Sam	morality\morality in recovery	26	26	0.91
Sam	transformation\transformation and conscience	26	26	0.91
Sam	conscience\conscience in recovery	26	26	0.91
Sam	transformation\transformation and abstinence	26	26	0.91
Sam	transformation\transformation and abstinence	27	27	2.16

Sam	morality\morality in recovery\virtues\humanity\love	27	27	0.06
Sam	conscience\conscience in recovery\principle of mutual respect (Golden Rule)	27	27	0.06
Sam	conscience\conscience in recovery\just to give back what I have been given	27	27	0.06
Sam	conscience\conscience's nature and functioning	31	31	2.45
Sam	conscience\conscience during the addiction	31	31	1.25
Sam	alcohol addiction\defining alcohol addiction	33	33	1.46
Sam	alcohol addiction\defining alcohol addiction\before I got one I want the next	33	33	0.05
Sam	alcohol addiction\managing alcohol addiction	35	35	0.84
Sam	alcohol addiction\personal realisation of addiction	35	35	0.07
Sam	morality\defining morality	37	37	1.45
Sam	morality\morality during the addiction	39	39	2.51
Sam	morality\morality during the addiction\with drinking it would take away all morality	39	39	0.09
Sam	conscience\conscience in recovery	39	39	0.12
Sam	spirituality\defining spirituality	41	41	0.32
Sam	spirituality\spirituality before the addiction	41	41	1.40
Sam	spirituality\spirituality in recovery	43	43	0.48
Sam	spirituality and religiousness	47	47	0.51

Appendices

Sam	religiousness\religiousness before the addiction\barrier—distorted belief about God	49	49	0.81
Sam	transformation\influential person in transformation	50	50	1.06
Sam	transformation\transformative process	50	50	1.06
Sam	transformation\influential person in transformation	56	56	1.69
Sam	transformation\transformative moment	58	58	1.30
Sam	transformation\transformative process	59	59	1.89
Sam	morality\morality in recovery\virtues\transcendence	59	59	1.89
Sam	transformation\transformative moment	61	61	0.25
Sam	conscience\conscience during the addiction	61	61	0.25
Sam	morality\morality during the addiction	61	61	0.06
Sam	morality\morality in recovery\virtues\humanity\love	61	61	0.20
Sam	transformation impact\transformation impact on morality	61	61	0.18
Sam	conscience\conscience during the addiction\suppressed—silenced	61	61	0.43
Sam	conscience\conscience development	63	63	0.78
Sam	conscience\conscience development\negative impact on conscience	63	63	0.11
Sam	conscience\conscience during the addiction\suppressed—silenced	65	65	0.19
Sam	morality\morality during the addiction\vices\gluttony	65	65	0.12

Appendices

Sam	morality\morality during the addiction\vices\greed	65	65	0.08
Sam	transformation impact\transformation impact on conscience	71	71	1.65
Sam	transformation impact\transformation impact on understanding	71	71	0.20
Sam	transformation impact\transformation impact on understanding	73	73	1.37
Sam	conscience\conscience in recovery\conscience and discipline	75	75	1.55
Sam	morality\morality in recovery\virtues\humanity	77	77	0.13
Sam	future plans in recovery\helping others in recovery	77	77	4.41
Sam	morality\morality during the addiction\vices\anger	78	78	0.09
Sam	morality\morality in recovery\virtues\justice\leadership	78	78	3.65
Sam	morality\morality in recovery\virtues\wisdom and knowledge	78	78	3.65
Sam	morality\morality during the addiction\vices\anger	80	80	0.17
Sam	alcohol addiction\personal realisation of addiction	80	80	0.14
Sam	alcohol addiction\impact of alcohol addiction\distorts reality and destroys life	80	80	0.13
Sam	conscience\conscience development\negative impact on conscience\difficult circumstances	81	81	0.02
Sam	conscience\conscience development\negative impact on conscience\abuse from others	81	81	0.28
Sam	conscience\conscience development\negative impact on conscience\difficult circumstances	81	81	0.04
Sam	morality\morality during the addiction	82	82	0.27

Appendices

Sam	morality\morality in recovery\virtues\courage\bravery	82	82	0.16
Sam	religiousness\religiousness during the addiction	82	82	0.53
Sam	transformation impact\transformation impact on religiousness	83	83	2.51
Sam	transformation impact\transformation impact on spirituality	83	83	2.51
Victoria	alcohol addiction\context of alcohol addiction\alcohol addiction and family	3	3	2.11
Victoria	religiousness\religiousness before the addiction	4	4	1.78
Victoria	alcohol addiction\context of alcohol addiction\alcohol addiction and relationships	5	5	1.47
Victoria	conscience\conscience development\negative impact on conscience	5	5	0.20
Victoria	alcohol addiction\development of alcohol addiction	6	6	2.86
Victoria	alcohol addiction\impact of alcohol addiction\distorts reality and destroys life	6	6	0.36
Victoria	alcohol addiction\development of alcohol addiction	7	7	2.92
Victoria	alcohol addiction\defining alcohol addiction	7	7	0.51
Victoria	alcohol addiction\context of alcohol addiction\alcohol addiction and occupation	8	8	2.62
Victoria	conscience\conscience during the addiction\suppressed—silenced	8	8	0.25
Victoria	alcohol addiction\managing alcohol addiction	8	8	2.62
Victoria	conscience\conscience during the addiction\exposing conflict	8	8	0.24

Victoria	alcohol addiction\defining alcohol addiction	9	9	3.16
Victoria	alcohol addiction\defining alcohol addiction\I felt justified to drink	9	9	0.08
Victoria	alcohol addiction\personal realisation of addiction	9	9	3.16
Victoria	alcohol addiction\impact of alcohol addiction\addiction and suicide	10	10	2.61
Victoria	conscience\conscience's nature and functioning\conscience and spirituality	11	11	2.87
Victoria	conscience\conscience during the addiction\exposing conflict	11	11	0.68
Victoria	spirituality\spirituality during the addiction	12	12	2.19
Victoria	transformation\transformative moment	13	13	2.87
Victoria	transformation impact\transformation impact on conscience\conscience empowerment	15	15	2.16
Victoria	morality\morality in recovery\virtues\temperance\self-regulation	15	15	2.16
Victoria	alcohol addiction\defining alcohol addiction\addiction and managing emotions	16	16	2.84
Victoria	alcohol addiction\context of alcohol addiction\alcohol addiction and relationships	17	17	3.46
Victoria	transformation\spiritual transformation	18	18	7.95
Victoria	transformation\transformative moment	18	18	7.95
Victoria	conscience\conscience during the addiction\suppressed—silenced	20	20	0.62
Victoria	conscience\conscience's nature and functioning	20	20	0.88

Appendices

Victoria	conscience\conscience's nature and functioning\inner voice	20	20	0.91
Victoria	conscience\conscience's nature and functioning\relation to emotions	20	20	0.47
Victoria	alcohol addiction\development of alcohol addiction	22	22	1.95
Victoria	alcohol addiction\personal realisation of addiction	24	24	1.96
Victoria	alcohol addiction\personal realisation of addiction\rationalisation of the drinking	24	24	0.09
Victoria	conscience\conscience during the addiction\suppressed—silenced	24	24	1.91
Victoria	morality\morality during the addiction\vices\lust	26	26	1.05
Victoria	morality\morality during the addiction\with drinking it would take away all morality	26	26	1.52
Victoria	spirituality\spirituality before the addiction	30	30	1.81
Victoria	spirituality\spirituality during the addiction	30	30	5.56
Victoria	spirituality and religiousness	32	32	0.41
Victoria	religiousness\religiousness during the addiction	36	36	0.72
Victoria	spirituality\influential person in spirituality	40	40	1.13
Victoria	transformation\transformative moment	40	40	2.99
Victoria	transformation impact\transformation impact on conscience	42	42	0.96
Victoria	transformation impact\transformation impact on religiousness	42	42	0.96
Victoria	transformation impact\transformation impact on spirituality	42	42	0.96

Victoria	transformation impact\transformation impact on morality	42	42	0.96
Victoria	conscience\conscience in recovery\conscience and peace	42	42	0.22
Victoria	transformation impact	44	44	1.12
Victoria	transformation impact\transformation impact on conscience	44	44	1.12
Victoria	morality\morality in recovery\virtues\courage\integrity	44	44	0.57
Victoria	conscience\conscience in recovery	44	44	0.98
Victoria	conscience\conscience during the addiction\suppressed—silenced	46	46	0.32
Victoria	transformation impact\transformation impact on conscience	46	46	1.54
Victoria	conscience\conscience during the addiction\exposing conflict	48	48	0.53
Victoria	transformation impact\transformation impact on conscience	50	50	0.69
Victoria	transformation impact\transformation impact on conscience\conscience empowerment	50	50	0.39
Victoria	morality\morality in recovery\virtues\courage\integrity	52	52	0.43
Victoria	conscience\conscience in recovery	52	52	1.30
Victoria	alcohol addiction\managing alcohol addiction	52	52	1.05
Victoria	transformation impact\transformation impact on conscience\conscience empowerment	52	52	0.87
Victoria	future plans in recovery\helping others in recovery	54	54	3.01
Victoria	future plans in recovery\spirituality in future plans	54	54	1.33
Victoria	main theme of narrative\main theme and transformation	58	58	3.94

Appendices

Analysis Identification Table of Memos and their Location in the Interviews

(Note: The numbering of paragraphs is according to MAXQDA and commences from the title of the interview)

Document	Paragraph	Memo title
Interview–Adam	3	main theme and spirituality
Interview–Adam	4	distorts reality and destroys life
Interview–Adam	5	rehabilitation and other treatments
Interview–Adam	6	defining alcohol addiction
Interview–Adam	7	personal realisation of addiction
Interview–Adam	7	spirituality during the addiction
Interview–Adam	8	blaming others
Interview–Adam	9	transformative moment
Interview–Adam	10	religiousness before transformation
Interview–Adam	11	spiritual transformation
Interview–Adam	12	anger
Interview–Adam	13	traumatic childhood
Interview–Adam	14	anger
Interview–Adam	15	alcohol addiction and family
Interview–Adam	16	addiction and managing emotions
Interview–Adam	17	before I got one I want the next
Interview–Adam	18	development of alcohol addiction
Interview–Adam	19	transformative process
Interview–Adam	20	distorts reality and destroys life
Interview–Adam	21	defining spirituality
Interview–Adam	22	solution vs. consequences
Interview–Adam	23	managing alcohol addiction
Interview–Adam	24	spiritual transformation
Interview–Adam	25	addiction and suicide
Interview–Adam	26	greed
Interview–Adam	26	transformation impact on understanding

Interview–Adam	27	conscience's cleanness
Interview–Adam	28	open-mindedness
Interview–Adam	28	integrity
Interview–Adam	29	humility and modesty
Interview–Adam	30	transformation impact on spirituality
Interview–Adam	31	transformation impact on addiction
Interview–Adam	32	spirituality in recovery
Interview–Adam	32	spirituality and religiousness
Interview–Adam	33	transformation impact on understanding
Interview–Adam	34	spirituality after transformation
Interview–Adam	35	conscience and spirituality
Interview–Adam	41	suppressed—silenced
Interview–Adam	42	conscience and spirituality
Interview–Adam	44	personal realisation of addiction
Interview–Adam	48	morality during the addiction
Interview–Adam	49	anger
Interview–Adam	50	transformation impact on morality
Interview–Adam	50	gratitude
Interview–Adam	52	spirituality during the addiction
Interview–Adam	54	religiousness during the addiction
Interview–Adam	56	transformative process
Interview–Adam	60	spirituality after transformation
Interview–Adam	66	transformative process
Interview–Adam	68	main theme of narrative
Interview–Alex	12	religiousness before transformation
Interview–Alex	17	religious support during childhood
Interview–Alex	19	alcohol addiction and relationships
Interview–Alex	19	rehabilitation and other treatments
Interview–Alex	20	addiction and managing emotions
Interview–Alex	21	addiction deterrents
Interview–Alex	23	defining religiousness
Interview–Alex	25	distorts reality and destroys life

Appendices

Interview–Alex	26	gluttony
Interview–Alex	26	spirituality in recovery
Interview–Alex	28	conscience during the addiction
Interview–Alex	30	addiction and managing emotions
Interview–Alex	31	addiction deterrents
Interview–Alex	32	spirituality in recovery
Interview–Alex	32	spirituality in recovery
Interview–Alex	34	transformative process
Interview–Alex	36	morality during the addiction
Interview–Alex	44	spirituality during the addiction
Interview–Alex	45	transformative process
Interview–Alex	47	transformative process
Interview–Alex	49	transformative process
Interview–Alex	53	spiritual transformation
Interview–Alex	55	helping others in recovery
Interview–Alex	57	main theme and spirituality
Interview–Ben	5	alcohol addiction and occupation
Interview–Ben	6	development of alcohol addiction
Interview–Ben	7	morality during the addiction
Interview–Ben	8	alcohol addiction and occupation
Interview–Ben	9	development of alcohol addiction
Interview–Ben	10	hurting others
Interview–Ben	11	suppressed—silenced
Interview–Ben	12	defining alcohol addiction
Interview–Ben	13	negative impact on conscience: parents' role
Interview–Ben	14	forgiveness and mercy
Interview–Ben	15	pride
Interview–Ben	16	suppressed—silenced
Interview–Ben	17	pride
Interview–Ben	18	spirituality during the addiction
Interview–Ben	19	transformative process
Interview–Ben	20	religious transformation

Interview–Ben	21	transformation impact on understanding
Interview–Ben	22	transformation impact on morality
Interview–Ben	23	transformation impact on religiousness
Interview–Ben	24	religiousness after transformation
Interview–Ben	25	transformation impact on addiction
Interview–Ben	26	personal realisation of addiction
Interview–Ben	27	transformation impact on morality
Interview–Ben	29	suppressed—silenced
Interview–Ben	35	religiousness during the addiction
Interview–Ben	39	influential person in transformation
Interview–Ben	41	transformative process
Interview–Ben	43	becoming a burden
Interview–Ben	47	influential person in transformation
Interview–Ben	49	religion and conscience in future plans
Interview–Ben	51	main theme and transformation
Interview–Jack	5	traumatic childhood
Interview–Jack	6	religiousness before the addiction
Interview–Jack	7	traumatic childhood
Interview–Jack	9	alcohol addiction and friends
Interview–Jack	10	addiction and managing emotions
Interview–Jack	11	anger
Interview–Jack	11	pride
Interview–Jack	12	addiction deterrents
Interview–Jack	13	development of alcohol addiction
Interview–Jack	14	addiction and suicide
Interview–Jack	14	religiousness during the addiction
Interview–Jack	15	rehabilitation and other treatments
Interview–Jack	16	addiction and suicide
Interview–Jack	16	conscience and understanding
Interview–Jack	16	conscience during the addiction
Interview–Jack	17	transformative moment
Interview–Jack	17	transformation impact on morality

Appendices

Interview–Jack	18	transformative process
Interview–Jack	19	moral degradation during addiction
Interview–Jack	19	transformation impact on conscience
Interview–Jack	20	transformation impact on spirituality
Interview–Jack	22	conscience's resurrection
Interview–Jack	22	dead conscience
Interview–Jack	24	personal realisation of addiction
Interview–Jack	26	morality before the addiction
Interview–Jack	29	spirituality before and after transformation
Interview–Jack	30	spiritual transformation
Interview–Jack	32	religiousness during the addiction
Interview–Jack	36	transformative process
Interview–Jack	38	influential person in transformation
Interview–Jack	42	transformation impact on spirituality
Interview–Jack	44	transformation impact on conscience
Interview–Jack	46	conscience and understanding
Interview–Jack	48	helping others in recovery
Interview–Jack	50	main theme and transformation
Interview–James	6	traumatic childhood
Interview–James	7	alcohol addiction and family
Interview–James	8	alcohol addiction and family
Interview–James	9	anger
Interview–James	9	managing alcohol addiction
Interview–James	10	gluttony
Interview–James	10	hurting others
Interview–James	11	alcohol addiction and relationships
Interview–James	12	personal realisation of addiction
Interview–James	13	anger
Interview–James	14	greed
Interview–James	14	managing alcohol addiction
Interview–James	17	transformative process
Interview–James	18	religious and spiritual transformation

Interview–James	19	conscience empowerment
Interview–James	22	transformative moment
Interview–James	23	transformation impact on religiousness and spirituality
Interview–James	24	transformation impact on addiction
Interview–James	32	dead conscience
Interview–James	32	conscience's resurrection
Interview–James	36	conscience and understanding
Interview–James	38	transformation impact on morality
Interview–James	40	transformation impact on spirituality
Interview–James	42	transformation impact on religiousness
Interview–James	44	transformative moment
Interview–James	46	influential person in transformation
Interview–James	48	transformation impact on religiousness
Interview–James	50	conscience's freedom
Interview–James	52	transformative process
Interview–James	54	spirituality in future plans
Interview–James	56	main theme and addiction
Interview–James	56	main theme and spirituality
Interview–John	7	traumatic childhood
Interview–John	8	alcohol addiction and culture
Interview–John	8	development of alcohol addiction
Interview–John	9	alcohol addiction and family
Interview–John	10	greed
Interview–John	10	envy
Interview–John	11	gluttony
Interview–John	11	spirituality during the addiction
Interview–John	11	before I got one I want the next
Interview–John	12	gluttony
Interview–John	12	distorts reality and destroys life
Interview–John	13	rehabilitation and other treatments
Interview–John	13	distorts reality and destroys life

Appendices

Interview–John	13	sloth
Interview–John	14	transformative moment
Interview–John	15	influential person in transformation
Interview–John	16	integrity
Interview–John	16	transformative moment
Interview–John	16	transformation impact on conscience
Interview–John	17	conscience and spirituality
Interview–John	17	spirituality and religiousness
Interview–John	18	transformation impact on understanding
Interview–John	19	influential person in transformation
Interview–John	20	transformation and abstinence
Interview–John	21	transformation impact on understanding
Interview–John	22	helping others in recovery
Interview–John	23	virtues
Interview–John	24	transformative process
Interview–John	30	conscience and spirituality
Interview–John	32	conscience and peace
Interview–John	34	suppressed—silenced
Interview–John	38	with drinking it would take away all morality
Interview–John	40	spirituality during the addiction
Interview–John	42	religiousness during the addiction
Interview–John	46	transformation impact on spirituality
Interview–John	48	conscience's freedom
Interview–John	54	helping others in recovery
Interview–John	58	main theme and transformation
Interview–Luke	7	alcohol addiction and friends
Interview–Luke	8	personal realisation of addiction
Interview–Luke	9	lust
Interview–Luke	10	hurting others
Interview–Luke	11	personal realisation of addiction
Interview–Luke	12	spirituality during the addiction
Interview–Luke	13	conscience during the addiction

Interview–Luke	13	religiousness during the addiction
Interview–Luke	15	managing alcohol addiction
Interview–Luke	16	hurting others
Interview–Luke	17	distorts reality and destroys life
Interview–Luke	19	religiousness during the addiction
Interview–Luke	20	gluttony
Interview–Luke	21	becoming a burden
Interview–Luke	23	suppressed—silenced
Interview–Luke	24	conscience during the addiction
Interview–Luke	25	religiousness during the addiction
Interview–Luke	26	gluttony
Interview–Luke	27	pride
Interview–Luke	28	transformative process
Interview–Luke	29	conscience in recovery
Interview–Luke	30	lust
Interview–Luke	30	transformative moment
Interview–Luke	34	morality during the addiction
Interview–Luke	36	becoming a burden
Interview–Luke	36	transformation impact on understanding
Interview–Luke	37	main theme and addiction
Interview–Luke	38	greed
Interview–Luke	48	personal realisation of addiction
Interview–Luke	56	spirituality before the addiction
Interview–Luke	58	influential person in transformation
Interview–Luke	64	transformation impact on morality
Interview–Luke	65	transformation impact on understanding
Interview–Luke	69	helping others in recovery
Interview–Luke	70	conscience in future plans
Interview–Luke	72	religion and spirituality in future plans
Interview–Luke	75	main theme and addiction
Interview–Luke	76	main theme and spirituality
Interview–Mary	5	traumatic childhood

Appendices

Interview–Mary	6	alcohol addiction and childhood
Interview–Mary	7	destroys progress
Interview–Mary	8	alcohol addiction and occupation
Interview–Mary	9	alcohol addiction and relationships
Interview–Mary	10	rehabilitation and other treatments
Interview–Mary	11	alcohol addiction and relationships
Interview–Mary	13	rehabilitation and other treatments
Interview–Mary	14	distorts reality and destroys life
Interview–Mary	16	distorts reality and destroys life
Interview–Mary	17	rehabilitation and other treatments
Interview–Mary	19	transformative moment
Interview–Mary	20	influential person in transformation
Interview–Mary	21	humanity
Interview–Mary	23	helping others in recovery
Interview–Mary	27	becoming a burden
Interview–Mary	28	conscience's nature and functioning
Interview–Mary	31	rehabilitation and other treatments
Interview–Mary	33	transformation impact on understanding
Interview–Mary	35	transformation impact on spirituality
Interview–Mary	41	transformative moment
Interview–Mary	43	transcendence
Interview–Mary	45	transcendence
Interview–Mary	48	transformation impact on religiousness
Interview–Mary	50	conscience during the addiction
Interview–Mary	54	principle of mutual respect (Golden Rule)
Interview–Mary	56	humanity
Interview–Mary	58	addiction and managing emotions
Interview–Mary	62	helping others in recovery
Interview–Mary	66	conscience in recovery
Interview–Mary	68	main theme and spirituality
Interview–Max	5	alcohol addiction and occupation
Interview–Max	5	religiousness before the addiction

Appendices

Interview–Max	6	alcohol addiction and family
Interview–Max	7	development of alcohol addiction
Interview–Max	8	exposing conflict
Interview–Max	9	distorts reality and destroys life
Interview–Max	9	conscience and spirituality
Interview–Max	9	rehabilitation and other treatments
Interview–Max	9	exposing conflict
Interview–Max	10	gluttony
Interview–Max	10	spirituality and morality during addiction
Interview–Max	11	conscience in recovery
Interview–Max	12	humanity
Interview–Max	13	conscience's cleanness
Interview–Max	13	transformative process
Interview–Max	15	parents' role
Interview–Max	15	conscience's nature and functioning
Interview–Max	17	development of alcohol addiction
Interview–Max	21	morality and conscience
Interview–Max	23	transformation impact on spirituality
Interview–Max	25	religiousness during the addiction
Interview–Max	26	religiousness in recovery
Interview–Max	28	influential person in transformation
Interview–Max	28	transformative moment
Interview–Max	32	transformation and abstinence
Interview–Max	36	transformation impact on spirituality
Interview–Max	38	conscience and peace
Interview–Max	40	conscience's nature and functioning
Interview–Max	42	conscience in future plans
Interview–Max	44	spirituality in recovery
Interview–Paul	3	context of alcohol addiction
Interview–Paul	4	traumatic childhood
Interview–Paul	4	morality before the addiction

Appendices

Interview–Paul	5	alcohol addiction and childhood
Interview–Paul	6	sexual immorality (lust)
Interview–Paul	7	envy
Interview–Paul	9	morality during the addiction
Interview–Paul	10	alcohol addiction and friends
Interview–Paul	11	impact of alcohol addiction
Interview–Paul	12	lust
Interview–Paul	13	rehabilitation and other treatments
Interview–Paul	15	lust
Interview–Paul	16	transformative process
Interview–Paul	17	spiritual transformation
Interview–Paul	18	transformation impact on understanding
Interview–Paul	20	conscience and consciousness
Interview–Paul	22	addiction as dependency
Interview–Paul	24	defining morality
Interview–Paul	24	conscience and consciousness
Interview–Paul	26	spirituality before the addiction
Interview–Paul	26	spirituality in recovery
Interview–Paul	28	defining religiousness
Interview–Paul	30	transformative moment
Interview–Paul	32	transcendence: spirituality (humour)
Interview–Paul	34	conscience in recovery
Interview–Paul	36	conscience in recovery
Interview–Paul	38	conscience in recovery
Interview–Paul	40	conscience and spirituality
Interview–Sam	3	traumatic childhood
Interview–Sam	5	addiction and managing emotions
Interview–Sam	5	distorted conscience development
Interview–Sam	5	dual addiction
Interview–Sam	6	alcohol addiction and relationships
Interview–Sam	9	solution for the emotional pain
Interview–Sam	9	personal realisation of addiction

Interview–Sam	11	disconnect from the emotional pain
Interview–Sam	11	distorts reality and destroys life
Interview–Sam	13	conscience during the addiction
Interview–Sam	13	conscience during the addiction
Interview–Sam	13	anger
Interview–Sam	13	anger
Interview–Sam	15	addiction and self-harming
Interview–Sam	19	moral failures of religious people
Interview–Sam	21	addiction and managing emotions
Interview–Sam	21	moral failures of religious people
Interview–Sam	22	impact of alcohol addiction: suicide
Interview–Sam	24	distorts reality and destroys life
Interview–Sam	24	influential person in transformation
Interview–Sam	24	spirituality in recovery
Interview–Sam	25	humanity
Interview–Sam	26	spirituality in recovery
Interview–Sam	31	conscience's nature and functioning
Interview–Sam	31	conscience during the addiction
Interview–Sam	35	addiction and managing emotions
Interview–Sam	35	personal realisation of addiction
Interview–Sam	39	conscience (morality) in recovery
Interview–Sam	41	defining spirituality
Interview–Sam	41	spirituality before the addiction
Interview–Sam	43	spirituality in recovery
Interview–Sam	49	barrier—distorted belief about God
Interview–Sam	58	transformative moment
Interview–Sam	61	transformative moment
Interview–Sam	61	conscience in recovery
Interview–Sam	63	conscience development
Interview–Sam	65	conscience during the addiction: suppressed (gluttony; greed)
Interview–Sam	71	conscience empowerment

Interview–Sam	77	humanity
Interview–Sam	77	helping others in recovery
Interview–Sam	78	wisdom and knowledge
Interview–Sam	82	morality during the addiction
Interview–Sam	82	religiousness during the addiction
Interview–Sam	83	transformation impact on religiousness
Interview–Victoria	3	alcohol addiction and family
Interview–Victoria	4	religiousness before transformation
Interview–Victoria	5	negative impact on conscience
Interview–Victoria	6	development of alcohol addiction
Interview–Victoria	7	addiction and managing emotions
Interview–Victoria	8	conscience during the addiction
Interview–Victoria	9	defining alcohol addiction
Interview–Victoria	10	addiction and suicide
Interview–Victoria	11	conscience during the addiction
Interview–Victoria	12	spirituality during the addiction
Interview–Victoria	13	transformative moment
Interview–Victoria	15	conscience empowerment
Interview–Victoria	16	addiction and managing emotions
Interview–Victoria	17	alcohol addiction and relationships
Interview–Victoria	18	transformative moment
Interview–Victoria	20	suppressed—silenced
Interview–Victoria	22	development of alcohol addiction
Interview–Victoria	24	personal realisation of addiction
Interview–Victoria	24	rationalisation of the drinking
Interview–Victoria	26	morality during the addiction
Interview–Victoria	30	spirituality during the addiction
Interview–Victoria	36	religiousness during the addiction
Interview–Victoria	40	influential person in spirituality
Interview–Victoria	40	transformative moment
Interview–Victoria	42	transformation impact on conscience
Interview–Victoria	44	transformation impact on conscience

Interview–Victoria	46	transformation impact on conscience
Interview–Victoria	48	exposing conflict
Interview–Victoria	50	transformation impact on conscience
Interview–Victoria	52	conscience in recovery
Interview–Victoria	52	managing alcohol addiction
Interview–Victoria	54	spirituality in future plans
Interview–Victoria	54	helping others in recovery
Interview–Victoria	58	main theme and transformation

Appendices

Reference Table of Direct Quotations from Transcripts Used in the Work with their Counterparts in MAXQDA

(Note: The table shows the number of direct quotations from the transcripts used in the work and presents their references to the transcript's material in the work with their counterparts in MAXQDA which differ in relation to their paragraph lines due to software incompatibility as well as in relation to their paragraph numbers which in MAXQDA include the title of the transcript)

No. in order of occurrence in the work	Reference in MAXQDA	Reference in the work
1	Mary, 2011, par 29:1; par 29:2–3; par 52:1–2	Mary, 2011, par 28:1–2; 2–3; par 28:3–8; par 51:3–4
2	Sam, 2011, par 31:3–4	Sam, 2011, par 30:9–10
3	Max, 2011, par 15:2–3	Max, 2011, par 14:6–7
4	Max, 2011, par 40:1–2	Max, 2011, par 39:4–7
5	Victoria, 2011, par 20:1–2	Victoria, 2011, par 19:3–7
6	Luke, 2011, par 24:1–3	Luke, 2011, par 23:1–9
7	Adam, 2011, par 35:7–8; 9–10	Adam, 2011, par 34:21–23; 28–30
8	John, 2011, par 17:1; 2–3; 3–4	John, 2011, par 16:2–4; 7; 10–11
9	John, 2011, par 30:1–2	John, 2011, par 29:4–6
10	Max, 2011, par 9:5–6	Max, 2011, par 8:19–22
11	Paul, 2011, par 20:1–2	Paul, 2011, par 19:2–4
12	Paul, 2011, par 24:2–3	Paul, 2011, par 23:6–8
13	Adam, 2011, par 42:7–9; 10–11	Adam, 2011, par 41:22–26; 29–33
14	Jack, 2011, par 16:6–7	Jack, 2011, par 15:19–20
15	Jack, 2011, par 46:1–2; 5	Jack, 2011, par 45:1–4; 15–16
16	James, 2011, par 36:1–2	James, 2011, par 35:1–4
17	Victoria, 2011, par 5:1	Victoria, 2011, par 4:2–3
18	Max, 2011, par 15:5	Max, 2011, par 14:15

19	Sam, 2011, par 63:1–2	Sam, 2011, par 62:3–4
20	Sam, 2011, par 5:7	Sam, 2011, par 4:12
21	Luke, 2011, par 13:6	Luke, 2011, par 12:19
22	Luke, 2011, par 24:3–5	Luke, 2011, par 23:9–14
23	Sam, 2011, par 13:8–9	Sam, 2011, par 12:16–18
24	Sam, 2011, par 13:4–5	Sam, 2011, par 12:13–16
25	Sam, 2011, par 31:7–8	Sam, 2011, par 30:20–22
26	Alex, 2011, par 28:1–2	Alex, 2011, par 27:3–4
27	Alex, 2011, par 28:4–5	Alex, 2011, par 27:12–14
28	Alex, 2011, par 28:3–4	Alex, 2011, par 27:9–10
29	Alex, 2011, par 16:3; 8–9	Alex, 2011, par 15:8–9; 25–27
30	Alex, 2011, par 23:1	Alex, 2011, par 22:1–2
31	Luke, 2011, par 13:3–5	Luke, 2011, par 12:9–15
32	Luke, 2011, par 21:2–3	Luke, 2011, par 20:5–10
33	Luke, 2011, par 36:5–6	Luke, 2011, par 35:15–19
34	Mary, 2011, par 27:1; 2; 3	Mary, 2011, par 26:1–2; 4–5; 8–9
35	Mary, 2011, par 52:1–2	Mary, 2011, par 51:1–4
36	Ben, 2011, par 43:1–3	Ben, 2011, par 42:1–7
37	Luke, 2011, par 23:3–5	Luke, 2011, par 22:10–14
38	Sam, 2011, par 61:4–5	Sam, 2011, par 60:11–15
39	Victoria, 2011, par 20:3–4	Victoria, 2011, par 19:10–12
40	John, 2011, par 34:1	John, 2011, par 33:1–3
41	Adam, 2011, par 41:3–4	Adam, 2011, par 40:8–10
42	Ben, 2011, par 16:1	Ben, 2011, par 15:1–3
43	Ben, 2011, par 29:1	Ben, 2011, par 28:1–3
44	Max, 2011, par 9:9–10	Max, 2011, par 8:33–36
45	James, 2011, par 32:1	James, 2011, par 31:1–3
46	Jack, 2011, par 22:1–2	Jack, 2011, par 21:1–4
47	Sam, 2011, par 82:1	Sam, 2011, par 81:1–3
48	Alex, 2011, par 38:1; 3	Alex, 2011, par 37:1–2; 9

Appendices

49	Paul, 2011, par 9:3	Paul, 2011, par 8:7–9
50	Adam, 2011, par 48:9	Adam, 2011, par 47:26–27
51	Ben, 2011, par 7:2–3	Ben, 2011, par 6:6–8
52	Luke, 2011, par 34:2–3	Luke, 2011, par 33:5–7
53	John, 2011, par 38:3	John, 2011, par 37:7–9
54	Max, 2011, par 10:10–11	Max, 2011, par 9:33–35
55	Sam, 2011, par 13:1; 5	Sam, 2011, par 12:2–3; 15–16
56	Adam, 2011, par 49:2; 3; 4	Adam, 2011, par 48:5–6; 9–10; 11–12
57	Jack, 2011, par 11:4–5	Jack, 2011, par 10:11–14
58	James, 2011, par 9:6–7	James, 2011, par 8:18–21
59	Paul, 2011, par 7:2; 2–3	Paul, 2011, par 6:4; 6–8
60	John, 2011, par 10:5; 6	John, 2011, par 9:15–17; 18–19
61	Alex, 2011, par 26:4	Alex, 2011, par 25:11–12
62	James, 2011, par 9:5	James, 2011, par 8:14–16
63	John, 2011, par 11:2–3	John, 2011, par 10:7–9
64	Max, 2011, par 10:6–7	Max, 2011, par 9:21–22
65	Luke, 2011, par 20:4	Luke, 2011, par 19:10–12
66	Adam, 2011, par 26:5–6	Adam, 2011, par 25:16–18
67	John, 2011, par 10:1–2; 3	John, 2011, par 9:3–6; 9
68	Luke, 2011, par 38:4–5	Luke, 2011, par 37:13–15
69	Paul, 2011, par 12:4	Paul, 2011, par 11:11–12
70	Luke, 2011, par 30:2	Luke, 2011, par 29:4–6
71	Adam, 2011, par 6:2–3; 5	Adam, 2011, par 5:5–7; 14
72	Mary, 2011, par 10:1–2	Mary, 2011, par 9:3–6
73	Jack, 2011, par 24:2	Jack, 2011, par 23:5–7
74	John, 2011, par 40:2–3	John, 2011, par 39:6–9
75	Mary, 2011, par 10:1; 4; 5	Mary, 2011, par 9:1; 11–12; 12–14
76	John, 2011, par 13:8–9; 10	John, 2011, par 12:27; 30–33
77	Jack, 2011, par 46:2	Jack, 2011, par 45:4–5

78	Victoria, 2011, par 8:4	Victoria, 2011, par 7:12–13
79	Victoria, 2011, par 11:4–5	Victoria, 2011, par 10:10–13
80	Max, 2011, par 8:1–2; 3	Max, 2011, par 7:3–5; 7–9
81	Luke, 2011, par 23:4–5	Luke, 2011, par 22:11–15
82	Paul, 2011, par 34:1–2	Paul, 2011, par 33:1–4
83	Sam, 2011, par 57:2–3	Sam, 2011, par 56:6–7
84	Sam, 2011, par 61:1–2	Sam, 2011, par 60:3–4
85	Paul, 2011, par 30:1–3	Paul, 2011, par 29:3–9
86	Victoria, 2011, par 13:4–5	Victoria, 2011, par 12:12–14
87	Victoria, 2011, par 18:4–5	Victoria, 2011, par 17:11–15
88	Mary, 2011, par 19:2	Mary, 2011, par 18:5–7
89	Adam, 2011, par 9:1	Adam, 2011, par 8:1–2
90	Jack, 2011, par 17:2–3	Jack, 2011, par 16:7–8
91	James, 2011, par 22:2–6	James, 2011, par 21:6–17
92	John, 2011, par 14:1–2	John, 2011, par 13:1–6
93	Max, 2011, par 28:1–2	Max, 2011, par 27:1–5
94	Luke, 2011, par 30:3; 4–5	Luke, 2011, par 29:8–9; 13–15
95	Alex, 2011, par 34	Alex, 2011, par 33
96	Paul, 2011, par 16	Paul, 2011, par 15
97	Paul, 2011, par 17:1–2	Paul, 2011, par 16:3–4
98	Adam, 2011, par 66:1	Adam, 2011, par 65:1–3
99	Ben, 2011, par 41:1–3	Ben, 2011, par 40:3–7
100	Jack, 2011, par 18:1–2	Jack, 2011, par 17:1–4
101	James, 2011, par 54:1–2	James, 2011, par 53:1–6
102	John, 2011, par 24:1–2; 6–7	John, 2011, par 23:1–5; 19–21
103	Max, 2011, par 13:3–4; 6–7	Max, 2011, par 12:7–12; 17–21
104	Victoria, 2011, par 46:1–3	Victoria, 2011, par 45:1–8

Appendices

105	Jack, 2011, par 19:10–11	Jack, 2011, par 18:30–33
106	John, 2011, par 16:10	John, 2011, par 15:30–32
107	James, 2011, par 50:2; 3	James, 2011, par 49:5–6; 6–7
108	John, 2011, par 48:1–2	John, 2011, par 47:2–4
109	Jack, 2011, par 44:1–2; 4–5	Jack, 2011, par 43:1–4; 12–14
110	Jack, 2011, par 22:1; 7	Jack, 2011, par 21:1–2; 20–22
111	James, 2011, par 32:1–3	James, 2011, par 31:3–9
112	Adam, 2011, par 27:7–9	Adam, 2011, par 26:21–26
113	Max, 2011, par 13:3; 4	Max, 2011, par 12:7–8; 9–13
114	Paul, 2011, par 40:3–4	Paul, 2011, par 39:8–11
115	Victoria, 2011, par 48:1	Victoria, 2011, par 47:1–3
116	Victoria, 2011, par 42:2	Victoria, 2011, par 41:4–5
117	Max, 2011, par 38:1; 1–2; 3–4	Max, 2011, par 37:1–2; 2–4; 5–10
118	John, 2011, par 32:4	John, 2011, par 31:11–13
119	Victoria, 2011, par 15:3–4	Victoria, 2011, par 14:8–11
120	Victoria, 2011, par 52:1–2	Victoria, 2011, par 51:3–7
121	Victoria, 2011, par 50:1–2	Victoria, 2011, par 49:2–4
122	James, 2011, par 19:5–7	James, 2011, par 18:17–25
123	Sam, 2011, par 71:1–2	Sam, 2011, par 70:2–6
124	Adam, 2011, par 42:1–2	Adam, 2011, par 41:1–6
125	Luke, 2011, par 29:2–3; 3–5	Luke, 2011, par 28:7–8; 8–15
126	Paul, 2011, par 34:1–2; 3	Paul, 2011, par 33:3–6; 7–8
127	Paul, 2011, par 36:2–4	Paul, 2011, par 35:4–10
128	Victoria, 2011, par 44:1–2	Victoria, 2011, par 43:1–6
129	Mary, 2011, par 66:1–2	Mary, 2011, par 65:3–5
130	Max, 2011, par 11:1; 2–4; 6–8	Max, 2011, par 10:1–3; 4–11; 18–25
131	Adam, 2011, par 69:4–5	Adam, 2011, par 68:11–14

132	Adam, 2011, par 70:11–13	Adam, 2011, par 69:35–39
133	Max, 2011, par 21:1; 2–5; 8–9; par 13:5–6; 6–7	Max, 2011, par 20:1; 6–15; 24–26; par 12:14–17; 19–20
134	Mary, 2011, par 54	Mary, 2011, par 53
135	Max, 2011, par 42:2–4	Max, 2011, par 41:4–11
136	Luke, 2011, par 70:4–5; 7; 8	Luke, 2011, par 69:12–14; 21–22; 25
137	Paul, 2011, par 38:1; 3	Paul, 2011, par 37:1–2; 7–9
138	Sam, 2011, par 39:6–8	Sam, 2011, par 38:18–23
139	Adam, 2011, par 50:1–2; 3; 5; 6	Adam, 2011, par 49:3–4; 6–8; 15–16; 16–17
140	Adam, 2011, par 28:4	Adam, 2011, par 27:11–13
141	John, 2011, par 16:2	John, 2011, par 15:4–6
142	Sam, 2011, par 77:1	Sam, 2011, par 76:2–3
143	Mary, 2011, par 56:3; 4	Mary, 2011, par 55:8–9; 11–12
144	Max, 2011, par 12:8	Max, 2011, par 11:24–25
145	John, 2011, par 23:4–5; 6; 7; 8; 8–9	John, 2011, par 22:12–15; 16–17; 22; 23–24; 25–26
146	Adam, 2011, par 29:1; 2–3; 4	Adam, 2011, par 28:1–2; 6–8; 11–12
147	Ben, 2011, par 14:3–4	Ben, 2011, par 13:10–12
148	Mary, 2011, par 46:3–4; par 43; par 45	Mary, 2011, par 45:10–11; par 42; par 44
149	Adam, 2011, par 66:3–4	Adam, 2011, par 65:9–11
150	Paul, 2011, par 32:1	Paul, 2011, par 31:2–4
151	Adam, 2011, par 50:14	Adam, 2011, par 49:43–44
152	James, 2011, par 23:3–5	James, 2011, par 22:8–13
153	Sam, 2011, par 78:7–11	Sam, 2011, par 77:22–33
154	Adam, 2011, par 28:4–6; 6–8; 9	Adam, 2011, par 27:13–16; 19–23; 26–28

www.ingramcontent.com/pod-product-compliance
Lightning Source LLC
Chambersburg PA
CBHW071147300426
44113CB00009B/1113